Richard Frederick Littledale

A Commentary on the Song of Songs

From Ancient and Mediaeval Sources

Richard Frederick Littledale

A Commentary on the Song of Songs
From Ancient and Mediaeval Sources

ISBN/EAN: 9783337020743

Printed in Europe, USA, Canada, Australia, Japan

Cover: Foto ©Lupo / pixelio.de

More available books at **www.hansebooks.com**

A COMMENTARY

ON

THE SONG OF SONGS.

FROM ANCIENT AND MEDIÆVAL SOURCES.

BY

RICHARD FREDERICK LITTLEDALE,
LL.D., D.C.L.

LONDON:
JOSEPH MASTERS, ALDERSGATE STREET,
AND NEW BOND STREET.
NEW YORK: POTT AND AMERY.
MDCCCLXIX.

LONDON:
PRINTED BY JOSEPH MASTERS AND SON,
ALDERSGATE STREET.

IN DEAR MEMORY

OF

JOHN MASON NEALE.

PREFACE.

THE Song of Songs, though for many centuries a favourite theme of the most eminent Saints and Christian writers, either by way of direct comment or of illustrative quotation, has fallen, during these latter times, into comparative neglect. It is rarely made the basis of sermons, or even of devotional treatises, and thus, as may be reasonably inferred, does not occupy any prominent place in private study of Holy Scripture.

Two attempts, both most valuable in their way, to reinstate it in its proper position as an element of religious teaching, and as affording ample subject-matter for practical meditation, have been recently made. The first is the well-known translation of Avrillon's devout book, *L'Année Affective;* the second is the series of *Sermons in a Religious House,* preached by the late Dr. Neale.

But the plan of each of these works excludes completeness of treatment, and leaves much of the ground still uncovered. Nor do any of the commentaries usually accessible supply the defect. The mystical exegesis, which is of the very essence of any true understanding of perhaps the most difficult book in Scripture, was either quite foreign to the temperament and method of the expositors; or when some genuine feeling of sympathy with patristic theology did manifest itself, as, for example, in the writings of Matthew Henry, the influence of eighteenth-century modes of thought, and the fear of being altogether out of harmony with the readers of their time, cramped and enfeebled their utterance.

It is only seven years since the late Mr. Thrupp endeavoured to revive intelligent interest in the religious study of the Canticles through the means of the devout and scholarly gloss which he published. But, while he admitted the truth of the main outlines of the traditional interpretation, he exhibited much timidity in following up the details, a timidity all the more remarkable when contrasted with the boldness with which he proposed conjectural emendations of the Hebrew text. His volume, therefore, though very useful in its degree to students, does not appear to have succeeded in its higher aim, that of promoting reverent perusal of the Canticles amongst the educated laity.

Nor could this class obtain assistance from foreign sources. Apart from colossal works like those of Ghislerius and Cornelius à Lapide, there is no book which presents in a compendious form the pith of ancient and mediæval exposition on the Song; though there are, no doubt, many, like that of Hamon the Port-Royalist and the briefer composition of S. Francis de Sales, which may be read with interest and profit.

The following Commentary is an attempt to fill this void, at least provisionally, until some more competent hand undertakes the task. Its chief claim to attention is that it is almost exclusively a compilation from the writings of the Fathers and Schoolmen, with just so much illustration from ascetic writers, hymnodists, and poets, ancient and modern, as seemed to give point to their comments, and to make the continuous perusal of the volume an easier task.

An attempt to bring to bear on the Canticles all the appropriate matter which exists, would simply have been to aim at turning into this one channel all the streams of the devotional theology of the Middle Ages, and would have defeated the intention with which the Commentary was undertaken, that of summarizing in brief and portable compass the results of seventeen centuries of loving meditation on the Book of Divine Love.

This work, therefore, does not aim, like the larger compilations already referred to, at making clerical readers independent of further study on the subject. Rather it is hoped that the extracts from the writings of Origen, S. Bernard, Gilbert of Hoyland, Henry Harphius, and others like-minded, may incite them to fuller perusal. But it does propose to give other students of the Canticles, and especially the inmates of Religious Houses (for whose instruction it was originally projected) a sufficient, though necessarily brief, insight into the treasures which have accumulated, in the course of centuries, around this shrine of sacred mysteries. To further this end, a suggestion made by a critic of the *Commentary on the Psalms*, too late so far as the plan of that work was concerned, has been here adopted, namely, the addition of English versions to the Greek and Latin quotations which occur in the course of the work. As these have been somewhat hastily executed, they are consequently not a little rugged, and aim merely at giving the sense approximately, without pretending to any literary excellence.

It would have been most desirable if a Commentary such as this, not designed for critical purposes, but of a purely devotional character, could have been kept absolutely free from polemical matter, yet, as the spiritual character of the Canticles has been freely impeached in our day, it has been necessary to make some protest against the method and arguments of its impugners; but this has been excluded so far as possible from the text, and relegated to the Introduction, in which a few of the literary problems connected with the Song of Songs are briefly discussed.

It remains only to request a lenient judgment on this tentative execution of a most difficult task, and to ask for such assistance at the hands of readers as may make a future edition, should it be required, less defective.

LONDON,
Nativity of Our Lady, 1869.

INTRODUCTION.

I. THE exceptional position occupied by the Song of Songs among the books of Holy Writ, standing as it does apart from Law and Prophets, Histories and didactic compositions, and having obviously on the surface but very faint relations to the remaining Scriptural Canticles, has naturally concentrated much attention upon it, and given rise to no little variety of comment on all the particulars connected with its external form and history, and its internal signification. One fact alone remains undisputed, that of its inclusion within the Canon, both Jewish and Christian, from the earliest times of which we have any record. Its place in the Septuagint testifies to its recognition as a sacred book by the Jews two centuries before the Christian era, and the language used concerning it by Rabbinical authorities puts it on a very different level from that accorded by them to the Deutero-Canonical Books. They classed it as one of the five *Megilloth* of the Bible, along with Ruth, Lamentations, Ecclesiastes, and Esther, and ranked it first among them, reading it at the Passover, the most solemn festival of the year. Fully in accordance with this position is the remark of Rabbi Akiba, a contemporary of the Emperor Hadrian, saying, "The entire history of the world does not present an epoch like the day when the Song of Songs was given to Israel, for though all the Hagiographa are holy, yet the Song of Songs is most holy." The corollary from these premises is that the Canticles have been regarded

Canonicity of the Song.

Rabbinical estimate of it.

all along as the work of an inspired writer, and as instinct with a spiritual meaning; both which views are explicitly asserted by the Targum, which begins its paraphrase with the words: "The songs and praises which Solomon the Prophet, king of Israel, spake by the HOLY GHOST, before the LORD the Creator of the universe."

First objection to mystical view

It has been objected in modern times against the alleged admission by the ancient Jews of a mystical import underlying the letter, that they prohibited the perusal of the Canticles by all persons below thirty years of age, whence it has been argued either that the book was given in vain so far as all who died in youth were concerned, or that the very fact of withholding it establishes the denial of its spiritual character. This objection, apart from its failing to settle

refuted.

whether the Jews were right or wrong in their discipline on this head, falls to the ground for two reasons; first, that the Rabbins extended the same prohibition to the beginning of Genesis and the earliest and latest chapters of Ezekiel, without any impeachment of their inspiration; and secondly, that the Eastern Church, like the Church of England, while avowedly upholding the mystical sense, refrains, on grounds of expediency, from public reading of the Canticles in divine worship, though the place of the book in the Old Testament Canon, as received by Christians, has been acknowledged ever since the earliest known list was drawn up by Melito, Bishop of Sardis, about A.D. 170.

Date and authorship.

II. The questions of date and authorship have both been hotly contested. The prevalent opinion amongst Jews and Christians until comparatively recent times, agreed with that of the Targum and Septuagint, and other ancient versions, in ascribing the Song to Solomon, son of David. There were, however, some exceptions. Some Talmudists assigned it to Hezekiah, R. Kimchi and a few others to Isaiah. On the other hand, the received tradition is supported by some important arguments. Apart from the title, which may of course have been added by a later hand (as is doubtless the case with several of the Psalms,) and from direct references to Solomon as a living person, which might be only poetical, there are two items of internal evidence which fix the date with tolerable accuracy. First is the passage in chap. vi. 4, "Thou art beautiful, O my love, as Tirzah, comely as Jerusalem." Tirzah, as the capital of the Northern kingdom under Jeroboam I. and his successors until the building of Samaria, (1 Kings xiv. 17 ; xv. 21; xvi. 8, 23,) would never have been coupled with Jerusalem, the head of the Davidic and Aaronic polity, by a poet of either Israel or Judah after the revolt of the ten tribes, owing to the political and religious hostility which immediately arose between the two realms, just as no poem before the union of the English and Scottish crowns praises both London and Edinburgh. Thus the furthest possible limit of date is the outbreak of war between Abijah and Jeroboam in B.C. 958. Another passage narrows the period much more. The eighth verse of the same chapter tells us of Solomon's harem, "There are threescore queens and fourscore concubines." But in 1 Kings xi. 3, we read, "And he had seven hundred wives, princesses, and three hundred concubines." Wherefore we conclude that the Song was not only written in Solomon's life-time, but at a comparatively early period of his reign, before he had fallen into the extravagant excesses of his old age. The plea which would deny the authenticity of the passage of the Book of Kings, treating it as a mere exaggeration of later times, to be corrected by the more reasonable estimate of the Canticles, may be dismissed at once, apart from any question of inspiration, as neither justified by what we know of the manners of Eastern sovereigns nor by the treatment which two equally compatible statements would receive if found in the pages of a secular historian. So far as style and diction are concerned, the chief modern critics are agreed in attributing the Song of Songs to the Solomonic age, in opposition to a somewhat earlier school, which post-dated it considerably, on grounds now admitted to be insufficient.

Internal evidence.

In the absence of direct internal evidence and of

historical testimony at all coeval with the date of the composition, it is impossible to lay down as a certainty that Solomon was author of the Song. But there is, at the very least, quite as much to be said in favour of the earliest known tradition as can be urged against it. The title goes for something, for it establishes that at the very remote period when it was affixed,—earlier at any rate than the LXX. version—no rival claimant had been effectually set up. Those who deny the Solomonic authorship urge that such an epithet as "Song of Songs" makes against the claim, because no author would venture on such a panegyric of his own work. The reply to this is twofold. The critics must either accept the inscription as synchronous with the poem, or reject it. If they accept the genuineness of the name "Song of Songs," they must take the remainder of the title into account also, and admit Solomon's claim. If they reject the whole inscription as a later interpolation, then Solomon is not to be charged with having qualified his poem with any epithet at all, and the count fails. And this without taking into account a further consideration, that of the inspired character of the book; since, if Solomon was divinely instructed what to write, there can be no more personal vanity in his using the title "Song of Songs" than there is blasphemy in a Prophet beginning a sentence with "Thus saith the LORD." There would be, at the outset, something unaccountable in the total loss of the most copious class of writings of the wisest and most powerful of Hebrew kings. Most copious, because the thousand and five songs attributed to him in 1 Kings iv. 32, must have necessarily exceeded in bulk those three thousand proverbs, of which such important remains exist. It is not unreasonable to suppose that the great majority of these poems were of merely passing and secular interest, but it is difficult to conjecture why utter oblivion should have come on them all, as the negation of his authorship in this case requires its supporters to maintain. This difficulty, no light one in face of the preservation of so many songs of David

Marginal notes: Probability of Solomon's authorship, from the title; from authorship of other songs;

and Asaph, is more readily solved by acceptance of the traditional view than by any other means.

The next plea in Solomon's favour is of small weight independently, but not without importance in a cumulative argument. He is praised, in the same passage which mentions the number of his writings, for his great skill in natural history : " And he spake of trees, from the cedar tree that is in Lebanon even unto the hyssop that springeth out of the wall : he spake also of beasts, and of fowl, and of creeping things, and of fishes." (1 Kings iv. 33.) There is no book of Scripture which dwells so much as the Canticles upon natural imagery, or which mentions so many names of animals and plants in terms implying familiarity with their habits. The only reply which has been suggested to this plea is that other people may have known these things as well as Solomon. No doubt; but the real point at issue, that the internal evidence is so far perfectly consistent with the traditional authorship, is not in the least weakened by such a demurrer. The like may be said of the analogies of idea and diction, admittedly existing between Proverbs and Canticles.[1] They do not fix with certainty the parts of the Book of Proverbs which are due to Solomon's pen, nor do they give any clue to the priority of date in either case. But allowing, as all do, that Solomon is author of part of the Proverbs, the coincidences lend additional weight to the traditional view, and, as must never be forgotten in discussions of the kind, make the burden of disproof heavier for the contesters of the claim in possession.

from love of natural history;

and from analogies with Proverbs.

Two other pleas are urged against Solomon from opposite sides. Those who allow the spiritual interpretation of the Song maintain that Solomon was not morally fitted to be the instrument of such teaching, while those who adhere to the newest modern literal

Further objections.

---

[1] Cant. i. 11=Prov. xxv. 11; Cant. iv. 5=Prov. v. 19; Cant. iv. 9=Prov. i. 9; Cant. iv. 11=Prov. v. 3, xvi. 24; Cant. iv. 12=Prov. v. 15; Cant. v. 1=Prov. ix. 5; Cant. v. 2= Prov. xx. 13; Cant. v. 6=Prov. i. 28; Cant. vii. 1=Prov. xxv. 12; Cant. vii. 9=Prov. xxiii. 31; Cant. viii. 7=Prov. vi. 31—35, &c.

view regard the poem as in some degree a satire against him, and therefore certainly not from his pen. The second of these objections will be considered later, while it is enough to say of the first one that it loses sight on the one hand of the admitted discrepancy between the youth and age of Solomon, to the former of which the Song may more probably be ascribed; and on the other of the frequent instrumentality of sinners in working out the designs of GOD, of which the prophecy of Balaam and the apostolate of Judas are sufficient examples.

Methods of Interpretation.

III. The third question, and that which has been most eagerly contested of all, concerns the interpretation of the Song, whether it is to be mystical, allegorical, or literal, and in each of these cases what is the method to be followed. As before, there is a

Traditional view.

traditional view in possession, which has the pleas of remote antiquity, continuous tenure, and perfect consistency with itself in its favour. This view, common to the Talmud and Targum and to all Christian writers (with a brief exception to be noticed presently) for sixteen centuries, is that the poem is wholly mystical, with no historical basis whatsoever, and that it denotes the relations between GOD and His Church, albeit there is much variety of detail in setting forth the particulars

Allegorical view.

of this relation. An intermediate view supposes an historical foundation for the Song, preferably the bridal of Solomon with Pharaoh's daughter, and holds that a superstructure of religious allegory has been raised on this basis, as in that other case of the Exodus, so frequently used as a type of spiritual deliverance from

Literalist view.

sin. And a third view, almost exclusively modern, denies all inner meaning to the poem, save of the most incidental kind, and maintains a literal exposition. The mystical interpretation, which forms the subject-matter of the commentary in this volume, and which traces the history of the Divine dealings with man under the Law and the Gospel, has in its favour a cumulative mass of evidence of a very cogent nature.

Arguments for traditional view.

In the first place, the relationship of marriage is very frequently used in Scripture to denote the union be-

tween GOD and the chosen people, the ornaments of a
bride and abundant progeny are the promised rewards
of devotion and obedience, barrenness and divorce
are the threatened punishments of spiritual adultery.
There is thus no antecedent improbability, as has been
alleged, in the nuptial imagery of the Song having a
mystical signification. This comes out most clearly in from the
that Book which has most obviously approached, if language of
not actually borrowed, the language of the Canticles, Scripture;
namely, the prophecy of Hosea, in which the marriage of
GOD to Israel, and her sins against the nuptial bond, are
steadily dwelt upon. A further illustration is afforded
by the language of the forty-fifth Psalm, which represents
a King, who is styled LORD and GOD, as the Spouse of
a Virgin Bride, and which is directly applied to CHRIST
in the Epistle to the Hebrews. As the structure of
this Psalm, like that of the seventy-second, absolutely
forbids its literal application to any mere human sovereign
ran, save at the hands of those who are resolved to
see no Messianic prophecies in the Old Testament, be
the evidence what it may, it contributes a most important item of proof to the tenability of the traditional view. This is further borne out by the Gospels,
the Pauline Epistles, and the Revelation. The Baptist
speaks of CHRIST as the Bridegroom, and of himself
as the Bridegroom's friend; while the SAVIOUR, in
defending His disciples from the charge of religious
laxity, applies the name Bridegroom to Himself, and
that of "children of the bridechamber" to His followers. S. Paul illustrates the metaphor further by
declaring that he has "espoused" his converts "as a
chaste virgin, to CHRIST," and that earthly marriage
is only a type of a heavenly mystery. The Apocalypse,
with its description of the heavenly Jerusalem as the
Bride of the Lamb, and of the final triumph of the redeemed as His marriage feast, completes the chain of
Scriptural evidence; and if the mystical interpretation
of the Canticles be set aside, it becomes exceedingly
difficult to explain the use of this peculiar imagery,
which cannot be traced to any other source.

The plea that not marriage, but courtship, which

leads to marriage, is the scope of the Song, has been urged against the Catholic view, but vainly in the face of the recurrent phrase "the Virgin of Israel" in the Old Testament, and the clear statement of the New that the marriage has not yet come, and only the betrothal has taken place. The next argument of weight is that which serves to repel the *à priori* objections taken to the form and diction of the poem as a vehicle for spiritual ideas. If it could be shown that the Song, if mystically explained, is an isolated pheno-

<small>from parallels in Arabic and Persian literature;</small>

menon, having no parallel in any literature, very much would be done towards discrediting the ancient view. But such is not the case. The Arab nation, which in blood and language is most nearly allied to the Hebrews, has preserved to the present day the custom of chanting in public worship songs in which the religious meaning is veiled under the ordinary terms of earthly love. The service at which these are recited is called a *Zikr*, the poems themselves (usually in honour of Mohammed) *muweshshah*. On this, Mr. Lane, in his *Modern Egyptians*, chap. xxiv. writes as follows : " He pointed out the following poem as one of those most

<small>Songs at Zikrs.</small>

common at Zikrs, and as one which was sung at the Zikr which I have begun to describe. I translate it verse for verse, and imitate the measure and system of rhyme of the original, with this difference only, that the first, third, and fifth lines of each stanza rhyme with each other in the original, but not in my translation.

> With love my heart is troubled;
>   And mine eye-lid hind'reth sleep:
> My vitals are dissevered;
>   While with streaming tears I weep.
> My union seems far distant:
>   Will my love ever meet mine eye?
> Alas! did not estrangement
>   Draw my tears, I would not sigh.
>
> By dreary nights I'm wasted:
>   Absence makes my hopes expire:
> My tears, like pearls, are dropping;
>   And my heart is wrapped in fire.

INTRODUCTION. xvii

>Whose is like my condition?
>　Scarcely know I remedy,
>Alas! did not estrangement
>　Draw my tears, I would not sigh.
>
>O turtle-dove! acquaint me
>　Wherefore thus dost thou lament?
>Art thou so stung by absence?
>　Of thy wings deprived, and pent?
>He saith, 'Our griefs are equal;
>　Worn away with love I lie.'
>Alas! did not estrangement
>　Draw my tears, I would not sigh.
>
>O First and sole Eternal!
>　Show Thy favour yet to me.
>Thy slave, Ahmad El-Bekree,
>　Hath no LORD excepting Thee.
>By Tá-Há,'the Great Prophet,
>　Do not Thou his wish deny.
>Alas! did not estrangement
>　Draw my tears, I would not sigh.

I must translate a few more lines, to show more strongly the similarity of these songs to that of Solomon; and lest it should be thought that I have varied the expressions, I shall not attempt to render them into verse. In the same collection of poems sung at Zikrs is one which begins with these lines:

>O gazelle from among the gazelles of El-Yemen!
>I am thy slave without cost:
>O thou small of age and fresh of skin!
>O thou who art scarce past the time of drinking milk!

In the first of these verses we have a comparison exactly agreeing with that in the concluding verse of Solomon's Song; for the word which, in our Bible, is translated 'a roe,' is used in Arabic as synonymous with 'ghazál' (or a gazelle,) and the mountains of El-Yemen are the 'mountains of spices.' This poem ends with the following lines:

>The phantom of thy form visited me in my slumber:
>I said, 'O phantom of slumber! who sent thee?'
>He said, 'He sent me whom thou knowest;
>He whose love occupies thee.'

> The beloved of my heart visited me in the darkness of night;
> I stood, to show him honour, until he sat down.
> I said, 'O thou my petition, and all my desire!
> Hast thou come at midnight, and not feared the watchmen?'
> He said to me, 'I feared, but, however, love
> Had taken from me my soul and my breath.'

Compare the above with the second and five following verses of the fifth chapter of Solomon's Song. Finding that songs of this description are extremely numerous, and almost the only poems sung at Zikrs; that they are composed for this purpose, and intended only to have a spiritual sense (though certainly not understood in such a sense by the generality of the vulgar;) I cannot entertain any doubt as to the design of Solomon's Song. The specimens which I have just given of the religious love-songs of the Moslems have not been selected in preference to others as most agreeing with that of Solomon, but as being in frequent use." To this may be added the statement of Major Scott Waring as to a kindred custom in Persia, "The Persians insist that we shall give them the merit of understanding their own language, that all the odes of their celebrated poets are mystical, and breathe a fervent spirit of adoration to the Supreme Being. They maintain that the Soofees profess eager desire with no carnal affection, and circulate the cup, but no material goblet, since all things are spiritual in their sect; all is mystery within mystery." And finally, European literature contributes its quota of parallel in the *Vita Nuova* of Dante.

Attempted reply, from absence of sacred names;   A twofold reply, of but little cogency, has been attempted to this proof that there is no inherent unlikelihood in the mystical interpretation. It is alleged, firstly, that the Song of Solomon contains no hint, no key, no direct reference to holy names and ideas, such as is certainly found in the first quotation from Arabic sources given above, and such as may possibly be found in the full text of the remainder, and that we are therefore not at liberty to interpret it otherwise than literally. This loses sight of a very important and familiar canon of composition, that an

allegory, in order to be perfect, ought *not* to con- *untenable*
tain its own key. So far as it does, or as any ob- *on abstract*
trusive clue is given, it is defective in structure. The *grounds.*
beast-fables of Bidpai, Æsop, and Krilof, supply familiar examples. Any distinct intimation of the purport in the body of the fable is simply destructive, and even an application tagged on is more than superfluous, ranking with the too audible stage-explanations in the tragedy of Pyramus and Thisbe. This charge against the Song of Solomon, then, merely proves its high literary excellence, and the skill with which the author avoided the defect into which the Arab poet has fallen. The only reason which would excuse deviation from this rule would be the imperative need of warning persons against being led astray by the literal sense; but as a fact, in the whole literary history of the Canticles for nearly nineteen hundred years, there is scarcely an example on record of the literal sense having held its ground anywhere for a moment. Surely, if the mystical exposition be so unnatural and far-fetched as some declare, this would not and could not be so, as we may learn from the total failure of the Alexandrine critics to establish their allegorical interpretation of the Iliad. Another objection, that urged by an American *Objection*
literalist, Professor Noyes, is more philosophical in *from dissimilarity of*
tone, but not more convincing. It is that the funda- *race and religion, and*
mental differences between the pantheistic system of the *from distance of*
Sufis and the religion of the Jews, and the great interval of time which lies between Solomon and Hafiz, *time;*
(even if it be conceded that the odes of the latter are religious poems at all) make it absolutely impossible to institute any parallel between them. This argument loses sight of the original question, which is not whether there is any close likeness between Sufism and Judaism, which might crop up in literary forms, but whether there is the least antecedent improbability in the human mind selecting amatory language to express devotional thoughts. The allegation that it is most unlikely to do so is disposed of by the parallels adduced, and the cogency of the argument would be un- *inadequate*
affected by the broadest divergency of race and creed, *as disproof.*

as all students of comparative mythology know full well. But, not to dwell on the constant intercourse between Canaan and Persia, from the days when Abraham met Chedorlaomer till those when John of Persepolis came with Macarius of Jerusalem to the Council of Nicæa, which allowed ample opportunity for Iranian ideas to enter Palestine, the proof from the kindred race and religion of Arabia remains unmoved by any exception based on the plea of diversity, weak as even that is.

Anthropomorphic language of the Song. Still less weight can be attached to objections drawn from the anthropomorphic language of the Song, which has been declared inappropriate in the highest degree to such august themes as those which the traditional interpretation finds in it. For this, again, is a mere *à priori* plea, and therefore of no logical force whatsoever, failing, besides, to take account of the manner in which the shadow of the coming Incarnation is cast over the Old Testament, occasioning, nay, necessitating such language in order to prepare the minds of the Jewish nation for the reception of the full Messianic idea of a GOD-MAN, which is gradually unfolded with advancing clearness as the prophetic series draws near its close. And as regards the question of the abstract fitness or unfitness of the language, it may be briefly observed that the "verifying faculty" of seventeen Christian centuries, exercised amongst others by men of such keen intellect, spiritual insight, and moral purity as Origen, Athanasius, Augustine, Gregory the Great, Alcuin, Bernard, Thomas Aquinas, and Gerson, may well be set against the conflicting opinions of the last hundred years in a matter of the kind.

Main difficulty of the literalist view. This portion of the controversy leads up directly to what is, after all, the main difficulty in the way of literalists, a difficulty which they have not hitherto even plausibly seemed to overcome. It is that of accounting for the presence of the Song, assuming it to be a mere love-poem, in the Canon of Scripture at all, whether as originally admitted by the Jews or subsequently adopted by the Christians. It would stand apart from all the rest of Scripture as alone without a directly religious signification, and be necessarily degraded into a secondary rank, if not altogether excluded from the list of inspired writings. The only semblance of answer to this plea is the allegation that the Song does not stand alone in this respect, because the Book of Esther belongs to the same category, being alike without those sacred names and phrases which mark all other portions of the Bible.   *Isolation of the Song from the rest of the Bible.*

But this phantom argument vanishes at a touch. The Book of Esther does stand in a very clear and definite relation to all the other historical books, because it gives the details of a most important crisis in the national life of the Hebrew people, serving as the chief link between the Captivity and the restoration of Israel. And further, though holy words are carefully excluded from the book (possibly through reserve in a writing designed for circulation amongst Gentiles,) yet the fast proclaimed by Esther and Mordecai points at once to a time of prayer to that Being Whose Name is left unspoken, and the Feast of Purim, celebrated by Jews everywhere for the twenty-three centuries which have since elapsed, testifies to the national sense of a deliverance scarcely second to that of the Exodus. The Song, however, cannot be so connected with other parts of Scripture on a literalist theory, but must remain as a startling and inexplicable anomaly.   *The Book of Esther not a parallel case.*

IV. The sense that this is so has prompted, at different eras, various tentative solutions of the difficulty. The earliest of these was propounded by Theodore of Mopsuestia in the first quarter of the fifth century, and represented the Song as merely an epithalamium on the marriage of Solomon with Pharaoh's daughter or with Abishag the Shunammite. This theory, after being condemned in express and forcible terms in the Fifth General Council, disappeared completely for more than eight hundred years, when it was reproduced for a moment by Gregory Abulfaraj. It rested again till revived by Grotius, who allowed it, nevertheless, to include an allegory; and it was finally developed into a very elaborate form by the celebrated   *Solutions proposed for this difficulty.*

Bossuet, in 1690, whose genius gave it a measure of popularity amongst scholars till the early part of the present century, when the ingenious criticisms of Dr. Mason Good (some of which had been anticipated long before by Natalis Alexander,) established the utter incongruity of the language of the Song with the circumstances of a State alliance and with the national surroundings of an Egyptian princess, to whom the pastoral character of the Bride could in no wise be accommodated. The eloquent words in which Theodoret expresses the mind of the Church in his day against the views ascribed to Theodore of Mopsuestia merit citation. In the preface to his commentary on the Canticles, he says: "Since the majority of those who slander the Song of Songs and deny it to be a spiritual book, weave fables unworthy of crazy old women, some of them saying that Solomon the Wise wrote it concerning himself and Pharaoh's daughter; a few authors of the same stamp alleging that Abishag the Shunammite is the Bride, and not Pharaoh's daughter; while others, taking a somewhat more philosophical view, call it the Royal Speech, so as to understand the people by the Bride and the King by the Bridegroom; we think that we shall be well employed in refuting at the outset of our exposition these false and mischievous theories, and then will proceed to set forth the true and clear meaning of the author. And yet these men ought to know that the holy Fathers, much their superiors in wisdom and spiritual insight, were they who placed this Book amongst the divine Scriptures, and approving it as full of the SPIRIT, pronounced it worthy of the Church. For had they thought otherwise, they would never have included a work whose subject was passion and desire in the number of Holy Writ. . . . Not only Eusebius of Palestine, and Origen the Egyptian, and Cyprian of Carthage, crowned with the diadem of martyrdom, and men earlier than they were and nearer to the Apostles, but also those who were afterwards famous in the Churches, Basil the Great in his exposition of the beginning of Proverbs, and the two Gregories, allied to Basil, one by blood

Rejoinder of Theodoret.

and the other by friendship, and that valiant champion of religion Diodorus, and John, who to this day waters the whole earth with the streams of his teaching, and they who came still later, all pronounced this Book to be spiritual. Seeing that this is so, let us consider whether it be reasonable for us to follow our own theories, paying no attention to so many eminent men, and despising the HOLY SPIRIT Himself, by not listening to him who says so well: 'The thoughts of mortal men are miserable, and our devices are but uncertain,' (Wisd. ix. 14,) and blessed Paul saying of certain persons, 'They became vain in their imaginations, and their foolish heart was darkened,' (Rom. i. 21.) But let us cry thus with blessed Peter, 'We ought to obey GOD rather than man,' (Acts v. 29.) Let us also say to them, 'Whether it be right in the sight of GOD to hearken unto you more than unto GOD, judge ye: for we cannot but speak the things which we have seen and heard by the HOLY GHOST.' . . . Coming then from the old to the new Bride, let us in this wise interpret the Song of Songs, and rejecting false and mischievous theories, let us follow the holy Fathers, and recognize one Bride conversing with one Bridegroom; and learn from the holy Apostles who that Bridegroom and Bride may be. For the inspired Paul teaches us that, writing thus, 'I have espoused you to one husband, that I may present you as a chaste virgin to CHRIST,' (2 Cor. xi. 2.) He calls her a Bride who is made up of many. For he does not say, 'I have betrothed *thee*,' but *you*, that is, holy souls, perfected in virtue. For Divine Scripture understands the Church by the Bride, and calls CHRIST the Bridegroom."

It is needless to heap up testimonies of the same kind from other Patristic writers, since their own comments on the Song will speak for them in due time. But it is worth while to dwell for a moment on one point of the citation just given. It has been alleged by some modern critics that the dazzling powers of Origen gave the tone to the traditional interpretation which has held its ground ever since his day, and that he drew it from Talmudic sources, being the first to

Origen not the author of the mystical view.

introduce it into the Church. Considering how embittered the opposition to Origen became even in his own life-time, this is not very probable in itself, but it is refuted by the contemporaneous language of S. Cyprian, who was not influenced by Origen's works, and also by Theodoret's incidental mention of an earlier and consentaneous tradition ascending much nearer to primitive times. Of this tradition but one written fragment has come down to us, a solitary note on Cant. iii. 9, by S. Theophilus of Antioch, who died between A.D. 178 and 189, a few years before Origen was born. But the fragment is decisive as to the method followed in the second century, and materially lessens the probability of Talmudic influence having affected a pre-existing literalism.

Omitting the various phases through which the literalist theory has passed since its revival in the sixteenth century by Castellio (who went to the length of rejecting the Canticles altogether) it will suffice to state briefly the view now in fashion, but soon to be discredited by its own supporters on the ground of its glaring improbability and self-contradiction, possessing, as it does, no shred of external evidence or internal plausibility. According to this hypothesis, invented by Jacobi in 1771, and accepted with further developments by the majority of subsequent literalists, the Song represents the adventures of a newly-wedded or betrothed Hebrew shepherdess, who is accidentally seen by Solomon in one of his progresses, is vainly solicited and tempted by him, and even carried off as a prisoner to the royal harem, whence she finally escapes with her beloved shepherd back to the scenes of her former life. The witnesses called in defence of this theory, like the elders who testified against Susannah, are agreed in the main outline of their story, but are so irreconcilably at variance with one another on points of detail essential to consistency, as to be destructive of each other's credit. For if anything might be fairly expected to be most unmistakably prominent, were the theory true, it would be the distinction between the language of the genuine affection of the shepherd-husband, and that of the seductive wiles of the royal tempter. But Ginsburg and Renan, Meier and Hitzig, are utterly at variance on this head, and interchange the speeches in the most bewildering manner. Can any one suppose, were the stage directions in Shakespeare absent, that there could be the least doubt in assigning their several parts with accuracy to Othello and Iago, to Postumus and Iachimo? Further, if the poem be intended, as has been suggested, as a satire upon Solomon, the difficulty is very much increased by the elaborate way in which the censure is concealed, so that the lapse of about two thousand eight hundred years has been necessary for its discovery. If a poet of the northern kingdom had written it with this intent, there is no conceivable reason why he should not have been more plain-spoken, because the fiercer his invective, the better would the kings of Ephraim have been pleased. And if he was a total stranger to the Aaronic worship, the men of the Great Synagogue, with whom Mosaic orthodoxy and loyalty to the House of David were first principles, would never have included his work in their Canon. If, on the other hand, a southern bard (and, by the hypothesis, an inspired one,) were the writer, there is at once a startling dissimilarity between the extreme caution employed, (worthy of a courtier epigrammatist under Domitian or Louis XIV.,) and the bold denunciations of royal guilt such as we know to have been the wont of Hebrew prophets, a Nathan, an Elijah, a Micah, or a Jeremiah. *The Song not a satire upon Solomon.*

As this commentary is not designed for critical, but for devotional purposes, it is beside its aim to go into the further disproof of this theory at length; but two items of the moral argument against it may be given, one from the pen of a favourer of it, and the other from that of an opponent. "Wherever," observes Dr. Davidson, "the doctrinal interest prevails, scientific exegesis declines in proportion, because it is overridden. The genuine spirit of interpretation is always favourable to the literal sense. For the same reason Hofman and Delitzsch have recourse to the typical. Though *Moral argument against literalism.*

they do not recognise the validity of the allegorical method, they are too much led by doctrinal prepossessions to embrace the literal, and are therefore fain to adopt a kindred mode of explanation." If for "doctrinal interest" we substitute the equivalent term "religious belief," the meaning of this sentence will be unaltered, but a little clearer, and it is in fact an admission that in exact proportion as men accept the tenets of Christianity, they will recede from "the letter that killeth" and draw near to "the spirit that giveth life." The other remark is that of Hengstenberg, who has said with biting truth: "The literal interpretation of this Book gained its honours in the age of Rationalism, when the Church was degraded to its lowest level, and when it was bare and void of sound ecclesiastical judgment, and of holy taste and tact." He might have gone further, had his position allowed it, and have pointed out that the Lutheran body, true to the animal and earthly instincts of its celebrated founder, has always been nearer the ground than any other large Christian community, and less capable of lofty spiritual views. The whole sect, in its three centuries of existence, though prolific in respectability, has not given birth to one man in whom the common consent of other men has recognized the marks of a saintly character, such as have not infrequently illustrated the members of other Communions, nor has it produced any book (with the possible exception of Gerhard's Meditations) which has been permanently added to the list of those devotional works that have really enriched religious literature. In the field of the outer letter of Biblical study, in textual and grammatical criticism, in historical elucidation, it has laboured in a spirit of diligence and zeal beyond all praise, yet as

>   the least erected spirit that fell
> From heaven; for even in heaven his looks and thoughts
> Were always downward bent, admiring more
> The riches of heaven's pavement, trodden gold,
> Than aught divine or holy else, enjoyed
> In vision beatific.

Consequently, from being thus always engaged with the outer shell, the inner sense and the religious aroma have always escaped it. It has expended much care and science on Holy Writ, but its spiritual chemistry has invariably been of the kind which turns the most lustrous diamonds into black and worthless lumps of carbon, never of that higher constructive type which makes the light of jewels flash on our eyes from the dark places of the Bible.

The necessity, after the gradual manufacture of the reigning literalist theory, for discovering some ground for the retention of the Canticles in the Canon, has led to the assertion that its design is to teach a higher morality with regard to love and marriage than that prevalent amongst the Jews of the Solomonic age, and in particular, to be a protest against polygamy and its attendant evils. There is a very sensible rule in English law-courts to the effect that whatever may be the apparent grammatical meaning of an old statute, the only rule which can guide a judge is the interpretation put on its wording by his predecessors in their decisions. If it can be shown by a series of precedents, that the meaning contended for was never so much as urged, not to say recognized and allowed by the Courts, the plea breaks down at once. So it is in this case. There is not the faintest hint in any writer, Jewish or Christian, before the nineteenth century, that such a lesson is inculcated by the Song of Songs, there is no trace of any influence having been exerted by it in this direction. *The Song not a treatise on wedlock.*

Conversely, the rule holds good that a series of decisions in agreement with one another, however little they may seem at first sight to outsiders to be logically deducible from the premises, are declaratory of the true force of a statute. Here, then, is a book which has exerted an exceedingly marked influence in Christendom ever since a Christian literature arose; which has materially affected the whole range of ascetic theology; which has powerfully contributed to the formation of that religious ideal which moulded ten centuries of Christian history; which continues to maintain its hold upon many thousands of believers, directly or indirectly. For all practical purposes, and for all philosophic investigation into the spiritual records of the world, no method is of any value save the mystical one, for no other has ever passed into the stage of energy, or has contributed anything to the religious consciousness of mankind. If the truth of Jacobi's hypothesis could be set beyond a doubt by the discovery of coeval documents, there would be at best but the same kind of languid antiquarian interest aroused which greets each fresh alleged Biblical testimony found in cuneiform inscriptions, because the theory has always been utterly barren and dead; and the graver problem would remain unsolved, how a literature so peculiarly limpid and emphatic in its utterance on moral and social questions should have suddenly changed its whole method, and have approached the question of marriage by a path so indirect, obscure, and enigmatic, as to be wholly inaccessible to all for whom the teaching was intended, and to owe its first survey to the chance guess of a stray traveller, eighteen centuries after another road had been opened, involving the total disuse of the older one. There have been many rival theories as to the road by which Hannibal's army crossed the Alps, but no one has yet conjectured that it came over the summit of Mont Blanc or the Matterhorn, much less that there was no other path for ordinary traffic till the Simplon was made practicable. And, it may be added, the upholders of this theory have shown by their own conduct how little they value the lesson they profess to have found. The marriage law of Prussia, under which most of them live, is perhaps the very laxest and least moral in the civilized world; only slightly, if at all, raised above the level of that of Imperial Rome in the days of Juvenal. Yet it does not appear to have elicited any protest based upon the Canticles, or, indeed, upon anything else, from the critics.

Form and unity of the Song. V. With regard to the form and unity of the Canticles, there have also been conflicting theories, but the earliest Christian view has, curiously enough, been reinstated by modern critics in both these respects, for they admit on the one hand that the poem is essentially one, and not a mere collection of odes loosely strung together, and on the other that its truest designation is that of a dramatic idyll. There is, however, the utmost disagreement amongst them as to the portions into which the Song is to be divided. Magnus, for example, makes twenty strophes of it; De Wette and Heiligstedt twelve, though disagreeing as to the points of division; Hitzig finds nine, Weissbach six, and several others five. There is a similar, though much slighter, discrepancy between the pauses recognized by the mystical interpreters (for in truth these pauses are, with but one or two exceptions, very indistinctly marked,) but there is a very great difference between the result of these contradictions in the two cases. The mystics, acknowledging the Song to be a drama only in the modified sense of a dialogue carried on between three speakers,—the Bridegroom, the Bride, and the leader of their friends,—during a certain change of action, of entrances and exits, are little disturbed by any difficulty in adjustment of the divisions, because the sense is quite unaffected thereby. But the literalists, who profess to see a regular plot evolved in accordance with the rules and the spirit of modern melodrama, are put out of court if they cannot agree amongst themselves as to the progress of the action, and few things in criticism are more instructive than the elaborate stage-directions and lavish creation of additional *dramatis personæ* to which Hitzig has been driven in order to harmonize the contradictions of their theory. The accepted Christian view, which acknowledges only one masculine speaker in the Song, that Solomon who is depicted as at once Shepherd and King, finds confirmation from the juxtaposition of these two ideas in relation to the same person more than once in the Old Testament, as thus in Ezek. xxxiv. 23, "And I will set up one shepherd over them, and he shall feed them, even My servant David; he shall feed them, and be their Shepherd. And I the LORD will be their GOD, and My servant David a prince among them; I the LORD have spoken it." Again, in Micah v. 2, 4, the

The Bridegroom, King and Shepherd.

"Ruler in Israel" Who is to come out of Bethlehem, is to "feed in the strength of the LORD." Accordingly, it is natural enough to find CHRIST claiming as His own the titles of Shepherd and King, and the Lamb of the Apocalypse crowned, and yet leading the redeemed to pastures and fountains, so that this portion of the imagery is as closely in accord with the teaching of the New Testament as that concerning the bridal relation was shown to be a little while back.

The Bride of the Canticles; threefold. In the following Commentary the Bride is usually depicted as the Church, whether Jewish or Gentile, or as the holy soul which is the microcosm of the Church. The Blessed Virgin, as the holiest of all elect souls, and as thus the most perfect type of the Church of GOD, is also given frequent prominence, in accordance with the teaching of the great mediæval divines. But a certain weight must be allowed to the twofold objection urged against absolute identification of her with the Bride throughout; namely, that the Bridegroom stands to her in the relation of Son, not of Husband; and further, that it is not till the twelfth century that any very large share is allotted her by the commentators. As a fact, Rupert of Deutz, and Honorius of Autun, who were the first to make her the leading figure in the Canticles, are frequently compelled to desert their path and return to the earlier track, and the four commentators, Denys à Rykel, Delrio, Ghislerius, and Cornelius à Lapide, who have professed to devote a section on each verse to her, are constantly obliged either to mere repetition of what they had already said concerning the holy soul, merely strengthening the epithets, or to pass over the paragraph with a few conventional phrases. Therefore, in the following pages no attempt has been made to pursue the formal tripartite division, and the Bride is presented under each aspect solely in proportion to what the text will reasonably bear, and to the really telling expositions of the Schoolmen.

Catena of Authors. VI. It remains now only to speak briefly of the authors whose works have been employed in the compilation of this volume, and at the outset it should be observed that one very marked difference is noticeable between the Commentaries on the Psalter and those on the Canticles. On the Psalter, possibly from its greater prominence in the Western Church, the Latin Fathers far surpass the Greek in beauty, depth, and fervour of exposition. In treating the Canticles, the case is re- Greek and Latin Commentators. versed. No Latin writer on this book, not even S. Bernard, approaches Origen; S. Gregory the Great is inferior to Philo of Carpasia; Aponius ranks below Theodoret; Rupert beneath S. Gregory Nyssen. To counterbalance this advantage, the Canticles have suffered very heavy losses, positive and negative. Negatively, they have never been treated by some of those whose genius was most adapted to such a task. Neither S. Albert the Great nor S. Bonaventura, for example, have included it in their labours. Positively, the losses have been much more serious. Of the great commentary of Origen but a few scanty fragments remain, breaking off before the close of the second chapter. S. Gregory Nyssen's work remains imperfect too, and Michael Psellus, who paraphrases him, is compelled to break off in consequence. Death seized S. Bernard while he was engaged in the composition of his wonderful sermons on the Song of Songs, when he was but a fourth of the way through his task, and the like destiny took away his continuator, Gilbert of Hoyland, before he had completed the fifth chapter. Some of the ancient commentators, as Eusebius and Polychronius, are reduced to the merest fragments; others have perished all but the name. Yet, after all such deductions, the quantity of material existing down to the close of the sixteenth century is very great, of considerable interest and value, and singularly homogeneous, apart from the open borrowing or recasting usual in commentaries of successive generations. Since that time the number of writings on the book has vastly increased in number, but not by any means in spiritual value, and the list subjoined, therefore, makes no pretence to be an exhaustive catalogue, but merely indicates the volumes which have actually been laid under contribution, or examined with that end, even if unsuccessfully.

xxxii   INTRODUCTION.

Third Century.

1. First in order, though perhaps not in actual date of present condition, comes the Targum on Canticles, valuable as exhibiting the current of Jewish tradition, and often illustrating remarkably the views of Christian theology. I cite it usually from Walton's Polyglot.

2. Origen, (+ 253) whose splendid genius and profound devotional instinct shone so conspicuously in his Biblical writings, left a commentary of great length on the Canticles, of which S. Jerome, a most competent judge, observed that whereas he had surpassed every one else in his other commentaries, he had surpassed himself in this. Only a few brief passages remain, carrying on the exposition to Cant. ii. 15.

Fourth Century.

3. Still more unfortunate has been Eusebius of Cæsarea (+ 340,) of whose commentary only the merest fragments exist, which were published by Meursius at Lyons in 1617.

4. S. Gregory Nyssen (+ 370) has left a commentary carried on as far as Cant. vi. 9. Its distinguishing peculiarity is that he represents the Bride throughout as the soul of man, and pays but little attention to the more usual theory. His defects of obscurity and involution are by no means absent from the work.

5. A Catena, known as that of the Three Fathers, SS. Nilus, Maximus, and Gregory Nyssen, drawn up at an early period, is of considerable value, and is one of the chief authorities for the tropological interpretation.

6. S. Epiphanius, the famous Bishop of Constantia (+ 403,) wrote a commentary on the Canticles, long supposed to be utterly lost, and not therefore cited by any of the chief compilers. It was translated, however, into Latin by his namesake Epiphanius the Scholastic, about a century after his death, and after lying neglected in manuscript for twelve hundred years, was at last published at Rome by Foggini in 1750. It is very terse, and not of much importance, because, for the one part, it follows Origen pretty closely; and for the other, it is followed in turn and happily expanded by the subject of the next notice. The Abbé Migne's edition, though professing to give all the works, genuine and spurious, of each Epiphanius, omits this commentary.

7. Philo, Bishop of Carpasia in Cyprus (+ 374,) the pupil and friend of S. Epiphanius, to whom he owed his see, has left one of the most valuable of the early commentaries on the Song of Songs. It is of considerable length, and contains many passages of great beauty, probably enshrining for us much of the teaching of Origen, and undoubtedly much of that of S. Epiphanius. It is noteworthy for another reason also, that S. Gregory the Great borrowed freely from it in his commentary, a circumstance which has led Cornelius à Lapide to allege that Philo must have been largely interpolated, rather than admit that the great Western Doctor could stoop to draw materials from the East.

8. S. Ambrose (+ 397) though not formally a commentator on Canticles, has, in fact, gone over nearly the whole ground in one or other of his books, and often with great beauty of illustration. A certain Abbat Guilielmus of S. Thierry at Rheims (+ circ. 1160) was at the pains to collect these scattered notices into a single volume.

9. Polychronius (+ 427,) Bishop of Apamea, has left a few fragments on the Song, in full agreement with the traditional interpretation, and noteworthy on that account, because he was brother of its first impugner, Theodore of Mopsuestia. They were published, along with those of Eusebius, by Meursius. *Fifth Century.*

10. Theodoret, Bishop of Cyrus (+ 430,) is one of the most important and able of the early expositors, and the calm judgment of his language adds much weight to his opinion.

11. S. Justus of Urgel (+ 540,) is the earliest extant Latin commentator, and, while following in the track of his Eastern predecessors, often adds a pithy remark of his own, which exhibits the germ of that kind of mystical exposition which culminated in the twelfth century. *Sixth Century.*

12. Next follows the commentary ascribed to Cassiodorus (+ 562,) though its authorship is disputed. The truth seems to be that it is his, though interpolated to some extent. Whoever the author may be,

the work is marked with great good sense and unquestionable piety.

<small>Seventh Century.</small>

13. S. Gregory the Great (+ 604,) has not sustained his usual level in his Commentary on the Canticles. That there are devout and beautiful passages in it, besides those drawn from Philo, is unquestionable, but it does not reach the standard of his Morals on the Book of Job.

14. S. Isidore of Seville (+ 636,) has compiled a very brief gloss on the Canticles, containing no fresh matter, and it may accordingly be passed over by students.

15. Aponius, an author of somewhat uncertain date, but probably about 680, wrote one of the very best of the early Latin comments. It is unfortunately imperfect, but an epitome of the missing portion, by Lucas, Abbat of Mount S. Cornelius, is extant, and in a great degree supplies the loss.

<small>Eighth Century.</small>

16. The Venerable Bede (+ 735) follows Cassiodorus almost invariably, but often expands his thought and adds some fresh touches which give additional vigour and fervency.

17. Alcuin of York (+ 750,) like S. Isidore of Seville, brings nothing new to the exposition of the Song, and may be safely omitted.

<small>Ninth Century.</small>

18. Angelomus of Luxeuil (+ 850,) compiled at the desire of the Emperor Hlothar I. a commentary in which he mainly follows Aponius and S. Gregory the Great, but not infrequently adds a few touches of his own, which have their value.

19. Haymo, Bishop of Halberstadt (+ 853,) a contemporary of Angelomus, has also compiled a terse gloss drawn from his predecessors, and selected with much judgment. It contains, however, very little original matter.

20. To the same period, about the middle of the ninth century, belongs the Ordinary Gloss, first drawn up by Strabo of Fulda, and gradually augmented. It will be found cited a few times in the following commentary.

21. The tenth century is an entire blank, so far as

expositions of the Canticles go, and the first book of the kind which meets us in the eleventh century is a mere epitome of S. Gregory the Great by S. Radulphus of Fontenelle, first Abbat of S. Vandrille (+ 1047.) His learned Augustinian editor, Hommey, retorts the charge which Cornelius à Lapide brings against Philo, for he claims for him the original authorship as against S. Gregory, but on very insufficient grounds. *Eleventh Century.*

22. Michael Psellus, a Greek physician and senator, (+ 1105,) wrote, about 1050, a metrical paraphrase of the Canticles in accentual iambic verse, based on the commentary of S. Gregory Nyssen, but occasionally introducing new matter of his own.

23. S. Anselm of Laon, the "Scholastic Doctor," (+ 1103,) is supposed to be the true author of a commentary of much interest which was originally printed under the name of his more eminent namesake and contemporary, S. Anselm of Canterbury. It has also been attributed to Hervé of Dol, and will be found often cited in the succeeding pages. *Twelfth Century.*

24. Marbod of Rennes, who died at a very great age in 1123, has left, like Psellus, a metrical paraphrase of the Song, executed in hexameters. Its closeness to the Vulgate text, however, and tolerable neatness of execution, are its chief merits, for it does not add anything to the exegesis.

25. S. Bruno of Aste, (+ circ. 1120,) is the author of a compilation on the Canticles, which contains scarcely a trace of new matter, and may therefore be passed over.

26. The wonderful sermons on the Canticles by S. Bernard, (+ 1130,) all too few, though eighty-six in number, do not quite complete the exposition of the first and second chapters. Their eloquence and fervour are far more conspicuous than the actual amount of direct illustration which they yield, though it is by no means scanty, and they not merely deserve, but compel perusal.

27. Honorius of Autun, the author of the famous *Gemma Animæ*, (+ circ. 1130,) has left two independent commentaries, one of them entitled *Sigillum B.*

Mariæ, both of them containing many beautiful, though fanciful passages.

28. Richard of S. Victor, (+ 1130,) has commented on portions only of the Canticles, and is not quite continuous in his work. What he has done is, however worthy of his great reputation as a mystical divine, and he will be found often cited.

29. Rupert, Abbat of Deutz, (+ 1135,) one of the very greatest of mediæval commentators on Scripture, has produced a gloss of considerable length, whose main feature is the presentment of the Blessed Virgin as the Bride, a rule only occasionally departed from throughout his work, and that under great stress.

30. The same holds of the Gloss by Philip Harveng, Abbat of Bona Spes, in Hainault, (+ 1150,) a celebrated mystic, but it is far inferior to that of Rupert in beauty and value, and will be rarely found referred to.

31. The sermons of Gilbert of Hoyland, (+ 1175,) on the Canticles, written in avowed continuation of S. Bernard, and approaching more nearly than any others to the beauty and fervour of his style, are well deserving of study, and have supplied many paragraphs to this book.

32. Irimbert, Abbat of Ambden, and previously of S. Michael at Bamberg, (+ 1177,) commented at some length on detached portions of the Canticles, and sometimes happily enough. His work was first published by the learned Bernard Pez in his *Thesaurus Anecdotorum*.

Thirteenth Century.

33. Alanus de Insulis, the Universal Doctor, (+1203,) has followed in the steps of Rupert, but not without leaving traces of his own marked individuality on his work.

34. William Little, of Newbury, or Guilielmus Parvus, (+ 1208,) the author of a well-known and sensible History of England, also wrote a commentary on the Canticles, now lost, but which Delrio, who saw it in MS. at Louvain about 1600, has largely cited. All quotations from this source are therefore at second-hand.

35. Thomas, Canon of S. Victor, and first Abbat of S. Andrew's at Verceil, (+ 1226,) wrote a mystical

comment on the Canticles, based on the Hierarchies of the Pseudo-Dionysius, for the most part difficult of comprehension by the uninitiated reader, but with occasional passages which are really suggestive and clear. It was published by Pez in the same volume as Irimbert.

36. John Hailgrin, Archbishop of Besançon, and Cardinal of S. Sabina, (+ 1237,) is author of a Gloss belonging to the same school as those of Rupert and Alan of Lille, but not, on the whole, of remarkable merit.

37. A more famous Cardinal, occupying the same title of S. Sabina, Hugo of S. Cher, (+ 1250,) is next to follow. His great work on the whole Bible includes the Canticles, and though mainly aiming at condensing and systematizing the patristic comments, often adds much of value to the older matter.

38. A Catena, passing under the famous name of S. Thomas Aquinas, (+ 1274,) but of more than doubtful authenticity, succeeds in order. It adds so very little to what had been done four centuries earlier by Haymo of Halberstadt, that it may be altogether pretermitted.

39. Nicolas de Lyra, a converted Jew, of Norman birth, and afterwards an ornament of the Franciscan Order, (+ 1340,) is the author of valuable Postils on the Bible, in which his knowledge of Hebrew is made to bear on the exegesis. The distinguishing peculiarity of his useful treatise on the Canticles is the renewed prominence into which he brings the forgotten thought of the spiritual identity between the Jewish and Christian Churches, thus striking at the root of that alleged severance of the Song from all relations to the Old Testament which has been charged by modern literalists against the mystical exposition. *Fourteenth Century.*

40. The Emperor Matthew Cantacuzene, (+ circ. 1360,) who, after a year's partnership of the Byzantine throne with his father John V., retired to a monastery on Mount Athos, wrote in his monastic state a commentary containing many beautiful passages, and noticeable as the only Greek one which depicts the Blessed Virgin as the Bride.

Fifteenth Century.

41. John Gerson, the "Most Christian Doctor," (+ 1429,) has directly treated the Song in his *Sympsalma in Canticum*, and indirectly in his more celebrated Treatise on the Magnificat. But his writings, though full of piety and fervour, contribute scarcely anything to the exposition.

42. Far different is the case with the beautiful comment of the Ecstatic Doctor, Dionysius Leewis à Rykel, better known as Dionysius the Carthusian (+ 1450.) He is the first to divide each chapter under three formal heads, according as he treats of the Church, or *Sponsa Universalis*, of the holy soul, or *Sponsa particularis*, or of the Blessed Virgin, or *Sponsa singularis*, a method which found several followers at a later time. I am not sure that this work does not rank above even his lovely exposition of the Psalms.

43. Contemporary with this is the work of Nicolas Kempf of Strasburg, Prior of the Carthusians at Gaming in Austria, and known as Nicolaus de Argentina, (+ 1450,) published by Pez, in the two closing volumes of the *Bibliotheca Ascetica*. Though mainly drawn from SS. Gregory the Great and Bernard, it is full of beautiful passages due to the compiler himself, and will amply repay examination.

44. The celebrated mystic, Henry Harphius, (+ 1478,) has left a treatise on the spiritual life, entitled *Theologia Mystica*, consisting of long expositions or meditations on detached verses of the Song, perfectly crowded with beauties, though not always available for separate citation. No edition after 1580 is trustworthy, as the book was tampered with by its later editors.

Sixteenth Century.

45. Jacob Parez de Valentia, Bishop of Christopolis, (+ 1507,) has treated the Canticles in a gloss which, though of little originality or power, contains not a few suggestive passages.

46. Francis Titelmann, a Franciscan, (+ circ. 1547,) a man of great learning and no mean critical skill, has written usefully on the Song, though not contributing much to the mystical exposition.

47. S. Thomas of Villanova, Archbishop of Valencia, (+ 1555,) was cut off by death after having merely

outlined his intended Commentary on the Song, and when but three chapters had been sketched. The patristic spirit shines, however, in the fragment, and causes regret at the incompleteness of the undertaking.

48. Martin Delrio, a learned Jesuit, (+ 1608,) is the first on the list of those commentators of the seventeenth century who began a twofold treatment of the books they discussed, first giving a literal and textual comment, and then a catena of earlier expositions. His own original matter is not striking, but he has collected much valuable material together. *Seventeenth Century.*

49. Michael Ghislerius, a Clerk Regular, (+ circ. 1615,) is the most ponderous of writers on the Canticles. He has bequeathed to us an enormous folio of nearly a thousand pages in double columns and small type, wherein he discusses every verse in five different ways; textually, taking the Church, the holy soul, and the Blessed Virgin, severally as the Bride, and closing with a long catena of ancient expositors, which is by far the most valuable part of his work, though even it is by no means exhaustive.

50. Henry Ainsworth, an English Independent (+ 1622,) is deserving of consultation, for the Rabbinical learning and the apt parallelisms from other books of Scripture which he has brought to bear upon the Song.

51. Luis de la Puente, or De Ponte, (+ 1624,) composed a huge volume of Sermons on the Canticles, intended for the use of Religious, but heavy and lifeless in treatment, and quite below his reputation.

52. It is unnecessary to do more than name the well-known commentary of Cornelius à Lapide (+ 1637) since its character is sufficiently well known to make criticism superfluous.

53. John Cocceius, a German Protestant theologian of enormous learning and diligence, and of great piety, (+ 1669,) of whom it was said, that "Grotius sees CHRIST nowhere, but Cocceius sees Him everywhere," recalls the spirit of the best mediævalists by his remarkable gift of mystical appreciation. His Commentary on the Canticles is injured by its exclusive reference to

the literal history of the Christian Church, and by occasional outbreaks of controversy, but it may be consulted with much profit.

With this author closes the period formally embraced in the following commentary, which does not profess to deal with the exegesis of the eighteenth and nineteenth centuries, properly beginning with Bossuet's commentary in 1690. But as textual criticism often throws new and valuable light on mystical interpretation, later writers have been freely consulted, and it will suffice to enumerate, amongst others, Harmer, Percy, Mason Good, Rosenmüller, Heiligstedt, Hitzig, Hengstenberg, Weissbach, and Thrupp. It would have been easy to have extended the catalogue largely, but at the sacrifice of unity of plan; and besides, the omitted authors are for the most part readily accessible and familiarly known, whereas the majority of those quoted in the succeeding pages have been hitherto practically confined to a very narrow circle of readers.

A COMMENTARY

ON

THE SONG OF SONGS.

CHAPTER I.

1 The song of songs, which is Solomon's.

Song of songs. "As we have been taught by Moses <small>Origen.</small> that there are not only holy places, but a Holy of holies, that there are not only other Sabbaths, but Sabbaths of sabbaths; so now we are taught, by the pen of Solomon, that there are not only songs, but a Song of songs. Blessed, truly, is he who enters into the holy place, but more blessed he who enters the Holy of holies. Blessed is he who keepeth the Sabbath, but more blessed who keepeth the Sabbath of sabbaths. So, too, blessed is he who understands songs, and sings them, for no one does sing save on high festivals, but much more blessed is he who sings the Song of songs. And as he, who enters into the holy place, still needs much ere he is able to proceed into the Holy of holies, and as he who keeps the sabbath enjoined on the people by the Lord, wants many things that he may keep the Sabbath of sabbaths, so too he who traverses all the songs of Holy Writ, finds it no easy thing to ascend to the Song of songs. Thou must needs go out of Egypt, and, issued thence, cross the Red Sea, that thou mayest sing the first song, saying, 'I will sing unto the Lord, <small>Exod. xv. 1.</small> for He hath triumphed gloriously.' And even though thou mayest have sung this first song, thou art still far from the Song of songs. Pass spiritually through the wilderness, till thou comest to the well, which the princes dug, that thou mayest there sing the second song. Afterwards approach the borders of the Holy Land, and, standing on Jordan's banks, sing the song of Moses, 'Give ear, O ye heavens, and I will speak; and hear, O earth, the words of my mouth.' Yet again, thou needest soldiers, and the inheritance of the Holy Land, and that a bee should prophesy to thee and judge thee—for Deborah is, by interpretation, a bee—that thou mayest utter that hymn also, which is contained in the Book of Judges. Ascending to the record of the Kings, come to the song when David escaped from the hands of all his enemies, and from the hand of Saul, and said, 'The LORD is my rock, and my fortress, and my deliverer.' Thence thou must reach Isaiah, that thou mayest say with him, 'I will sing to my Beloved a song of my Beloved touching His vineyard.' And when thou hast traversed all these, go up yet higher, that thou mayest with pure soul cry unto the Bridegroom this song of songs." The Targum counts up ten songs, adding to Origen's list those of Adam, sung after his fall and pardon; Joshua's at Ajalon; and a tenth, never yet uttered, to be sung by the people of GOD at the end of their long captivity, to which applies that prophecy, "Ye shall have a song, as in the night when a holy solemnity is kept." This one, however, is the *Song of songs*, because as CHRIST our LORD, as Man, surpassing all Apostles, Patriarchs, Prophets, and heavenly powers, is King of kings, and LORD of lords, so this song, since entirely concerning Him and His Bride, excels, and includes in itself, all the hymns of victory, of thanksgiving, of instruction, and of lamentation in Holy Writ, just as the bridal feast surpasses all others, and since no blessing which other songs commemorate can be compared with the Incarnation. And as the Apostle tells his hearers to speak to themselves "in psalms, and hymns, and spiritual songs," we understand that psalms, accompanied by an instrument, denote the active life of charity, and hymns the contemplative life, and songs, embracing these two, are the life of the righteous, who give soul and body to GOD; while the *Song of songs*, that holy secret which only GOD's unction can teach, only spiritual experience can make clear, is the life of the perfect. The Song is Solomon's, the third in order of his books, following Proverbs and Ecclesiastes, to teach us that after the have passed the purgative way, by following the moral precepts of the first of these; and the illuminative way, by learning in the second that all earthly things are vanity, and GOD alone to be desired; we attain in the third place to the unitive way, and by it make our entrance into the Holy of holies, where the High Priest, our Bridegroom, stands, that we may there learn and sing the song of perfect love,—there only, for "how shall we sing the LORD'S song in a strange land?" It is *Solomon's,* for Solomon means Peaceful, and CHRIST, to Whom it in truth appertains, is "our Peace," having been "made unto us wisdom, and righteousness, and sanctification, and redemption." S. Greg. M.
Origen.
Nic. Argent.
Ps. cxxxvii. 4.
S. Greg. Nyss.
Eph. ii. 14.
1 Cor. i. 30.

2 Let him kiss me with the kisses of his mouth: for thy love is better than wine.

First, say the Fathers in general, it is the cry of the Synagogue, GOD'S ancient Church, yearning for the Incarnation of CHRIST, and desiring that GOD would no more speak to her only by the voices of angels and prophets, but face to face. I care not, she says, to hear Moses, who is slow of speech to me, the lips of Isaiah are unclean, Jeremiah cannot speak, for he is a child, and all the Prophets are tongueless. Let Him of Whom they speak, Himself speak, *let Him kiss me with the kisses of His mouth.* And His answer is set down for us by the Apostle: "GOD, Who at sundry times and in divers manners spake in time past unto the fathers by the prophets, hath in these last days spoken unto us by His SON." She asks for His *kiss,* because as two separate bodies unite in the act of kissing, so CHRIST, by His becoming flesh, united GOD and man together, two natures in One Person. And as a kiss denotes peace and reconciliation, it is the fit greeting of Him, our peaceful Solomon, Who came to us as GOD and SAVIOUR. It is also the cry of the Gentile world, yearning for the teaching of the HOLY SPIRIT, for as the breath of one that kisses is felt by the one that is kissed, so by the kiss of CHRIST, we understand the inspiration of the HOLY GHOST Whom He hath sent. Next, the words belong to every faithful soul which desires the presence of its LORD. See, exclaims a Saint, how sudden is the opening of her address. Asking a great thing from a mighty Person, she uses no customary flattery, she takes no indirect Omn. Patr.
S. Bernard.
Dion. Carth.
Heb. i. 1.
The Gloss.
S. Justus Orgel.
Hen. Harph.
S. Ambros.
S. Greg. M.
S. Bernard. Serm. vii. in Cant.

way to that which she longs for. She makes no preface, she seeks not to conciliate good-will, but breaking out from the abundance of her heart, says, in plainest and boldest words, *Let Him kiss me with the kisses of His mouth. His mouth.* Yes, but it is not every one who dares ask this, but only such as have already received the pledge of love, and desire it again. For us sinners it is fitter to fall down trembling at the feet of our righteous LORD, like the publican, not daring to look up, but like the sinful woman, content to kiss His feet, and to bathe them with our tears. Then, when He hath said, "Thou art made whole, sin no more, lest a worse thing happen to thee," we may dare to rise a little, and kiss the Hand which has cleansed and lifted us, giving Him the homage and glory which are His due. At last, after many tears and prayers, we may, in fear and trembling, lift our heads to His glorious mouth, not merely to gaze upon it, but to kiss it. To Thee, O LORD JESU, to Thee has my heart fitly said, Thy Face, LORD, will I seek. For Thou madest me to hear of Thy mercy betimes in the morning, when, as I lay in the dust, kissing Thy sacred footsteps, Thou forgavest me the sins of my life. Then, as the day grew on, Thou madest glad the soul of Thy servant, bestowing on me the grace of holy living in the kiss of Thy Hand. And now what remains, O gracious LORD, save that in the fulness of light, in the fervour of the Spirit, Thou, mercifully admitting me to the kiss of Thy mouth also, wouldst fill me with joy with Thy countenance? Note, too, how it is said *Let HIM kiss me*, with no name particularized, no context to explain who is meant. And that because to the Bride there can be but One to think of, because her word ever is, "Whom have I in heaven but Thee? and there is none on earth I desire in comparison of Thee." She asks, too, not for a single kiss, but for *kisses*, for those seven great gifts of the SPIRIT which CHRIST bestows, and for other graces besides. And He gives them in four ways, by His Incarnation, by His conversation amongst men as their Teacher, by mystical incorporation with us for our redemption, and by the final glory which He promises. Peace with GOD in CHRIST, is then the scope of the Bride's longings, as she prays for illumination, for love, for perfect union with Him of Whom she says, "Full of grace are Thy lips, wherefore GOD hath blessed Thee for ever." His lips, which give the kiss, are His truth and sweetness, hers, which receive it, are her understanding and affection. And He has heard the cry of His Bride, and answered it, giving her more than she asked, giving her Himself again and again in the Holy Sacrament of the Altar. "The soul," observes an ancient writer, "sees herself cleansed from all her sins, and fitted to approach the Altar of CHRIST. She sees the wondrous Sacrament and saith, *Let Him kiss me with the kisses of His mouth,* let CHRIST Himself impress His kiss on me." And Simeon Metaphrastes, in that hymn which the Eastern Church puts in the mouth of her children before Communion, speaks of the kiss which the penitent soul offers in turn to her LORD in that sacred rite: _{Henr. Harph.} _{Pseudo-Ambros. de Sacr. 2.}

More than the harlot I have erred, who, learning Thine abode, _{Σύνοψις.}
Made purchase of the precious nard, and boldly took her road
To seek and to anoint Thy feet, O CHRIST, my GOD and LORD,
And, as she came with love to greet, was not by Thee abhorred.
So, WORD of GOD, calm Thou my fears, and give me, not despised,
Thy feet to clasp, and kiss, and wash with tears, that nard unpriced.

The soul may kiss her LORD also by acts of love and compassion towards His poor, and will be rewarded by Him therefor with that last kiss which He will give at the Doom, saying, "Come, ye blessed." But they who have not so kissed Him here, shall see His face no more, for He will turn His back upon them. And that which is true of the Church, and true of every believing soul, is especially true of her who is the Church's fairest ornament, the purest and most blessed of Saints, the Virgin Mother of GOD. The words are her prayer to GOD the FATHER, that by the breath of His mouth, which is the HOLY GHOST, He may give her that ineffable kiss, His Only-begotten SON. When the Angel brought her the marvellous tidings of her true betrothal, then by her answer, "Behold the handmaid of the LORD, be it unto me according to thy word," she did in truth say, *Let Him kiss me with the kisses of His mouth.* And after His nativity, the prayer was yet more literally answered, when the tender Mother hung over her infant LORD, and clasped Him to her breast. And His love so endured that even at the last moment of life He bent to offer His kiss. "He bowed His head to His Mother," says a holy writer, "and to all mankind, as though bidding His last farewell, and _{Nic. Argent.} _{Rupert.} _{S. Luke i. 38.} _{Corn. à Lap.} _{Tauler, de Pass. Dom.}

offering the kiss of peace. See here, O faithful soul, the unspeakable love of thy GOD, that He loved us unto the end." And we learn hereby the pain as well as the sweetness of His kiss.

<small>Keble, *Lyra Innocent.*</small>
Three Saints of old their lips upon the Incarnate SAVIOUR laid;
And each with death or agony for the high rapture paid.
His Mother's holy kisses of the coming sword gave sign,
And Simeon's hymn full closely did with his last breath entwine.
And Magdalen's first tearful touch prepared her but to greet
With homage of a broken heart His pierced and lifeless feet.

<small>Theodoret.
S. Greg. M.</small>
For Thy love is better than wine. The change from the third person to the second, from speaking *of* the Bridegroom to speaking *to* Him, denotes, some Fathers say, His swift appearing in fulfilment of His Bride's desire, coming even before He is actually called; showing how more than ready GOD ever is to answer our prayer, according to that saying of the Prophet, "Before they call, I will answer: and while they are yet speaking, I will hear." The LXX. and Vulgate have *Thy breasts.* And some tell us that the gentle teaching of CHRIST, drawn from the secret treasures of His wisdom and knowledge, is meant thereby, milk fitted for babes, *better than the wine* of human wisdom or even of the old Law. Philo of Carpasia and several others see in the *breasts* the two Testaments, both given by CHRIST, whence the sincere milk of the Word, refreshing, and not hurtful like wine, is granted to mankind. And a kindred explanation is found in those writers who will have the Apostles and Doctors of the Church to be meant here. The ancient exposition of the Three Fathers interprets the words of the hidden grace of the Holy Eucharist, with which agrees well that passage of S. Chrysostom: "See ye not with what eagerness infants seize the breast, with what pressure they fix their lips upon the teats? Let us approach with no less desire to this Table, and to the spiritual breast of this Chalice, nay, with yet greater longing, let us, as sucking children, drink in the grace of the SPIRIT; let it be our one sorrow, our one grief, if we be stinted of this spiritual food." Some of the interpretations, however, bring us back to the true meaning of the literal Hebrew, *Thy loves.* Thus S. Bernard bids us see here the long-suffering of CHRIST in bearing with sinners, and His loving-kindness in receiving

<small>Isa. lxv. 24.

Origen.
S. Greg. Nyss.
Haymo.

Philo Carp.
Cassiodorus.
Beda.
S. Just. Org.
S. Greg. M.
S. Greg. Nyss.
S. Nilus.
S. Maximus.
Hom. in Mat. 83.

Serm. ix.</small>

them when they return to Him. S. Gregory speaks of the love of GOD and of our neighbour as supplying that stream of charity which is the necessary food of the soul. And we may take it also of that sweetness of CHRIST, which is the HOLY SPIRIT Himself, given in twofold manner, for the remission of sin and for the increase of grace. However it be explained, we come back to the one thought of union with Him Whose loving kiss is beyond all earthly blessedness. S. Greg. M.

Rupert.

> Νέκταρ ἔην τὸ φίλημα· τὸ γὰρ στόμα νέκταρος ἔπνει,
> Νῦν μεθύω τὸ φίλημα, πολὺν τὸν ἔρωτα πεπωκώς. Anthol.
Græc. v. 305.

Nectar to me was the kiss, for the mouth was breathing of nectar,
Now am I drunk with the kiss, having quaffed off love in abundance.

They inquire at much length, too, (unnecessarily so far as the Hebrew is concerned,) why the Bridegroom's breasts are commended, while we should expect such praise to be given only to the Bride. And the happiest answers are, first, that CHRIST, Himself the source of all true and pure love, unites in His own Person a mother's affection for us with a father's, whence the Book of Sirach, speaking of the Eternal Wisdom, says, " I am the mother of fair love ;" and secondly, that as mothers feed their babes from their own bodies, so CHRIST feeds His children, and poured forth, like the fabled pelican, His very Blood for our refreshment as He hung upon the Cross. Corn. à Lap.

Ecclus.
xxiv. 18.

S. Chrysost.

> Et nunquam sine lacte charitas,
> Lac non uberat, uberat cruorem.

> And never without milk is charity,
> It is not milk it yields for us, but blood.

The Bride sums up the fruits of that kiss in a fourfold manner. She has obtained from it the sweetness of milk, the warmth of wine, the fragrance of odour, and the gladness of unction. She is refreshed by the first, which is light to her understanding; she is inflamed by the second, which is heat to her affection ; she is excited to appetite by the third, which is the foretaste of glory to her longing ; she is consecrated by the last, which is joy of spirit in the Passion. S. Thomas
à Villanovâ.

3 Because of the savour of thy good oint-

ments thy name is as ointment poured forth, therefore do the virgins love thee.

The first clause here does not exactly represent the existing Hebrew text, nor yet any of the chief versions. The true rendering is, *Pleasant for odour are Thine ointments.* The LXX. reads, *The perfume of Thine ointments is above all spices.* And the Vulgate, connecting the words with the previous verse, has [*Thy breasts are*] *fragrant with the best ointments.* The Bride, observes Origen, had already some acquaintance with spices, to wit, the words of the Law and the Prophets, wherewith, before the Bridegroom's coming, she was partially instructed and trained for the service of GOD, as still in her early youth, and under tutors and governors, for "the Law was our schoolmaster, to bring us unto CHRIST." All these were spices, wherewith she seems to have been nourished and made ready for her Bridegroom. But when the fulness of time was come, and she came of age, and when the FATHER sent His Only-begotten into the world, anointed by the HOLY GHOST, the Bride, smelling the fragrance of the divine unction, and perceiving that all those spices which she had been hitherto using were far inferior compared with the sweetness of this new and heavenly ointment, saith, *The perfume of Thine ointments is above all spices.* Of this anointing the costly unguent wherewith Aaron was consecrated is but an earthly type, as inferior as the earthly High Priest is to the heavenly one, yet having a mystical reference to it. And note, that the Bride speaks of *ointments,* in the plural, as confessing the many gifts and graces which come from CHRIST as their one source. And thus is said in another place touching this same unction: "Thou hast loved righteousness, and hated iniquity, wherefore, O GOD, Thy GOD hath anointed Thee with the oil of gladness above Thy fellows. All Thy garments smell of myrrh, aloes, and cassia." The Latin Fathers, following the Vulgate, explain the passage somewhat differently. As they often speak of the Apostles and Doctors of the Church as the breasts of CHRIST, so they call them here *fragrant,* because eminent for miracles and holiness, so that the perfume of their righteousness came abroad, giving delight and refreshment to their hearers. And in this sense we may take the words of S. Paul: "Now thanks be unto

GOD, which always causeth us to triumph in CHRIST, 2 Cor. ii. 14.
and maketh manifest the savour of His knowledge by
us in every place, for we are unto GOD a sweet savour
of CHRIST." S. Bernard, who supposes the breasts to
be of the Bride as well as of the Bridegroom, tells us
that she is fragrant with the triple unction of contri- Serm. x.
tion, devotion, and of piety; the first pungent, causing pain, the second lenitive, soothing pain, the third
healing, and even expelling disease. The first is made
by the soul breaking and grinding her sins in the mortar of conscience, and then distilling them within the
crucible of a glowing heart with the fire of penitence
and grief, that she may say, "My heart was hot within Ps. xxxix. 1.
me, and while I was thus musing, the fire kindled."
That is the ointment wherewith the sinner anointed
the feet of CHRIST. The second ointment is not to be
found on earth, but has to be sought afar. "Every S. James i.
good gift and every perfect gift is from above, and 17.
cometh down from the Father of lights," and the unguent of devotion is formed of the blessings which
the Divine bounty has bestowed on man, pondered in
the vessel of the heart, heated with the fire of longing,
and blended with the oil of gladness. With this we
anoint not the feet of CHRIST, but His head. The Serm. xii.
third ointment, of piety, or lovingkindness, is made
from the sufferings of others, from the wants of the
poor, the burdens of the oppressed, the troubles of the
sad, the errors of the sinful, blended with the oil of
mercy, heated with the fire of love. This is the ointment which we must buy, as Mary Magdalene, and
Mary the mother of James, and Salome did, and
anoint therewith the whole Body of JESUS, by helping
every suffering member of It. Returning to the truer Ghislerius.
sense of the passage, we see how true of the holy soul
which desires CHRIST is that saying of the Wise Man,
"Ointment and perfume delight the heart." And this Prov. xxvii.
twofold gladdening is set forth by S. Peter, saying, 9.
"GOD anointed JESUS of Nazareth with the HOLY Acts x. 38.
GHOST and with power," and He in turn gives us these
same blessings, "doing good, and healing all that were
oppressed of the devil," giving that consolation which
earthly wisdom cannot bestow, and that healing which
human physicians know not. And Rupert, dwelling Rupert.
in his wonted manner on the graces of the Mother of
GOD, does not fail to point out the correspondence of
the Angel's words to her with those of S. Peter spoken

of her SON: "The HOLY GHOST shall come upon thee, and the power of the Highest shall overshadow thee," so that she was truly the house filled with the odour of the ointment, and, rejoicing in the fragrance of that perfume granted to her, might say, "I yield a pleasant odour like the best myrrh, as galbanum, and onyx, and sweet storax, and as the fume of frankincense in the tabernacle."

Thy Name is as ointment poured forth. Before the coming of CHRIST the Name of GOD was inclosed, as in a vial, amongst the Hebrew people alone, as it is written, "In Jewry is GOD known, His Name is great in Israel." But now we can more fitly say, "O LORD our Governor, how excellent is Thy Name in all the world." "That ointment," says S. Ambrose, "existed eternally, but it was with the FATHER, in the FATHER. Its perfume was known to Angels and Archangels above, as inclosed within the vase of heaven. The FATHER said, 'I will give Thee for a covenant of the people, for a light of the Gentiles.' The SON came down, and all things were filled with the new fragrance. . . . . The SON of GOD kept that fragrance at first in His Body, as though in a vase, biding His time, as He saith Himself, 'The LORD GOD hath given Me the tongue of the learned, that I should know how to speak a word in season.' The time came, He opened His mouth, and the ointment was poured forth when power went out of Him. This ointment was poured forth upon the Jews, and gathered up by the Gentiles, was poured forth in Judæa and perfumed all lands." Origen, pressing the exact meaning of the LXX. version, *emptied out,* reminds us how "CHRIST JESUS *emptied* (ἐκένωσε) Himself, and took upon Him the form of a servant." "He Who is full," exclaims S. Gregory Nazianzen, "is emptied, drained of His glory for a short time, that I might be partaker of His fulness."

But it is not merely the knowledge of GOD which is so poured forth, but His Name. What name? And first they answer that it is the Name of CHRIST, itself denoting "anointed," which is poured forth, not only by being widely preached, but because it is poured on all the faithful in the waters of Baptism, wherein they are given the title of Christians. And this is what the Prophet foretold, saying, "I will pour out My SPIRIT upon all flesh." *Pour* out, not *drop* out, for "GOD giveth not the SPIRIT by measure." Poured forth,

---

S. Luke i. 35.
S. John xii. 3.
Corn. à Lap.
Ecclus. xxiv. 15.

Didymus.

Ps. lxxvi. 1.
Ps. viii. 1.

Lib. de Virgin. 3.

Isa. xlii. 6.

Isa. l. 4.

Origen.

Phil. ii. 7.

Orat. de Nativ.

Eusebius.
S. Just. Org.

Theodoret.
Beda.
Joel ii. 28.
S. John iii. 34.

adds S. Gregory the Great, because whoso are Christians in truth as well as in name, abound with the streams of holy charity, which soften them, and make them fit for kindling, so that they break forth in the flames of good example; and, as another expositor remarks, also with that love for the Creator kindled in the creature when CHRIST died for us. He was known but little before His Passion, says one more Greek Father, but when His life was poured forth upon the Cross, when the alabaster shrine of His most sacred Body was broken, the Apostles, filled with the perfume of that sweet ointment, traversed sea and land, filling the whole world with its fragrance. S. Augustine calls Jerusalem the vase wherein that ointment, which he takes to be GOD's mercy, was first shut up, but when the rebellious city was broken and destroyed, then the unguent pervaded all nations. And, as when the precious oil which has been in a vase is poured forth, we can only guess at its nature by the few remaining drops and the perfume, so the Name of GOD is mysterious, and no title which divines can invent discloses His nature and excellence. We conjecture Him only by the effects of His working, by the fragrance which He diffuses, and therefore He is like *ointment poured forth.* But the Name of CHRIST, royal, priestly, holy though it be, is yet only a title of office, by which all His servants may address their King. His Bride must have some dearer, closer, more personal name by which to call Him. "If you write," says she in the words of S. Bernard, " it has no savour for me unless I read JESUS there. If you argue or discuss, it has no savour for me, unless the sound of JESUS be there. JESUS is honey in the mouth, melody in the ear, gladness in the heart. And it is medicine too. Is any of you sad? Let JESUS come into his heart, and thence leap into his mouth, and lo, as the Name of Light issues forth, every cloud disperses, and the clear sky returns. Does any fall into sin, and hasten thence in despair to the snare of death? If he invoke the Name of Life, will he not breathe again to life? Who ever found hardness of heart, torpor of sloth, rancour of soul, languor of indifference, able to stand before the face of that saving Name? Who is there, whose fountain of tears has chanced to dry up, that does not burst forth more plentifully and flow more gently into weeping, when he invokes JESUS? Who

S. Greg. M.

Philo Carp.

Theodoret.
Tauler.

S. August.
in Ps. xxx.

S. Greg.
Nyss.

Serm. xv.

is there, quivering and trembling in peril, to whom that Name of Might invoked has not straightway given confidence and banished fear? Who, I ask, swaying and wavering in doubt, has not at once seen certainty shine forth at the invocation of that Name of Renown? Who, fearing in adversity and already fainting, has ever lacked strength if the Name of Help has sounded? These are all diseases and weaknesses of the soul, and that is their medicine. And you may prove it. 'Call upon Me in the time of trouble, so will I hear thee, and thou shalt praise Me.'" That Name is truly oil poured forth, for it refreshes the weary, heals the sick, lightens the blind, and floats high above all other names, for "GOD hath given Him a Name which is above every name, that at the Name of JESUS every knee should bow, of things in heaven, and things in earth, and things under the earth."

<small>Ps. l. 15.</small>

<small>Nic. Argent.</small>

<small>Phil. ii. 9.</small>

<small>The Hymn, *Gloriosi Salvatoris*.</small>

> Name of gladness, Name of pleasure,
>   By the tongue ineffable,
> Name of sweetness passing measure,
>   To the ear delectable;
> 'Tis our safeguard and our treasure,
>   'Tis our help 'gainst sin and hell.
>
> 'Tis the Name for adoration,
>   'Tis the Name of victory,
> 'Tis the Name for meditation
>   In the vale of misery:
> 'Tis the Name for veneration
>   By the citizens on high.

<small>Targum.</small>

Therefore do the virgins love Thee. The earliest of all comments on this Song, the Chaldee paraphrase, explains these words in full accordance with the spirit of Christian writers, as denoting the righteous who follow after the goodness of GOD. And first it is to be noted that the Hebrew word עֲלָמוֹת *alamoth* implies not only virginity, but youth, and accordingly the LXX. gives νεάνιδες, and the Vulgate *adolescentulæ*. What then are these *young damsels* who love the Bridegroom? They answer, in the first place, that they are souls newly born in Baptism, having put off the old man and the wrinkles of sin, and renewed their youth as an eagle. And they are well called *damsels*, because the Saints, conscious of their own weakness, love all the more for that reason CHRIST their strength. Others, dwelling yet more on the admission of fragility, see here souls yet imperfectly taught, and only beginning

<small>S. Greg. M.
S. Ambros.
Ps. ciii. 5.
Cassiodorus.

Aponius.
S. Anselm.
Laudun.</small>

to run their course, being still weak in the faith. Whereupon Rupert aptly remarks, "Had not the ointment been poured forth, had not the WORD been made flesh, imperfect souls never would have dared to love GOD, nor even to hear Him, as they said, when it had not yet been poured forth, 'Let not GOD speak with us, lest we die.'" And S. Thomas of Villanova bids us remark further, that the Bride saith that the virgins love Him because His Name is as oil poured out, because their fire of devotion is but newly kindled, and needs this fuel. She does not say this of herself, because her fire has long since been kindled to a clear flame, and she loves Him for Himself alone, and even when He gives no oil. They want Thine, she cries to Him, I want Thee. And some extend the meaning yet further, to newly planted Churches, not as yet fully established, but zealous in their first love. Others again, looking rather to the idea of purity than of weakness, prefer to see here the holiest and most perfect Churches and souls. Martyrs who have attained their crown, says one Father. All healthy and vigorous souls, says another, neither in their infancy, too young to understand love, nor in their dotage, too old to retain it, but in the mid flower of their spiritual life and beauty, not having spot, or wrinkle, or any such thing. And thus the words tell us of the early zeal of the Christian Church, when the memory of the Apostles was still fresh in the minds of the faithful, and the crown of martyrdom was often sought and won. Wherefore the Apostle saith, "I have espoused you to one husband, that I may present you as a chaste virgin to CHRIST." "Literally, too," notes the Ecstatic Doctor, "it means the consecrated virgins, those elect maidens, those virtuous damsels, many of whom, for Thy sake, despised not only the riches of the whole world, its delights, its honours, and all its outward pomp, its vanity and lightness: but most manfully endured the cruelest deaths, and happily triumphed; as the holy Katharine, the famous Ursula, and countless others like them, who served Thee most constantly in virginity of soul and body, and to the present day unnumbered others, abandoning in their youth this evil world with all its deceit, enter convents and holy retirements, wherein abiding always inclosed, they give themselves up to Thy pure embraces in the spirit." And of such we may cite the words of a great

Rupert.

Exod. xx. 19.

S. Thomas à Villanovâ.

S. Just. Org.

Philo Carp.

S. Greg. Nyssen.

Corn. à Lap.
2 Cor. xi. 2.

Dion. Carth.

Saint and Martyr in the early Church: "The flower of the Church's bud, the glory and ornament of spiritual grace, the joyous disposition, the perfect and untarnished work of honour and praise, the image of GOD answering to the holiness of the LORD, the more illustrious portion of the flock of CHRIST. The glorious fruitfulness of our Mother the Church exults through them, and abundantly blossoms in them, and by how much the more the great band of virgins adds to its own number, so much does it increase its Mother's joy."

<small>S. Cyprian. De Hab. Virg. 1.</small>

4 Draw me, we will run after thee: the king hath brought me into his chambers; we will be glad and rejoice in thee, we will remember thy love more than wine: the upright love thee.

Draw me. They say, some of them, that the speaker is now changed, that whereas the Synagogue expressed in the former verses her longing for CHRIST's Advent, now we have the Gentile Church eager to come to Him. But it is far better to hold here by the view which recognizes the substantial identity of the Jewish and Christian Churches, and sees but the one Bride throughout, at first expecting, and then receiving, her Spouse. She says *draw me,* because she knows herself to be too weak to reach Him of herself, for He hath said, "No man can come to Me, except the FATHER Which hath sent Me draw him." *Draw me* to Thy Cross, whereof Thou hast said, "And I, if I be lifted up from the earth, will draw all men unto Me." *Draw me* yet further, after Thee in Thine Ascension, that I may not be left desolate here on earth, but rest and be with Thee evermore. And so the hymn:

<small>Cassiodorus. Beda. Haymo.</small>

<small>Lyranus.</small>

<small>S. John vi. 44.</small>

<small>S. John xii. 32. S. Bruno Ast.</small>

> O CHRIST, Who hast prepared a place
> For us beside Thy throne of grace,
> Draw us, we pray, with cords of love,
> From exile to our home above.

<small>Santolius Victorinus, The Hymn, *Nubis, Olympo.*</small>

But why *draw?* Does the Bride need to be drawn after the Bridegroom, as though she followed Him unwillingly? Nay, it denotes no reluctance, any more than an invalid feels in being drawn to his bath or to his food, though a criminal may well need being drawn to judgment or to execution. She longs to be drawn, and therefore prays for it, which she would not do were she able to follow her Beloved at her will. But why can she not?

<small>S. Bernard. Serm. in Cant. 21.</small>

Are we to call her at once weak and the Bride? If one of the virgins complained of weakness and asked to be drawn, we should not marvel, but does it not seem strange that the Bride, who ought to seem able to draw others, as being strong and perfect, should herself need, as weak and feeble, to be drawn? But it is that she may follow the steps of His conversation, imitating His example, learning His discipline. And to do all this she needs His aid, that she may renounce herself, take up her Cross, and follow CHRIST. What marvel if she need to be drawn, who runs behind a Giant, who seeks to overtake Him Who "cometh leaping upon the mountains, skipping upon the hills?" For, she saith, "His WORD runneth very swiftly." She cannot run at an equal pace, nor rival His swiftness "Who rejoiceth as a giant to run His race:" her strength is insufficient, and she prays to be drawn. I am weary, she saith, I faint, leave me not, but *draw me after Thee*, lest I should wander after other lovers, lest I should run uncertainly. *Draw me*, for it is better for me that Thou shouldst use any force against me, awing me with threats, chastening with scourges, than, sparing me, leave me perilously secure in my sloth. *Draw me*, even if I be unwilling, to make me fain, draw me when slothful, to make me run. "Behold, O Heavenly Bridegroom, O sweetest JESU," exclaims a true servant of His, "my spirit strives to cling faithfully unto Thee, to rest in Thee, to give itself up to Thee alone in loving contemplation, but a thousand hindrances draw me back, delay me, stop my way. My understanding is wavering, my reason weak, my will inclined to vain and evil things, sensuality drags me down, the needs of daily life keep me busy with earthly and tangible cares, the temptations of the senses beset me, the world and the hosts of evil spirits attack us on every side, and I walk in the midst of snares, in the thick of grievous perils, and, besides, the weight of my sinful flesh depresses me. What then am I to do save fly to Thy most gracious help, and with the deepest longing of my heart pray, *Draw me after Thee*, evermore hold, bedew, enlighten, aid, and comfort my heart. For Thou hast said in Hosea the Prophet, 'I drew thee with cords of a man, with bands of love;' and in Jeremiah, 'I have loved thee with an everlasting love, therefore with loving-kindness have I drawn thee.'" And in this drawing, which

Cant. ii. 8.
Ps. cxlvii. 15.
Ps. xix. 6.

Dion. Carth.

Hos. xi. 4.
Jer. xxxi. 3.

consists in leading the human will into union with the Divine will, as the magnet draws the iron to itself, the Three Persons of the Holy Trinity co-operate, the FATHER drawing by His power, the SON by His wisdom, the HOLY GHOST by His goodness, a threefold cord which is not quickly broken. "And even to be drawn by your will is but little," says the Doctor of Grace, "you are drawn by pleasure also. What is to be drawn by pleasure? 'Delight thou in the LORD, and He will give thee thy heart's desire.' There is a pleasure of the heart to which that heavenly Bread is sweet. And if the poet could say,

—Trahit sua quemque voluptas,

not necessity, but pleasure; not compulsion, but delight; how much more forcibly may we say that a man is drawn to CHRIST, when he delights in truth, delights in blessedness, delights in righteousness, delights in everlasting life, all which is CHRIST?" The LXX. reading, *They have drawn Thee*, referring to the virgins who love CHRIST, comes in fact to the same thing, for they do not draw till they have first been drawn. And an ancient writer compares this drawing of GOD towards us to men in a ship pulling at a rope which is attached to a rock. They seem to draw the rock to them, but they are in fact drawing themselves to it.

We will run after Thee. And first it is to be noted how the address changes. Draw *me*, and *we* will run. Why does the Bride thus speak? It is, answers S. Bernard, because *drawing* tells of weakness, of trial, of suffering, all which the Bride prefers to bear alone, as better able to endure them than the tender virgins. She is willing that they should partake of the consolations which are implied in *running*, that they should share her joy, but not her sorrow. But this is forced and poor compared with the simpler explanation of an older writer, who says that the Church uses the singular form at first, as denoting her unity, and then the plural, because she is made up of many faithful, nay, of many ranks and degrees of the faithful. *Draw me*, then, she says, in my corporate character, draw my prelates and pastors, that they may in their turn draw on the virgins, the tender flock committed to their charge. Secondly, whereas the Bride's weakness made it needful for her to be drawn, her confidence in the strength to be given her is such that she does not say,

"We will follow," nor "We will walk," but "We will *run*," and therein she is like the Apostle, who said to his children, "So run, that ye may obtain." Origen.
S. Greg. M.
1 Cor. ix. 24.

The LXX. and Vulgate here add some words not in the Hebrew, and read the whole sentence thus: *Draw me after Thee, we will run for the odour of Thine ointments.* When we think on those gifts of grace, faith, hope, and charity, which all come from CHRIST, and strive to imitate the examples of His Saints and Martyrs, who displayed them in their lives, we are running, says an ancient Father, *after the odour of His ointments.* When those same gifts are vouchsafed to ourselves, notes another, we do not thereby cease to run, rather we are kindled with longing for the Beatific Vision, and haste eagerly towards the source of the fragrance which delights us. And in this sense S. Augustine takes it: "Let us love and copy Him. Let us run after His ointments; for He came and gave forth perfume, and His fragrance filled the whole world. Whence was that fragrance? From heaven. Follow Him then to heaven, if thou givest no false answer to those words, 'Lift up your hearts,' lift up your thoughts, lift up your love, lift up your hope." "If His Name alone can do all this," exclaims Origen, "if its perfume so cause and strengthen the virgins to run, what will be the virtue and height they shall attain when they reach His very self, incomprehensible, ineffable? I think if they do so attain, they will walk no more, nor run, but cling closely to Him, bound with the cords of love, that no more removal shall be possible, but they may be one with Him." And they inquire further what are these various ointments of His which draw eager souls, like gallant hounds, upon His track. S. Bernard replies by quoting the Apostle, "CHRIST JESUS, Who of GOD is made unto us wisdom, and righteousness, and sanctification, and redemption;" and shows how different Saints ran for each of these, as Nicodemus, seeking to learn the deep things of GOD, desired wisdom; Mary Magdalene and S. Peter in their penitence, seeking righteousness; S. Paul and those who like him had left all, that they might be like unto CHRIST, sought for sanctification; and the Martyrs, eager to share in the Passion of CHRIST, yearned for that redemption which was paid upon the Cross. Akin to this is another interpretation, which names the ointments as three. First, CHRIST's preaching, giving Philo Carp.

Angelomus Luxov.

In Ps. xc.

Origen.

Hugo Card.
Serm. 22 in Cant.
1 Cor. i. 30.

Nic. Argent.

light and healing error, after which Saints run wisely. Secondly, CHRIST's conversation, kindling affection, and healing our moral nature, for which one needs to run sweetly. Thirdly, CHRIST's miraculous working, which strengthens, and keeps in the course of good works, and this makes us to run mightily. And as GOD led the Hebrews in the wilderness after the Ark of the Covenant, fragrant with incense, so CHRIST, the True Ark of the LORD, goes before us in the desert of this world, perfumed with holiness and power, and we can do no less than follow Him. Or you may take the words in a more literal sense, referring them to the various anointings used in the Church, as in Baptism, whereby we are made CHRIST's soldiers, and begin to run our race; in Confirmation, when we receive additional strength, that we faint not in our course; in Ordination, when priests and prelates are given especial charge to follow close upon CHRIST, and to draw the people after them in the same way by setting them a holy and fragrant example. Thus, quaintly observes S. Basil, pigeon-fanciers catch doves, by sending out a dove smeared with perfume, which attracts others to it by the fragrance, and allures them into the dove-cot.

The King hath brought me into His chambers. Here is the first explanation of who that *He* is Whose kisses the Bride desires. The Bride does not yet call Him her Bridegroom, nor her Beloved, but her *King,* that she may glory in His power and riches. He, like David, is Shepherd and King, and appears in both characters in the Song. *Into His chambers.* Doubtless royal ones, as befits a king, and heaped with riches. The words used by the LXX. and Vulgate (ταμιεῖον, *cellaria,*) denote a store-room, or place where treasures or provisions are kept. And much of the traditional interpretation is in accordance with this view. The Targum, which sees throughout the Song a history of GOD's dealings with Israel, explains this passage of the people being brought to the foot of Sinai, there to be given the Law out of the Treasury of the Most High. And most of the Christian Fathers see here the revelation of GOD's mysteries to the Church, or to the faithful soul, differing, however, as to the exact meaning of the *chambers.* Some take them of Holy Writ, the storehouse of GOD's oracles. S. Bernard and Cardinal Hugo, accepting this view, amplify it by dwelling on the four senses of Scripture, as separate chambers with various stores. The first chamber is the Historical sense, containing the coarser food intended for the slaves and cattle. Secondly, comes the Tropological, with its three compartments, severally containing oil and wine for refreshment, balms and spices for delight, and ointments for healing. The third chamber is Allegory, wherein are the arms of the warriors, the golden shields, and the spears of Solomon, to wit, the mysteries of CHRIST and the Church Militant. Fourth is Anagoge, wherein is nought but pure gold and precious stones, that is, whatever belongeth to everlasting life. Others will have it that the foretaste of the joys of heaven, granted to certain Saints by faith or by direct revelation, is intended. S. Ambrose takes it of the mystery of the Atonement, revealed to the Bride after the Passion and Resurrection of CHRIST, by the preaching of the Apostles; and in another place, of the visions and joys granted in contemplation or trance, as to S. Paul, when he was caught up to the third heaven; and in yet a third passage, of the Sacrament of the Holy Eucharist. Philo stands alone in understanding the *chamber* to be that human Body of CHRIST wherein the Eternal WORD tabernacled. And note, that whereas it is said, "*We* will run after thee," here we read, "The King hath brought *me* in," implying that He withdrew her for a time from the virgins which be her fellows, and that she now returns to tell them what great things He had done for her, wherein they rejoice. All run, but only one is perfect, who so runs as to obtain, and alone receives the palm, and becomes a Queen. Here they tell us not only, as before, of the unity of the Church, and of the rarity of perfect souls, but point out how there is one in especial of whom the words are most true, even her to whom the King gave Himself as a Son, and who, entering into the house of Elizabeth, was greeted by her cousin and the unborn babe, saying, in effect, *We will rejoice and be glad in thee.* Whether these latter words be addressed by the Bride to CHRIST, or by the virgins to Him or her, they are alike thanksgivings and not boastings. If they be addressed to the Bridegroom, they are the joint voices of the Spouse and her companions, she for what she has already obtained, they because of that promise, 'The virgins which be her fellows .... with joy and gladness shall they be brought, and enter into the King's palace." If they be congratulations to the

Cassiodorus.
Aponius.
Beda.
S. Ans. Laud.
S. Ambros. in Ps. cxix.
Lib. de Isaac.
2 Cor. xii.

Philo Carp.

Origen.
S. Greg. Nyss.
S. Bernard.

Origen.

Rupert.
Philipp. Harveng.
Cassiodorus.
S. Greg. M.
V. Beda.
Origen.
S. Greg. Nyss.
S. Bernard.
Ps. xlv. 15, 16.

Bride, they are, observes S. Anselm of Laon, a promise on their part to make themselves ready in body and spirit for her fellowship, that they may enter in also.

We will remember thy love more than wine. Here again they differ as to whether these words are spoken to the Bridegroom or to the Bride. Taking the former view, we note first that it is said, "We *will* remember." It is a promise for the future, on the part of those who have not yet attained so high a spiritual level as to care little for earthly wine. Here too, as in the second verse, the A. V. reading *love*, appears in the LXX. and Vulgate as *breasts.* As before, too, it is explained of the lowly and gentle teaching of CHRIST, contrasted with the austerity of the Law, and S. Gregory the Great dwells here on the tender love which CHRIST showed the Church when He hung dying on the Cross. If the words be addressed to the Bride, then it is the voice of her children, saying, Because thou hast loved the breasts of CHRIST above the wine of pleasure and of worldly wisdom, we too will love thy teaching, because the *Righteous loveth thee.* Two of the Fathers allegorize the passage of S. John the Divine, who leant on the breast of JESUS at the Last Supper. *The upright love thee.* Here they all dwell on the intimate and necessary connection between true holiness of life and the love of CHRIST, showing that the latter never can be in any great measure in the soul which does not aim at the former. The *upright*, not those who always stand, for "the just man falleth seven times," but those whose intention is right, even when their performance is imperfect. *Upright*, because they stand looking up to their Creator, not bowed down to the creature. S. Bernard dwells at some length on the form of the human body as enforcing this thought, but does not in effect say more than a heathen poet had said before him:

> Pronaque quum spectent animalia cœtera terram,
> Os homini sublime dedit: cœlumque videre
> Jussit, et erectos ad sidera tollere vultus.

> While other creatures downward look on earth,
> He gave to man a towering face, and bade
> Him lift his upward gaze to sky and stars.

Right, also, because they keep to the middle of the King's highway, never swerving aside, but journeying straight on towards heaven, and seeking GOD for His own dear sake.

5 I am black, but comely, O ye daughters of Jerusalem, as the tents of Kedar, as the curtains of Solomon.

The Targum takes this of the fall and rising again of Israel, when the golden calf was made, whereby the chosen people became as *black* as the Æthiopians in idolatry, but afterwards, repenting, became *comely* once more, and returned to the service of GOD, making *curtains* for His tabernacle. And similarly many Christian writers see in it the Church, or the penitent soul, speaking of her past sins and present conversion to GOD. S. Gregory the Great recognizes here the conflict of the higher and lower wills in the soul. She is *black*, not only by reason of past sins, but of present ones, and yet *comely*, because she is striving after that righteousness of which she is conscious within. It is the soul of a catechumen, says Origen, already comely through repentance, but not yet white, because not admitted to the cleansing of Baptism. Or again, black by nature, comely by grace. Yet once more, the Church is black with suffering and persecution, and nevertheless comely in holiness and in reward, nay, adds S. Bernard, even more comely because of that blackness. The address to the *daughters of Jerusalem* has led more than one Father to see here the Gentile Church, confessing her lowly and heathen origin, and yet asserting the truth of her calling in CHRIST, and therefore claiming acknowledgment from the Synagogue, or even from the Jewish Christians, just as the Æthiopian wife of Moses made good her claim against Aaron and Miriam. Not very dissimilar is the view of those Greek Fathers who, taking the words of the whole Church, see in the blackness the Gentile element, and in the comeliness the Hebrew. Akin to this in spirit is the interpretation that the mixed character of the Church, as made up of saints and sinners, is implied. And finally, Rupert reminds us how Our Lady's purity was doubted, when she was found to be with child, so that she was blackened by injurious thoughts, while comely indeed, as full of grace, the tabernacle of our true Solomon. Black, too, as the Mother of Sorrows, when she stood by the Cross, despised

Targum.

Origen.
S. Hieron.
ad Eustoch.
22.
S. Bernard.

S. Greg. M.

Origen.

S. August.
de Verb.
Dom. 201.
Cassiodor.
S. Ans. Laud.
Hugo Vict.
Monast.
Instit. 84.
S. Athanas.
Theodoret.

Numb. xii.

S. Nilus.
Philo Carp.
Theodoret.

S. August.
Doct. Christ.
iii. 32.
S. Eucher.
Beda.

Rupert.

Guilelm.
Parv.

with her Son, comely in the joy of His Resurrection. *Daughters of Jerusalem.* Which Jerusalem, that which now is, and is in bondage with her children, or that which is above, and free, the mother of us all? Origen takes the former view, and makes it a call to the Jewish nation. Cardinal Hugo and others refer it to the Angels and spirits made perfect, the appeal of the Church Militant to the Church Triumphant. *As the tents of Kedar.* The tents of the Ishmaelites, formed of coarse goats' hair, and black, or dark, as *Kedar* means, are taken as the types of sin, of suffering, or of Gentilism, and contrasted with the costly hangings, or *curtains of Solomon*, made for the adornment of the temple, or, following the Arabic Version, the monarch's own *pavilions* of state. And so the Church is despised outwardly by her persecutors, yet is glorious and adorned within. Even Kedar, as descending from Abraham, was not altogether without a share in the Divine blessing, and Solomon inherited the sure mercies of David, therefore, O daughters of Jerusalem, despise not me, says the Gentile Church, who am that Æthiopian woman whom Moses took as his wife. Others, remembering that it is written, "Woe is me that I am constrained to dwell with Mesech, and to have my habitation among the tents of Kedar," take these *tents* to be the sojourn of the soul in the pilgrimage and wars of the body, while the *curtains* speak to us of that temple of which it is written that he which entereth in shall go no more out. The Church, says another, most deeply, is like the *tents of Kedar*, for she shelters under her wings penitents stained with their sins. She is like the *curtains of Solomon*, as surrounding wise, and peaceful, and holy Saints. *Curtains of Solomon.* The Body of CHRIST, touchingly notes the Gloss, is truly called a curtain, because it was stretched out upon the Cross to shelter us. For *curtains* the LXX. and Vulgate have *skins.* And that, says Cassiodorus, because as tabernacles are made from the skins of dead animals, so the Church, which is GOD's tabernacle, is framed of those who have mortified themselves with the affections and lusts. Yet again, the verse tells us of the hardships and repulsiveness of the higher Christian life, as it appears to the world, rough, sombre, and uncomely, whereas those who are within see round them, not the black goats' hair of the tent of warfare, but the purple, gemmed, and golden tapestry of the Prince of Peace, into Whose chambers of the celestial life they have entered. Honorius.

6 Look not upon me, because I am black, because the sun hath looked upon me: my mother's children were angry with me; they made me keeper of the vineyards, but mine own vineyard have I not kept.

They take the first clauses in various senses, according as they explain the *sun* to be the heat of temptation and of suffering, or the warmth of CHRIST. Wonder not that I am black, though not created so, because the fire of evil temptation hath scorched me, and dried up that once green germ in me which lacked root. Marvel not at the persecutions which I have to endure, and "faint not at my tribulations, which is your glory," for those very trials have given me patience and constancy. And just as bodies which habitually rest in the shade wither up in the broad glare of day, whereas those which move about and labour in the light scarcely feel the effects of heat, so those toilsome ones who prepare themselves for struggles and temptations, overcome the world, and win that blessing, "The sun shall not burn thee by day, neither the moon by night." If the sun be CHRIST, then the words may denote that the sufferings which the Church endures at the hand of her enemies are for His sake, Who is the Sun of Righteousness; or again, that burning zeal for His house hath eaten her up, or longing for Himself hath consumed her. Or you may take it with S. Gregory, that Saints, whatever progress they may seem to make in holiness, and however they may be looked on by men as burning and shining lights, yet feel themselves to be utter blackness when compared with the perfect righteousness of CHRIST, for the nearer we draw towards grace, the more we learn our sin. And there are not wanting those who apply the words to CHRIST Himself, despised and rejected in His Passion, so that He was "as a root out of a dry ground; He hath no form nor comeliness."

S. Greg. Nyssen.
Aponius.
Beda.
Eph. iii. 13.
S. Hieron. in Amos, iii.
Ps. cxxi. 6.
S. Ans. Laud.
S. Bernard.
S. Greg. M.
Angelomus Luxov.
Irimbert.
Isa. liii. 2.

My mother's children were angry with me. They take it first of the trials of the Primitive Church, oppressed by Jewish persecutors, once headed by S. Paul, and children of the Church's mother, the Synagogue, Origen. Beda. S. Bernard. Gloss.

but not her brethren. And next, of the Judaizing party within the Church herself, who endeavoured to impose the ceremonial Law on the Gentile converts. And they dwell on the forcible wording of the LXX. and Vulgate, which translate thus: *They fought against me.* It was true also of those heretics and evil Christians who arose in later days in the bosom of the Church, the Arians and schismatics, and evil rulers, especially unworthy Bishops, who rend instead of guarding the flock. And, taking the words of the soul, instead of the Church, we may see here either the strife carried on against it by its own passions and desires, akin as these are to its higher and better aspirations; or, more generally, the resistance of lax and worldly Christians to those who strive to serve GOD more perfectly, and that especially in the Religious life; for those who are without resist the vocation of such as feel themselves called thereto, and those within but too often war against such as would recall them to the full strictness of their rule, as many a reformer, like S. Gregory VII. or S. Teresa, has proved. And therefore it is written in another place, "I am become a stranger unto my brethren, even an alien unto my mother's children." We may, however, take the words in a good sense also, of those wise teachers, Apostles and others, who seek to war against the sins of Christians, and who give them a charge to keep.

They made me the keeper of the vineyards. In their very attempt to crush the infant Church, the Jews were the involuntary cause of its rapid spread beyond the limits of Palestine into every part of the Gentile world; *but,* adds the Church, *mine own vineyard have I not kept,* because I have been forced to abandon the Jews to their own devices. And so the Apostles, "It was necessary that the Word of GOD should first have been spoken to you: but seeing ye put it from you, and judge yourselves unworthy of everlasting life, lo, we turn to the Gentiles."

There are some who see here the story of Adam's fall. Made by GOD the keeper of the garden of Eden, he was fought against by the serpent and by Eve, and kept not his vineyard. Others explain it of the great peril of high office in the Church, lest, when men are set, not merely to labour in this vineyard, but to oversee other labourers, and to prevent the incursions of robbers, they neglect the care of their own souls, and, after preaching to others, become castaways. There is another sense, however, in which the words may be taken, of that Good Shepherd Who laid down His life for the sheep, and was not careful of Himself, so long as His peril might be the salvation of others, and Who, because He thus gave up His own vineyard, was made keeper of all others. And so speaks the aged Apostle, in the very strongest sense: "I could wish that myself were accursed from CHRIST for my brethren, my kinsmen according to the flesh." S. Ambrose, referring the vineyard to the state of consecrated virginity, warns the brides of CHRIST lest they should suffer any Ahab or Jezebel to turn their vineyard from a place wherein sweet fruits grow, into a mere garden of pot-herbs, into a secular form of life, good in its degree, but not comparable to the better way. And if so, much more does it befit Religious to beware lest when their LORD comes, He should say, "I went by the vineyard of the man void of understanding; and, lo, it was all overgrown with thorns, and nettles had covered the face thereof."

^{Irimbert.}
^{Rom. ix. 3.}
^{Exhort. ad Virg.}
^{Prov. xxiv. 30.}

7 Tell me, O thou whom my soul loveth, where thou feedest, where thou makest thy flock to rest at noon: for why should I be as one that turneth aside by the flocks of thy companions?

Thou whom my soul loveth. "So I call Thee, for Thy Name surpasseth all thought and understanding, nor could all creation reach so high as to express or comprehend it. Thy Name, then, that by which Thy goodness is known, is the affection of my soul to Thee, for how should I not love Thee, Who so lovedst me, even when I was so black, as to lay down Thy life for Thy sheep, which Thou feedest. For greater love than this cannot enter into thought, that Thou boughtest my salvation with Thine own life." *Where Thou feedest.* Not Thyself, but Thy sheep. And where is it save in that Sacrament of the Altar, in which Thou givest the nourishment of Thy Passion and the fountain streaming from Thy side to all devout souls? *To rest at noon.* They take it in many ways. And first, let us see here, with the old Cypriote Bishop, that mysterious time when JESUS, wearied with His long journey of thirty-three years, and its last blood-printed

^{S. Greg. Nyssen. Hom. ii.}
^{Idem.}
^{Philo Carp.}

footsteps along the Way of Sorrows, sat thus on the Well of our salvation, and it was about the sixth hour, and there was darkness until the ninth hour.

The Hymn, Patris Sapientia.

He upon that Cross at Sext for our sake was mounted;
By the passers-by reviled, with transgressors counted:
Vinegar and gall they give to His thirst to slake it,
Which, when He had tasted of, He refused to take it.

Cassiodor. Beda.

S. Greg. M.

Origen. Hom. 1.

Theodoret.

S. Ambros. in Ps. cxix.

Idem.

Aponius.

Again, *noon*, as the time of greatest warmth, fitly denotes especial seasons of trial and persecution in the Church, urging her to call on her LORD to be a shadow from the heat, lest she faint therein. S. Gregory applies it rather to the fiery assaults of sin, when the Bride seeks the coolness of sanctifying grace. Once more, the Bride would fain see the full glory of her Beloved, would see Him in the clear light of faith and love, undimmed by any darkness. "I ask not," she says, "as to other times, where Thou feedest at evening, or morning, or at sunset. I ask of that time when, in the flower of the day, Thou art in the fullest light clothed in the splendour of Thy Majesty." Others will have it that the Church, in her clear brightness as the light of the world, is intended by the noon-day. For as she preaches the doctrine of CHRIST everywhere throughout the world, and is therefore fitly styled Catholic, contrasting with the dark heretical sects which lurk in the corners of single nations, she is like the noon spread over the heavens. And, because it is noon when the sun is in mid-sky, so as CHRIST, the Sun of Righteousness, is the Head of the Church, directly over her, giving her light and warmth, the epithet suits her well. And if it be objected that she is not yet all clear and bright, that dark spots of sin mar the beauty of her face, yet the words hold good of her Saints. "They," says the Father last cited, "who have received Thee as the Author of salvation, are in the noon-day. Thou shinest on them, Thy grace, as the noon, warms them. Thou hast become the noon of them who feed on Thy riches, and trust in Thee." And another tells us that these especial sheep of CHRIST, whom He keeps with Himself in the noon-day warmth of His love, whom He does not merely guide with His staff, but cherishes in His bosom, are those virginal souls which have given themselves to Him alone, forsaking earthly ties for Him. Yet again, you may take the passage, with two great mystical writers, to denote the two chief divisions of spiritual life, the active being typified by the feeding of the Bridegroom, and the contemplative by His rest. At *noon*, too, because there are three hours of contemplation. The first is thought, like the early morning, having but little radiance or heat. Of this is written, "Early in the morning I will direct my prayer unto Thee, and will look up." The second period is meditation, like the third hour, when the sun begins to get high, and to glow. Whence the Psalm, "While I was thus musing the fire kindled." The third time is foretaste, like the noon-day, "when it parcheth the country." This, the true fervour of contemplation, is the place where the Beloved resteth at noon-day. "O place of true repose, not unfitting the name of bed, where GOD is seen, not in His wrath, nor as though wrapped in His providential love, but as a Will altogether merciful, loving, and perfect. This vision affrights not, but soothes; calms all anxious restlessness; arouses not, wearies not, but tranquillizes. The tranquillity of GOD makes all things tranquil, and to look upon His rest, is rest itself." Another most striking interpretation is that of Irimbert, who sees in the *rest*, the descent of CHRIST into the grave, when He made the place of darkness bright with the glorious rays of His Divinity, and fed the hungering flock of Patriarchs which had waited so long in Hades for the coming of its Shepherd, till— *[margin: Hugo Victorin. Henr. Harphius. Ps. v. 3. Ps. xxxix. 4. Ecclus. xliii. 3. Henr. Harph. Irimbert.]*

> Lumen clarum tenebrarum
> Sedibus resplenduit.
>
> Splendour lighted the benighted
> Seats of darkness with its ray.

[margin: S. Pet. Ven. The Hymn, Mortis portis.]

And Cardinal Hugo, with scarcely less beauty, applies the words to that noonday of the Church, when the Pentecostal fires descended on the Apostles, enlightening them with all the radiance of the HOLY GHOST, after the night of the Passion, the dawn of the Resurrection, and the first warmth of the Ascension had all passed over the young Bride of CHRIST. Lastly, we may take the question to be that of the Church Militant, feeling that her portion here, though sweet, is insufficient for her cravings, and desiring the full fruition of CHRIST in that Land *[margin: Hugo Card.]*

> Where no cloud nor passing vapour
> Dims the brightness of the air,

[margin: The Hymn, Jerusalem luminosa.]

> Endless noonday, glorious noonday,
> From the Sun of suns is there,
> There no night brings rest from labour,
> All unknown are toil and care.

<small>Serm. 33.</small> And on this let us hear S. Bernard: "O true noonday, fulness of glow and light, abiding of the sun, dispeller of shades, drier up of marshes, ejector of evil odours! O perennial solstice, when the day shall no more go down! O noontide glory! O vernal mildness! O summer beauty! O autumnal plenty, and lest aught should be lacking to my tale, O rest and festival of winter! Or, if thou wouldst rather have it so, winter alone is over and gone. Show me, says the Bride, the place of such love and peace, and fulness, <small>Gen. xxxii. 30.</small> that as Jacob, yet abiding in the flesh, saw GOD face to face, and his life was spared, so I too may look on Thee in Thy light and glory, by contemplation in trance of soul, as Thou feedest more abundantly, and restest more securely. For here too Thou feedest, but not in security, nor canst Thou rest, but Thou must needs stand and watch, because of the terrors of the night. Alas! here is no clear light, nor full refreshment, nor safe dwelling, and therefore tell me where Thou feedest, where Thou restest at noon. Thou callest me blessed when I hunger and thirst after righteousness. What is that to their happiness who are filled with the good things of Thy house, who feast and rejoice before GOD, and are merry and joyful? When wilt Thou fill me with joy with Thy countenance? Thy Face, LORD, will I seek. Thy Face is the noon. Tell me where Thou feedest, where Thou restest at noon. I know well where Thou feedest, but restest not, tell me where Thou dost both rest and feed." There will be, even in the noonday radiance of Heaven, cool waters and <small>Ps. xxiii. 2.</small> green pastures for the flock of the Good Shepherd, and so the type of heathen poetry shall be fulfilled:

<small>Virgil. Culex, 103.</small>
> Et jam compellente vagæ pastore capellæ
> Ima susurrantis repetebant ad vada lymphæ,
> Quæ subter viridem residebant cærula muscum.
> Jam medias operum partes evectus erat sol,
> Quum densas pastor pecudes cogebat in umbras.

> The roaming she-goats, at their herdsman's will,
> Resought the low fords of the whispering stream,
> Which rested blue beneath the verdant moss.
> And now the sun had reached his midmost toils,
> When to the thick shade drove the swain his flock.

For why should I be as one that turneth aside by the flocks of Thy companions? This is the reason, say they all, assigned by the Bride for her question. It is not merely for herself, that she may find her Beloved, that she asks Him to tell her His abiding-place, but for His sake too, lest He should lose her. And they agree in the main, also, to interpret the second clause of bodies other than the One Church, but bearing a specious resemblance to it. *Turneth aside.* The Vulgate reads, *Lest I begin to wander.* The LXX., agreeing with the margin of A.V., and with most modern critics, has *As one that is wrapped up,* or *veiled.*[1] Of this there are various expositions. First and most probably, we may take it of the customary veiling of harlots. Why should I, the Virgin Bride, by wandering near other shepherds than Thee, appear as though a shameless courtezan? Again, it may be, Why should I, who look on Thee face to face, and have felt Thy kiss, be compelled to veil myself in modest bashfulness, lest any eyes save Thine should see me? If Thou tell me where Thou restest, I can come at once to Thee, unveiled, but if Thou tell me not, I must needs cover my face while I am seeking Thee among strangers. Or, why should I, missing Thee, be forced to put on the garments of mourning, and appear as a widow instead of a bride? Origen, who gives various explanations of the passage, remarks that several of the philosophical schools and sects assumed the title of *Veiled*, implying thereby their possession of hidden truth, and that the Church here beseeches that she may know and teach the truth openly, so as not to appear like one of them; nor, adds S. Augustine in the same sense, like the obscure and localized communities of heretics. And last, we may take *veiled* as practically coming to the same thing as the *wandering* of the Vulgate, understanding it to mean putting on the walking-dress of the East over the attire worn within doors. *Thy companions.* Origen says that the *companions* of CHRIST are the Angels placed in charge of the various Gentile nations of the earth, those

<small>Gen. xxxviii. 14.
Vatablus.
Origen.
S. Hieron. ad Eustoch.
Corn. à Lap.
Origen.
S. August. Ep. ad Vincent. 48.
S. Greg. Nyss.
Cassiod.
S. Bernard.
Origen.</small>

---

[1] The root עטה, *texit*, whence עֹטְיָה, the word in the original, is derived, includes the idea of circular motion, as a garment is wrapped about the person, and thence may be transferred to the notion of wandering round and round a place. Hence Symmachus translates, in this sense, ὡς ῥεμβομένη.

"other sheep" which are not yet of CHRIST's fold. But the great majority of commentators see in the *flocks of the companions* the sects of heretical Christians. They are called CHRIST's *companions*, though they are not His friends, because they assume the Christian name, and profess to teach the same truths as the Church, and promise the like blessings. And as *companions* is the special Eastern title for those who feast at the same table, so these profess to feed their disciples with the same banquet of Sacraments and Holy Writ, though they poison it by perverting its sense, "having a form of godliness, but denying the power thereof." S. Gregory extends the application of the words to all false brethren, all evil Christians, who are in a sense CHRIST's companions, as having a place in His Church and a share in His Sacraments, but are not truly His elect. Rupert stands alone in seeing here a reference to the Scribes and Pharisees, and therefore a petition of the Church to be guarded from Judaizing. Another, not very dissimilarly, applies the passage to the Patriarchs and Prophets of the Old Testament, *companions* indeed of CHRIST, as loving and following Him as far as they knew, but still wandering uncertainly, and with no clear noontide revelation. S. Bernard takes the words, very singularly, of the evil spirits, transforming themselves into angels of light, and pretending to be CHRIST's servants and friends in order to deceive the soul which seeks Him.

S. John x. 16.
Theodoret.
S. Just. Org. Cassiod.
S. August. de Verb. Dom. 50. Aponius.
2 Tim. iii. 5.
S. Greg. M.
Rupert.
Irimbert.

8 If thou know not, O thou fairest among women, go thy way forth by the footsteps of the flock, and feed thy kids beside the shepherds' tents.

If thou know not. The simple meaning of these words has been obscured by the LXX. and Vulgate, which endeavour to reproduce the pleonastic Hebrew idiom, and read *If thou knowest not thyself*, and nearly all the ancient commentators have interpreted this of self-ignorance. And thus S. Justus of Urgel, taking the words in close connection with those that follow, observes, that CHRIST thus addresses the Church, If thou know not that thou art *fairest* amongst all Christian bodies, since all except thee have lost their purity, then go forth to seek Me; but if thou truly knowest what thou art, and with what grace I have dowered

S. Just. Org.
S. Athanas. Philo Carp.

thee, then look within thyself, and thou wilt find Me there. S. Bernard, also taking the words as those of the Bridegroom, interprets them in a far sterner sense, as a rebuke to the Bride who, ignorant that she is yet but in the body, and merely *fairest among women*, (that is, amongst secular and carnal souls, having no true vigour or constancy,) yet dares to ask GOD to show her the place of His glory. She is therefore recalled to herself, and convinced of her ignorance, and chastised for her boldness, and to teach her humility, she is commanded to go forth out of the sanctuary of her heart, away from holy contemplation, and to busy herself again in the lower service of external cares. And not dissimilarly S. Jerome, addressing the Abbess S. Eustochium, explains the passage, "Though thou be fair, and thy beauty be loved by Me thy Bridegroom more than that of all other women, yet, unless thou know thyself, and keep thy heart with all watchfulness, unless thou fly from the glances of youth, thou shalt go forth from My chamber to feed the goats, which are to stand on My left." Yes, adds S. Augustine, carrying on the same argument, to feed them not as Peter feeds My sheep, not to be in My fold, Who am the One Shepherd, but by the tents of other shepherds, not of unity but of division. A second view puts the words into the mouths of the Bride's virgin friends, as though of encouragement to her, lest she should be too much cast down with thoughts of her marred beauty, and not knowing herself to be fairest, doubt of retaining her Spouse's love. *By the footsteps of the flock.* That is, observes one, follow up all the traces of those Saints of the Old Covenant who belonged in faith to the New, lead on, and *feed thy kids*, thy weak and sinful members, by the *tents of the shepherds*, the Churches of the Apostles, that there they may be healed. And this is, in fact, the Christian view of the old Jewish gloss, which says here, "The Holy and Blessed One spake to Moses the Prophet: Thou askest that their exile may be ended. Let the Synagogue, which is compared to a most beautiful virgin, and whom My soul loveth, walk in the paths of the just, and direct its prayer in the mouths of its rulers, and lead its generations and lead its sons, (who are compared to kids of the goats,) to walk in the house of the congregation, and in the house of doctrine, and because of that good deed they shall be supported

S. Bernard, Serm. 38.

S. Hieron. Epist. 22.

Serm. 50, de Verb. Dom. Cf. Origen.

S. Greg. Nyss.

Theodoret.

Targum.

in their captivity, till I send them Messiah the King, Who shall lead them into rest to their own tabernacle, which is that House of Sanctuary which David and Solomon, Shepherds of Israel, shall build for them. Aponius, too, takes the words as spoken by CHRIST to the Synagogue, urging her to come to the knowledge of the truth. The common view sees in the *flock*, *kids*, and *shepherds*, the heretical, sinful, and schismatic companionship into which a Church or a soul which does not strive after self-knowledge is certain to fall. There is not wanting, however, a nobler and more cheering interpretation, which is, in fact, the truest meaning of the passage. When the LORD asked Peter, "Simon, son of Jonas, lovest thou Me?" and was answered, "LORD, Thou knowest that I love Thee;" His further speech was, "Feed My sheep." So, the way for the Church or the soul to find CHRIST is to go forth from herself, to follow the traces of the straying flocks, to feed more especially the *kids*, weak and sinful servants of His, and so to reach the tents of the shepherds, the wise and holy teachers to whom He intrusts His sheep. And again, the *kids* may well denote the petulant and unrestrained desires of the heart, which need to be checked, ruled, and fed, not in the tabernacles of the body, but in those of the spirit, whereof is written, "How goodly are thy tents, O Jacob, and thy tabernacles, O Israel."

9 I have compared thee, O my love, to a company of horses in Pharaoh's chariots.

The obvious reference here is to the Egyptian breed of horses, chiefly esteemed in Solomon's time, as we read in Scripture; and the Church, or the faithful soul, is compared to a gallant steed, first, because of the swiftness of her running after CHRIST; next, because of her ready obedience and submission to His yoke; thirdly, because of her bearing the Gospel chariot into all lands; and lastly, because of her fruitfulness, bringing forth young abundantly by preaching. And much in this same sense the Greek Fathers understand it, explaining, as they do, that CHRIST compares the Gentile Church, in its zeal and holiness, to His great steeds the Apostles, who drew Him in *Pharaoh's chariots*, that is, amongst all the nations of the earth. And so a Saint has said, "Those swift-limbed steeds, the Apostles, from Sion as from their starting-point, went forth into the whole world." — *S. Chrysos. in Ps. xlix. 1.*

O Guider of Thy chariot fleet, mount, LORD, these steeds of fire, and make a pathway for their feet through our hearts' deepest mire; That we, borne safely in this car from out the troubled sea, May reach our country's haven far, and ever dwell with Thee. — *The Sequence, Regnum tuum. Hab. iii. 15.*

Origen, dwelling on the word *Pharaoh* as the Scriptural type of evil, comments thus: "As in Egypt, when Pharaoh, pursuing after the children of Israel, went forth with horses and chariots, *My* (LXX. and Vulg.) chivalry far surpassed and excelled Pharaoh's chariots, in that it overcame them and drowned them in the sea, so thou, My Love and Bride, excellest all women, and art made like to My chivalry, which, compared with the chariots of Pharaoh, proved stronger and more glorious." He further proceeds to remind us what that chivalry of GOD is, by citing the vision at Dothan, when Elisha's servant saw the "mountain full of horses and chariots of fire round about." And thus the sense would be, I have matched thee against the horses and chariots of Pharaoh. I have set thee, My Church, to war against the chief priests and scribes who denied Me. I have set thee to fight against all the darkness and idolatry of the spiritual Egypt. Others would turn it, I have likened thee, who wast once in Pharaoh's chariots, in bondage and misery, to My own chivalry, for I have brought thee through the Red Sea of Baptism, and made thee clean and free. A yet deeper mystical sense, seeing in the white horse of the Apocalypse, on which He Who is Faithful and True rides, the Manhood of CHRIST bearing His Godhead as Its Ruler,—finds here the manner in which CHRIST makes His Bride like Himself, in that He "will change our vile Body that it may be like unto His glorious Body." And this He will do, when He makes us go up, as He did, "with a merry noise, and the sound of the trump;" when we are "caught up to meet our LORD in the air;" caught up, as Elijah was, by the fiery "chariot of Israel and the horsemen thereof;" which are those cherubim on which He rides, "ministering spirits sent forth to minister for them also, who shall be heirs of salvation;" horses terrible to Pharaoh's chariots in the battles of the soul, going on to meet the armed men, mocking at fear, and turning — *Origen. 2 Kings vi. 17. S. Bernard. Aponius. Beda. Haymo. Ricard. Victor. in Apoc. xix. Theodoret. Philip. iii. 21. Irimbert. Ps. xlvii. 5. 1 Thess. iv. 17. 2 Kings ii. 12. Ps. xviii. 10. Heb. i. 14. Job xxxix. 21.*

not back from the sword. Yet another view is that GOD makes His Saints like His chivalry the Angels, even while He suffers them to be driven by Pharaoh in his chariot; that is to say, that He gives them grace whereby they lead a life of angelic purity and holiness even while in the prison of the flesh, and sorely tried by temptations of the evil one. "And you will not marvel," adds S. Bernard, "that one soul is here compared not to one horse only, but to a *company of horses*, if you remark how many armies of virtues there are in a single soul which is holy, what orderly array in affections, what discipline in habits, what equipment in prayer, what vigour in action, what dreadfulness in resolution, what steadiness in fight, what aggregate of triumphs." That matching against Pharaoh is no light struggle, as the Saint goes on to say: "There Israel is brought out of Egypt, here man out of the world, there Pharaoh is routed, here the evil one; there Pharaoh's chariots are overwhelmed, here the carnal and secular desires which war against the soul; those went down in waves, these in weepings. And I believe that now the demons, if they encounter such a soul, cry out, 'Let us flee from the face of Israel, for the LORD fighteth for him.'"

S. Thom. à Villanov.

S. Bernard. Serm. 39.

Exod. xiv. 25.

10 Thy cheeks are comely with rows of jewels, thy neck with chains of gold.

This rendering is sufficiently close to the Hebrew text, save that the word "pearls" might perhaps be well substituted for "gold." The simile of the horse continues, and now the costly trappings with which the swift and docile steed is decked are described. First comes the headstall, to which the bit and bridle are attached, and this is said to be made with *rows* תֹּרִים *torim*, a word akin to *Torah*, the Law, and denoting orderly arrangement. Thus, the first adornments of the Church of GOD are the precepts and statutes by which He guides her, because "the fear of the LORD is the beginning of wisdom," and when "the LORD of Hosts hath visited His flock, and hath made them as His goodly horse in the battle," He adorns the neck which bears His yoke with those additional instructions of which is written in another place, "They shall be an ornament of grace unto thine head, and chains about thy neck." So too the Targum explains it;

Ps. cxi. 10.
Zech. x. 3.

Prov. i. 9.

and we have in Ezekiel a fuller enumeration of this adorning: "I decked thee with ornaments, and I put bracelets upon thine hands, and a chain on thy neck: and I put a jewel on thy forehead, and earrings in thine ears, and a beautiful crown upon thine head: thus wast thou decked with gold and silver." But the LXX., Arabic, and Vulgate, taking the word *torim* in its frequent sense of *turtle-doves*, translate here, *Thy cheeks are comely as those of a turtle.* The words are spoken by the Bridegroom, says Origen, to comfort the Bride, deeply blushing at the rebuke she has just received. And he explains the *cheeks*, as the seat of modesty, to be those members of the Church who are eminent for purity and shamefastness. They are cheeks of a *dove*, because of the faithfulness of those birds to one another when they have paired; and so the Church keeps herself faithful to her one Beloved, and mourns for Him when He is absent from her. Of a *dove*, says another, because CHRIST is Himself that Dove, and those Doctors of the Church who are eminent for holiness, are her *cheeks*, and are like Him. Again, they lay stress on the well known habit of the turtle-dove of dwelling in retired and shady places, to point out the need of solitary retirement for the holy soul. And thus S. Bernard: "It is far above one's own power to be plighted to the LORD of Angels. Is it not beyond thee to cling to GOD, and to be one spirit with Him? Sit then solitary like the turtle, have nothing to do with crowds and multitudes, forget also thine own people and thy father's house, so shall the King have pleasure in thy beauty. . . . Withdraw, then, but in soul, in resolve, in devotion, in spirit, not in body." The unvarying note of the turtle suggests to the Greek Fathers the grave and steadfast discourse of true Christians, as distinguished from the frivolous loquacity of the heathen world. And others dwell on its mournful sound, as typifying the tears of pity and intercession flowing down from the contemplative Saints, called the *cheeks* of the Church, because close to the *eyes*, which are the enlightening gifts of the HOLY SPIRIT. *Thy neck as collars.* If of "pearl," as suggested above, then the points of likeness will be three, roundness, whiteness, and orderly arrangement, typifying the Religious Life, *round*, in the vow of poverty, because as a sphere touches other bodies at one point only, so the profes-

Ezek. xvi. 11.

Origen.
Theodoret.
S. Greg. M.
S. Bernard.
Rupert, &c.

Aponius.

Serm. 40.

Tres Patr.

Nic. Argent.

sion of poverty detaches Religious almost completely from earthly things; *white,* in the profession of chastity; and *regular,* in the pledge of obedience to rule. The flexibility of the neck too, as also denoting obedience, has been dwelt on by several expositors, and, as some add, it is therefore said, "as a necklace," because of the pliancy of that ornament. And, S. Ambrose observes, the law of GOD is not a bond or a yoke upon the obedient neck, but a collar, which even dumb animals take pride in wearing. Most early commentators, however, explain the *neck* to mean the chief Doctors and preachers of the Church, because, as the throat is the passage for food from the head to the stomach, and is also the channel of speech, so they communicate the doctrine of CHRIST to the people, and utter it in their discourse. S. Anselm of Laon adds another reason, that they are the link of union between CHRIST the Head, and the faithful laity of His Body. And as a necklace goes all round the neck, so true obedience embraces all the actions of the Christian life, especially amongst Religious. Again, as necklaces are made of jewels set in gold, so the true adornments of Saints are good works undertaken in wisdom. Once more, as jewelled collars are made of many separate parts, all united in one flexible band, so the decoration of the Bride of CHRIST is made up of many virtues, twined with humility. And it is not to be forgotten that in ancient days the jewelled necklace was not merely the ornament of virgins (wherefore a Saint says, addressing women, "Let your collar and chains be modesty and shamefastness,") but also the especial prize of conspicuous valour,

Ut qui fortis erit sit felicissimus idem,
Ut læti phaleris omnes et torquibus omnes.

That whoso valiant is in fight, the same may richest be,
And all be glad with costly gauds and collars fair to see.

11 We will make thee borders of gold with studs of silver.

We will make. First they ask, Who are these that speak? And the answer of the Targum is the best, that it is the same Who said in the beginning, "Let us make man in our image;" to wit, the Most Holy Trinity, FATHER, SON, and HOLY GHOST. The Chaldee paraphrast thus continues, "Then was it said unto Moses,

Get thee up into the mount, and I will give thee two tables of stone, cut from the sapphire throne of My glory, shining as the finest gold, ruled with lines traced by My finger, wherein are written ten sayings, purified more than silver which has been purified seven times, and I will give them by thy hand to the people of the house of Israel." But this sense, beautiful as it is, refers to the past, long before the time of the Canticles. It is not *We have made*, but *We will make*, and is therefore a promise to the Bride of some good things she has not yet obtained. So then we may compare the similar promise in another place: "Though ye have lien among the pots, yet shall ye be as the wings of a dove, that is covered with silver wings, and her feathers like gold," and are led on from the harsh, stern dictates of the Law to the grace and truth of the Gospel, according to that saying of the Prophet, "For brass I will bring gold, and for iron I will bring silver." We may see here in the word *border*, a reference to Him Who standeth "round about His people for evermore," and then, as it is written, "A word fitly spoken is as apples of gold in pictures of silver," the gold may denote the Godhead of the WORD, the pictures or studs of silver the pure Manhood of CHRIST. Several of the Fathers agree with the general spirit of the Chaldee interpretation, and take the golden borders to denote the knowledge of Holy Scripture, intertwined with silver threads of types, prophecies, counsels, and the like, or even with the human eloquence of devout preachers; silver, as pure and holy, but not golden with direct inspiration. They vary, however, in attributing the words to the Bridegroom or to His friends. Origen, taking the latter view, and following the LXX. rendering, which is *similitudes of gold with spots of silver*, holds that the speakers are the Angels, who ordained the Law in the hand of a Mediator, and the Prophets who expound that Law. *While the King is in His lying down*, and has not yet come to deck His Bride Himself, they desire to do something for her adornment. They have no gold, because of "the Law having a shadow of good things to come, and not the very image of the things," and therefore they can give only *similitudes of gold*, the Ark of the Covenant, the altar of incense, the shew-bread, and the like, mere types of future mysteries. They have *silver*, the

Ps. lxviii. 13.

Ainsworth.
Isa. lx. 17.

Ps. cxxv. 2.

S. August.
S. Greg.
Nyss.
Theodoret.
Aponius.
Beda.

Origen.
S. August.
de Trin. i. 8.
Gal. iii. 19.

Heb. x. 1.

moral precepts and counsels to guide man's life, but only in very small quantity, so that they can bestow merely *spots* of it, unlike the true Solomon, of whom it is written, "And the king made silver and gold at Jerusalem as plenteous as stones." Others, agreeing with Origen in taking the clause *While the King is in His lying down* with the present sentence, explain it of the current dispensation, to end when He arises to judgment, and they interpret the *similitudes of gold* and the *spots of silver* to be the imperfect foretaste of eternal joys granted to the Church Militant on earth. Again, they take the golden ornaments to signify the cleansing of the Church by fiery persecutions, and in this sense one commentator declares that the Martyrs are the golden jewels of the Church, marked with silver spots denoting the torments and sufferings they endured, as the Apostle writes, "I bear about in my body the marks of the LORD JESUS."

The Vulgate rendering, *necklets* (*murenulas*, literally, *little eels*, named from their flexibility and cylindrical form) *damascened* (*vermiculatas*) *with silver*, has given rise to much comment from the Latin Fathers. Thus S. Gregory observes, "The eel is a fish which, when taken, twists itself into a circle, in resemblance of which an ear-ring is made, called *murenula*, by which is denoted preaching, which hangs to the ears, and enters them. Collars (*monilia*) are fastened to the neck with *murenulæ*, just as wisdom and religion are united by preachers with Holy Writ. For by these necklets we understand Holy Writ to be meant. It is well said to be damascened with gold and silver, because it shines with wisdom, and is heard, by clear preaching, throughout the world." Another Saint, looking to the twinings of the eel, says that the golden necklets denote the more involved and difficult sayings and doctrines of Scriptures, and the silver threadings the expositions of the Saints thereon. Not very dissimilarly, another holy writer sees in the gold the contemplation of Divine mysteries, and in the silver the created channels through which we are here obliged to make that contemplation. Or, as yet another puts it, the gold is CHRIST's benefits of love: the silver, the good works and wisdom with which we carry them out. After these explanations, that of Parez seems poor, who takes the golden necklaces to be the spiritual graces of the Church, the silver threadings her temporal endow-

ments. Lastly, S. Jerome says that gold denotes the
Virgin life. Before CHRIST came, the Church had the
silver of chaste marriage and widowhood, but the ^{S. Hieron.}
more precious metal of virginity was His gift. And ^{cont. Jovin.} ^{1.}
the words therefore point to that especial aureole re-
served for maiden brows.

> They say, who know the life divine,   *Keble,*
> And upward gaze with eagle eyne,   *Christian*
> That by each golden crown on high,   *Year.*
> Rich with celestial jewelry,
> Which for our LORD's redeemed is set,
> There hangs a radiant coronet,
> All gemmed with pure and living light,
> Too dazzling for a sinner's sight,
> Prepared for virgin souls, and them
> Who seek the Martyr's diadem.

12 While the king sitteth at his table, my
spikenard sendeth forth the smell thereof.

They assign four principal meanings to this *sitting* ^{S. Aug. de}
of the King, or rather, following the original idiom, ^{Trin. i. 8.}
and that of the ancient versions, His *lying down.* ^{S. Greg. M.}
First; it is taken of the repose of CHRIST's Godhead
in heaven. "The lying-down of the King is the ^{S. Bernard.}
Bosom of the FATHER, for the SON is ever in the FA- ^{Serm. 42.}
THER. And thou canst not doubt Him to be a merciful
King, whose everlasting down-lying is the dwelling of
the FATHER's lovingkindness. Fitly does the cry of
the lowly ascend to Him, Who is the fount and habitation of gentleness." And this is the sense in which
Origen and those other Fathers who attach the words ^{Origen.}
to the previous verse understand them, taking, as they
do, the Incarnation of CHRIST to be His *standing up* to
help mankind in the battle. But others will have it ^{Cassiodor.}
that the Incarnation itself is here meant, called *lying* ^{Beda.}
down because of the humility with which the LORD ^{Aponius.}
emptied Himself of His glory. Thirdly; the Passion ^{S. Just. Org.}
and Death of CHRIST, His lying down on the Cross and ^{S.Ans.Laud.} ^{Theodoret.}
in the grave, is the view of more than one Saint and ^{S. Greg.}
Father. And lastly; there is the indwelling of CHRIST ^{Nyss.}
in the holy soul. They vary also as to the meaning of ^{Tres Patr.}
the *spikenard.* The older interpretation explains it of
CHRIST Himself, "It is no marvel," says Origen, "if ^{Origen.}
CHRIST, as He is the Fountain, and streams of living
water proceed out of Him; and as He is the Bread, and ^{Theodoret.}
gives life; so He is the Spikenard also, and gives odour,

and is the ointment wherewith those who are anointed become Christs, as He saith in the Psalm, 'Touch not My Christs.' And it may be that as the Apostle saith, unto 'those who by reason of use have their senses exercised to discern both good and evil,' CHRIST adapts Himself for each of the soul's senses. Therefore He is called the True Light, that the soul's eyes may have illumination; therefore He is the WORD, that the ears may hearken; therefore He is the Bread of Life, that the soul's taste may perceive savour. Therefore also He is called spikenard or ointment, that the soul's sense of smell may receive the fragrance of the WORD. Therefore, too, He can be touched and handled with the hand, and the WORD was made flesh, that the hands of the inner soul might handle the Word of Life." Next; the spikenard will denote the lowliness of the Church, or of the soul which draws near GOD. "Good," exclaims S. Bernard, "is that odour of humility which, ascending from the vale of tears, and impregnating all the regions round about, perfumes with grateful sweetness the royal chamber itself. The spikenard is a lowly plant, which they who have carefully studied the properties of herbs state to be of a warm nature, and thus I hold it not unsuitable to understand here that virtue of humility which is hot with the exhalations of holy love." And if it be true of all humble saints, whether of the Old or New Covenant, as they allege, much more is it so of her, the holiest and most exalted of all, in whose hallowed womb the King vouchsafed to lie down. "The King Himself," says a saintly writer, venturing, with holy boldness, to put words into the pure mouth of the Mother of GOD, "SON of the Most Highest King, Himself of no lesser dignity, from His equal throne with the FATHER, from His royal seat, from the secret dwelling of His unapproachable Majesty, where the Angels see and desire His Face evermore, vouchsafed to come hither to earth for the salvation of perishing souls, and rested in my chamber. In my womb, I say, that King gladly laid Himself down, and found nought in me to make His dwelling displeasing to Him. And there lying, He filled me marvellously with His grace: While preserving my virginity, He took away my maiden barrenness, and His forceful fire consumed me as a whole burnt-offering, and filled the entire house with the most fragrant perfume of ointment."

> Only her spacious soul, the blessed Sea,
> Where all those floods of precious things did meet,
> Knew what it comprehended; Glorious, she
> Did taste the relish of each mystic sweet
> In one miraculous instant, and did try
> The various dainties of Divinity.
>
> J. Beaumont, *Psyche*, vii. 98.

And so, too, it was not till He came in the flesh, that the sweet odour of the Church went up to GOD, filling His house, the earth, and no longer shut up in the narrow casket of Judea. Thirdly; they explain the spikenard of repentance, and here, most naturally, that other Mary, who anointed the feet of JESUS with ointment of spikenard, very precious, when her King sat at table, is taken as the type of all true penitent souls. Origen. Beda. Aponius.

> In prædulci unctione,
> Nardum ferens pisticum,
> Et unguenti fusione
> Typum gessit mysticum,
> Ut sanetur unctione,
> Unxit ægra Medicum.
>
> The Hymn, *Pange, lingua, Magdalenæ.*
>
> She, in that anointing sweetest,
> Bearing spikenard rich and pure,
> In its pouring-out completest,
> Showed us mystic types and sure,
> Sick, she gave that Healer meetest
> What she sought herself for cure.

Next; it is taken to denote the faith of the Church in her Incarnate, suffering, and risen LORD, and her preaching of that faith till its perfume filled the world. Fifthly; it is explained of all good works, especially of prayer. And following this view in connection with that which sees in the *lying down*, the Passion and Burial of CHRIST, we may remember not only the spices with which the Sacred Body was interred, but also those which the holy women brought to the sepulchre, deeming Him to be still there, and may take upon our lips those words of the Holy Eastern Church: S. Ambros. in Ps. cxix. S. Just. Org.
Cassiodor. Beda.

> Let us rise in early morning,
> And instead of ointments, bring
> Hymns of praise unto our Master,
> And His Resurrection sing,
> We shall see the Sun of Justice
> Risen with healing in His wing.
>
> S. Johann. Damasc. *The Golden Canon.*

And this especially when we approach the sacred Banquet wherein the King indeed *sitteth at His table*, to feed His guests with His own most precious Body

S. Greg. M. and Blood. We greet Him, however, not only in His glorious Resurrection, but in His wonderful Ascension, so that the odour of our petitions and holy deeds may be wafted upwards to His feet as He sits on the great white throne. When the fires of Pentecost came down after CHRIST went up and entered His chamber once more, then the words of salvation and the holy examples of the Saints of GOD sent their fragrance over all the earth, because the incense was kindled by the flame of the SPIRIT.

13 A bundle of myrrh is my wellbeloved unto me; he shall lie all night betwixt my breasts.

Theodoret. Honor. Aug.
Origen.
S. Ambros. in Ps. cxix.
S. Greg. Nyss.
Origen.
2 S. Pet. i. 20.
Aponius. Cassiodor. S. Greg. M.

As we had in the *spikenard* the Incarnation of CHRIST, so here we have His Passion set before us in the *myrrh*. And observe, this myrrh is not loose, but in a bundle, tied up. First then, CHRIST is a *bundle* for us, because He was not content to be with us in the Omnipresence of His Godhead, but came to us also bound in human form, and with like passions to ours. He is a bundle, again, because He ties Himself to our souls with the cords of His most tender and unfailing love. And thirdly; because each group of CHRIST's sayings, and each doctrine or miracle of His, is bound up with others, with the cord of truth, and cannot be taken separately. And this is what the Apostle means when he says that "no prophecy of the Scripture is of any private interpretation." Next; the bundle is of *myrrh*, because that bitter herb typifies the suffering and death of CHRIST, and also the share in that suffering which must be the lot of all who follow Him. Myrrh, they remind us, was used in the burial of the dead, to preserve the body from corruption.

Prudent. Cathem. x. 51.

Aspersaque myrrha Sabæo
Corpus medicamine servat.

And myrrh which is sprinkled preserveth
With unguent of Saba the body.

S. John xix. 39.

And therefore the Church, mindful not only of the mixture of myrrh and aloes which Nicodemus brought for the burial of the LORD, but of her own preservation from the rottenness of sin by His dying, dwells in thankful love on the story of His Passion. *He shall lie all night.* The words *all night* are not necessarily implied in the Hebrew, nor are they expressed in the old versions, but the verb לין *lūn* here used, so often has this sense,[1] that we need not hesitate to apply their mystical import. *All night*, then, in all time of our tribulation, in every sorrow, and throughout the darkness of this world, till the day break, CHRIST shall be with us, closest and dearest. *Betwixt my breasts*. And that because He is *My Well-beloved*. "Just now," says S. Bernard, "He was King, now He is Well-beloved. Just now, He was in His lying down, now betwixt the breasts of His spouse. Great is the might of humility, to which the majesty of Godhead so readily bows itself. The name of reverence is quickly changed into that of love, and He Who was far off, speedily is near. *A bundle of myrrh is my Well-beloved unto me*. Myrrh is a bitter thing, harsh and rough; it denotes tribulation. She, knowing that it awaits her for her Beloved's sake, utters that saying thankfully, trusting that she can valiantly bear it all. 'The disciples departed,' she says, 'from the presence of the Council, rejoicing that they were counted worthy to suffer shame for His Name.'" *Betwixt my breasts*. The metaphor is taken from the Eastern custom of carrying a small posy or bag of myrrh in the bosom, to scent the clothes, and also as a safeguard against infection, and thence it is fitly transferred to them who keep in their heart the memory of CHRIST's death. *My breasts*. Of the Church, the Old and New Testaments, one with its prophecies and types of the Passion, the other with the history and the results of it, between which lies the scarred form of the Man of Sorrows. *My breasts*, of the holy soul, which carries CHRIST between the two great commandments, the love of GOD and the love of one's neighbour. *A bundle of myrrh betwixt the breasts* of His most dear Mother, in His Incarnation, because He preserved her then pure from all taint of her virginity; and again in the hour of His Passion, when the sword passed through her bosom, and she tasted the bitterness of death with Him. And it is because of all these reasons that it has been the delight of Christians for many centuries, and especially of those Virgin souls which are dedicated to their LORD, of whom it is written,

S. Bernard. Serm. 43.

Acts v. 41.

Cassiodor.

Philo Carp.

S. Greg. M.

Parez.

Rupert.

Dion. Carth.

> In earum pectore cubat in meridie,
> Inter mammas virginum collocans cubiculum;

Godeschalcus. The Sequence, *Virgines castæ.*

[1] Gen. xix. 2; Judg. xix. 6, 9; Ruth iii. 13; Job xxix. 19, &c.

> He lieth on their bosom in the noontide,
> Making His couch betwixt the breasts of the virgins;

to wear the crucifix upon their breasts in memory of their suffering Bridegroom.

14 My beloved is unto me as a cluster of camphire in the vineyards of En-gedi.

Dion. Carth. And now we have the Resurrection. There is no doubt as to the plant intended here, which is the famous *henna* of the East, worn by the women in posies on their breasts, because of its beautiful and fragrant blossoms, and employed as a dye to give the favourite golden red tinge to their nails. And the word כֹּפֶר *Corn. à Lap.* *copher*, here read in the Hebrew, means also *expiation* or *ransom*, so that we have here a confession from the *Thrupp.* Bride of the preciousness and fragrance of that Redemption wrought for her, which makes the traces of CHRIST's Passion appear even in her humblest members. This camphire can be gathered only in the *vineyards*, where the wine of the Passion is produced, vineyards truly of *En-gedi*, the "fountain of the kid," *Cassiodor.* because when the mingled tide flowed from the spear *Philo Carp.* wound on the Cross, then the prophecy was fulfilled, *S. Greg. M.* *S. Bernard.* "In that day there shall be a fountain opened to the *Zech. xiii. 1.* house of David and to the inhabitants of Jerusalem for sin and for uncleanness," and the waters of Baptism were provided to wash away our guilt. *En-gedi* now, because of the clear sweet waters of the Gospel, but once *Gen. xiv. 7.* Hazazon-Tamar, the "pruning of the palm," by reason *2 Chron. xx. 2.* of the stern precepts of the Law, cutting off, rather than cleansing, the sinner. An ambiguity in the LXX. and Vulgate rendering of אֶשְׁכֹּל הַכֹּפֶר *eshcol ha-copher*, which they both turn *botrus Cypri*, has led to much difficulty and variety of exposition amongst both Greek and Latin commentators. With the single exception of Origen, who rightly explains the words of a thickly flowering shrub, (though he prefers, after all, to follow the less correct rendering,) they agree in taking *botrus* to mean a *cluster of grapes*, and the Latins, for the most part, suppose *Cypri* to denote the island of Cyprus, then, as now, famous for its wine, and thus merely an epithet of excellence. Others, nearer to the truth, take it to be the proper name of a *balsam-tree*, resembling the grape in its clusters, and therefore said to grow in *vineyards*.

It is not a little curious that the error of rendering *grape* for *cluster* is found not only in those who followed the ambiguous rendering, but in the Chaldee Targum itself. The Greeks generally suppose *Cypri* to denote *blooming* or *flowering*, from the verb κυπρίζω, and interpret the whole phrase, *a grape in flower*, i.e., before the fruit is developed. "And this," says Origen, "because those to whom the WORD is the True Vine, do not find Him giving them all at once ripe and sweet grapes; nor does He suddenly become to them that rich wine which makes glad the heart of man, but first He gives them only the pleasant odour of blossoms. This flowering grape is said to be in the vineyards of Engaddi; that its grateful fragrance may at the very beginning be poured into the soul; that she may afterwards endure the bitterness of trials and temptations which beset believers for the sake of the WORD of GOD; and at last He gives them the sweetness of His maturity, till He brings them to the wine-presses, where is poured out the blood of the grape, the blood of the New Testament, which shall be drunk on the festal day above, where the great banquet is prepared .... And in that this flowering grape is said to be of the *vineyards of Engaddi:* the word Engaddi is interpreted, *the eye of my temptation*.[1] Any one, then, who understands how men's life on earth is a temptation, and who also knows how one is delivered in GOD out of temptation, and who detects the nature of his own special temptation, so that it may be said of him that in all these things he hath not sinned with his lips before GOD: to such a man the WORD of GOD becomes a flowering grape in the vineyards of Engaddi." *Origen.*

Some of the Latin Fathers, remembering the vine-bunch borne on the pole by the spies, see in the *grape of Cyprus* the Crucifixion of CHRIST; and in *Engaddi,* the Scribes and Pharisees who surrounded and *tempted* *S. Ambros. Aponius. S. Just. Org.*

---

[1] This curious rendering may thus be accounted for: *En* or *Ain* is strictly the *eye*, and is merely transferred by metaphor to a *pool* or *fountain*, as an eye of the earth. *Gaddi* is explained, "my temptation," by following the LXX. interpretation of Gen. xlix. 19, where is read, "Gad, a temptation shall tempt him," instead of our reading, "a troop shall overcome him." From the verb גוּד or גּוּד, properly "to press violently on," with the pronominal suffix, comes Origen's view. Another explanation, "my cutting," referred to later, comes from another sense of the same verb, "to prune," or "make an incision."

Him; but the majority prefer to take it of the Resurrection. And thus, amongst several others, S. Bernard: "If He be well-beloved in myrrh, much more in the sweetness of the grape-bunch. Therefore my LORD JESUS is myrrh to me in His death, a grape-bunch in His Resurrection. He mingled Himself for me as the most healthful of drinks, in tears, in a measure. He died for our offences, and rose again for our justification; that dead unto sin, we might live unto righteousness. Therefore, if thou hast mourned for thy sins, thou hast drunk bitterness; but if thou hast revived with holier conversation in hope of life, the bitterness of the myrrh is changed for thee into wine, which maketh glad the heart of man." Aponius, contrariwise, from finding here in the meaning of *Cypri* a reference to the funereal cypress, explains that CHRIST is the *grape of sorrow* to sinners, when He pours the spirit of grief and compunction into their souls, according to His own saying, "Blessed are they that mourn, for they shall be comforted." And that in *Engaddi*, because it is the fount of penitential tears which washes the rank-smelling kids. Again; if Engaddi be explained *fount of my cutting*, it may be taken of the precious *balsam* for all our hurts, flowing from the wounded side of CHRIST, as balm from the incisions in a tree. They are also careful to dwell on the fact that En-gedi was the place whence the choicest balsam came. And thus S. Ambrose, though explaining one word differently: "Engaddi is a place in Judæa, where opobalsam grows. If you ask its meaning, it is in Latin, *temptation*. In those vineyards is a tree which yields ointment if pierced, and this is the product of that tree. If it be not cut, it is not so fragrant and penetrating in odour, but when it has been skilfully pierced, it drops a tear. So CHRIST, crucified on that Tree of temptation, weeps over His people, to wash away our sins, and from the bowels of His mercy pours ointment upon us, saying, 'FATHER, forgive them, for they know not what they do.' Then He was pierced with a spear on the Tree, and there came forth from Him blood and water, sweeter than any ointment, a victim acceptable to GOD, pouring the odour of sanctification throughout the world; and as balsam from a tree, so power went forth from His Body." Beda, following up a reference of S. Gregory the Great to the use of balsam in chrism, tells us that the balsam denotes the graces of the Holy Spirit, and bids us note the collocation of ideas. The Bride first says, that her spikenard yielded its odour while the King was lying down, then she compares Him to a bundle of myrrh; and thirdly, calls Him a grape-cluster of Cyprus; declaring lastly, that He is in the vineyards of Engaddi. And that because a devout woman first anointed the LORD with spikenard when He lay down at supper. After that, the disciples wrapped in fine linen His crucified Body, anointed with myrrh for burial, and after this, He, in the joy of His Resurrection, which came so soon, bestows spiritual gifts on the faithful. And it is said *in the vineyards,* denoting the Churches and faithful souls which rejoice in the redemption bought for her by CHRIST. Nowhere, save in *Engedi,* adds another, for just as many kings tried in vain to transplant the balsams of that place successfully, so there is but the one faith wherein the Bride can find her Beloved, and the life of CHRIST, outside His Church, withers away in the soul. Philo Carp.
Aponius.
S. Bernard.
Serm. 44.

15 Behold, thou art fair, my love; behold, thou art fair; thou hast doves' eyes.

"This," notes Origen, "is the second address of the Bridegroom to the Bride. In his former speech He invited her to learn to know herself, telling her that she was fairest among women, but that unless she did know herself, she should certainly undergo sufferings. And as she at once hasted in thought and understanding to self-knowledge, He compares her to His horses or chivalry, whereby He overcame Pharaoh's chariots. So too He compares her cheeks to turtle-doves because of her great modesty and her swiftness in action, and her neck to jewelled collars. Now, He declares her to be fair, and not as before, merely fair among women, but as near Himself,[1] and lifts her to a still higher title of praise, and affirms that she is not *fair* merely when near to Him, but *fair* even if He be absent. For this is denoted hereby, that after saying, *Behold thou art fair, My companion,* (A. V. marg.,) He adds after this absolutely, and without any addition, *Behold, thou* Origen.

---

[1] The LXX. translate רַעְיָתִי, *my neighbour,* ἡ πλησίον μου. The root is רָעָה, *he fed,* and the primary meaning of the word is "one who eats at the same table."

art fair." Man, comment other Greek Fathers, is like a mirror, which appears beautiful or hideous according to the object closest to it, which it reflects, and therefore in this life CHRIST's Bride can be fair only by nearness to Him, that His countenance may shine on and in her, His *companion.* But in the world to come, when the Church is no longer militant, but Triumphant, she will have perfection and beauty, not as now by imitation, but inherently of her own. Others, including some Western expositors, take the words of the double holiness in act and thought, in labour and contemplation, in body and soul, vouchsafed by CHRIST to His Bride. S. Gregory the Great sees here, as in the two breasts of a former verse, the love of GOD and of one's neighbour as the double beauty of the Church; while S. Bernard prefers to find in the words a reference to the grace of penitence, whereby pardon, and thereby renewed beauty, has been won, and that of humility, whereby it is retained. "The repetition," says the Ecstatic Doctor, "is a token of affirmation, of love, of seriousness, and to arouse attention, as though He were saying, Thou, My Bride, My holy and elect Church, for which I gave Myself up to death, thou art fair in soul and in chastity of body. Fair by the gifts of nature, fairer by the blessings of grace. Fair within by the brightness of thy virtues, gifts, and merits: fair without, in thy most lovely ways. Fair in the beauty of the Sacraments, adorned with the manifold divisions of thy ministry, the varied order, station, and ranks of thy prelates, religious, and doctors, decked not only with those supernatural gifts of that grace which maketh us graceful, but of that grace which is given freely." And that, comments another, because the first fairness is of the purgative way, which brings us to know ourselves and love GOD; the other, the illuminative, which makes perfect, because we see GOD as He is. Another explanation, not without some beauty, sees here the twofold Church, Hebrew and Gentile, the first having been long GOD's *companion,* the other but lately come to Him, but both alike fair in His sight.

Thou hast doves' eyes. First, they take it of the enlightening graces of the HOLY GHOST, granted to the Church and to every faithful soul. Then, of the inner vision of the soul herself, fixed on heavenly things. *Doves' eyes,* not only because of the Dove that came to Jordan, but as the type of meekness and purity, and conjugal faithfulness. Thus, for the one part, Venerable Bede observes: "CHRIST's love has *doves'* Beda. *eyes*, because every soul which truly loves Him internally, is not fired, like hawks, with greed for things without, nor plans evil against any living things; for it is said to belong to the meek nature of the dove, to look on everything that may happen with simple, gentle, and lowly heart." And for the other view, let us hear S. Gregory: "Her eyes are well said to be S. Greg. M. *doves' eyes*, because whilst she sighs amidst passing things, and is borne aloft to eternal longings, she guards her senses in simplicity, and abhors fleshly desires. For the dove, when loving, utters sighs instead of songs. Fitly, then, is the holy soul compared to a dove, for whilst the ungodly prate and rejoice in their love of the world, the elect soul pines in her longing for heaven, because she fears to lose that which she loves so long as it is delayed." And Psellus turns it Psellus. prettily of the virgin life, looking to the Creator and not to the creature:

> Ἰδοὺ, φησὶ, καλὴ τυγχάνεις, ὦ παρθένε,
> ἔχεις γὰρ ὄμματα τερπνὰ περιστερᾶς παρθένου
> ὁπόταν σοῦ τοὺς ὀφθαλμοὺς ἀπέστρεψας τῆς πλάνης,
> καὶ πρὸς ἐμὲ τὸν πλαστουργὸν τὸν σὸν ἐνατενίζεις·
> περιστερᾶς δὲ μέμνηται νῦν ὀφθαλμοὺς ὁ λόγος,
> τὸ καθαρὸν τοῦ βλέμματος σημαίνων τῆς παρθένου,
> καὶ γὰρ τοσοῦτον καθαρὸν ἔσχεν ἐκείνη βλέμμα,
> ὥστε κατεῖδε καθαρῶς τὸν κάλλιστον νυμφίον.

> Behold, He saith, O Virgin, thou art fair,
> Thou hast the sweet eyes of a virgin dove,
> When thou hast turned thine eyes from wandering,
> And gazest upon Me, thy fashioner.
> The Word now maketh mention of doves' eyes,
> Noting the pureness of the virgin's mien;
> For she hath just such pureness in her mien
> As she hath purely scanned her fairest Spouse.

Another interpretation sees in the *eyes* of the Church, Aponius. the Prophets and Apostles of earlier times, and the S. Greg. M. great Doctors and preachers of later days. And thus S. Anselm of Laon: The dove lives beside streams, that S.Ans.Laud. when she sees the hawk she may plunge in and escape, she chooses the better grains, she nourishes young ones not her own, she wounds not with her beak; she has no gall, she makes her nest in the holes of the rock, she has a sigh instead of a song. So too, holy preachers Honorius dwell beside the streams of the divine Scripture, where- Augustod.

with their hearts are watered, that by their aid they may escape the devil's assaults; they choose the better grains, that is, the better doctrines, not those of heretics; they nourish the young of others, that is, they train with precept and example men who were formerly aliens from CHRIST and children of the evil one. They do not rend with their beak, that is, they do not, like heretics, pervert and rend sound doctrines; they are free from gall, that is, unreasonable anger. They build in the clefts of the rock, that is, they make their nest in the death-wounds of CHRIST, Who is the firmest of all rocks. They have sighing for singing, because as others delight in song, so do they in tribulation. Besides, the dove flies in flocks, and so the Church strives to draw many with her to the joys of heaven. Finally, they expound this whole verse of the Blessed Virgin, *fair* in her purity, *fair* in her lowliness, *fair* in the beauty of her earthly body, *fairer* in the loveliness of her stainless soul, *fair* in her virginity, *fair* in her childbearing, and, as she was full of grace, and especially dowered by the HOLY GHOST, she has *doves' eyes*.

S. Bernard.
Hugo Vict.
Rupert.
Dion. Carth.

The Hymn,
Regina misericordiæ.

Tu columba nubilis,
Turtur subarrhata,
Tu domus eburnea,
  Civitas murata;
Tu sic dicta viola,
Quod inviolata,
Ager, rosa, lilium,
  Mater, uxor, nata.

Mary, thou art bridal dove,
  Thou art turtle dowered,
Ivory abode of love,
  City strongly towered;

Thou, inviolate by stain,
  Name of violet bearest,
Rose-bud, lily-flower, plain,
  Child, spouse, mother fairest.

16 Behold, thou art fair, my beloved, yea, pleasant; also our bed is green.

It is now the Bride who speaks in answer to the praises which the Bridegroom has just uttered to her. And here at once arises the question so much debated in the Early Church, as to the physical aspect of CHRIST. The Eastern Fathers, almost universally, press the literal sense of such texts as that in Isaiah. "He hath no form or comeliness, and when we shall see Him there is no beauty that we should desire Him." But the Western doctors, with more than equal unanimity, explain these and the like phrases as denoting only the lowliness and suffering of His earthly life, Who yet was "fairer than the children of men." The Bride, remarks Origen, now that she is gifted with the spiritual insight of doves' eyes, recognises the beauty of her Spouse, namely, the Godhead hidden under the veil of Humanity. *Thou*, she says, *art fair*. She does not qualify the words as He did, by adding *among men*, for she knows of none other beauty save His, not even her own, as she ascribes it all to Him. "To us who now believe," exclaims S. Augustine, "the Bridegroom ever seems fair. Fair was GOD the WORD with GOD, fair in the Virgin's womb, where He lost not His Divinity and took on Him Manhood. Fair was the WORD born an Infant, for when He was an Infant, when He sucked, and was carried in arms, the Heavens spake, and the Angels uttered praise. A star guided the wise men, and the Food of the meek was worshipped in the manger. Fair was He then in heaven, fair on earth, fair in the womb, fair in His parents' arms, fair in His miracles, fair in His scourges, fair inviting us to life, fair recking not of death, fair laying down His life, fair taking it again, fair upon the Tree, fair in the tomb, fair in heaven, fair unto the thought."

Isa. liii. 2.

Ps. xlv. 3.
Origen.
Theodoret.
Tres Patr.

S. Greg.
Nyss.
Angelomus.

S. August.
in Ps. xlv.

He is not *fair* only, but *pleasant*, a yet stronger word, denoting, as they say, far more than mere beauty of feature, that winning grace in expression, voice, gesture, and act, which attracts affection even as harmonious regularity of countenance compels admiration. And they delight in finding twin sources of beauty in the Redeemer in the most various ways. First, and most obviously, we may take it of the two Natures in His one Person, the first being *fair* by reason of its Divine essence, the second *pleasant* for its tender pardoning grace. "How fair art Thou unto Thine Angels, O LORD JESU," cries a Saint, "in the form of GOD, in Thine eternal day, in the splendour of the Saints, Thou splendour and image of the FATHER's substance, begotten before the morning star, Thou truly everlasting and undimmed radiance of unending life! How pleasant art Thou to me, my LORD, in the very

Ghislerius.

S. Greg. M.
Beda.

S. Bernard.
Serm. 45.

seat of this pleasantness of Thine! For where Thou didst empty Thyself, where Thou didst strip Thine unwaning light of its natural rays, there Thy loving-kindness shone forth the more, there Thy charity blazed out more brightly, there Thy grace shed its rays further. How bright to me is Thine arising, O Star out of Jacob; how gleaming is Thy coming up, O Flower of Jesse's Root; how joyous is Thy light, visiting me in darkness, O Dayspring from on high! How fascinating and wondrous is Thine heavenly might, in Thy conception by the HOLY GHOST, in Thy Virgin-birth, in Thy stainless life, in Thy streams of doctrine, in the flashings of Thy miracles, in the revelations of Thy Sacraments! How brilliantly, O Sun of righteousness, dost Thou arise from the heart of the earth after Thy setting, how beautiful in Thine apparel! At last, O King of Glory, Thou ascendest to the highest heavens. Wherefore then should not all my bones say, 'LORD, who is like unto Thee?'"

Ps. xxxv. 10.

He was *fair*, observes an Eastern Father, in the Prophets, but *pleasant* in the Apostles; *fair* in keeping those good things which He gave under the Law, *pleasant* in the abundant promises of better things in the Gospel. *Fair* in His pure Body, *pleasant* in His stainless human soul.

Philo Carp.

Aponius.

Also our bed is green. This, the true sense of the Hebrew, is not found either in LXX. or Vulgate. The former has two readings, each adopted by certain expositors. *Our bed is shady,* and *Thou art a shadow to our bed.* The Vulgate has, *Our bed is flowery.* Origen, taking the first reading, explains that the Bride says *our* bed, because her members are CHRIST's members, and adds that it is *shady* because of His promise, "The sun shall not burn thee by day, neither the moon by night," and shady too because of the thick growth of good works from souls watered by His grace, and not parched up with spiritual dryness, under which shade we may avoid the hot breath of sin. Theodoret, who takes the same reading, expounds the bed to be the divine Scriptures, shady because guarded by the grace of the HOLY SPIRIT, and sheltered from the heat of wickedness. The other LXX. reading, which is the received one, is followed by several Eastern Fathers, but they do not take it, as might be expected, in the sense of those words, "He shall defend thee under His wings, and thou shalt

Origen.

Ps. cxxi. 6.

S. Ambros.

S. Greg. Nyss.
Tres Patr.
Ps. xci. 4.

be safe under His feathers," but of the Human Nature of CHRIST, mercifully shading from our eyes the dazzling glory of His Godhead, on which man cannot look and live. The Latin commentators, for the most part, expound the *bed* of the tranquillity of the Church, *flowery* with the many virtues of the Saints. Beda, reproducing in a Christian form the explanation of the Targum, adds that the Church is flowery not only with good works, but with the abundant offspring of faithful, produced to GOD from water and the SPIRIT, and blooming with the flower of faith. And it is to be noted, continues he, that throughout this book the Bride always expresses a desire to be with her Spouse in the house, on the bed, or any other inner place, whereas the Bridegroom is always summoning His love to outer tasks, to the labours of the vineyards or of the gardens. And that because Holy Church, if it might be, would ever gladly converse with her LORD in the quiet of earthly peace, and bring forth and train up for Him a heavenly progeny. But He ordains her to be tried by constant sufferings in the present life, that she may arrive, all the purer, at everlasting blessings, and lest, if all temporal things should be too prosperous, she might take pleasure in her exile, and sigh less after the Heavenly Country. Another sees in the flowery bed that hallowed womb where the Incarnate LORD rested for nine months, and the same idea, substituting the overshadowing trees (denoting darkness and mystery) for the blossoming flowers of beauty and lowliness, is seen in the way in which the Greek Fathers explain the LXX. reading of Habakkuk ii. 3: "GOD shall come from Teman, and the Holy from the thick and shady mountain of Paran." Thus in the Eastern Office for Christmas Day: {S. Greg. M.} {Beda.} {Rupert.}

> Rod of the Root of Jesse,
> Thou, Flower of Mary born,
> From that thick shady mountain
> Cam'st glorious forth this morn:
> Of her, the Ever-Virgin,
> Incarnate wast Thou made,
> The immaterial Essence,
> The GOD by all obeyed!

{S. Cosmas.}

"I think," observes S. Bernard, "that the Church's *bed*, whereon one may rest, means cloisters and convents, where one lives free from the cares of the world {S. Bernard. Serm. 46.}

and the anxieties of life. And it is declared to be flowery, when the conversation and life of the brethren are beautified with the examples and precepts of the Fathers, as though with fragrant flowers." And note, that this bed is flowery, rather than made of cedars and firs, for another reason, that as cut flowers fade quickly, and need to be renewed daily, so it is needful for Religious constantly to renew the vows and resolutions of their profession, so as to offer them fresh and sweet to GOD. Two other writers see here, by a somewhat forced interpretation, the tomb in which CHRIST lay down, called *flowery* by reason of the fragrant myrrh and spices used at His burial. Far more beautiful is the view of Nicolaus de Argentina, who dwells on the Vulgate diminutive *lectulus*, "little bed," in the text here, and bids us remember that hard and narrow bed of the Cross, which was the bridal couch of CHRIST and His Church. And precisely in this sense runs the hymn:

Vieyra. Serm. do S. Francisco Xavier.

Aponius. Angelomus.

Hugo Card.

Nic. Argent.

The Hymn, Huc ad jugum Calvariæ.

> The fox hath where to lay his head,
> Her nest receives the sparrow:
> Thy Monarch, for His latest bed,
> One plank hath, hard and narrow.

Isa. xxviii. 20.

Of it the Prophet spake, saying, "The bed is shorter than that a man can stretch himself on it." It was once dry and leafless, but now, because of the Resurrection, it is the delight of the Western Church to represent it as fleury or pommée, breaking out into blossom and fruit. And so in the great Passiontide hymn:

Venantius Fortunatus. The Hymn, Pange lingua.

> Faithful Cross, above all other
> One and only noble Tree,
> None in foliage, none in blossom,
> None in fruit thy peer may be.

And lastly, as this is not our rest, we may take the green or flowery bed of those pastures of heaven, where the Sabbath remaineth for the people of GOD when they have ended their weary pilgrimage and warfare.

Heb. iv. 9.

Francis Baker.

> Thy vineyards and thine orchards are
> Most beautiful and fair,
> Full furnished with trees and fruits
> Exceeding rich and rare.

> Thy gardens and thy gallant walks
> Continually are green;
> There grow such sweet and pleasant flowers
> As nowhere else are seen.
>
> Jerusalem! my happy home!
> Would GOD I were in thee,
> Would GOD my woes were at an end,
> Thy joys that I might see!

17 The beams of our house are cedar, and our rafters of fir.

The first inquiry here is, Who is the speaker? All save Origen, who varies from himself on this head, agree that the Bride still speaks. Next, What is the *house* (LXX. and Vulg. *houses*) thus described? The more usual interpretation is that the local Churches on earth are the joint dwelling-place of CHRIST and of the elect soul. Theodoret, however, explains it of Holy Scripture, incorrupt as *cedar*, perfumed as *cypress* (LXX. and Vulg.,) and several Fathers say that the soul itself is the house intended. Taking the common exposition, they tell us that the *beams*, the most important part of the Church's building, are her Prelates and great preachers, *cedar* because of their incorruptness, and that the *rafters* or *fretted ceilings* (LXX. φατνώματα, Vulg. *laquearia*) denote the clergy in general, or else the faithful laity, resting, as Beda reminds us, upon the beams, and lifted high from earthly things by their precept and example. Another interpretation sees in the *beams* the great dogmas on which the Church's structure rests, and in the *panels* the practical virtues with which the Saints who rest on these doctrines adorn their dwelling. Not remote from either of these is the view of Honorius, who takes the *houses* to be the cloisters, whose *beams* are the Abbats and other superiors, and whose *panels* are the Religious; of *cypress*, because that tree does not revive when cut down, and was therefore borne anciently before the bier of the dead, and thus typifies the death to the world of those who seek to be hidden in the tabernacle of GOD. Yet again, taking the *house* to be the soul wherein CHRIST dwells, its *beams*, they tell us, are the inner virtues, its main strength and support; the *panels*, less important, but more ornamental, the outward beauty of a devout life. It is to be noted, fur-

[margin: Theodoret. S. Greg. Nyss. S. Just. Org. S. Bernard. Beda. Tres Patr. Hon. Aug. S. Greg. Nyss. S. Bernard.]

ther, that both the Temple and palace of Solomon were built of cedar and fir or cypress, and that a reference to that fact is intended here. But, whereas they were framed with beams and planks cut from the wood, and therefore dead, here, on the other hand, the Hebrew implies that whole trees, living evergreens, *cedars* and *firs*, formed the house and shadowed the bed of the Bridegroom, which was therefore more beautiful and enduring than the former temple and palace. And so the Targum: "Solomon the Prophet said, How fair is this house of the sanctuary of the LORD, which is builded by my hands, of cedar wood! But fairer shall be the house of the sanctuary which shall be builded in the days of Messiah the King, the beams whereof shall be of the cedars of the garden of Eden." And what was that cedar shrine and palace, incorrupt, repelling all evil, save the most pure womb of His immaculate Mother? *Cedar*, in her utter purity, *cypress* in her sorrows by the Cross of her Son; wherefore it is written, "I was exalted like a cedar in Libanus, and as a cypress tree upon the mountains of Hermon."

Tu fons, hortus, platanus,
 Cedrus exaltata,
Tu palma, tu olea,
 Cypressus plantata.

1 Kings vi. 15; vii. 2, 7.

Hengstenberg.

Targum.

Dion. Carth. Parez.

Ecclus. xxiv. 13.

The Hymn, *Regina clementiæ*.

CHAPTER II.

1 I am the rose of Sharon, and the lily of the valleys.

The first clause here is rendered in the Syriac, LXX., and Vulgate, *flower of the plain*, and modern critics, for the most part, hold that the narcissus, not the rose, is the plant intended. The commentators differ as to the speaker. The Targum, followed by some Greek Fathers, assigns the verse to the Bride, but the majority of the Westerns, with some great Eastern names too, hold that it, as well as the succeeding one, belongs to the Bridegroom, claiming to be Himself the chief

Targum. S. Greg. Nyss. Theodoret. Philo Carp.

glory of that flowery bed of which the Bride had delightedly spoken just before. Following this interpretation first, let us hear Origen: " The *plain* is level ground, cultivated, and tilled by husbandmen. The *valleys* denote rocky and untilled places. We may thus understand the *plain* of that people which was cultivated by the Law and the Prophets, and the *valleys* of the rocky and untilled dwelling of the Gentiles. The Bridegroom was therefore the *Flower* among the Jewish people, but because the Law brought no man to perfection, therefore the WORD of GOD could not there pass beyond the stage of *flower*, and arrive at the perfection of fruit. But He was made a *Lily* in the *valleys* of the Gentiles. What kind of Lily? Such, no doubt, as He describes in the Gospels, which the Heavenly FATHER clothes. The Bridegroom becomes then a Lily in this valley, because His Heavenly FATHER clothed Him with such a garment of flesh as Solomon in all his glory could not have. For Solomon had not a body pure from all desire and from fleshly enjoyments, and thus liable to no sin. But He seems to set forth why He, Who was the Flower of the field, willed to be the Lily of the valleys. Though He had long been the flower of the field, yet He never says that any flower imitating or resembling Him had sprung from that field. But when He became the Lily of the valleys, immediately His beloved became a lily too, in imitation of Him; so that the result of His labour is, that as He is made a lily, so His neighbour, that is, every soul which draws near Him and follows His example, becomes a lily also. What He then says, 'As the lily among thorns, so is My love among the daughters,' we may take as spoken of the Gentile Church, either because she arose from the midst of unbelievers, as out of thorns, or because set in the midst of thorns by reason of noisy heretics around her, attacking her with their teeth." And the same great Father in another place expounds the words of CHRIST's Incarnation. For my sake, he says, who was in the valley, the Bridegroom comes into that valley, and becomes a Lily there. Instead of being the Tree of Life, planted in the Paradise of GOD, He became the Flower of all the plain, that is, of the whole world, of the entire earth. For what could so truly be the flower of all the world as the Name of CHRIST? His Name is ointment poured out. Aponius sets be-

[marginalia: Origen. Cassiod. Aponius. Beda. S. Mat. vi. 28. Hom. 2.]

fore us this same idea from another point of view. CHRIST was, he comments, the *flower of the field* before His Incarnation, because in His glory He was the worship of the heavenly spirits in all the plain of the heavens, but after His Incarnation He became the *Lily of the valleys,* when He came down into the vale of tears, and brought with Him three things, the doing-away of sin, the wiping out of falsehood, and the cooling of desire, just as the lily exhibits three qualities, whiteness, fragrance, and medicine for certain complaints after it has been parched in the fire. S. Cyril of Alexandria sees in the perfume of the flower, invisible in the visible blossom, the Godhead united with the Manhood of CHRIST, and inseparable from It. Theodoret, agreeing with many others that the words *flower of the plain* denote CHRIST's coming to earth, explains the *lily of the valleys* of His further humiliation, when He went down into the lower parts of the earth, and preached in Hades the Resurrection. Yet again, they take the plain to be His most holy Mother, from whom He sprang by no human will, as the flower grows in spots no man has tilled. And thus S. Ambrose: "CHRIST was the Flower of Mary, and sprang from the virgin womb to shed the sweet perfume of faith throughout the world. A flower, though cut down, retains its fragrance, and if pounded, collects it, nor does it lose it by being torn up. So too the LORD JESUS withered not when ground upon the Cross, nor did He disappear when so torn away from us, but when wounded with that piercing of the spear, He, Who cannot die, bloomed yet more beauteously with the Precious Blood He shed, breathing forth the gift of eternal life to them which were dead."

"The human Nature of CHRIST," says one of the greatest of the Schoolmen, "is called a *plain,* for as a variety of flowers spring up in a plain, so are there many virtues in the human nature of CHRIST. Herein was the violet of lowliness, the rose of patience, the lily of purity. CHRIST was the flower of this plain; that is, its glory because of His Godhead, since He had by reason of that Godhead the fulness of gifts in His human nature. Fitly is that human nature of CHRIST denoted by a plain, because of its width and smoothness, for in Him was no roughness of sin. Whence also He is said to be *Lily of the valleys.* For as there was perfect humility in Mary and in CHRIST's human nature, therefore the person of the Virgin and the Manhood of the WORD are called *valleys*." In the lily, beautifully notes another, there are five things observed. It is white, having a projecting anther of golden hue, it is fragrant, and expanding, and ever curving downwards. So was CHRIST white in His Manhood, golden in His Godhead, fragrant in His preaching, open in receiving penitents, bowed down in His condescension to sinners, and in lifting them up. Another writer dwells somewhat variously on some of these same qualities. "CHRIST was a lily," says he, "because of the glory of His Resurrection, externally white because of the glory of His Body, golden within by reason of the resplendence of His soul. And before His Passion He was as it were a closed lily, but when crowned with glory and honour because of that Passion, He was thereafter an open lily, because He disclosed in His assumed humanity the power of that divine radiance which He had with the FATHER before the world was." So far we have considered how CHRIST is Flower and Lily in Himself, and may next turn to ponder how He is these to us. And first, Origen tells us that the words mark different stages of spiritual progress, that He is the Flower of souls which are like a plain by reason of their simplicity, gentleness, or equity, in that He is in them the beginning of good works, the promise of fruit, while to those who search into deeper and more hidden things, as though in the valleys, He becomes a Lily, either in the brightness of purity or the sheen of wisdom, that they too may be lilies, breaking forth from the midst of thorns, that is, fleeing from the thoughts and cares of the world. S. Gregory teaches that CHRIST is the Flower of the plain, in that He gives the soul the beauty of heavenly desire; the Lily of the valleys, because of the purity He infuses into the lowly. And they delight to tell us how He is the crown and glory and loveliness of the Virgin Life. CHRIST, observes S. Jerome, (writing of one who had given herself to her LORD,) as the author and Prince of virginity, confidently speaks, "*I am the flower of the plain and the lily of the valleys.*" The order of Virgins in the Church, comments another, is a plain, that is, an untilled soil whose flower is CHRIST, because He is its delight, its crown, and its reward. He is, notes a third, the Lily of the valleys, not of the fields of the

Hon. Aug.

Eucherius, in Lib. iii. Reg.

Origen.

S. Greg. M.

S. Hieron. Ep. ad Demetr. Cf. S. Ambros. de Virgin. iii.

S. Just. Org. Hon. Aug.

Nic. Arg.

active life, much less the lily among the thorns, but of those who dwell in the lowly and sequestered life of contemplation, whereon the rays of the sun pour the heat of love, unstayed and undisturbed by any words of temptation, while the mountains stand around, and the rivers of grace flow down them into the valleys, so that there is abundance of corn there, and the Lily, finding the water it loves, flourishes abundantly.

<small>Ps. civ. 10.</small>

Following the other interpretation, which ascribes the words to the Bride, they tell us how the Church is the *flower of the plain* so far as she consists of believing Israel, levelled to the smoothness of a field by the Law and the Prophets, watered by the rain of heavenly knowledge, bright with the flowers of holiness. The Gentiles, uneven and rough through unbelief, and depressed by the weight of sin, are the valleys out of which the Lily springs from the depth, so high that she cannot be hid even in the lowest parts of the vale, lifting up her head in the grace and beauty of faith, of purification, and of contemplation of GOD. The Church under the Law, remarks another Greek Father, not dissimilarly, calls herself a flower, when she has listened to the voice of the Prophets, and striven to serve GOD. But when she has heard the voice of CHRIST Himself in the Gospel, telling His disciples to cast away all worldly anxiety, and saying, "Consider the lilies how they grow," then, attaining to the loveliness and fragrance of true devotion, she is bold to say, *I am the lily.* They take it too, of any holy soul growing in the plain of this world, exposed to wind and storm, but lifting itself up to heaven and diffusing perfume around. And the words *plain* and *valleys* denote twofold humility; the first, that whereby any one humbles himself to his superiors, and does not try to rise above his equals: and the second, that more perfect lowliness whereby he humbles himself to his equals, and strives to descend below his inferiors. Not any flower, but especially a *lily*, because it is white externally and with a golden spike within. Such is the soul, which is compassed with the glory of righteousness, and which carries within its inmost shrine the spiritual gift of wisdom and knowledge. How much more then is it true of her who was herself that pure calyx within which the golden glory of the Eternal Wisdom tabernacled! Well may the Ecstatic Doctor say, "The most Blessed Virgin is the most blooming,

<small>Tres Patr.</small>

<small>Philo Carp.</small>

<small>S. Mat. vi. 28.</small>

<small>S. Greg. Nyss.</small>

<small>Card. Hailgrin.</small>

<small>Dion. Carth.</small>

fairest, and most fragrant flower of the field, that is, of this world, wherein we are placed as in the arena of contest, for our life on earth is a warfare. She is also the flower of that other field, the garden of delights, the heavenly Paradise. And again, she is the flower of the field, that is, of the Church Militant in its pilgrimage here on earth, whose mother, flower, queen, and advocate she is, obtaining by her prayers and merits the ornaments and perfume of merits for the Church. Then, she is the flower of every devout soul which loves her, into whose thought she never enters without fruit, and without shedding her sweetness around. She is the Lily of the valleys, that most sweet and peerless Virgin Mother of GOD, the blooming offspring of her lowly parents, from whom she sprang as a most fair Lily, nor was Solomon in all his glory arrayed as that fair Lily was." And lastly, taking our own version, we may see in the rose and lily the double grace of martyrdom and chastity which forms the choicest coronal of heaven. Thus S. Bernard observes, "The flower is virginity, the flower is mar- Serm. 47. tyrdom, the flower is good deeds. In the garden, virginity; in the field, martyrdom; in the chamber, good works. He is the flower of the garden, the Virgin sprung from a virgin stem. He too is the flower of the field, the Martyr, the Crown of Martyrs, the force of martyrdom." Wherefore the Paris Breviary fitly sings in the Common of Virgin Martyrs:

> Roses and lilies are the Bridegroom's portion, Sant. Vict.
The Hymn,
Quid sacram,
Virgo.
> Thou, to thy Bridegroom evermore found faithful,
> Gavest Him roses as a Martyr, gavest
> Lilies, a Virgin.

2 *As the lily among thorns, so is my love among the daughters.*

Noting the contrast, so strongly marked in the first Theodoret.
S. Just. Org. clause, they observe that as the lily surpasses thorns, so does the Church of GOD excel the Synagogue, the schools of philosophy, and the parties of the State. Again, the Church was a lily among thorns in the time of her greatest purity and beauty, when she was the victim of repeated persecutions. Whereupon Hono- Honor.
August.
S. Ambros. rius: "As I, saith the Bridegroom, am the Lily of the valleys, the ornament of the lowly, so thou, My love, shalt be the lily among thorns, the glory of the Gentiles; and as I am the Lily among thorns, that is, the Jews who pierce and wound Me, so thou, O Church, My love, shalt be among the Gentile daughters of Babylon, which is confusion, who shall pierce thee with many a thorn, and rend thee with many a suffering." The words are true also of that inner Church of the elect, compassed by the outer Church of the called, wherein are many reprobates who show no grace or beauty in their lives, but are like thorns, flowering quickly in temporal prosperity, withering swiftly in goodness, wounding the devout with their evil habits, cut down and given to feed the fire. Such as these are *daughters*, indeed, but not of GOD, rather of the evil one, carnal and worldly souls, given up to the wounding and torturing pleasures of the senses. And observe further, that a lily growing amongst thorns ensures the wounding of him who would gather the flower for his very own. On which a devout writer comments thus: "As the Bride's love for her Spouse is signified here, so also is His love for her. For he that would gather a lily amongst thorns, necessarily suffers their pricks; which is evidently true of the Bridegroom Himself, for He, gathering that lily from the midst of the reprobate, suffered the prickings of the thorns, whilst He underwent the rendings of the persecutors as He was assembling His elect by His own preaching and that of His disciples. Whence it is written, 'Whoso breaketh a hedge [the synagogue of the people,] a serpent shall bite him.' The LORD acted like a hunting dog, which pursuing wild game, thrusts its head amongst the prickles of thorns, fearing no wounds so that it may take its prey. He drew forth the Church, lurking like a wild beast amongst thorns, that is, amongst the reprobate; but He endured the piercings of the thorns even to bloodshedding, in token of which He wore a thorny crown upon the Cross." The soul which clings to CHRIST amidst the troubles, cares, and persecutions of an ungodly world, is also fitly called a lily among thorns. But all these cannot really hurt the lily, rather do they set off her beauty. "The thorn," expounds S. Bernard, "is sin, the thorn is punishment, the thorn is a false brother, the thorn is evil hard at hand. 'As the lily among thorns, so is My love among the daughters.' O shining lily, O frail and delicate flower, the unbelieving and destroyers are with thee, see then that thou walk cautiously amongst the thorns. The world is full of thorns. They are in the earth, in the air, in thy flesh. To be amongst them, and not to be hurt by them, comes of the Divine power, not of thine own strength. 'But be of good cheer,' saith He, 'I have overcome the world.' Therefore, although thou seest the prickles of tribulations, like those of thorns, aiming at thee on every side, let not thine heart be troubled, neither let it be afraid, 'knowing that tribulation worketh patience; and patience, experience; and experience, hope; and hope maketh not ashamed.' Consider the lilies of the field, how they flourish and bloom among the thorns. If GOD so guards the grass which to-day is, and to-morrow is cast into the oven, how much more His love and dearest Bride?" And another holy writer treats at much length of the various thorns which must be overcome by patient continuance in well-doing. The truly patient soul is likest to the beauty of CHRIST, to the measure of a perfect man, in that it bears all cheerfully, and loves those who put it to pain; first, by words of slander and calumny, then by actual wrong-doing. How is this patience to be attained? Hearken, O lily among thorns. "My soul hath long dwelt among them that are enemies unto peace. I labour for peace." And again: "They that went about to do me evil, talked of wickedness, and imagined deceit all the day long. As for me, I was like a deaf man and heard not, and as one that is dumb, who doth not open his mouth." And this is effected by loving contemplation of our Maker, because the soul that looks on GOD is deaf and blind to meaner things, and is filled with such delights in thinking on Him that pain becomes of no moment, or even a source of pleasure, as the Cross was to S. Andrew, the fire to S. Laurence, the stones to S. Stephen, the dungeon and rack to S. Agatha. And this patience is threefold, in heart, word, and deed, indisposing men to vengeance, leading them on to entire forgiveness of their enemies, and thence to hearty interest in and affection for them. Those who begin by checking their own impulse to revenge, at first from the lower motive of fear of results, and then for the sake of salvation, and at last from true love of GOD, attain even on earth the "peace to men of good will," promised by the Angels at the Nativity, and, tried by many sorrows and tribulations, reach at last the per-

S. John xvi. 33.

Rom. v. 3.

Henr. Harph.

Ps. cxx. 5, 6.

Ps. xxxviii. 12, 13.

S. Luke ii. 14.

fect tranquillity of the children of GOD, in their own beloved Home. *Among the daughters.* That is, among all elect souls, loving GOD the FATHER with filial tenderness, but yet *thorny,* as beset with the pricks of original and actual sin, and unable to fulfil His commandments perfectly. And therefore there is only one of whom it is truly written, "Many daughters have done virtuously, but thou excellest them all," and yet again, "Of all the flowers Thou hast chosen one lily."

<small>Irimbert.</small>

<small>Prov. xxxi. 29.
2 Esd. v. 24.</small>

<small>Keble, Christian Year.</small>

> Ave Maria! blessèd Maid,
> Lily of Eden's fragrant shade,
>   Who can express the love
> That nurtured thee, so pure and sweet,
> Making thy heart a shelter meet
>   For JESUS' holy dove!

<small>Dion. Carth.</small>

Whereupon the Carthusian: Although there were many holy virgins, yet in respect of the Most Blessed Virgin they seem as though but thorns, in that they had some sinfulness, and though pure in themselves, yet the embers of evil were not utterly quenched in them. But the Virgin Mother of GOD was perfectly freed from all sin, the embers of evil were completely quenched in her, and yet she was filled with the intensest love. Another reminds us that she was indeed among thorns, in that she, like her Son, was a mark for slanderous tongues, she, with her Son, suffered at the Cross. "As a rose groweth among thorns," says the great Swedish Saint, "so grew the Blessed Virgin in this world among troubles; and as the rose increases, so do the thorns likewise; thus as Mary, the choicest of roses, advanced in age, so much the more deeply was she wounded by the thorns of tribulation." Another Saint refers the thorns to Our Lady's kinship to the unbelieving Hebrews. "Sprung from the thorny race of Jews, she shone bodily with the pureness of virgin modesty, and she glowed in soul with the warmth of double charity, she was ever fragrant in good works, and with the unvarying impulse of her heart she soared up towards heavenly things." A Christian poet, six hundred years before the great Bishop of Ostia, had expressed nearly the same thoughts in verse:

<small>Rupert.</small>

<small>S. Birgitt. Serm. Angel. 16.</small>

<small>S. Pet. Dam. Serm. 3, de Nat. B.V.M.</small>

<small>Sedulius.</small>

> Et velut in spinis mollis rosa surgit acutis,
> Nil quod lædit habens, matremque obscurat honore;
> Sic Evæ de stirpe sacrâ veniente Mariâ,

Virginis antiquæ facinus nova Virgo piavit,
Sicut spina rosam, genuit Judæa Mariam.

As from the sharp thorns springs the gentle rose,
Stingless, and hides its mother with its bloom ;
So blessèd Mary, come of Eva's stem,
A new Maid, purged that elder Maiden's sin.
Thorns bear the rose, Judea Mary bore.

3 As the apple-tree among the trees of the wood, so is my beloved among the sons. I sat down under his shadow with great delight, and his fruit was sweet to my taste.

When CHRIST took the nature of man, He came down into the wood of this life, and became one of its trees, but a fruitful one, nay, able to make fruitful trees of men however evil and wild. And human life is called a *wood*,[1] because in it are found many things which beset the soul, lurking as wild beasts do in a forest, sluggish when the sun is hot, but active in the darkness. Because the "singular beast" which feeds in the wood had sorely hurt the beautiful vine of human nature, therefore the *apple-tree* was planted in the wood ; which, in that it is a tree, is of like nature with the wood of humanity ; for CHRIST was tempted in our likeness, though without sin. But in that it bears such fruit as to gratify the senses, it is more unlike the rest of the wood than the lily is unlike the thorns. For the pleasantness of the apple is common to three senses, it is beautiful to the sight, fragrant to the smell, and sweet to the taste. So CHRIST is more than the Bride, for He is the joy of our eyes, and the ointment to our smell, and life to us who eat of Him ; but human nature, even if perfected in virtue, is but a flower, not feeding the husbandman, but merely decking itself. For He needs not our good things, whereas we do need His. Therefore the purified soul beholds her Bridegroom made the apple-tree in the wood, that

S. Greg. Nyssen.

Ps. lxxx. 13, Vulgate.

---

[1] It is almost a commonplace to note that this figure is used by Dante in the very opening of the Divine Comedy.

Nel mezzo del cammin di nostra vita,

Mi ritrovai pel una selva oscura,

Chi la diritta via era smarrita.

Ahi quanto a dir qual era è cosa dura

Questa selva selvaggia ed aspra e forte,

Che nel pensier rinnova la paura.

graffing into Himself all the wild boughs of that wood, He may cause them to bring forth fruit like His own. They assign other reasons too why CHRIST is called an *apple-tree*,[1] and several of them dwell on His feeding us with the Gospel, while the Holy Eucharist is the idea which suggests itself to others, as the juiciness of the apple makes it both food and drink, and so CHRIST gives us His Body and Blood in the Sacrament of the Altar. A Greek and a Latin commentator, in distant centuries, following up this view, understand here, to make the simile more perfect, a *pomegranate-tree*, (therein agreeing with the Arabic version,) because the juice of that fruit is ruddy and watery, typifying that which flowed from CHRIST's side upon the Cross. They have pushed the metaphor further, and remarked how the grains from which the fruit is named lie enclosed in the ruddy flesh within the rind, just as the members of CHRIST, in the One Church, are united in His Body, crimson with His life-blood:

margin: Theodoret. S. Ambros. S. Bernard. Philo Carp. Origen. S. Ans. Laud.

margin: Aponius. Psellus.

margin: Ovid. Ep. ex Pont. 15.

    Quæ numero tot sunt, quot in horto fertilis arvi
        Punica sub lento cortice grana rubent.

    Many, as in a fertile orchard's soil
        Beneath their slight rind blush the Punic seeds.

Among the sons. They vary much in expounding these words. Some will have it that the Angels, or Angels and men together are meant, but S. Bernard protests against this view, on the ground that CHRIST is spoken of as He appeared when made lower than the Angels, and thus, though fairer and more fruitful than the *trees of the wood*, than all mankind, not so glorious to the eye as many trees of the orchard or park. The praise given Him here, observes the Saint, is poor and small, as coming from one who is small. It is not the mighty LORD, highly to be praised, that is commended, but the LORD, small, yet highly to be loved, the little Child Who was born for us. Limiting, then, the word *sons* in this wise, some will have it that the Apostles and Prophets, and the elect generally, GOD's special children by adoption, are here intended, those trees of Eden around the Tree of Life. Others, taking it in a bad sense, refer it to evil men generally,

margin: Origen.

margin: S. Bernard. Serm. 48.

margin: Cassiodor. S. Greg. M. Beda.

margin: Theodoret. Tres Patr.

---

[1] It may be observed that modern critics, generally speaking, say that the *citron*, not the *apple*, is the tree denoted by תַּפּוּחַ, but the mystical sense is not affected thereby.

as having the wildness and brute terrors of the forest in them, or to the Jews in particular; or, with further restrictions of meaning, many of them see a reference to the crucified Redeemer, hanging on the tree between the two thieves, suffering Himself, as S. Thomas observes, to be fastened to a tree as its fruit, in order to atone for the first sin of man, in plucking the fruit from the tree of knowledge of good and evil. *I sat down under His shadow with great delight.* The Hebrew of the first clause, closely followed by the LXX. is, *I delighted, and sat down under His shadow.* The Vulgate, a little differently, *I sat down under the shadow of Him Whom I desired.* There are three things, comments Henry Harph, which cause a shadow, light, medium, and object. CHRIST, in His Divinity, is the Light whence is cast the shadow of GOD. The medium, whose form this shadow takes, is His Manhood, by the fulness of His grace, and the abundance of His merits. The object of the light, which becomes the shadow, is our will, lying, of its own glad accord, under the light divine. And as the shadow moves with every motion of the interposed body which causes it, and accompanies it wherever it goes, so the will which has become the shadow of GOD follows within the guiding of His SPIRIT in everything, and externally imitates the Manhood of the LORD JESUS, and His teaching in all the paths of perfection. Again; the *shadow* denotes CHRIST's providential care and guardianship of His Church, and of every soul which puts its trust in Him, according to that saying of the Psalmist, "My soul trusteth in Thee, and under the shadow of Thy wings shall be my refuge." Or you may take it, with S. Gregory, of the HOLY SPIRIT, "The Shadow of CHRIST," says he, "is the protection of the HOLY GHOST. For the HOLY GHOST overshadows the soul which He fills, because He allays the heat of every temptation, and while He gently fans the soul with the breeze of His inspiration He banishes whatever baneful heat it had been enduring." Yet again, S. Bernard tells us that faith, being the evidence of things not seen, is shadowy and dark, as we walk by faith and not by sight, although that very shadow is leading us to the full glory of the heavenly vision. And whereas it is not said *I delight*, and *I sit;* but, *I delighted*, and *I sat;* we may understand the Church speaking of the time when she was yet in the Syna-

Rupert.
Aponius.
S. Bernard.
Psellus.
S. Thomas Aquinas, Comp. Theol. c. 228.

Henr. Harphius.

Origen.
Cassiodor.
S. Ans. Laud.

Ps. lvii. 1.

S. Greg. M.

S. Bernard. Serm. 49.

Origen.
Philo Carp.
S. Ambros.

gogue, abiding under the Law, which is but the shadow of the Gospel, and even then by anticipation rejoicing and trusting in CHRIST alone, looking hopefully for the Man who should "be as an hiding-place from the wind, and a covert from the tempest; as rivers of water in a dry place, as the shadow of a great rock in a weary land." And they remind us how Elijah lay down under the shadow of a juniper-tree, and arising, found a cake baken on the coals, and a cruse of water at his head. So, those who come near to the Cross, find the *shadow* of CHRIST fall on them in the mysterious sacramental veils wherewith His Body and Blood are hidden from our eyes. Another reminds us that the dark sayings and hidden things of Holy Scripture, the chosen meditation of the faithful soul, are the shadow of CHRIST Himself; and the further explanation that every foretaste given us here in contemplation, is but the shadow of the Beatific Vision, has not been forgotten. Again; as the Cross is the Tree which throws the shadow, every sorrow and trouble endured for CHRIST's sake in this world is not merely endured, but *delighted* in by the faithful soul, which desires to be conformed to His Passion.

<blockquote>
Oppressed with noonday's scorching heat,
  To yonder Cross I flee;
Beneath its shelter take my seat,
  No shade like this for me!

Beneath that Cross clear waters burst,
  A fountain sparkling free;
And there I quench my desert thirst,
  No spring like this for me!

A stranger here, I pitch my tent
  Beneath this spreading tree;
Here shall my pilgrim life be spent,
  No home like this for me!

For burthened ones a resting-place
  Beside that Cross I see;
Here cast I off my weariness,
  No rest like this for me.
</blockquote>

And so resting, she advances in holiness and in likeness to Him, because as the day passes from noon towards evening, the shadows become longer, and cover a greater space. Of none is it so truly said,

I sat down under His shadow, implying long and happy rest, as of her concerning whom the Angel spake, "The power of the Highest shall overshadow thee," for her abiding in the peace of GOD was of no brief hour, but for all time. They tell us too how the Saints, striving to imitate the Sun of Righteousness, are His shadows, a delight to those who hearken to their teaching and follow their examples. *And His fruit was sweet to my taste.* There are many such fruits, for the Tree of Life bears twelve, besides those fruits of the Spirit which the Apostle counts up for us. And first, it is the preaching of CHRIST's Passion, and that which comes thence, the remission of our sins. Then, there is the meditation on GOD's love, a true sustenance of the soul, and the contemplation of the Godhead, Manhood, and Life of CHRIST, whereof a Saint tells us: "CHRIST Himself is a fruitful Tree, planted in our hearts by faith, which tree, if our soul love as it deserves, and tend carefully, brings forth sweet and wholesome fruits. When the soul eagerly gathers and eats of these, she esteems all worldly pleasures as inferior to their sweetness." Again; the Holy Eucharist, as noted above, is the *fruit* of that Tree which gives us both food and drink. He Himself, when born for us, the fruit of the overshadowing SPIRIT, was sweet to His Mother as she pressed her lips to Him. Further; as fruit is the ultimate product of the tree, so action is the ultimate product of man's will put into exercise, and when that will is moved by a higher influence than any of earth, then man's good works are the fruit of the SPIRIT, pleasant to the palate, and not biting, and yet palling, like earthly delights. Words are but leaves; devout thoughts and inward devotion are the flower; but only the perfect Christian life is the fruit. And they tell us, too, that the deeper insight into the things of GOD which is attained by contemplative Saints in mystic vision is, in an especial manner, the fruit of that same Tree which gives us the other fruits of refreshment and consolation in our hungering and thirsting after righteousness here below, and who are bidden to "taste and see how gracious the LORD is," and find Him indeed *sweet* to their *taste* or *palate*, that spiritual understanding without which the choicest dainties are insipid.

Rupert.

S. Luke i. 35.

Tres Patr.

Rev. xxii. 2.
Gal. v. 22.
S. Ambros. in Ps. cxix.
Origen.

S. Greg. M.

Aponius.
S. Bernard.
Rupert.
Dion. Carth.

Henr. Harph.

Dion. Carth.
Thom. Vercell.

Ps. xxxiv. 8.

Tres Patr.

4 He brought me to the banqueting-house, and his banner over me was love.

The banqueting-house. More exactly, with LXX. and margin of A. V., *the house of wine.* The Vulgate is but little different, *the chamber of wine.* They take Theodoret. Cassiodor. Hugo Victorin. S. Greg. M. Targum. the words, firstly, of admission into the Catholic Church, wherein alone is the wine of the Spirit to be found. Next; it is explained of Holy Scripture, a view not very remote from that of the Targum, which calls Mount Sinai the house where the wine of the Law was stored up for Israel. That, after all, remarks Cardinal Hugo, was only the chamber of water, the mere outward and typical sense. Not till Christ came for His bridal with the Church, was the water turned into wine, and the inner mystical meaning revealed. But as the revelation was not completely given till the advent of the Paraclete, some explain the *house of wine* to be that upper chamber in Jerusalem where the disciples were gathered together on the Day of Pentecost. "Do you not think," asks S. Bernard, "that the *chamber of wine* is that dwelling where the disciples were assembled, when 'suddenly there came a sound from heaven, as of a rushing mighty wind, and it filled all the house where they were sitting,' and fulfilled the prophecy of Joel? Might not each of them, going forth inebriated with the plenteousness of that house, and given to drink of such pleasure as out of a river, truly say, 'The King hath brought me into the chamber of wine?'" This was that new wine put into new bottles, of which the Lord spake, so that the Jews were in one sense right when they said, "These men are full of new wine."

Hugo Card.

S. Just. Org.

S. Bernard. Serm. 49.
Acts ii. 2.

Beda.
S. Bernard.
Acts ii. 13.

Adam. Vict.
The Sequence, Lux jucunda for Pentecost.

> Utres novi, non vetusti,
> Sunt capaces novi musti;
>   Vasa parat vidua;
> Dat liquorem Helisæus,
> Nobis sacrum rorem Deus,
>   Si corda sint congrua.

> Bottles new, no longer olden,
> Hold that wine, so new and golden;
>   Lo, the widow's jars are here:
> Oil Elisha is renewing,
> God gives us His own bedewing,
>   If our hearts prepared appear.

Again; remembering that it is written, "Wisdom hath

builded her house, she hath hewn out her seven pillars: she hath killed her beasts; she hath mingled her wine; she hath also furnished her table," some explain the *house of wine* to be the Altar of GOD, where the Cup of Salvation, the Wine which truly maketh glad the heart of man, is given by the Bridegroom to His love. And with this sense the *banqueting-house* of the A. V. best accords. Also they see here a reference to the progress of the soul in prayer and contemplation, when GOD bestows the wine of comfort, joy, love, and fervour. First, as the Greek Fathers tell us, by meditation on the mystery of the Incarnation, because CHRIST'S Human Body is the house wherein dwells GOD the WORD, the true Wine of the soul. Then, as a great Latin Doctor adds, "What can we better understand by the *chamber of wine* than the hidden contemplation of eternity? In this eternity the holy Angels are inebriated with the wine of wisdom, when, beholding GOD face to face, they are filled with every spiritual delight. Into this the holy soul enters, if it leave all temporal things behind, and be brought in by the Bridegroom, and there tastes whatsoever is bestowed upon it of those delights of the Angels. And if as yet, because still detained in a corruptible body, she cannot fill herself completely; nevertheless, even from that very little which she can hurriedly take, she understands how much she ought to love that which she does love." Nay, more, add others, for the draughts she there imbibes make her utterly forget everything else, and take from her all wish, yea, all power, of returning to her former life. And lastly; the *house of wine* is interpreted of the heavenly mansion where the marriage-feast of the Lamb is made ready. And the Church says of this, not, *He will bring me in*, but, *He brought me in*. And that for two reasons, first, because His promise is so sure, that a thing pledged by Him is as certain as though it were already past; and again, He has bestowed so many foretastes of everlasting blessedness even here on earth that we may truly say, *He brought me into the banqueting-house*, where the Saints assemble from the East and the West, and sit down with Abraham, Isaac, and Jacob, in the kingdom of GOD.

And His banner over me was love. Little doubt what that banner is, the sign of that love greater than which no man hath, that a man lay down his life for his friends.

[margin notes: Prov. ix. 1, 2. S. Greg. Nyss. Rupert. Psellus. S. Pasch. Radb. Tres Patr. S. Greg. M. Honorius. Hugo Card. Dion. Carth. Origen.]

> Salve Crux, arbor
> Vitæ prœclara,
> CHRISTI vexillum,
> Thronus et ara.

> Hail, O Cross, Life's Tree
> Glorious alone,
> CHRIST JESUS' banner,
> Altar, and throne.

But it will not be the token of warfare in the House of Wine on high, as it is in the Church Militant on earth. There it will be, as the same hymn continues, the emblem of past victory, the pledge of everlasting peace, and the glory of the triumphant Saints:

> Crux cœlestis
> Signum victoriæ,
> Belli robur
> Et palma gloriæ.

> Cross of the heavens,
> Victory's crown,
> Strength in the battle,
> Palm of renown.

Ghislerius. Here, the office of the banner is manifold. First, it is the summons to the nation, to assemble the host. And *Isa. lxii. 10.* so it is written, "Lift up a standard for the people." *Jer. li. 27.* Next, it is the signal for the battle: "Set ye up a standard in the lands, blow the trumpet among the nations, prepare the nations against her." Thirdly, the great banner marks the tent of the Leader, for *Numb. ii. 2.* "Every man of the children of Israel shall pitch by his own standard, with the ensign of their father's house." And in all these ways the Cross of CHRIST is the banner of the Church. But the Vulgate reads, less exactly, *He set love in order over me. Ordinavit* *S. Hieron. in me charitatem.* "Love," observes S. Jerome, writ-*Ep. ad* ing to Marcella, "has no order, and impatience knows *Marcell.* no measure, and therefore this is a hard thing." But GOD is the author of order, not of confusion, and therefore the first way in which we are taught His love in order is by contemplation of the Three Persons of *Aponius.* the Holy Trinity, wherein we learn first, the Name of the FATHER, Who so loved the world that He gave His Only-begotten SON for it; secondly, the Name of the SON, the Eternal Wisdom Who loved us and gave Himself for us; thirdly, the Name of the HOLY GHOST, the SPIRIT of love, Who comforts and strengthens us. And our order is therefore that we are to love the LORD our GOD with all our heart; with all our mind; and with all our strength. He *set love in order*, for He loved us first, and thus drew us on to love Him. S. Bernard understands the gift of spiritual tact and discretion, which regulates and guides our zeal, teaching us what things are to be preferred to others,—the love of GOD to the love of man; heaven to earth; eternity to time; the soul to the flesh. But love is also divided into active and affective, and it is after the order of GOD's law that active love has to busy itself with less perfect things, and persons, for their sakes, rather than for its own, when it would prefer rising with affective love, to the contemplation of heavenly things. It is to be noted that the LXX. takes this whole verse as addressed by the Bride to the companions of the Bridegroom, and reads, *Bring ye me into the house of wine, set love in order over me,* applying the words first to the Jewish Church calling on the Prophets to lead her to CHRIST, then of the Christian Church appealing to the Apostles and Doctors; and afterwards of faithful souls asking for further instruction in divine mysteries, and for guidance in their affections. It has thus been not inaptly applied to postulants for the Religious Life, asking for admission from Superiors, and instruction in the rule and order which they propose to follow. The Vulgate may also be explained to mean, *He set love in array over me;* that is, as my chief and leader in the battle, teaching me that in all things charity is the more excellent way. Or, again, *He arrayed his love against me*, attacking the fortress of my heart with power which I could not resist, entering it as its Lord and Conqueror, and setting His banner in token of victory over its highest battlements.

Cassiodor.
Beda.
S. Bernard.
Serm. 49, and 50.

Origen.
Philo Carp.

De Ponte.
Ghislerius.

Hugo Card.

Sanchez.

> O generous love! that He who smote
> In man for man the foe,
> The double agony in man
> For man should undergo;
>
> And in the garden secretly,
> And on the Cross on high,
> Should teach His brethren, and inspire,
> To suffer and to die.

J. H. Newman, *Dream of Gerontius.*

5 Stay me with flagons, comfort me with apples, for I am sick of love.

The version before us seems to be the intreaty of

the Church for the Holy Eucharist under its two forms, the *flagons* denoting the chalice, and the *apples* the species of Bread, true medicine of the soul which longs for CHRIST. But there is a twofold difficulty in accepting this apparently obvious meaning. In the first place, the Bride speaks not to the Bridegroom, but to His friends, for the verbs are in the plural, and He alone would be asked to give Himself. Next, the A. V. is at variance with the older translations and with modern criticism. The LXX. reads, *Strengthen me with ointments, strew me with apples, for I am wounded with love.* The *ointments* are those which have been poured forth, the *apples* are the fruit of that Tree under whose shadow the Bride sat down.

Theodoret. And the words are thus, notes Theodoret, a petition to the Bridegroom's friends to heap up about her every memory of His love, to guard her against herself, to hinder her from straying to any other than Him.

S. Ambros. in Ps. cxix. Thus too a Western Doctor, following the same reading, tells us that the *ointment* is that which CHRIST shed, the *apples*, what hung upon the Tree. Others, however, explain the *ointments* to be the graces of the HOLY SPIRIT, and particularly that of ghostly strength,

Tres Patr. while the *apples* are discourses on divine things, sweet to the palate of the Bride. The Vulgate is somewhat different: *Prop me with flowers, surround me with*

S. Greg. M. *apples.* It is, says S. Gregory, the mother calling her children round her bed, that in seeing their beauty and growth she may find some comfort, the *flowers* being the younger and weaker offspring, the beginners in the spiritual life; the *apples*, those who have gone on further towards perfection. And with this agrees

Origen. Origen's interpretation, which sees catechumens and faithful souls in the two, and also that of Aponius, who

Aponius. explains the *flowers* of all pure souls, and the *apples* of the Apostles, growing out of CHRIST, as out of a tree, by His teaching. Again, the words have been aptly

Titelmann. taken to denote severally the words and the deeds of CHRIST, which the Bride beseeches His companions to recall to her memory, lest she should fail to bear them in mind; and thus she looks at them and turns them over lovingly as the letters and gifts of her absent Bridegroom. Hermann Hugo reminds us that

Pia Desid. iii. 2. it is no earthly flowers and fruits that she desires, but roses and lilies and apples, such as S. Dorothea in the legend sent to Theophilus by the hand of an Angel, to tell him of her arrival after martyrdom in the garden of GOD, blooming in its pride when earth was lying frozen in the grasp of winter. The Bride would fain have many such flowers heaped around her,—roses by the martyrs; lilies by the virgins; violets by the confessors and penitents; and apples by all who do good works in the Church, and bring forth fruit to perfection. And yet again, the flowers may well be the prayers of the faithful, and the apples their works, by which the Church in general, or any soul in particular, may be aided. Modern criticism translates the first clause of the verse, *strengthen me with raisin-cakes,* and the latter, *strew my bed with apples,* (i.e. probably, apple-leaves.) The *raisin-cakes,* made of dried grapes, out of which the wine has been pressed, but still retaining much sweetness, and amongst the most satisfying of foods, and the *apples,* or their *leaves,* used, not for sustenance, but for a bed whereon to recline, most fitly typify that spiritual communion of the faithful soul which is cut off, by one cause or another, from opportunities of Sacramental feeding at the Altar of GOD. Strength and rest are to be had even thus, and the sick may be healed by touching the hem of JESU's garment. Hugo Card.
De Wette.
Hitzig.
Cf. 1 Sam.
xxx. 12.

> LORD, I cannot seek Thee
>   At Thine Altar-throne,
> Yet may I receive Thee,
>   Friendless and alone.
>
> Far from Priest and Altar,
>   CHRIST, to Thee I cry,
> Come to me in spirit,
>   Let me feel Thee nigh.
>
> In my silent worship
>   Let me share the Feast,
> Be Thy Love the Altar,
>   Be Thyself the Priest.

Lyra Eucharistica.

For I am sick of love. O happy infirmity, where the "sickness is not unto death," but unto life, "for the glory of GOD!" O happy fever, that proceedeth not from a consuming, but a perfecting fire! O happy disorder, wherein the soul relisheth no earthly things, but desires only the savour of heavenly food! The LXX. reads, *wounded with love;* that is, as all the Easterns agree, with the love of GOD. And thus S. Augustine says, "She calls herself wounded with love. For she loved, and did not yet possess; she grieved, Gisten.
S. John xi. 4.
Origen.
Tres Patr.
S. Basil. M.
S. Aug. in
Ps. xxxvii.

because she had not yet; therefore, if she grieved, she was wounded, but the wound hurried her to true healthfulness. For he who is not wounded with this wound, never can attain to true health." Every virtue, observes Origen, wherewith the soul is affected, is as it were an arrow of GOD shot at the soul, arrows that are very sharp, so that it is subdued unto Him. "GOD," says an ancient Father, "hurled His SON at me, His Bride, as at a target, a javelin whereof is said by the Prophet, 'In the shadow of His hand hath He hid Me, and made Me a polished shaft.' That arrow, piercing me with its point of faith, hath brought its Archer together with it, according to that saying, ' I and My FATHER are one.' 'We will come unto him, and make our abode with him.'" And so a quaint old English poet says:

<small>Origen.
S. Hieron.
Ep. 140.
Ps. xlv. 6.
S. Greg.
Nyssen.
Isa. xlix. 2.

S. John x. 30; xiv. 23.</small>

<small>Francis Quarles, *School of the Heart*, 33.</small>

> LORD, empty all Thy quivers, let there be
> No corner of my spacious heart left free,
> Till all be but one wound, wherein
> No subtle sight-abhorring sin
> May lurk in secret, unespied by Thee,
> Or reign in power, unsubdued by Thee,
>   Perfect Thy purchased victory,
>   That Thou may'st ride triumphantly,
> And leading captive all captivity
> May'st put an end to enmity in me.
>
> Then, blesséd Archer, in requital, I
> To shoot Thine arrows back again will try;
>   By prayers and praises, sighs and sobs,
>   By vows and tears, by groans and throbs,
> I'll see if I can pierce and wound Thine Heart,
> And vanquish Thee again by Thine own art;
>   Or, that we may at once provide
>   For all mishaps that may betide
> Shoot Thou Thyself, Thy polished shaft, to me,
> And I will shoot my broken heart to Thee.

<small>Cassiodor.
S. Greg. M.
Beda.

Hugo Card.</small>

The interpreters of the Vulgate reading, which is also that of A.V., explain the words to denote the eager, restless longing of the exiled soul for the Heavenly Country, which gives her strong distaste for earthly things, and makes her languid in all that regards them. And her sickness, adds another, is threefold. She is sick because of her own vileness, which she fears will repel her Spouse; sick with anxiety, lest she should fall short in those good works which He desires; sick by reason of her frailty, lest she should become cold and lax through want of perseverance. And accordingly, she asks for three remedies against these,—*flowers*, to give her beauty; *apples*, to give her fruit; and, in the next verse, His own *Hand* to be her stay. None has expressed this yearning for heaven, this sickness of earth, both springing from love, better than S. Teresa.

> Ah, what a length does life appear,
> How hard to bear this exile here,
>   How hard from weary day to day
>   To pine without relief:
> The yearning hope to break away
> From this my prison-house of clay
>   Inspires so sharp a grief,
> That overcome I weep and sigh,
> Dying because I do not die.
>
> *   *   *   *
>
> Ah, LORD, my Light and living Breath,
> Take me, O take me from this death,
>   And burst the bars that sever me
>   From my true life above.
> Think how I die Thy Face to see,
> And cannot live away from Thee,
>   O my eternal Love.
> And ever, ever weep and sigh,
> Dying because I do not die.

<small>S. Teresa. The Rhythm, *Vivo sin vivir in me*.</small>

And in this sickness of love, comments a great master of the ascetic life, the Bride passes out of herself, and falls into a death which is life, a trance wherein, no longer able to sustain herself, she is stayed up in the everlasting Arms, and therefore adds, as she feels them, <small>Gerson. Sympsalma in Cant.</small>

6 His left hand is under my head, and his right hand doth embrace me.

"The Bridegroom cannot bear the suffering of His Bride, He is at hand; for He cannot delay when called by such longings. And because He finds that she was faithful in her tasks, and eager for gain while He was absent, in that she desired to have flowers and apples to be added to her, He returns to her now with an even more spontaneous reward of grace. He supports her reclining head with one of His arms, holding the other ready to embrace her, and cherish her in His bosom." And on the difference between these two hands, let us hear the Doctor of Grace: "*His left hand is under my head*, for He will not leave me even <small>S. Bernard. Serm. 57.</small> <small>S. August. in Ps. cxliv.</small>

in temporal needs and desires, but nevertheless the left hand will be *under* my head, not put before it, but beneath it, that *His right hand* may *embrace me*, promising me everlasting life. Thus is fulfilled that saying of the Apostle: 'Having promise of the life that now is, and of that which is to come.' What of that which now is? *His left hand is under my head.* What of that to come? *His right hand doth embrace me.* Do ye seek things for time? 'Seek ye first the kingdom of God,' that is, the right hand, 'and all these things shall be added unto you.' Ye shall have, saith He, riches and glory, and in the world to come life everlasting. With the left hand I will sustain your weakness, with the right I will crown your perfection." Again, the same Saint in another place observes that the right hand is above, the left hand below; the left for consolation, the right for protection. Our head, that is, our faith, where CHRIST dwells, rests on the left hand, because we set that faith above all temporal things, and then, truly, the right hand embraces us. But, writes another Father, even the temporal things here intended are not earthly, rather they are Divine. " GOD'S *left hand* means the pledge of the HOLY SPIRIT, the understanding of the sacred Scriptures, and such like gifts and graces whereby Holy Church is comforted in the present life. By the *right hand* is denoted the blessedness of the Heavenly Country, and by the *head* the guiding principle of the soul. Therefore the Bridegroom's left hand is under the Bride's head, because the Church receives all these gifts to the end that she may learn to sigh for things eternal. And the right hand of the Bridegroom embraces her, because the whole aim of the Church or of the faithful soul is that she may at length attain everlasting blessedness, and rejoice in the vision of her Maker. It is well said, therefore, that the Bridegroom's left hand is under the Bride's head, and then that His right hand embraces her, because no one can arrive at the embraces of eternal bliss, unless he strive to be partaker here of heavenly mysteries and Divine gifts." And thus too, more tersely, S. Bernard: "The left hand raises, the left clasps. The left heals and justifies, the right embraces and blesses. In His left hand are merits, in His right rewards. In His right, I say, delights; in His left, medicines." Another view sees in the left hand, under the head, as giving a certain degree of support, the old Law, but in the loving embrace of the right the tidings of the Gospel. Again, the left hand is taken to denote punishment and suffering, the right to be blessings and rewards. And in this sense an Eastern Father writes: "*His left hand* Theodoret. *is under my head,* that is, I am lifted up above sufferings, and not pressed down under them, because I am united to my Bridegroom, and heed Him eagerly. *His right hand shall embrace me;* that is, He will deck me with His bounties, and as though embracing, and grasping, and fulfilling my desire, heap me therewith." So too S. Bernard tells us that when we have attained that S. Bernard. Serm. 51. love which casteth out servile fear, GOD's left hand of threatening is *under* our heads, and we are bold enough, in confident hope, to draw close to that right hand wherein are His promises; but that when we fear Him more than we love or hope, when dread of wrath to come is our chief sentiment, then His left hand is *over* our heads. Another, accepting the view Aponius. that the left hand denotes punishment and suffering, applies it in a different and very beautiful way. "The scaffold, and torments of divers punishments, seemed to the foolish and ungodly shameful and hateful, but to the Martyrs, and to all who have been brought into the hall of wisdom, to be joyous delights, and beds of rest for the weary. Beds whereon fire rouses only a sportive smile; whereon the amphitheatre of the tried soul is turned into a paradise, the gratings and frying-pans become the softest feathers, the balls of flame turn to the sweetest flowers, melted lead into balmy unguents, the scourges, and rods, and toothed irons, become the most delicate brushes, wherewith the soul, cleansed from every stain of sin, and called back to her former beauty, is restored to her Creator. For death undergone for CHRIST's sake is preferred as more precious than any joy, any pleasure, or the most costly gem. These, then, are the delights of holy souls for winning everlasting joys, where the Church, fainting in delight, is glad of being held in the embrace of CHRIST her Beloved, that she may be counted worthy to bear the most savage tortures for her Maker. The left hand under her head may well be the shield of faith, held in the warrior's left hand as he fights; and by the embrace of the right hand we may understand the sword of prayer, wherewith he is ever armed on the right. With one of these arms the enemy is parried, with the other he is laid low." Others see in the first clause the highest grade of mystic contemplation, which is GOD's left hand under the head of intellectual meditation in the illuminative way, while the embrace of the right hand denotes the close union of the loving will with Him in the unitive way. But the loveliest interpretation of all is that which sees in the left hand the Manhood of the Eternal WORD, and all the works wrought by Him after His Incarnation, when He was indeed *under* our head, made lower not only than the Angels, but than men, a Man of Sorrows, acquainted with grief, despised and rejected, marred more than any other, with no beauty that we should desire Him, so that we esteemed Him not; and in the Right Hand the Godhead of the Crucified One, full of Divine gifts, the place of everlasting glory and blessedness. And thus Origen says: "That part of the WORD of GOD which existed before His taking flesh in this dispensation, may well be His Right Hand; that which exists through His Incarnation may be called the left. Whence the left hand is said to have riches and honour. For through His Incarnation He sought for riches and honour, that is, the salvation of all. In His right hand is said to be length of days, whereby without doubt that part which was in the beginning with GOD, which was GOD the WORD, is denoted as eternal. This left hand then, the Church, whose Head is CHRIST, desires to have under her head, that it may be protected by faith in the Incarnation; but to be embraced by His right, that is, to know and to be taught those things which were dark and hidden before the time of the dispensation which began when He took flesh. The right hand is there where we must hold that all things are wherein is nought of the misery of sin, nought of the fall of weakness. Here is the left hand, where He cured our wounds, and carried our iniquities, made Himself sin and a curse for us. All these, although they do as it were support the head and faith of the Church, may fitly be called the left hand of the WORD of GOD." And in the same strain S. Bernard observes, "In the left hand the holy soul recalls to mind that love, greater than which none is, that He laid down His life for His friends; in the right she remembers the Beatific Vision which He promised to His friends, and the joy in presence of His majesty." And therefore the Church looks forward in hopeful awe for the coming of that Great Day when the sheep and the goats shall be portioned, the one on His right hand, and the other on His left, trusting that then He will set her on His right hand in a vesture of gold, wrought about with divers colours, denoting the various graces and merits of the holy souls whom He has purified by suffering here. Ps. xlv

7 I charge you, O ye daughters of Jerusalem, by the roes, and by the hinds of the field, that ye stir not up, nor awake my love, till he please.

The Vulgate and LXX. are both at variance with this version. The former reads, *I adjure you, O ye daughters of Jerusalem, by the she-goats, and by the stags of the fields, that ye stir not, nor awake My love* (fem.) *until she please.* "It is," observes Cassiodorus, [Cassiodor.] "the voice of the Bridegroom, adjuring the daughters of Jerusalem, that is, souls bent on everlasting desires, and seeking the Vision of Peace, not to rouse or disturb the reposing Bride. That is, do not disturb or try to engage in outer works the soul which is busied in Divine contemplation, prayers, or reading, *until she will*, to wit, until at the close of her time of contemplation, she desires, warned by her bodily weakness, to be roused from her sleep of everlasting rest, and to proceed to her temporal duties. Let us see then by what He adjures the daughters of Jerusalem. By the *she-goats* and the *stags of the fields*. She-goats and stags are clean beasts, hostile to serpents and poisons. [Beda.] They denote the virtues of the Saints, which shine with spiritual clearness, and are not merely on their guard against the venom of the devil's craft, but actually pursue it and bring it to nothing." S. Gregory, [S. Greg. M.] agreeing with most of this explanation, prefers to understand the *daughters* to be weakly and effeminate souls, who prefer the temporal aspects of religion to the eternal ones, and therefore are eager to engage the Church chiefly in external works, instead of trusting to her better judgment as to the share to be given to each. S. Justus of Urgel applies the words very [S. Just. Org.] aptly to the wisdom of Christian teachers in not forcing the wills of the faithful towards counsels of perfection, but leaving, instead, some room for voluntary and spontaneous offering. And he cites S. Paul's counsel, [1 Cor. vii. 25, 35.] not command, to virgins, and his advice to Philemon, [Philem. 14.]

as also the LORD's own language respecting eunuchs, and to the young man whom He told to sell that he had, and give to the poor, in illustration of his comment. The palace of CHRIST, as another tells us, has not only many chambers and a banqueting-house, but also a great park, wherein are many souls, once wild in the woods of Gentile philosophy, but now captured by the hunters of the Church, and tamed for the delight of the daughters of Jerusalem, and set to disport themselves in the fields of Holy Writ, retaining their old swiftness and acute senses, but employing them better than before, when, as Platonic and Stoic teachers, they were only seeking after that GOD whom they have now found. They are urged to be patient with the Church, and to let her have her sleep out, to recruit her strength, when they would fain see their own intellectual eagerness in the pursuit of Divine knowledge universally shared. Again, it may be an appeal to all devout and peaceful souls, in the name of the Patriarchs and Seers of the Old Testament, and of the Apostles and Doctors of the New, not to interfere with the pious employments of their brethren on any pretext, but to rejoice in any spiritual advantage they may gain therein. Or you may take it as the address of CHRIST to the children of the earthly Jerusalem, the Scribes and Pharisees, not to interfere with or persecute the Christian Church, and this in the name of those swift ministering spirits, the Angels, who might otherwise be agents of punishment to them, as they had been of old to the Egyptians and Canaanites, when they meddled with the Synagogue. Cardinal Hugo, viewing the text as a warning against spiritual impatience to arrive at results before the means have been got ready, compares the necessary pause to the filling of cups before a feast can begin, to the tuning of instruments before a concert, to the whetting of arrows and hooks before a hunting-match, with other similes of the kind. And Rupert, taking the *daughters of Jerusalem* literally, interprets the passage of a warning to them, in the name of the Patriarchs, not to interrupt the silence of the Mother of GOD touching the mysterious burden of her womb, till it should please her to speak, lest Herod should learn the truth too soon, and find the Child to slay Him.

The LXX. read, *I adjure you, O ye daughters of Jerusalem, by the forces and powers of the field, if ye shall stir up or awake the love so long as she* (or *he*) *please*. And this is explained by Origen to mean that the Church is God's husbandry, but that each soul has its own plot in the great field, to till for Him and plant with virtues and good works. The Bride urges the daughters of the heavenly Jerusalem, by all that is dearest to them in these gardens of their souls, that if they have once begun to stir up and rouse love, which was sleeping, they are not to check its rising within any narrower bounds than those of the Bridegroom's will, because there should be no other measure to our love of God. It matters not what patience or suffering on the Bride's part this may involve, for it is her part to obey His will so long as He manifests it. S. Gregory Nyssen, agreeing in other respects with this, will have the forces and powers of the field to denote the Angels, whom the elect souls are hereby enjoined to imitate. Psellus, on the other hand, sees here a continuance of the former intreaty of the Bride that she may be decked for her Bridegroom, and represents her as calling on the Angels to increase in every way her love for Him, until His will for the salvation of all mankind may be fulfilled in her. Another very singular view is that of Philo, who takes the words as those of a holy soul beseeching other Saints not to urge God, Who is love, to call her to Himself by death, until His own good time, that she may employ herself in His service here below, according to that saying, "Until I have showed Thy strength unto this generation, and Thy power to all them that are yet for to come." The Greek Fathers, it will thus be seen, agree with the A. V. in ascribing the words to the Bride, and represent Love himself, whether God, or a faculty of the soul, as the sleeper. Herein they are also in accord with the Targum, which represents the words as an address of Moses, after the return of the spies, adjuring the people of Israel by the Lord of Hosts and the powers of the land of Israel,[1] not to rouse the Lord, nor to attempt to enter Canaan until

Origen.

S. Epiphanius.
S. Greg. Nyss.

Psellus.

Philo Carp.

Ps. lxxi. 16.

Targum.

---

[1] Hence it appears that the Targum accepts the LXX., "forces" and "powers," for "gazelles" and "hinds," obviously referring צְבָאוֹת to the root צָבָא "he went out to war" and taking אֵילוֹת *hinds*, as though it were equivalent to אֵילִים (from the same ultimate root אול) *princes* or *chieftains*. 2 Kings xxiv. 15.

His will should allow of it, at the end of the forty years. This, taken in conjunction with some of the patristic comments given above, will lead us on to what is probably the true mystical import of the words. The Bride urges all devout souls, in the name of those other souls which, though less perfect, and not yet as meek and docile as the sheep of CHRIST's fold, are yet dear to the Good Shepherd, not to hasten GOD's good time by impatience, but to let patience have her perfect work. Storms and persecutions may rage round the ship of the Church, but if He be in the ship, even though asleep on a pillow, it is the truest faith to await His waking, instead of rousing Him entirely from slumber, only to rebuke our incredulity. Again; as the word is not *Beloved*, but *Love*, we may well see here counsel against hurrying on souls too fast in religious growth, lest undue forcing should make them weakly exotics, rather than hardy, vigorous, and fruitful plants. It is, in other terms, the Apostle's counsel to give milk to babes and meat to the full-grown only, and not to urge immature Christians to apply to themselves language and usages fitted only for the tried athletes of the Faith. Still further is it a warning *Ainsworth.* against arousing CHRIST, by our sins, to stand up in judgment against us, because each of us has not been *Prov. v. 19.* in soul a true Spouse to Him, " as the loving hind and pleasant roe."

8 The voice of my beloved! behold, he cometh leaping upon the mountains, skipping upon the hills.

9 My beloved is like a roe or a young hart:

S. Ambros. The first act of this dramatic idyl closed with the preceding verse, wherein the Bride warns her companions against disturbing the slumber of the Bridegroom. Now, His time for waking has come, she hears His voice and sees Him, from a distance, hastening to her, and the second stage of the action—wherein some commentators not unfitly see typified the first efforts of the Pentecostal Church—begins with await- *Targum.* ing His nearer approach to perfect union. The Targum, which refers the words to GOD's message by Moses to Israel in Egypt, and to His Passover, as He went slaying the first-born of the Egyptians, while sparing the houses marked with the blood of the Lamb, gives, as it were, the key to all subsequent expositions. *The voice of my Beloved!* At first it was only by His voice that CHRIST was known by the Church, for He sent it before Him by His prophets, and was only heard, not seen; while His people had merely the promise of His Advent announced to them, according to that saying of the Apostle, "GOD, Who at sundry times and in divers manners spake in times past unto the fathers by the prophets, hath in these last days spoken unto us by His SON." And therefore, as the present verse represents the last few moments before His Advent, rather than that very time itself, this *Voice* has been aptly said to be that of the great Forerunner, the "Voice crying in the wilderness, Prepare ye the way of the LORD." And this exposition receives support from a saying of the Baptist himself, wherein he most plainly refers to this very passage of the Song: "He that hath the Bride is the Bridegroom: but the friend of the Bridegroom, which standeth and heareth Him, rejoiceth greatly because of the Bridegroom's voice." Another and singular view is, that the Voice of the Beloved is that call of the dead to resurrection, which will precede His second Advent to judge the world. A Latin Father, following the reading which makes the Bride the sleeper, bids us note how light her slumber is, how she is roused at once by the first tones of the Bridegroom's voice, heard in Holy Writ, in prayer, or in meditation, according to His own saying, "Every one that is of the truth heareth My voice." A Greek commentator, on the other hand, bids us observe how difficult true contemplation is, how we do but hear the voice, without seeing the form, of the WORD of GOD, and how, even when He does appear, the swiftness of His movements is such as to dazzle the eye, as He does not remain fixed that we may gaze, but comes rapidly on. And from this is drawn counsel, where the Western writer does but state a fact, to wit, the need of the soul being on the alert to catch the first intimation of her Bridegroom's presence. If He will but speak to her, it is enough, because "the sheep follow Him, for they know His voice." Again; as the time of silence and waiting was said above to be applicable to the abiding of the Apostles in Jerusalem during the ten days of expectation; the Voice here may fitly be taken of the mighty rushing wind of Pentecost,

Marginal references: Origen. S. Greg. Nyssen. Heb. i. 1. Tres Patr. Isa. xl. 3. S. Mark i. 3. Hengstenberg. S. John iii. 29. S. Just. Org. Aponius. S. John xviii. 37. S. Greg. Nyss. S. John x. 4. Ghislerius.

which gave the Apostles utterance, called the Voice of the Beloved, because of the mission of the Comforter from the SON. And so it is written: "He shall glorify Me: for He shall receive of Mine, and shall show it unto you." *Behold, He cometh leaping upon the mountains, skipping upon the hills.* "I long," cries a Saint, putting words into the mouth of the Bride, "that love should be stirred up for me. I count myself wounded with love, and love itself hastens to me the more. I said, Come, it leaps and skips. I ask Him to come with grace. He worketh the increase of graces, and as He comes, brings with Him additional grace; nay, He gains it Himself in coming, because even He desires to please His beloved. He leaps upon the high places, that He may ascend to His Bride. For the chamber of the Bride is the Judgment-seat of CHRIST." He leaps on the Church, He skippeth on the Synagogue. He leaps on the Gentiles, He skippeth on the Jews. Let us behold Him leaping. He leaps from heaven into the Virgin's womb, from the womb into the manger, from the manger into Jordan, from Jordan to the Cross, from the Cross to the grave, from the grave into heaven. And there is an ancient tradition of the Church, that the LORD, in the course of His Ascension, tarried one day with each of the nine orders of the Angelic hierarchy, arriving on the tenth at the right hand of the FATHER, and thereupon sending the HOLY GHOST down on the Apostles. For this reason, they say, it is that the *Kyrie Eleison* is said nine times in the Mass, and ended with the *Gloria Patri.* All this, observes S. Gregory, was *leaping on the mountains,* because beyond man's reach, though for the most part visible to him, and also because surpassing, in the might of His loving-kindness, all that the greatest Saints have ever done. S. Bernard, pointing out that the Bridegroom is said first to leap over *mountains,* and then over *hills,* refers the verse to the humiliation of GOD the SON, passing from His throne in the highest, revealing, as He goes down through the choirs of angels, the wonderful mystery of His love, hidden from all generations. He reaches the mightiest Spirits, still unspeakably below Himself, and passing by them, comes to the lowlier powers, and leaves even these far above Him, made, as He was, lower than the Angels for our sakes, and found in fashion as a man. Not only so, but He is said to leap over the Angels for another cause also, His far greater eagerness to minister to the heirs of salvation, rejoicing as a giant to run His race. "He leaped over Gabriel, and came before him to the Virgin, as the Archangel himself beareth witness, saying, 'Hail, full of grace, the LORD is with thee.' What? dost thou find Him in the womb Whom thou leftest but now? How is this? 'He did fly, yea, He did fly before on the wings of the wind.' Thou art vanquished, O Archangel; He who sent thee forward hath leaped over thee." And the same Saint reminds us in another place how often the LORD literally chose a mountain for His manifestations, preaching His first discourse to the people on one, praying on another, transfigured on a third, crucified on a fourth, and ascending again from that Mount of Olives which had been His frequent resort. Ps. xix. 5. Serm. 54. Ps. xviii. 10, Vulg. Serm. 4, in Ascens.

> Thrice for us the WORD Incarnate high on holy hills was set,
> Once on Tabor, once on Calvary, and again on Olivet,
> Once to shine and once to suffer, and once more, as King of kings,
> With a merry noise ascending, borne by cherubs on their wings.

Again; He leaped over mountains and hills by His conquering the kingdoms and provinces of the earth through the conversion of the Gentiles in the person of His messengers, of whom is written, "How beautiful upon the mountains are the feet of him that bringeth good tidings." And, as another aptly points out, He overthrew the idol temples, so often set upon hills in the midst of groves, a meaning enforced, as is noted, by the version of Symmachus, who reads, *Going against the mountains, leaping against the hills.* Origen. Vieyra. Isa. lii. 7. Theodoret.

> The lonely mountains o'er,
> And the resounding shore,
> A voice of weeping heard and loud lament;
> From haunted spring, and dale
> Edged with poplar pale,
> The parting genius is with sighing sent;
> With flower-inwoven tresses torn
> The nymphs in twilight shade of tangled thickets mourn.

Milton, Hymn on the Nativity, 182.

He comes leaping also to holy souls, not only to those more perfect ones, like His Apostles, who are lofty and strong as mountains, rooted deep in love, and kissed by the first rays of the sun; but also to the lowlier hills which court His presence. "Behold, He cometh, not upon the plains, nor upon the valleys, but leaping upon the mountains. If thou be a mountain, S. Ambros. in Ps. cxix.

He leapeth on thee. He leaps on Isaiah, He leaps on Jeremiah, He leaps on Peter, John, James. The mountains are round about Him. If thou canst not be a mountain, if thou art not strong enough for that, be at least a hill, that CHRIST may go up on thee, and if He pass, let Him so leap over thee, that the shadow of His transit may be thy safeguard." And another Saint reminds us that the Bridegroom is said to leap, and to leap over the hills, to teach us that though He comes often to His Saints, yet that the sweetness of internal contemplation is very brief and rare for each one even in the case of those most advanced in holiness, because we are weighed down with the burden of the flesh. He comes leaping to us as we study Holy Scripture, appearing in passage after passage on the hills of the Old Testament, and the loftier and more conspicuous mountains of the New. And in this sense we may take that saying, "I will lift up mine eyes unto the hills, from whence is my help." *Like a roe or a young hart.* For *roe* the LXX. reads δορκάδι a *doe.* And because this word is derived from δέρκω, "I see," by reason of the animal's large and beautiful eyes, Origen tells us that CHRIST is compared to it because He comes to us in contemplation, and that He is like a young hart, because the stag hates and destroys serpents, and thus figures the active Saints who imitate their LORD in making war upon evil. There is a crowd of other yet more fanciful interpretations, amongst which it is unnecessary to specify more than two, which seem really to illustrate the words, to wit, the swiftness of the creatures named, and their delight in climbing among the mountains, symbolising the working of CHRIST in the soul; and the harmlessness of the young hart, which has not yet put out its horns, denoting the gentleness of the SAVIOUR.

Behold, he standeth behind our wall, he looketh forth at the windows, showing himself through the lattice.

This wall, observes De Lyra, is that thick darkness in which the Law was given on Sinai, through which pierced the lightning-flashes from the hidden glory of GOD. CHRIST Incarnate stood, notes another, as though *behind our wall,* because the Godhead lay hid in our humanity. And because human weakness could not endure His infinity, were He to disclose it, He interposed the barrier of flesh, and whatever great work He wrought among men, He did as though hiding behind a wall. He who looks through windows and lattices, is partly seen and partly hides himself: so too our LORD JESUS CHRIST, when He was working miracles by divine power, and enduring insults in the weakness of the flesh, looked forth as it were through windows and lattices, because while hiding Himself in one way, He showed in another way who He was. S. Greg. M.

Again, He stands behind *our* wall, that is, our sin and fleshly weakness prevent us from seeing Him constantly, and yet He gives glimpses of Himself, by making, as it were, openings in that wall whereby we can contemplate Him partially. This is the wall to which Hezekiah turned his face and wept, because he could not yet behold his SAVIOUR. The *windows* whereat we see Him, observes a Greek Father, are our powers of understanding, chiefly exercised when we pray or read Holy Scripture, and as we are so engaged, we see Him at intervals. And whereas the LXX. word for *lattice* is *nets*, the same Father tells us that it is just when we are in the midst of temptation and snares that we see CHRIST'S Face shining on us through the meshes, to bid us be of good courage, for He is at hand to free us. Another, remembering how S. Paul describes that mid-wall of partition which stood between Jew and Gentile till the Passion, tells us that the wall is the Law, which hid CHRIST altogether under type and shadow. The *windows*, which gave fitful glimpses of Him, are the Prophets; and the *lattices*, through which He looks *out* (LXX.) denote the Apostles, who had seen Him in the body, and were able to preach His full revelation. S. Epiphanius, however, not very dissimilarly, takes the chief Messianic Prophets, Isaiah, Jeremiah, and Daniel, to be these windows. S. Bernard applies the words *windows* and *lattices* very touchingly to the weaknesses and suffering of our mortal bodies, as though gaps and crevices in a ruinous wall, and tells us that through these same windows of His own human Body the LORD looked out on suffering mortality, and learned to share and pity its deepest sorrows. The Chaldee paraphrase helps us to another deep mystical meaning, applying, as it does, the verse to the LORD looking through the windows of Cassiodor.
Card. Hailgrin.
2 Kings xx. 2.
Theodoret.

Origen.

Philo Carp.

S. Epiphanius.

S. Bernard. Serm. 56.

the Israelites in Egypt as they slew the Paschal Lamb, sprinkled its blood, and ate its roasted flesh with bitter herbs. So the LORD JESUS looks out steadfastly on faithful souls from behind the wall of the species of Bread and Wine in the Holy Eucharist, showing Himself in part to them even there, as they feed on Him in faith, and gives them joy with the light of His countenance. And again, they remind us how His love looked out upon us through the lattices of those Five Wounds He bore for us upon the Cross. The time will at last come when our wall shall be swept away, and all, especially sin, which now hinders us from beholding CHRIST face to face, shall vanish. Our sins separate between us and GOD. Would there were no barrier against me save that of the body, exclaims S. Bernard, and the sin which is inherent in the flesh, and not many another source of evil besides. I fear that besides that sin which is of my nature, I have added many, very many, of my own unrighteousness, whereby I have driven the Bridegroom too far from me, so that were I to speak truly, I should confess rather that He stands behind several walls than behind one. But it is written, " With the help of my GOD I shall leap over the wall." Till that blessed time come, we may pray in the language of a devout writer : " O my Beloved, Thou standest behind the wall of my mortality, blindness, and sloth, and I cannot see Thee, nor love Thee, as I would. Look upon me, then, through the lattices of all the powers of my soul, that I may know and love Thee as much as Thou vouchsafest. Look at me also, sometimes, through the windows, through those partial images of Thyself in my soul. So, though I cannot see Thee perfectly and wholly, yet I may ever in part behold Thee more clearly, and love Thee more truly, when and how far Thou willest, that I may thus learn by experience that Thou standest behind my wall, looking at me through the windows, and gazing on me through the lattices, and that no barrier parts Thee and me save that wall of mortal flesh, after whose dissolution I may see and know Thee perfectly, even as I am now known unto Thee."

Corn. à Lap.

S. Just. Org. Cantacuzene.

Isa. lix. 2. S. Bernard. Serm. 56.

Ps. xviii. 29.

Nic. Argent.

10 My beloved spake, and said unto me, Rise up, my love, my fair one, and come away.

Spake. The word עָנָה *anah*, here rendered *spake*, is very much more frequently used in the Bible in the sense of *answered.* Accordingly the LXX. turns the sentence, *My beloved answereth and saith unto Me*, which suggests at once the constant occurrence of the same phrase in the Gospels, applied to our LORD, and by no means always denoting a reply to spoken words, but rather to unspoken thoughts, which He reads as in an open book. *Rise up.* The LXX. in some copies, and the Vulgate add, *hasten*, and also insert the word *dove* among the epithets of the Bride in this verse. Rise up, the LORD says, and come, My love; rise up from the pleasures of the world, rise up from earthly things, and come to Me, thou who art still labouring and heavy laden, because thou art careful about things of the world. Come away above the world, come to Me, for I have overcome the world. Come near to Me, now fair with the beauty of eternal life, now a dove, meek and gentle, and altogether full of spiritual grace. And why, another Father asks, does he say, *Rise up, hasten?* Because He would say, I bore for thee the tempest's rage; I met the waves which were thy due. My soul, for thy sake, was exceeding sorrowful unto death; I arose from the dead, breaking the gates of death, and loosing the fetters of hell. Therefore I say unto thee, *Rise up, and come away.* He calls her out of the house into the field, and saith, *Rise up* from thy pleasant couch, from that repose, wherein thou seekest to please Me alone with psalms, and hymns, and prayers, *hasten and come*, that is, hasten to the help of thy neighbours, that by preaching, and the example of good works, thou mayest make them true imitators of thee, and lead them to salvation with thyself. She is His *love*, observes S. Justus, because reconciled to Him by His death, His *fair one*, because washed from her sins. Or, as S. Bernard, at fuller length, comments, She is fitly called His *love*, who seeks her Bridegroom's profit by earnestly and faithfully preaching, counselling, and ministering. Fitly is she His *dove*, who unceasingly seeks to gain the divine pity for her loved ones, sighing and entreating for them in prayer. Fitly also is she His *fair one*, who shining with the heavenly longing of lofty contemplation, at any rate when it may be timely and suitably done, clothes herself in its beauty. It may also be taken of any holy soul which GOD calls to Himself out of the troubles of the world. And thus

S. Matt. xi. 25.
S. John v. 19, &c.

S. Ambros. de Isaac et Anima, cap. 4.

Origen.

Cassiodor. Beda.

S. Just. Org.
S. Bernard.

S. Jerome speaks of one who had served her Master well, and was ready when He came and called for her. "The moment she heard the Bridegroom calling, Rise up, come away, My love, My fair one, My dove; for lo, the winter is past and over, the rain is gone; she joyfully answered, The flowers are seen in the land, the time of pruning is come. I believe verily to see the goodness of the LORD in the land of the living." His calling is not merely away from the world, but into heaven. "See," He says, "the middle wall of separation, which parted the concord of our inner affections and roused the bodily passions to strife, and to contrariety, is taken down. Come then, unfearing, to see Me no longer through the lattice, but face to face, O My love, to enjoy My loving countenance." And it is also taken in especial of the summons to the holiest of Saints by the voice of the Archangel. "Thou, the Heavenly Sender of the message would say, My love for thy lowliness, My dove for thy gentleness, My fair one for thy purity, come. Come, Mary, come, for Eve hath fled to a hiding-place. Come, and believe the Angel bringing thee glad tidings; for Eve believed the whispering serpent. Come, and crush the serpent's head, for Eve was deluded with the head, and tempted with the belly, and tangled in the tail of the serpent. Come, and say, Behold the handmaid of the LORD. For Eve hid and excused herself alike. The serpent, said she, deceived me, and I did eat. This is the Voice of my Beloved, and He saith this to me, Rise up by faith, hasten by hope, come by charity." The words are applied to the Blessed Virgin in another sense also, used as they are by the Gallican Church as one of the Antiphons for the Feast of the Assumption. And how does the Bride treat the call? She hears the command, replies a Saint, she is established by the word, she is aroused, she advances, she draws near. She becomes fair, she is called a dove. Fair, because drawing near GOD she has received the image of the Divine beauty in herself as in a mirror; a dove, in that she is lovely with that image of the HOLY GHOST she has received.

S. Hieron. Epitaph. S. Paulæ.

Ps. xxvii. 15.

S. Ambros. in Ps. cxix.

Rupert.

Brev. Paris. et Rotomag.

S. Greg. Nyss.

11 For lo, the winter is past, the rain is over and gone;

12 The flowers appear on the earth; the

time of the singing of birds is come, and the voice of the turtle is heard in our land;

Here, as so often, the Chaldee anticipates the true mystical sense, by explaining these words of the ending of the bondage of Israel in Egypt, and of the Voice of the HOLY SPIRIT of redemption, promised to Abraham, and now heard by his descendants. For *singing*, it reads, with the old Versions, *pruning*, and interprets the phrase of the circumcision of the firstborn. And the first general exposition of the verse by the Fathers takes it of the Gospel revelation, ending the rigour and harshness of the Jewish Law on the one hand, and of Gentile idolatry on the other. The *rain is over*, because the Sun of Righteousness, shining out, has dispersed the mists and clouds of error and sin, the earliest Saints, Apostles and Martyrs, spring up as flowers in the new field of the Church, as Prudentius sings of the Holy Innocents: Targum.

Origen.
Theodoret.
S. Greg.
M., &c.

> All hail! ye infant martyr flowers,
> Cut off in life's first dawning hours:
> As rose-buds snapt in tempest strife,
> When Herod sought your SAVIOUR's life.

Prudentius, The Hymn, *Salvete, flores martyrum.*

The Voice of the Holy Dove descends in tongues of fire on the disciples at Jerusalem, and the time of *pruning* away all ignorance, unbelief, and love of the world, has come, when the FATHER purges the branches of that True Vine which He hath planted. And observe that there are three stages of pruning the choicer vines. First the thick and hurtful branches are cut away. Secondly, the useless shoots, at the time when the vines flower. Thirdly, the superfluous leaves, which hinder the ripening of the grapes, that their removal may suffer the sun's rays to shine on the fruit. So too, it is needful in the soul first to prune away the more serious faults; secondly, lighter offences, or even things which are not offences, but merely useless and superfluous; and thirdly, things which are useful, lawful, and permitted, have to be cut away, that the precious and beautiful fruit may be ripened by the Sun of grace. Nic. Argent.

One ancient Father, however, takes the word in a yet wider sense, that of reaping, and explains the whole passage to be only another form of those words of the S. Epiph.

LORD, "The harvest truly is plenteous, but the labourers are few, pray ye therefore the LORD of the harvest, that He will send forth labourers into His harvest."

<small>S. Mat. ix. 37.</small>

And next, they take the winter and rain to be the time of the LORD'S Passion, when the floods came about Him, and the joyous shining which follows them denotes His Resurrection. So in many a hymn, as for example, Adam of S. Victor:

<small>Philo Carp.</small>

<small>The Easter Sequence, *Mundi renovatio*.</small>

> Cœlum fit serenius,
> Et mare tranquillius;
> Spirat aura levius,
>   Vallis nostra floruit.
> Revirescunt arida,
> Recalescunt frigida
>   Postquam ver intepuit.

> Now the heaven from clouds is free,
> And more calmly rests the sea,
> While the air breathes balmily,
>   In our valley flowers appear:
> Green is now the dried-up plain,
> And the chilled earth glows again
>   Since the genial spring is here.

And similarly a yet older poet:

<small>Venant. Fortunat. The Hymn, *Salve, festa dies*.</small>

> Hail, festal Day, for evermore adored,
> Wherein GOD conquered Hell, and upward soared!

> See the world's beauty, budding forth anew,
> Shows with the LORD His gifts returning too!

> The earth with flowers is decked,—the sky serene,
> The heavenly portals glow with brighter sheen.

> The greenwood leaves, the flowering meadows tell
> Of CHRIST, triumphant over gloomy Hell.

<small>Cassiodor. S. Greg. M. Angelomus.</small>

<small>Parez.</small>

<small>Psellus.</small>

<small>Nic. Argent.</small>

They give other interpretations of the *voice of the turtle* besides that of the Pentecostal Advent. First, that it denotes the preaching of the Apostles, and this is followed by many. Then, that it refers to the song of the Blessed Virgin, chanting the glory of the Incarnation. The loneliness and sorrowful note of the bird lead some to see in it a type of the Baptist, crying in the wilderness: and lastly, these same qualities cause another writer to remind us of the sad and desolate life of that turtle-dove whose Soul GOD did indeed deliver out of the hands of His enemies, but whose Body suffered pain for three and thirty years, and Who uttered His voice in the land in the Seven

Words upon the Cross. And the Gloss bids us notice Gloss.
a difference between the use of the words *turtle* and
dove. The turtle is a solitary bird, the dove a gregarious one; and accordingly the voice of the *turtle*
always denotes the revelation of those more secret
mysteries, the knowledge of which is confined to a few
great Saints, whereas the *dove* implies whatever is
made known to the lowliest, and therefore it was a
Dove, not a turtle, which descended on CHRIST at the
waters of Jordan, because His consecration to His
Priestly office was to be known to all mankind. And
there is a resurrection of CHRIST in every faithful soul S. Ambros.
also, when the winter of spiritual coldness, the rain of
temptation, are past and over, when the blossoms of Dion. Carth.
holy words and works spring out of the heart, when
the time comes for pruning away all luxuriant and
unprofitable growths:—or, if you take the word to be
singing,[1] the time for making melody in the heart with
spiritual song,—when the dove-like voice of pure,
faithful, and retired prayer goes up in supplication to
the LORD. Only One Dove, not many, as a Saint tells S. Bernard.
us, because the Inspirer of penitential prayer, Who Serm. 59.
Himself maketh intercession for us with groanings
which cannot be uttered, is but One. They take the Rom. viii. 26.
words also of the Annunciation, in the spring-time of
the year, when Mary heard the heavenly message: "O
fairest of the daughters of Jerusalem, thou heardest Hugo Victorin. Serm. de Assumpt.
the voice of the turtle, thou heardest and didst understand. He spake within, and thou wast within, therefore thou didst hear and understand, saying, It is the
voice of my Beloved." And, lastly, they take the
winter to be all the sorrowful exile of earth; the spring,
with its tokens of rejoicing, to denote the bliss of the
Heavenly Country, the true Land of GOD's people.
Our Land, as the Bride calls it, for her Bridegroom,
Who is LORD of it, gives it to her as a marriage present. The flowers are said to appear in the land because holy souls are received into heaven when they S. Greg. M.
depart from earth. And because they did not remain
slothful in good works in this life, winter though it
were, they blossom gloriously in the Land of the living.
It well follows: *The time of pruning is come,* because
the larger the number of the elect that is gathered into
heaven, the more swiftly are the reprobate cut off

---

[1] The Hebrew may denote singing, but not that of birds, as suggested by the italics of A. V.

from the Church as 'useless branches, that the world may come to an end. The great Portuguese preacher, in a touching funeral sermon delivered on the death of a young lady of rank, dwells on the juxtaposition of *flowering* and *pruning* in this verse. "The flowers," says he, "appear in our land, and Death grants them no longer time. They appear, they disappear. Behold the flowers, how the spring of their life is the autumn of their death. The pruning knife which is in his hand, is a tool for August, and not for April, but Death, with unseasonable activity, arms himself therewith, and threatens the buds, that the flowers may not guard themselves. O the sternness of it, O the disappointment! It is not the blow I grieve for, but its date. That there should be a time to bloom, and a time to prune, is natural, but that the time of blooming and of pruning should be the same, that the very flower of life should be the most frail, is hard indeed." The turtle which utters her voice is the Church, the land of the Bridegroom is the life of blessedness, her voice is heard therein, because her prayers, uttered in longing here, are received by CHRIST in heaven. And even here she has her flowers of promise, the foretaste of that bliss which, in its perfection, will be abundance of fruit.

<small>Vieyra, Serm. de las Exequias de Dona Maria de Atayde.</small>

<small>S. Greg. M. Hom. 16, in Ezek.</small>

13 The fig-tree putteth forth her green figs, and the vines with the tender grape give a good smell. Arise, my love, my fair one, and come away.

It is still only the promise of fruit. The fig-tree of the Synagogue, though unable to bring fruit to maturity, yet trained souls imperfectly to some degree of spiritual advance; reared its Nathaniels and other seekers after GOD, soon to be ripened in the sun of CHRIST's presence, and to develop into Apostles and Saints of His Church. And whereas the green figs, for the most part, fall from the tree before they ripen, so, though multitudes listened to CHRIST and His Apostles' preaching, comparatively few clung steadfastly to the Faith, or brought fruit to perfection. Others, however, take this falling away of the immature figs to denote the disappearance of the ceremonial rites of the Law. And taking the fig-tree to be the Christian, rather than the Jewish Church, they

<small>Cassiodor.</small>

<small>S. Ambros. Lib. vii. in S. Luc. c. 13.</small>

<small>Beda.</small>

tell us that its young fruits, soon to be so sweet, are the early Martyrs and Saints, and that the Vine of the Church put forth the grapes with a good smell, when the multitude of new converts filled the world with the fragrance of their holy works. S. Bernard prefers to distinguish two classes of Saints here, the meek and gentle, typified by the sweetness of the fig; the zealous and fervent, denoted by the glowing produce of the grape. Others, applying the words to the devout soul, tell us that the green figs denote the firstfruits of faith, immature, but the pledge of better things to follow. These grow, some allege, on the tree of human nature, not able of itself to achieve ripeness; but others tell us that the only tree which bears such fruit at all is the Cross, which bore no flowers, but at once gave the fruit of salvation to the world. And as the Chaldee paraphrase interprets the words as a summons to Israel to enter the Land of Promise, of which it is written, "They shall sit every man under his vine and under his fig-tree; none shall make them afraid," the words are also explained of the blessedness of heaven, and the foretaste of it which a holy life yields us even on earth. And therefore the Bridegroom again says, *Arise, my love, my fair one, and come away,* because in this pilgrimage and race, incessant advance and progress are needful, and the soul that has risen can go on rising, can come ever nearer to her GOD, finishing her course. And the repetition denotes, on His part, His tender affection, His eager longing for the salvation of mankind, wherefore He calls His beloved once more to her labour in the vineyard. So long as it is winter He suffers her to rest, He permits that in seasons of distress and tribulation quietness and confidence should be her strength, but the moment the time is again favourable, she must be up and doing His work upon the earth.

<small>Philo Carp. S. Greg. M.</small>
<small>S. Bernard. Serm. 60.</small>
<small>Theodoret. Psellus.</small>
<small>Corn. à Lap.</small>
<small>Targum.</small>
<small>Micah iv. 4. 1 Kings iv. 25. Zech. iii. 10.</small>
<small>S. Greg. Nyss. Hom. 5.</small>
<small>S. Bernard. Serm. 61.</small>
<small>Parez.</small>

14 O my dove, that art in the clefts of the rock, in the secret places of the stairs, let me see thy countenance, let me hear thy voice; for sweet is thy voice, and thy countenance is comely.

The Greek Fathers, remembering how the Apostle has said that the Rock is CHRIST, interpret the dwelling of the dove as the sure doctrines of the Faith, the mysteries of the Gospel. For the *secret places of*

<small>1 Cor. x. 4. Origen. Theodoret. Tres Patr.</small>

the stairs, the LXX. reads *having a bulwark,* or *outer wall,* which, Origen tells us, implies that the Bride is called out of the city, beyond its fortifications, to her labour, but is told that her path shall not be unsheltered, seeing that the shadow of the Rock will be over it. Others tell us that this *outer wall* is the old Law, and that we are called to pass from it to the safer refuge of the Gospel Rock. So too, a Western commentator bids us see in the *clefts of the Rock* the four Gospels, in the *cavern of the wall* (Vulg.,) the doctrine of the Apostles and the examples of the Saints. But he gives also that which is the favourite interpretation of the Latin Fathers, namely, that we are to see, in the clefts and cavern, the Five Wounds of the LORD's crucified Body. "I would understand by the *clefts of the Rock,*" observes S. Gregory, "the wounds of CHRIST's hands and feet as He hung upon the Cross; and in the same way, I should call the wound in His side, which was made with the spear, the *cavern of the wall.* Rightly is the dove said to be in the clefts of the Rock, and in the cavern of the wall, because when in meditating on the Cross she imitates CHRIST's patience, and calls His words to mind for her example, she is a dove in the clefts." They shall look, observes another, on Him whom they pierced. And He says, that the soul which sighs because of His piercing with the nails, is a dove in the clefts, and when grieving for the wound in His side, she is in the cavern of the wall. I was a *wall,* the LORD continues, when I was mortal and passible, but now that I have risen from the dead, I am a most strong Rock, nevertheless, the clefts are still to be seen in Me. "O happy clefts," exclaims the great Abbat of Clairvaux, "which build up faith in the Resurrection and in the Divinity of CHRIST! 'My LORD,' saith Thomas, 'and my GOD.' Whence came this oracle, save out of the clefts of the rock? Herein the sparrow hath found her an house, and the turtle a nest where she may lay her young. Herein the dove guards herself, and fearlessly looks on the wheeling hawk." He is here in unconscious accord with Homer:

φύγεν, ὥς τε πέλεια,
ἥ ῥάθ' ὑφ' Ἴρηκος κοίλην εἰσέπτατο πέτρην.

she fled; as flies a dove,
Shunning the falcon, to the hollow rock.

And he goes on to remind us how the bowels of

CHRIST's mercy may be seen by us through His gaping wounds, and how the Martyrs found their rest therein when their own bodies were but one huge wound under the torturer's hand. And so runs the hymn,

> Here is the heart's true bulwark found,
>   And here is rest secure,
> And here is love's most certain ground,
>   And here salvation sure.
> In this cleft Rock, once rent for all,
> And in this Heart's protecting wall,
>   May I confide, may I abide,
>   O JESU, SAVIOUR glorified.

The Hymn, Cor meum tibi dedo.

Again, while the *rock* must always mean CHRIST, the wall may be taken as the guard of Angels round about the elect, or as that wall of the Communion of Saints built up with living stones, wherein the soul may tarry for a time in contemplation of the holy lives of Saints departed. But if she will be perfect, she must pass from the disciples to the Master, from active imitation of the servants to loving gaze upon the face of the King. The wall may be insecure, the Rock never. And therefore it is well said to the Church Militant by the Prophet, "O ye that dwell in Moab, leave the cities, and dwell in the rock, and be like the dove that maketh her nest in the side of the hole's mouth." The words are taken by S. Bernard in yet another sense, as denoting the hidden mysteries of GOD's glory, wherein the contemplative soul makes her dwelling. The A. V. reading, *secret place of the stairs*, supported by the Chaldee paraphrase, but not by any of the old versions, accords very well with this last meaning, as the clause will then denote the gradual ascent of the soul towards GOD, up the steps of that ladder which Jacob saw in his dream, set up on the earth, and its top reaching to heaven, denoting the Manhood and Godhead of the One Mediator between GOD and man. It is in this latter sense of secret retirement and meditation on the mysteries of Divine love that we shall best apply the words to the Blessed Virgin, although more fanciful reasons are given by various commentators when explaining them of her, to whom is then said, *Show Me thy countenance*, in pure love and trust, not like Eve, who hid her face from Me in the garden after her sin, *let Me hear thy voice*, saying, "Behold the handmaid of the LORD, be it unto me according to Thy word," unlike Eve too, who was silent and uttered no word of

Beda. S. Bernard. Serm. 62.

Jer. xlviii. 28.

Ainsworth. S. Greg. M. Gen. xxviii. 12.

Philipp. Harveng.

Rupert.

Dion. Carth.

Rupert.

penitence when charged with her guilt, nor song of thanksgiving when I gave her the promise that her Seed should crush the serpent's head. The *face* and *voice* are, they tell us, the works and prayers of the Church or of the holy soul. As the face is the outer expression of our nature, so our purity of life and devoutness of zeal must be exhibited in action; and GOD requires our preaching of His kingdom, and our prayers and praises also, because "with the mouth confession is made unto salvation." Another and singular view sees here CHRIST calling on the Jewish Church, which had turned away its face from Him, to turn it back to Him now, though all stained with His Blood, that He may cleanse it with that very stream which has reddened it; to utter again in His ears that voice which had but lately yelled out the harsh and bitter cry, "Crucify Him, Crucify Him," that with the medicine of that same Blood, He may restore to her the power of celebrating His praises in sweet and musical tones. And He shows His love by telling the sinner that it is for His own sake as well as ours that He asks this, by adding of our harsh voice that it is *sweet*, of our disfigured countenance that it is *comely*. Some of the Greek Fathers take all the latter clause of this verse as the words of the Bride, desiring to see and hear CHRIST in the flesh, and no longer in prophetic mystery.

Origen.
Theodoret.
Beda.
S. Just. Org.

Rom. x. 10.
Aponius.

S. Epiphan.
S. Greg. Nyssen.
Philo Carp.
Psellus.

15 Take us the foxes, the little foxes, that spoil the vines: for our vines have tender grapes.

S. Bernard. Serm. 63.

The Bride has now obeyed her Bridegroom's summons, and they two have gone on together to the vineyards, but in no leisurely fashion, as the companions are at once called to the work of capturing the mischievous fox-cubs. And note that the Bridegroom speaks in the same terms as the Bride. She had spoken, but just now, of *our* land, claiming as hers what is His. He, in turn, says, Take *us* the foxes. "He might have said, Take *Me*, but through love of His fellowship with man, He says, Take *us*. O sweetness, O grace, O might of love! Is the Most Highest of all thus become one of all? Who hath done this? Love, that knows nothing of dignity, yet rich in dignity, powerful in affection, mighty in persuasion."

The Targum, explaining the little foxes to be the Amalekites, of whom is written, "Remember what Amalek did unto thee by the way, when ye were come forth out of Egypt; how he met thee by the way, and smote the hindmost of thee, even all that were feeble behind thee, when thou wast faint and weary; and he feared not GOD;" gives the key to the mystical sense. Accordingly, the primary interpretation is that heretics, spoiling the vineyard of the Church, but not actually striving to root up the vine, like the wild boar of Paganism or open unbelief, are intended. They are called *foxes* from their craft and deceit; *little* foxes, because of their external show of humility. They assign as another reason for the simile, that one well-known trick of foxes is to simulate death, lying stiff and extended, till their prey, taking courage, approaches near enough to be seized; resembling heretics, who make a special show of sanctity and deadness to the world, in order to deceive the unwary. And note, that the command is not to kill them, nor even to drive them out, but to *take* them. That is, comments the Doctor of Grace, to convince them of error, to convert them, and that, not only for their own sakes, adds another Saint, but for that of the Church in general. If the heretic be truly convinced of his sin, and so repent and be converted, we have gained him for GOD; if not, at any rate, the weaker members of the Church have been put on their guard by his detection, and are stablished in the true faith. S. Ambrose, citing that text, "the foxes have holes," says that heretics are aptly compared to foxes for this amongst other reasons, because they do not dwell in a house, but prefer a burrow of their own making, where they lie in wait for that hen of the Gospel which gathers her chickens under her wings. Secondly; it is said that the words are addressed by the Bridegroom to His companions, the Angels, directing them to extirpate the evil thoughts which the craft of the powers of darkness introduces into the vineyard of the soul in order to spoil its fruits. They *take* them, when they suggest to the spiritual understanding their true origin, and teach it, by the discerning of spirits, to know what is from GOD and what from the devil. They take them when *little*, by repressing them at once, before they have effected a lodgment in the soul, and before they have grown to maturity by being willingly dwelt on. They are called

Targum.
Deut. xxv. 17, 18.

Origen, &c.

Ps. lxxx. 13.

S. Greg. M.

Hugo Card.

Dion. Carth.

S. August. in Ps. lxxx.

S. Bernard. Serm. 64.

S. Ambros. lib. vii. in S. Luc. c. 9.

Origen.

Tres Patr. S. Greg. Nyss.

foxes, too, and *little* foxes, by way of contempt, to make us learn that they are no formidable enemies, lions, tigers, bears, endowed with gigantic strength, that we have to encounter, but rather skulking foes, whose whole resource is craft, needing only watchfulness as the sole weapon to repel it. S. Bernard, applying the passage to the Religious Life, remarks that the words do not refer to the spiritual perils which beset novices, because their vocation is only in its flower, and the foxes wish for fruit. The danger of novices is, that a frost of spiritual coldness may blight the promise of their early zeal, but the peril of the professed is more subtle, namely, that Satan will transform himself for them into an angel of light, and suggest ideas to them which look like virtues, but which lead to sin. He specifies such examples as a Religious leaving the convent and returning to the world for a time, in the hope of converting kindred and friends, and bringing them to the same haven, but being, instead, led back by them into secular habits. Or, on the contrary, withdrawing for the opposite reason of desiring a solitary life in a hermitage, and then falling, either because of the removal of the external constraining discipline of a community or from spiritual pride. Again; excessive and unprescribed fasting and penances are more likely, adds the Saint, to lead to evil than to good, because they give rise to scandal in one way or other by introducing a different standard of practice into the house from that recognized by authority. On the other hand, the *little foxes* of a Religious house are petty relaxations and violations of the rule, such as breaking silence, lack of punctuality, and other seeming trifles, which, if not checked at the outset, finally subvert the whole discipline and order of the community. And observe, it is not merely necessary to take the foxes which have already made their way into the vineyard, but to keep others out for the future, and this must be done with a wall or fence. Not with one so low and so slightly put together that our enemy can say of it, "Even that which they build, if a fox go up he shall even break down their stone wall." The stones must first be laid in close order, so that no crevices shall be in the wall; next, they must be built up to a considerable height, so as not to be climbed over; thirdly, they must be cemented with mortar, that they may not be dislodged. So the prayers and good works of a soul which seeks to keep the enemy aloof must be regular and continuous, not intermittent and casual; they must be numerous, so as to fill up the day in such wise as to leave few idle moments for temptation, they must be bound together with that binding cement of love towards GOD and our neighbour, whose chief ingredient is the precious Blood of CHRIST. Again; they remind us how the LORD, speaking of Herod Antipas, said, "Go, tell that fox," and thereby showed another class of enemies of the vine to be here intended. "See you not how that wild beast has eaten the tender shoots, how that cruel monster hath slain the infants in Bethlehem of Judah, the city of David? *Take the foxes, for our vineyard hath flowered.* (Vulg.) Its fruit is yet in flower, and not in grape; it is not yet ripe, and therefore it is most destructive to the vineyard that its flower should be cut down or spoiled. Let it grow first and let fruit come of the flower, let the Gospel be founded, and let it be known by signs and wonders that the Holy of Holies hath come,—this will be the coming of the flower to fruit, of the grape to ripeness. Then, if this grape be cut down, it will be kept, and carried on the pole of the Cross; that by the proof of its Resurrection and sweetness, men may learn what is the Land, what is the Kingdom, with which the little foxes, which spoil the vines, have nought to do." The Syriac, LXX. and Vulgate translate the last clause more correctly than the A. V., rendering it, *our vines (vineyard,* Vulg.) *are in flower.* This is the time to take the foxes, for when the time of ripeness has arrived, the LORD of the vineyard will come Himself for the vintage of the mature grapes, and then there can be no more peril from the craft of the enemy. And, finally; the words may be explained as spoken to the Angels in the Day of Judgment, according to that saying of the LORD, "So shall it be in the end of the world. The Son of Man shall send forth His angels, and they shall gather out of His kingdom all things that offend, and them which do iniquity, and shall cast them into a furnace of fire." Especially is it spoken of the evil spirits, who strive to injure His vineyard. And then truly will His vine flourish in luxuriant beauty for evermore.

S. Luke xiii. 32. Rupert.

Cf. Hengstenberg, in loc.

Honorius.

S. Mat. xiii. 40.

16 My beloved is mine, and I am his: he feedeth among the lilies.

"For they two shall be one flesh. This is a great mystery: but I speak concerning CHRIST and the Church." Her Beloved is hers, because He is her Head; she is His, because she is His Body. "My Beloved is mine, saith the holy soul, He gives me the grace of vocation, the badge of redemption, the glorious liberty of adoption. And what do I give Him? Obedience of will, the desire of preserving that purity which He gave me by nature. What gives He to me? A perfect example of guarding virginity, by His Virgin birth. What give I to Him? Singular gladness by my being born again in Baptism, by keeping His precepts with all my heart, by imitating the nature of angels and heavenly spirits." And whereas the Hebrew, as well as the LXX. and Vulgate, reads simply, *My Beloved to me, and I to Him,* they delight in supplying words to complete the idea variously. *My Beloved* is careful *for me,* anxious for my salvation. *I* am careful *for Him,* to obey Him in all things. *He* co-operates *with me,* by His assisting grace, *I with Him* by my free will, thus being a "labourer together with GOD." *My Beloved* is like *to me,* in nature, having taken on Him the form of a servant. I am like *to Him* by grace, being made holy and pure, and wise through His gift. *He is* the reward *to me* of all my toils, suffering, and weariness. *I am* the reward *to Him* of all the sorrows of His life, and of His Passion. *He* lived and died for me wholly, and *to me.* *I* will live and die *to Him,* "for whether we live, we live unto the LORD, and whether we die, we die unto the LORD." *My Beloved* drank *to me* in the Cup of His Passion; *I* drink It *to Him* in His honour and glory, taking the Cup of Salvation, and calling on the Name of the LORD. *My Beloved* spake *to me,* revealing to me the mysteries of His law, *I to Him* in psalms, and hymns, and spiritual songs. *My Beloved* is wisdom *to me : I* am heart *to Him. He* comes from heaven *to me, I* from the Gentiles *to Him.* And S. Bernard bids us note the briefness, and as it were incoherence, of the Bride's words. She is too fervent and eager to be altogether silent; she is too deeply and inexpressibly happy to say much. And thus infrequent speech is a mark in Scripture of that especial soul which could more truly than any other say, My Beloved is mine, and I am His, because I am she of whom is written, "A Virgin shall conceive, and bear a Son, and shall call

His Name Immanuel;" and therefore, "all genera- *S. Luke i. 48.*
tions shall call me blessed." There is an old poem,
written with a lower intent, which, taken in a better
meaning, makes a good comment on this verse:

> My true-love hath my heart, and I have his,   *Sir Philip*
> By just exchange one to the other given: *Sidney.*
> I hold his dear, and mine he cannot miss,
> There never was a better bargain driven,
>   My true-love hath my heart, and I have his.
>
> His heart in me keeps him and me in one,
> My heart in him his thoughts and senses guides,
> He loves my heart, for once it was his own,
> I cherish his, because in me it bides,
>   My true-love hath my heart, and I have his.

He feedeth among the lilies. What are denoted by *S. Greg. M.*
the lilies, asks a Saint, save pure souls? which retain the whiteness of chastity, and by their fair fame
give their pleasant fragrance to all near them. The
Bridegroom *feedeth among the lilies*, doubtless because
He delights in purity of souls, which both preserve
bodily chastity, and are pleasant unto Him by their
stainless thoughts, giving, at the same time, a pattern
to their neighbours, as though a grateful savour. And
so runs the hymn for the Common of Virgins:

> Who feedest where the lilies spring,   *The Hymn,*
> Surrounded by the Virgin ring,   *Jesu,*
> With glory decking them, Thy brides,   *Corona*
> And granting spousal gifts besides.   *Virginum.*

Our Beloved is fed, when we love Him, for His food *Nic. Arg.*
is our love; and our sighs, affections, desires, and aspirations are His chosen dainties. He is among the
lilies, says S. Bernard, of His own truth, and meek- *S. Bernard.*
ness, and righteousness, lilies which have sprung out *Serm. 70.*
of the earth, shining thereon, conspicuous amongst the
other flowers, fragrant beyond all spices. As many
virtues as there are, so many are His lilies, and they
are countless, all snowy white, all sweetly perfumed.
Our lilies of good works are few and poor, and much *Serm. 71.*
intermingled with flowers of less account, yet He loves
them, and is fain to dwell amongst them, continuing
as He began, for He dwelt first on earth between the *Rupert.*
lilies of the pure lives of Joseph and Mary in the car-
penter's dwelling at Nazareth. So far, the text has
been taken of CHRIST feeding Himself. But its fuller

sense appears to be that He is here spoken of as the Good Shepherd, feeding us in His pleasant pastures. "The divine Mysteries," comments S. Ambrose, "are good pastures. There thou mayest gather that new flower which gave the sweet odour of the Resurrection, there pluck the lily, wherein is the brightness of eternity; there too the rose, the Blood of the LORD's Body. The books of Holy Writ are also good pastures, wherein we are fed by daily reading, wherein we obtain refreshment and strength, when we taste what is written in them, or chew the cud of frequent thought over it. In these pastures the LORD's flock is fattened. Good too are the pastures of CHRIST, Who feeds us among the lilies, that is, in the glory of the Saints." In this last sense the Cluniac also, speaking of the joys of Paradise:

In Ps. cxix.

Bern. Cluniac. Rhythm.

> While through the sacred lilies,
> And flowers on every side,
> The happy dear-bought nations
> Go wandering far and wide.

Esth. ii. 8. And that, because "when the King's commandment and His decree was heard, many maidens were gathered together unto Shushan the palace," for Shushan is by interpretation, "Lily."

17 Until the day break, and the shadows flee away, turn, my beloved, and be thou like a roe or a young hart upon the mountains of Bether.

S. Greg. M.

S. Bernard. Serm. 72.

Until the day of Resurrection, the *day* of the revelation of eternal glory, dawns, until the *shadows* of this world's night *flee away*, so long does the Bridegroom feed amongst the lilies of pure souls obeying Him truly upon earth. But why, asks S. Bernard, is it said *Until?* Should we not rather expect that He would feed more among the abundant lilies of heaven than amongst the rare ones of earth? And the saint replies that the reason is twofold. First; we sinners here have to be incorporated into CHRIST's mystical Body, and that we may be so, have to be ground with His teeth of suffering and trial, but there will be no sinners and no suffering in heaven, wherefore the LORD speaks not of eating there, but says that He will drink new wine in His kingdom, and that, because the Saints, after their full refinement from all dregs, which cannot be accomplished in this life, will be the sweet and pure wine of the marriage feast. The Carthusian, more simply, bids us see here a warning to us to cultivate the lilies of purity in our hearts by holiness of thought, word, and deed, until the close of our lives, that the Lamb may find His accustomed pasture in some few spots at least of the world. When the day comes, we shall no longer need to tend our gardens, for their flowers will be perennial, their dangers gone. Others take the *day* to be the preaching of the Gospel, before which the *shadows* of the Law disappeared, though even under that Law CHRIST was feeding His people as their Shepherd. But the literal sense of the Hebrew is somewhat unlike all this. It points to the coming-on of the evening, not to the dawn of day, and runs, *Until the day breathe*, that is, till the cool evening breeze sets in, *and the shadows flee*, that is, lengthen out before us, becoming vaguer in their outline. And this is the sense of both LXX. and Vulgate, though most of the commentators have followed the other view. And so rendering the passage, we shall follow the traditional Hebrew construction, and take it with the clause which follows, rather than with that which precedes. The Bride is called to her labour, and the Bridegroom, after the summons, departs, leaving her alone. She, knowing herself unable to accomplish her labour unaided, calls on Him to *turn* back again to help her, and that so long as the working-day continues, remembering that it is written, "Man goeth forth unto his work and to his labour until the evening." The nearer the night is, the shorter the time that remains for completing our appointed task, the greater need have we of His help, and we therefore say, "Abide with us, for it is toward evening, and the day is far spent." And S. Anselm therefore applies the word *turn* to the LORD's co-operation with His Church in the conversion of the heathen. Others see rather a prayer to Him to visit our souls, even if only in the sudden and rare semblance of a stag appearing at intervals upon the hills. Again; some take it of His return to judgment, coming in that same human form which He took of us, and His Resurrection and Ascension have been also thought to be here referred to. *Upon the mountains of Bether*. Some take these to be

S. Mat. xxvi. 29.

Dion. Carth.

S. Just. Org.

Sanchez.

Hugo Card.

Ps. civ. 23.

Hengstenberg.
S. Luke xxiv. 29.
S. Anselm.
Cassiodor.
Beda.
S. Greg. M.
S. Bernard.
Serm. 73.
Aponius.
Rupert.
S. Just. Org.
Theodoret.
Philo Carp.

the proud and haughty, to be brought low when CHRIST appears and sets Himself above them, while others, conversely, take it of His visits to lofty and contemplative souls. *Bether*, meaning "division," a region cut up by a chain of hills pierced with valleys in every direction (whence the LXX. *mountains of hollows*,) denotes here anything which parts us from CHRIST, and we, unable to surmount the obstacle ourselves, pray to Him to *turn*, and show the light of His countenance, that we may be whole. Further than this, it is a prayer to Him to break down the mid-wall of partition between Jew and Gentile; and yet more, to come from the mountains of division, parting believers from idolaters, into that wide place of the Church Universal, "where there is neither Greek nor Jew, circumcision nor uncircumcision, Barbarian, Scythian, bond nor free, but CHRIST is all, and in all." And De Lyra, who, according to his wont, explains the mountain to be those of Sinai, when Israel's sin in the matter of the calf caused GOD to threaten that He would abandon and destroy them, thereby points the lesson that all occasions of sin are necessarily gulfs opened between the soul and GOD. Finally; in the petition of the Bride for the perfect bliss of heaven, it is not enough for her longing that she should merely enter in there, unless her Bridegroom come close to her Himself, leaping over the nine divisions of the Angelic hierarchy, in order to come to her who is of His own nature, bone of His bone and flesh of His flesh.

CHAPTER III.

1 By night on my bed I sought him whom my soul loveth : I sought him, but I found him not.

While mankind lay on its bed of sickness, smitten with the deadly disease of sin, and in the midst of the darkness of ignorance, it looked eagerly on every side for the coming of the Great Physician, but could nowhere find Him, till the time when He, our true Elisha, came of His own loving-kindness to stretch Himself on the couch of our mortality, to rouse the lifeless sleeper. So too, until His Advent, the Synagogue lay on the bed of the Mosaic Law, looking for her LORD in the dark shadows of the ceremonial types and of the hidden prophecies, and found Him no more than the Gentiles did. And as night denotes the time of rest as well as of darkness, so here we may see the Church in its earliest days resting after Pentecost, and confining itself and its preaching to Jerusalem and Judea, but not finding CHRIST in the hard hearts of the Jews, who refused to hear the glad tidings and to put on Him. And therefore she was compelled to rise up from that brief repose, and begin the long journey of her mission to the heathens, never ended since. Taken of the soul, rather than of the Church at large, it may be variously interpreted. They say, for the most part, that it denotes the impossibility of finding CHRIST while we lie down in carnal pleasure, and in the darkness of sin. Or, again, not quite so sternly, but still in a voice of warning, they tell us that it is not in bodily ease and quiet that we can find CHRIST, Whose bed was not of down, but the hard Cross: *[S. Ambros. in Ps. cxix. Corn. à Lap. Cassiod. Beda. Philo Carp. Angelomus. Vieyra.]*

> Ah, malè te placido quæsivi, Sponse, cubili; *[Hugo. Pia Desid. ii. 10.]*
> Qui Crucis in thalamo reperiendus eras.
> Pax mihi lectus erat. Tibi Crux erat aspera lectus.
> Hoc te debueram quærere, Sponse, toro.
>
> Ill sought I Thee in my hushed place of rest,
> Spouse, Whom the Cross's bridal-chamber shrined,
> My bed was peace, the rough Cross Thou hast pressed,
> That is the couch where, seeking, I shall find.

There are many, observes S. Ambrose, who seek CHRIST in ease, and find Him not, and then seek Him in persecution, straightway finding Him; and for this reason they find Him after temptations, because He is always at hand in the peril of His faithful ones. "Alas, LORD," exclaims one of the greatest of penitents, "I went very far to seek Thee, and Thou wast very near. I may find Thee in mine eyes, by modesty and purity; in my mouth, by confession of Thy greatness and my sins; in my memory, by the remembrance of my iniquity and Thy mercies; in my mind, by holy thoughts and meditations on Thy Divine Law; but above all, I shall find Thee in my heart, because, if I love Thee, it cannot be but that Thou shouldest rest there." There is *[S. Ambros. de Isaac. 5. S. August. Confess.]*

a happier sense, however, in which we may look at the words, as agreeing with that saying of David, "Have I not remembered Thee in my bed; and thought upon Thee when I was waking?" We seek our Beloved on our *bed*, when during any brief repose in this life we sigh with longing for our Redeemer. We seek *by night*, because though the soul is watchful in it, the eye is clouded. And on this a devout author speaks: "Fear not, O Bride, nor despair; think not thyself despised if thy Bridegroom withdraw His face awhile. All things work together for good. Both from His absence and His presence thou gainest light. He cometh to thee and He departeth from thee. He cometh to comfort thee; He departeth, to make thee careful, lest thine abundant consolation should puff thee up. He cometh, that the languishing soul may be comforted. He departeth, lest, if the Bridegroom be always with thee, thou shouldest despise His companions, and thou shouldest ascribe this constant visitation not to grace, but to nature. He departs therefore, lest, if too continually with thee, He should meet with contempt, that, being absent, He may be more desired, and being desired, be more eagerly sought; and being long sought, may be more gladly found." There are many ways, then, in which we may seek Him; there are many reasons why we should seek Him. And first, we may seek in the quiet of still contemplation. Thou art well placed on thy bed, observes a famous English Abbat, if thy soul keep free holiday in repose from its occupations, for what suits love better than repose and freedom? And night is good, which covers in wise oblivion all temporal things, that we may seek Him Who is Eternal; a convenient time, unfolding favourable opportunities, and hiding from us the desire, the care, and the very thought of the world. Even in the night of trouble and sorrow we can still seek Him in contemplation. But as the words are spoken by a still imperfect soul, she does not say, On *our* bed, denoting completed union with her Spouse, nor on *His* bed, but on *my* bed. Still, even so, it is the place where her passions have been hushed to sleep, and where victory after strife has come. She seeks Him then, pondering on His works, following His traces through creation, from stones to plants, from plants to animals, from them to man, thence to the Angels, but finds Him not, because He is exalted above all, and she must soar to the highest before she can reach his throne. *I found Him not*, only because He dwells in that light inaccessible which is night to man's eyes, not because I failed to search diligently. So Mary Magdalene sought Him in the bed of His sepulchre, coming before the dawn, and found Him not, because she looked for the living among the dead, and yet was blessed in her seeking. And thus S. Bernard couples the two ideas in his lovely hymn: *[S. Dionys. Areop. S. Greg. Nyss. Thom. Vercell.]*

> JESUM quæram in lectulo,
> Clauso cordis cubiculo ;
> Privatim et in populo
> Quæram amore sedulo.
>
> Cum Mariâ diluculo
> JESUM quæram in tumulo ;
> Cordis clamore querulo
> Mente quæram, non oculo.
>
> I seek for JESUS in repose,
> When round my heart its chambers close ;
> Abroad, and when I shut the door,
> I long for JESUS evermore.
>
> With Mary, in the morning gloom,
> I seek for JESUS at the tomb ;
> For Him, with love's most earnest cry,
> I seek with heart, and not with eye.

[S. Bernard. Rhyth. Jubilus.]

So then, the sleep, thus taken, does not typify spiritual sloth, but that fulness of love which makes the Bridegroom present even in the dreams of the Bride. And that because she knows so many reasons for seeking Him when she wakes. Upon these let us hear S. Bernard again: And first, because He is not always to be found, as He has Himself said: "Ye shall seek Me, but ye shall not find Me;" and that from seeking at the wrong time, by the wrong way, or in the wrong place. Wherefore the Prophet says, "Seek ye the LORD while He may be found," before He shuts the door against the foolish Virgins. Now is the accepted time, before the bed of death, before the night of the grave, in which there is no redemption. And here He must be sought eagerly, carefully, in no half-hearted and leisurely fashion. Not after the flesh either, in the bed of His tomb, His manger-cradle, or His Mother's womb, but in Heaven His dwelling-place. *My* bed is mortal weakness: *His* bed is Divine power. I *sought* Him there in the night of my ignorance, in the feeble-

[Aben Ezra. S.Ans.Laud.]

[S. Bernard. Serm. 75.]

[S. John vii. 34.]

[Isa. lv. 6.]

ness of my spiritual night. And yet, even so, it was good to seek Him, for it is written truly, "Seek His face evermore," even after He is found, seeking Him with desire when He need no longer be sought with the step. It is good for the lost sheep to seek the Shepherd who first sought it; good for seven reasons. First, for correction; agreeing in time with that Adversary who wars against our sins. Next, for enlightenment, that the WORD may be a lantern to our feet. Thirdly, for ghostly strength, that He may comfort us according to His Word, that we fall not when the world, the flesh, or the devil attempts to cast us down. Fourthly, for the sake of learning wisdom, only to be learnt from Him Who is Himself the Eternal Wisdom. Fifthly, to recover the beauty lost by sin. Sixthly, for fruitfulness in spiritual wedlock, bringing forth good works abundantly, and rearing fresh children for CHRIST. And lastly, because of the perfect gladness to be found in the enjoyment of the WORD. O whoever thou art that wouldst fain know what this means, to enjoy the WORD, prepare for Him thy soul, not thine ear. The tongue teaches it not, but grace. It is hidden from the wise and prudent, and revealed unto babes. It is sweet, remarks another, taking up the subject just where the dying Abbat of Clairvaux laid it down, to seek Thee, O good JESU, it is sweeter to hold Thee. The one is loving toil, the other perfect gladness. Good it is to seek Him on the bed in contemplation, for "in peace is His habitation, and His dwelling in Sion." *By nights* (Heb. LXX. Vulg.) I sought Him. The nights are many, the bed is but one. Many are the sorrows and trials of the righteous, but they bear them all on the one bed of their calling, saying, "I will lay me down in peace, and take my rest." So it may be taken too of the bed of sickness, when the LORD makes the bed of the patient.

    O how soft that bed must be,
    Made in sickness, LORD, by Thee,
    And that rest,—how calm, how sweet,
    Where JESUS and the sufferer meet!

    It was the Good Physician now,
    Soothed my cheek and chafed my brow,
    Whispering, as He raised my head,
    "It is I, be not afraid."

And, once more, the *bed* may be taken to denote the

quiet, as the *night* does the coolness and obscurity of the Religious Life, wherein many a soul has sought the Bridegroom, and found Him too at the last, though He may have at first concealed Himself to incite a closer search, according to His own saying, "In a little wrath I hid My face from thee for a moment; but with everlasting kindness will I have mercy on thee, saith the LORD thy Redeemer." The Bridegroom hides Himself when He is sought, that He may be more eagerly sought when not found, and the searching Bride is put off in her quest, that made more capable by the very delay, she may at length find in manifold more ways that which she sought for. Ghislerius.

Isa. liv. 8.

S. Greg. M. Moral. v. 4.

2 I will rise now, and go about the city in the streets, and in the broad ways I will seek him whom my soul loveth : I sought him, but I found him not.

I will rise now. The A.V. here implies a resolve to instant action; but the Hebrew נָא, *na*, does not denote this, but rather, *I will therefore rise*, or, *Come now, I will rise*. Because I cannot find Him on my bed, I will seek Him elsewhere. And observe first that the exertion determined on is considerable. The Bride does not make a small effort, and say, I will go about *my chamber*, but, I will go about *the city*. The Targum, which takes the preceding verse to denote the withdrawal of GOD's presence in the Shechinah from the congregation of Israel when they made the Golden Calf, explains this of the people going round the camp from tribe to tribe, and outside it to the tabernacle of the Covenant, seeking vainly for any trace of the cloud of glory. So too, the primary sense given by ancient Christian writers to the *City* here is that it denotes the Church. Literally, it may be taken of the Apostles preaching in the earthly Jerusalem, but finding Moses, not CHRIST, in the hearts of its people; or, with S. Bernard, of the eager looking of many imperfectly instructed hearers, searching if CHRIST might be seen again in those streets and ways through which He had passed teaching and healing, unknowing that He had gone up from the earthly to the Heavenly Jerusalem. And so Jeremiah had spoken, saying, "Run ye to and fro in the streets of Jerusalem, and Targum.

Corn. à Lap.

S. Bernard. Serm. 76.

Jer. v. 1.

see now, and know, and seek in the broad places thereof, if ye can find a Man, if there be any that executeth judgment, that seeketh the truth; and I will pardon it." And it was foretold in type that the Eternal Wisdom should so be found, for it is written in another place, "Wisdom crieth without, she uttereth her voice in the streets; she crieth in the chief place of concourse, in the openings of the gates, in the city she uttereth her words." Nor are we left in doubt as to the fulfilment of this saying, for in the Gospel we read, "Thou hast taught in our streets." But they did not listen when He was there, and now He must be sought elsewhere, in another city, to wit, the Church Militant here in earth. Some say that the streets and ways denote the two kinds of life within the Church, secular and religious, each having its Saints, and its profitable examples, but the one narrower and more spiritual, the other broader and more carnal. In each of these the Bride seeks for examples and counsels which may help to bring her to her Beloved. Another takes the Holy Scriptures to be the ways of the Church, through which the soul seeks her LORD, but finds Him not, so long as she looks to the letter alone, and not the spirit. Again, remembering that there are two cities, Jerusalem on high, and Babylon below, some think the latter to be meant here, as signifying the whole world. And then the streets and ways denote the weary pilgrimage by land and sea of Gentiles seeking the LORD everywhere, if haply they might find Him, in sects of philosophy, in mysterious rites, in cloudy speculations, yet not discovering Him, save in such rare cases as those of Cornelius and the eunuch of Queen Candace. But that He is not to be found in the pursuit of secular things is a lesson which they enforce with much care. "CHRIST is no haunter of the market. For CHRIST is peace, in the market is strife. CHRIST is righteousness, in the market is iniquity. CHRIST is good faith, in the market is fraud and deceit. CHRIST is a worker, in the market is idle leisure. CHRIST is charity, in the market is disparagement. Then the market is often a place of thieves, CHRIST is in the Church, idols in the market. In the Church the widow is justified,[1] in the market she is cheated. Let

---

[1] The theological use of this famous term in this passage is noteworthy. It plainly means "justly dealt with,"

us then shun the market, shun the ways. For it is not only bad for you not to find Him whom you seek, but it is generally hurtful to have sought Him in the wrong place." One cannot but agree with S. Ambrose in the earlier portion of this comment, but a profounder intellect than his takes a widely different view of the influence of the search itself upon the soul. Hear Richard of S. Victor on this point: " The Bride sought her Beloved through the streets and ways, and found Him not at her wish. She did not yet feel His presence, did not yet win the grace for which she longed. But I have no doubt that she gained much by her journey, and greatly increased her inner grace; since no slight longing after righteousness was kindled in her from her recognition of good men and their virtues. For she drew near those who burned with that fire which the LORD JESUS came to send on earth, and willed earnestly that it should be kindled. And in drawing near to them the lukewarm begins to glow, and the fervent takes fire more eagerly." Again, the *city* is taken by some in the yet wider sense of the whole creation, whose streets and ways are all things visible and invisible. The *streets*, narrow, and easily learnt, are visible, tangible, earthly things; the *ways* or *broad places*, (Heb. LXX. Vulg.) are heavenly and invisible things, harder for the mind to take in with its glance, but He Who is Uncreate is not even there, no, not in the highest: <small>Ricard. Vict.</small>

<small>Psellus. Gillebert. Nic. Argent.</small>

> Thou art not here, . . . for how should these contain Thee ?
> Thou art not here, . . . for how should I sustain Thee ?
>   But Thou, where'er Thou art,
> Canst hear the voice of prayer,
> Canst read the righteous heart.

<small>Southey, *Curse of Kehama*, xix. 10.</small>

Descending with rapid plunge from the contemplation of the whole universe, we come, with the Greek Fathers, to the search in the microcosm of a single human soul. This *city*, "whose builder and maker is GOD," has its *streets* of action, its *broad places* of contemplation, wherein the Beloved is sought. And thus Saints may look. But sinners have to do it in another <small>Heb. xi. 10.

Tres Patr.</small>

"fairly treated," and is opposed to injustice and fraud. It is obvious that S. Ambrose understood "justifying faith" to be that which puts a man	in the way of becoming just and righteous, not a quibble which calls him innocent when he is defiled with sin.

way, by carefully going over every year, nay every action, of past life, with examination of conscience by the rule of Scripture, looking not merely in the *streets*, or their own more personal and private sins, but in the *broad ways* of corporate offences, and of conformity to conventional rules of right and wrong, trying if CHRIST be visible in any part of their old conversation, in order that, learning that He is not there, they may turn utterly away from it, and seek Him in that holiness where only He may be found, " in the city of our GOD, even upon His holy hill." And so the Apostle saith: "Awake, thou that sleepest, and arise from the dead, and CHRIST shall give thee light." *I will arise*, then, not from evil works, not from bad habits, but from good to better; from habits to mysteries, from things hidden to things manifest, from calm to sweetness. *I will arise*, for CHRIST hath risen. Why should I not rise when I know of the resurrection of my Beloved? O happy me, if I had risen together with CHRIST, setting my affections on things above, and seeking Him not below, but above, for I should doubtless have found Him at the right hand of the FATHER. When once we enter into the gates of the Heavenly Jerusalem, there will be no need to seek Him any more, for He, as its Light, will pervade all its streets and ways. And observe that it is well said, I sought Him through the *streets* and *ways*, and found Him not, for there is only one Way to the City where He dwells, and that Way is Himself. And therefore, as we search vainly here, He tells us, "This is not the way, neither is this the city: follow Me, and I will bring you to the Man Whom ye seek." And so, after our journey away from Him, after our vain search in the company, after our retracing every step of our former way, we shall find Him, as His Mother did, in the Temple of GOD.

Philo Carp.
Ps. xlviii. 1.
Eph. v. 14.
Gillebert.
S. Bernard. Serm. 75.
S. August.
2 Kings vi. 19.
Rupert.

3 The watchmen that go about the city found me: to whom I said, Saw ye him whom my soul loveth?

The watchmen that guard (Vulg.) *the city*, who find the soul thus longing and seeking, are the holy Angels, who guard the Church, or the faithful, and by whose guardianship the mercy of CHRIST protects His own.

They are well named *watchmen*, because they watch <small>Ricard. Vict.</small>
and are careful about the elect, that they may be defended from temptation, may advance in good, and
may attain salvation. And so the Breviary hymn:

> Custodes hominum psallimus Angelos,   <small>Hymn. in</small>
> Naturæ fragili quos PATER addidit   <small>Fest. Ang.</small>
> Cœlestis comites, insidiantibus   <small>Cust.</small>
>   Ne succumberet hostibus.

> The Angel Guards of men we hail,
> Sent by our GOD to mortals frail
> As aids, lest we in battle fail
>   Before the crafty foe.

The soul, then, searching for GOD, is found by these, and after going round the city and making her quest, she attains to the appearance of the blessed Angels, she perceives their approach, and is received by them, for they are forerunners of the Bridegroom, and they disclose their presence, revealing themselves. For they are Angels of light, and come with light, whereby she is flooded and illuminated, and reached all at once, so that she is aware of their approach, and feels their presence. Before, she was blind, and felt only herself, now, the grace given her teaches her more. Then her longing breaks out into words, and she complains that her door is open for Him, and yet He does not enter, that she stands knocking at His door, and He does not open. He has promised to come, and promised to open, yet He seems to fail. Where then is He? for ye, who ever behold His face, must surely know. *They found me*, and set to work to purify me by action, <small>Theodoret.</small> and to enlighten me by contemplation, dead as I was in sin and ignorance, and the pupil of evil spirits. They did this, and more, for me; but they could not answer my question, because my Bridegroom is as incomprehensible to Angels as to men.

Again, the *watchmen of the city* are the teachers raised up by GOD in His Church at various times. Patriarchs, Prophets, Apostles, Doctors, of whom is written, " I have set watchmen upon thy walls, O Je- <small>Isa. lxii. 6.</small> rusalem, which shall never hold their peace day nor night;" and in another place, "Also I set watchmen <small>Jer. vi. 17.</small> over you, saying, Hearken unto the sound of the trumpet." With this view, which is the more usual one, agrees the Chaldee paraphrase, explaining the words of Moses and Aaron watching over the congre- <small>Targum.</small>

gation of Israel. What good watchmen, exclaims S. Bernard, who keep long watch while we are sleeping, as having to give account for our souls! What good guards, who watching in soul and passing the night in prayers, skilfully track out the ambushes of the enemy, forestall the counsels of the malignant, detect the snares, avoid the springes, break 'the nets, frustrate the schemings. These are lovers of the brethren and of the Christian people, who pray much for the people, and all the holy city. These are they who, careful for the LORD's sheep committed unto them, give their heart to resort early unto the LORD Who made them, and will pray before the Most High. And though they do all this, and instruct the soul which is seeking CHRIST, yet it is not enough that she should passively drink in their teaching. She must exhibit eagerness, longing, must actively search for herself, not merely let them search in her behalf, and therefore she asks, *Have ye seen Him?* For when the soul fixes herself on these mere teachers and watchmen, looking to them, and setting them up as her standard, and not searching further for her LORD, she does not find Him. She must *pass from them* to Him. And in saying, *The watchmen found me,* rather than *I found them,* the Bride marks the vigilance and zeal of good pastors of the Church, who themselves seek out souls that are looking for CHRIST, that they may bring them to His feet. They take the whole passage also of the Church of the Gentiles, asking the philosophers and idol priests, who disputed with her, the one unanswerable question, *Have ye seen Him?* It is the Jewish Church also, looking for Him in the City of Holy Writ, in its broad prophecies, and narrow dark types, and accosting its watchmen, the Chief Priests, Scribes, and Pharisees, with the same inquiry, *Have ye seen Him?* And they get no reply in either case, for "unless the LORD keep the city, the watchman waketh but in vain." The world knew Him not, and His own, to whom He came, received Him not. I asked my senses, *Have ye seen Him?* And my sight said, Nay, unless He be an image. But He is Truth itself, and no mere image or phantasm. I asked my hearing, and it replied, Unless He be a sound or a melody, I know Him not. And yet He is this too, the WORD Who is music to His own. I asked my touch, and it answered, Unless He be smoothness or roughness, I have not seen Him. Yet this also He is, gentle to others, harsh to Himself in His suffering life. I asked my sense of smell, and it rejoined, If He be not a perfume, I know Him not. Yet He is this too, an offering to GOD for a sweet-smelling savour. I asked my taste, and it replied, If He be not a flavour, I cannot tell. This also is He Who is our Food, sweet to our taste. All, and more than all, yet the senses cannot find Him. I asked all creation, Sun, I said, moon, and stars, sky, earth, and sea, *Have ye seen Him?* And they answered, We are not the Beloved, we are but His works, and we cannot contain nor comprehend Him.

4 It was but a little that I passed from them, but I found him whom my soul loveth : I held him, and would not let him go, until I had brought him into my mother's house, and into the chamber of her that conceived me.

But a little, whether spoken of time or of place. And yet CHRIST's coming was nine hundred years after the utterance of this Song; four hundred years after Malachi, the last of the prophetic watchmen, sealed up the oracles of GOD; but they seemed but as a few days to the Church because of the love she bore to Him. *I passed from them*. That is, observes one Father, when I had learnt fully all they had to teach me, when I had *gone through* this course of instruction, I found Him. But the majority take it more deeply: When I had left them all behind in search of Him Who is above and beyond them all, when I had left Gentile philosophers, as Justin and Cyprian did; when I had quitted Scribes and Rabbis, like S. Paul; when I have found the wisest Doctors, the holiest Apostles, still far beneath Him Who is co-equal with the FATHER : when I have pierced beyond the highest choir of Angels, likest to Him in nature, in beauty, wisdom, and purity ; then, and not till then, can I find Him, for love enters in when understanding waits without. It is *but a little*, however, that I have to wait, for He comes Himself to meet me, the very moment I have forsaken self and sin, and have been washed clean from my offences. *But a little*, for the knowledge of GOD is granted with small toil, since the moment He

Thrupp.

Cassiodor.

S. Just. Org. Parez.

S. Greg. M.

Ricard. Vict. Nic. Argent.

Philo Carp.

<small>S. Ans. Laud.
S. Bernard.</small> perceives the affection of the seeker He gives Himself freely, and throws Himself into our arms. *But a little,* for the Creed which sums up the mysteries of salvation is soon communicated, and easily learnt. *But a <small>2 Cor. iv. 17.</small> little,* for our light affliction, which is but for a moment, worketh for us a far more exceeding and eternal <small>Philipp. Harveng.</small> weight of glory. *But a little,* and yet ascending up far above all heavens, from the depth of sin and sorrow to the exalted throne of the SON of GOD, whereon He seats and crowns His Bride.

<small>Ric. Vict.</small> *I held Him, and would not let Him go.* GOD is *held,* observes Richard of S. Victor, by devotion in prayer, by longing, importunity, memory, intreaty, faith, and expectation of being heard, and He is *not let go* if there be no intermission of intention, if the countenance of the petitioner has not turned any more to other things. She holds her Beloved therefore, though it be morning, and does not let Him go until He bless her. She wrestled with Him all the night wherein she slept; but her heart was waking, because it had ceased from outer cares, and toiled in seeking the Beloved. For though she came through the night unto morning, she ceases not from her wrestling, that is, her steadfastness in prayer, and does not let her Beloved go until <small>Ps. lxxxiv.
S. Bernard.
Serm. 79, 83.
Guilelm.
Parv.</small> He give His blessing that she may go from strength to strength and behold the GOD of Gods in Sion, and be no more called Jacob, but Israel. She wants as her one blessing, Himself, as she holds Him by her love.

<small>Charles Wesley.</small>

  In vain Thou strugglest to get free,
   I never will unloose my hold,
  Art Thou the Man that died for me?
   The secret of Thy love unfold;
  Wrestling, I will not let Thee go,
  Till I Thy Name, Thy nature know.

  Yield to me now, for I am weak,
   But confident in self-despair;
  Speak to my heart, in blessings speak,
   Be conquered by my instant prayer;
  Speak, or Thou never hence shalt move,
  And tell me if Thy Name is Love.

  'Tis Love, 'tis Love! Thou diedst for me;
   I hear Thy whisper in my heart;
  The morning breaks, the shadows flee;
   Pure, universal Love Thou art;
  To me, to all, Thy bowels move,
  Thy nature and Thy Name is Love.

And now that the Bride holds Him, and prevails in her prayer of intercession, as she clasps Him in the arms of love, that she may bring comfort to the feeble of heart, the sorrowing cry of Isaiah is no longer true: "There is none that calleth upon Thy Name, there is none that stirreth himself up to take hold of Thee." Rather she exclaims, in the words of the Apostle: "For I am persuaded, that neither death, nor life, nor angels, nor principalities, nor powers, nor things present, nor things to come, nor height, nor depth, nor any other creature, shall be able to separate us from the love of God, which is in CHRIST JESUS our LORD." O how the faithful soul holds and, so to speak, constrains Him, whilst it does what is pleasing and acceptable unto Him! For the Bridegroom, like the Bride, delights in the life, the ways, the fellowship, and the familiarity of the righteous, and He is held by virtuous deeds, not by the hands of armed men, not by the pomp of the wealthy, nor the boastfulness of the rich, not by the stateliness of the haughty, not by any who suffer from the disease of gluttony, sloth, avarice, luxury, or envy, but by works of mercy, lovingkindness, continence, humility, temperance, good-will, purity, and by the prayers of the just. Then the Bridegroom comes freely and gladly to be brought into our *mother's house*. And of this *house* they speak variously. First, the speaker may well be the Gentile Church, resolving never to cease her hold on the LORD by prayer and zeal till He turns, and has mercy on the Synagogue, the spiritual parent of Christianity, by entering into the heart of the Jews, and dwelling there. "Great is the might of love. The SAVIOUR had gone forth in wrath from His house and His inheritance, and now, softened by her fervour with Him, He is prevailed upon to return not merely as SAVIOUR, but as Bridegroom. Blessed art thou of the LORD, O daughter, who both restrainest wrath and restorest the inheritance. Blessed art thou of thy mother, for whose welfare anger is turned away, salvation cometh back: He cometh back Who saith, I am thy salvation." Another devout writer, taking the *mother* to be the Christian, not the Jewish Church, explains the words similarly of the resolute zeal with which holy men labour for the reformation of spiritual abuses, not ceasing their labours in their several places, and in Synods, until CHRIST returns to that dwelling whence the sins of

Card. Hailgrin.

Isa. lxiv. 7.

Rom. viii. 38, 39.

Philo Carp.

*S. Greg. M.
Beda.
Aponius.
Rupert.*

S. Bernard.

Dion. Carth.

Christian priests and people seem to have driven Him. And observe that it is not enough to bring Him into the *house*. He must come not as a mere visitor, but as the most intimate of guests, into the *chamber*, conferring no common gifts, but His full grace. Again; they explain the grace and wisdom of GOD to be as it were our *mother*, and that the soul is the house wherein this dwells, with an inner chamber for the reception of the deeper mysteries. The soul says, *I will bring Him in.* "Therefore," comments a great mystical writer, "GOD will enter in unto thee that thou mayest enter in unto Him. When His love enters and penetrates thy heart, and affection for Him reaches its innermost recess, then He enters thyself, and thou enterest thyself too, that thou mayest go in unto Him. For He must needs come as far as the chamber and enter the bower itself, arriving at thine innermost habitation, there to rest." And lastly; they take it of the Bride, saying with the holy boldness of love, that she will not let her Bridegroom go until she bring Him into her true mother's house, in the city of "Jerusalem above, which is free, and the mother of us all." And this, because CHRIST is Himself the dweller in holy souls, which are His temple and habitation, "for ye are the temple of the living GOD: as GOD hath said, I will dwell in them and walk in them." And so we read in the Acts of S. Ignatius, who, when Trajan asked him, Who is Theophorus? —"GOD-bearer," a name by which the Saint had just designated himself—replied "He who has CHRIST within his heart." Trajan said, "Dost thou then carry within thee Him that was crucified?" Ignatius answered, "Truly so, for it is written, 'I will dwell in them, and walk in them.'" The words then are a pledge on the part of the Bride that she will so tenderly, purely, and jealously guard CHRIST in her soul, that He will have no mind to go thence, but will tarry in it, so that when she presents herself before the gates of the heavenly city, the warders will be fain to admit her, because they cannot refuse her without at the same time repulsing their King. And whereas it is said, *Until I had brought Him*, it is not implied that she then will let Him go. Rather she will hold more closely than ever, because then there will be no temptation to part her from Him, nor any desire on His part to withdraw. She will not let Him go till that other *until* is ended: "Sit Thou on My right hand *until* I make Thine enemies Thy footstool." These four verses were fulfilled by Mary Magdalene, who sought her LORD during the night of His absence from His Church, came with spices to His tomb, was found there by the Angels, questioned them about Him, passed them, found Him whom her soul loved, and did not let Him go till He sent tidings of His Resurrection back to Jerusalem by her. Accordingly, this passage forms the first Lesson at the Nocturns of S. Mary Magdalene's Day in the Breviary.

^{Beda.}

5 I charge you, O ye daughters of Jerusalem, by the roes, and by the hinds of the field, that ye stir not up, nor awake my love, till he please.

The old versions take these words here, as in chap. ii. 7, to be spoken by the Bridegroom, and it is well to observe again that the Hebrew admits of either construction. It is repeated, says Cassiodorus, because in the earlier verse reference was made to the Primitive Church of the Jews, but here to the Gentile Church, bound far more closely to Him in love. But the same words are used to denote the identity of GOD's love and care for His Saints under both dispensations. And whereas the Church has just been described not as sleeping or resting, but searching eagerly, she is nevertheless here said to sleep, because search after CHRIST is the sweetest of all sleep. The Church sleeps, therefore, and seeks for CHRIST, sleeps to earthly desires and worldly affairs, but wakes to her Bridegroom and seeks Him, because she clings to contemplation of Him, desires Him only, and strives to reach Him. And it is repeated here for another reason, because the Bridegroom has pity on His Bride, who had been searching and toiling all the night to find Him, and therefore needed repose more than she did before. And, accordingly, the words may well represent to us those seasons of repose and comparative tranquillity which always intervened between the persecutions suffered by the Early Church, giving her time to repair her shattered strength, and to rear up children instead of the fathers she had lost by the sword, or rack, or fire, or the wild beast, man. If taken, as by the A. V., of the Bride, it will then denote the appeal for a brief time of peaceful contemplation, after she has

Cassiodor.

Rosenmüller.

drawn her Beloved into the inner chamber. Or it may be explained, again, as a warning to the persecutors not to break rudely in upon the calm and silent spreading of the Word, so as to force that LORD Whose still small voice was well-nigh quiet like slumber, to speak to them in His wrathful judgments, in the wind, and fire, and earthquake, taking vengeance for His elect. This point marks the close of the second phase of the action, wherein the search for and discovery of the Bridegroom are described. The third stage of the drama, detailing the espousals, now begins.

Cocceius.

6 Who is this that cometh out of the wilderness like pillars of smoke, perfumed with myrrh and frankincense, with all powders of the merchant?

The ambiguity of the A. V. does not exist in the Hebrew, nor in the old translations, which, by employing feminine words here, tell us at once that the Bride is intended. And the Targum, as so often, furnishes a clue, putting the words into the mouth of the Canaanite nations, looking in wonder and awe at the mighty people which came out of the wilderness into the Land of Promise. Similarly too, most Christian writers ascribe the words either to the Patriarchs of the Jewish Church, the old possessors of the spiritual Canaan, looking in wonder on the Gentile Church, coming up out of the wilderness of heathenism, or else to the citizens of a yet holier Land, the Angels, marvelling at the progress of the soul which clings to CHRIST. If it be asked how she comes to be in the wilderness at all, Hosea gives the answer: "I will allure her, and bring her into the wilderness, and speak comfortably to her." Not unfitly, observes Theodoret, is the devout soul said to be like the smoke of incense, for she, as the Apostle saith, hath presented her members a living sacrifice, holy, acceptable unto GOD, and constantly offers the sacrifice of praise, and mortifies her members which are on earth, and is buried together with CHRIST, and presents herself as a whole burnt-offering to GOD. And she is said to be *perfumed with myrrh and frankincense, with all powders of the merchant,* because she worships CHRIST's Manhood, signified by myrrh, and His Godhead, denoted by frankincense; for she at once believes in the death of her

Targum.

Cassiodor. Philo Carp. S. Just. Org.

Card. Hailgrin.

Hos. ii. 14.

Theodoret.

Rom. xii. 1.

Bridegroom and in His eternal being. Therefore they select for praise the *myrrh* and *frankincense* out of all the powders of the merchant. For she has other virtues drawn from Holy Scripture as though from the merchant's shop, but the myrrh and incense, the knowledge of GOD and of His dispensation, are chief among them. The Church, or the holy soul, comments a Latin Father, dwells in the *wilderness* in the world, whilst it is an exile from the kingdom, and amongst the wild beasts, that is, the evil spirits. Herein, though she is not altogether deserted by her Spouse, yet while she is in the flesh, she is not yet admitted to the certain vision of Him, during her pilgrimage of exile and temptation. Wherefore she always toils to *come up,* in order to reach Him Whom she loves. For there are some who care nothing for all visible things, and lift up their hearts to the heavens, who strip themselves of their evil habits, despise this world's wealth and desires, and aim in hope at the unseen. They are well said to come up *like a pillar of smoke,* because they have both the sweet perfume of fair fame, and buoyancy of spirit. *Myrrh* denotes mortification of the flesh, *frankincense* purity of prayer; for the one is, as it were, applied to the body dead to the sinful pleasures of the world, and the other burned in the censer of the heart, on the coals of virtue, with the fire of GOD's love. And the other virtues are called *powders,* to denote the way in which they are spread over every, each, and all the good works of the faithful soul, not lying here and there in lumps, but uniformly distributed, and also because it is needful to grind all our actions down in order to find if any evil thing lies hid in them. And this grinding is contrition.

S. Greg. M.

S. Greg. M. in Ezek. Hom. 22. Ric. Vict.

> In mine own conscience then, as in a mortar,
> I'll place mine heart, and bray it there;
> If grief for what is past, and fear
> Of what's to come, be a sufficient torture,
> I'll break it all
> In pieces small:
> Sin shall not find a sherd without a flaw,
> Wherein to lodge one lust against Thy law.

Francis Quarles, *School of the Heart,* 14.

All the powders of the merchant also, because every virtue is united in the one fragrance of a holy life, every nation is united in the one Catholic Church, indistinguishably sending up their blended perfume to heaven. The *wilderness,* remarks Hugh of S. Victor,

Aponius. Beda.

Hugo Vict.
de Erud.
Theol. i. 111.

denotes a good heart, far from noise and tumult, untrodden by the concourse of earthly thoughts, but green and flowery, bringing forth the germs of holiness. There is heard the voice of the turtle dove, the HOLY GHOST, but no sound of man, nor of aught pertaining to man. This is the "barren and dry land" in which the soul thirsteth after GOD, in which the only food is the heavenly manna, the only drink is water from the spiritual Rock. From this, no less than from that other desert of the world, the Church and the faithful soul *ascend*, as the fume of a sacrifice, as a cloud drawn up towards heaven by the warmth of the sun, and as part of the train of the ascended SAVIOUR. *Like a pillar of smoke*, slender by reason of poverty, straight in right intention, buoyant because unweighted by sin, rising through desire of heavenly things. And on the word *pillars*, they note that the word תִּימְרוֹת *timeroth*, is derived from תָּמָר *tamar* the *palm*, a tree which, slender and straight below, spreads out a wide crown of foliage, perennially green, amidst which hang luscious fruits; and, because it never bends before the winds, it is a familiar type and ensign of victory. So the Church, beginning with a mere handful of believers, shot up into stately height, spread abroad in perpetual youthfulness and fecundity through the world, and, unshaken by persecutions, stands now as the memorial of CHRIST's triumph over the grave. And the holy soul *ascends* from the *wilderness*, in remembrance of her sins, like a *slender wand (virgula)* in holy confession of the same sins; and that wand one of *smoke*, because as the fumes of a censer pass up in one column out of the many orifices of the lid, so one act of confession includes the acknowledgment of many sins. There is *myrrh* there, in penitence, *frankincense* in the intreaty for the Divine mercy and pardon, and *all the powders of the merchant* in the minute sifting and examination of conscience. The *merchant* is that same One Who came seeking goodly pearls, and gave His all for one pearl of great price, bought with His own Blood, while He sells to us without money and without price. The LXX. and Vulgate, however, looking rather to the context than to the original word רֹכֵל *rokel*, translate it *ointment-maker*. Still it is the same. "The sons of the priests made the ointment of the

Beda.
Ps. lxiii. 1.

Cocceius.
Corn. à Lap.

Card. Hugo.

S. Bernard.
Serm. 59, de diversis.

S. Greg. M.
Hom. 22 in Ezek.
Cassiod.

1 Chron. ix. 30.

spices," and He Who is both a Son and a Priest, alone makes that unguent which can heal our wounds, that "ointment poured forth" of which we heard in the beginning of the Song. Only *His* powders, all those graces and sufferings which He added in His Life and Passion to His myrrh and frankincense, (as cinnamon, and cassia, stacte and onycha, galbanum and calamus, were blended with the holy oil and the incense of the Temple,) only they are the perfume of the Church, because she puts no trust in herself or her works, but only in the redemption which the Merchant purchased for her at so vast a cost; and she knows that if she strive to ascend from the pillar of her carnal desire, of her own will and presumption, the cold winds will soon drive its smoke back to earth, because its thick, gross vapours are not light enough to ascend into the higher and clearer air. The verse is also applied to the Assumption of the Blessed Virgin, in a letter printed amongst the works of S. Jerome, in this wise: This festival is peerless amongst the festivals of the Saints, as Blessed Mary is peerless amongst other Virgins, and it is a marvel even to the Angelic powers. Wherefore in the person of the heavenly citizens, the HOLY GHOST saith in the Canticles of her ascension: Who is this that ascendeth through the wilderness as a slender wand of smoke from spices? Rightly as *a slender wand of smoke*, because slight and delicate, as worn with holy discipline, and because kindled within, as a burnt-offering, by the fire of devout love and the longing of charity. As a slender wand, He saith, of smoke from spices, doubtless because she was filled with the perfumes of many virtues, so that the sweetest fragrance, grateful even to angelic spirits, flowed from her. The Mother of GOD once ascended from the desert of this world as a Rod sprung from the root of Jesse; but now the souls of the elect marvel, in very gladness, who she might be that surpasseth the dignity of angels in the holiness of her merits.

<small>Exod. xxx. Thrupp.</small>

<small>Nic. Argent.</small>

<small>Pseudo-Hieron. ad Paulam et Eustoch. Ep. 10.</small>

> Heaven with transcendent joys her entrance graced,
> Next to His throne her Son His Mother placed;
> And here below, now she's of heaven possessed,
> All generations are to call her blessed.

<small>Bishop Ken, *Christian Year*, 1st Sunday after Epiphany.</small>

7 Behold his bed, which is Solomon's; threescore valiant men are about it, of the valiant of Israel.

Targum.	The Targum sees here the sanctuary of Solomon's temple, and the orderly array of priests, standing ministering and stretching out their hands to bless the people, who derive from that blessing strength and protection, as it compasses Israel like a strong and lofty
Cassiodor.	wall. "The *bed of Solomon,*" comments Cassiodorus, "is the holy Church, because therein the Saints of GOD, when the tumult of sin is hushed, delight in the embrace of the true Prince of Peace. The *threescore valiant men* are the Doctors, who either protect the Church by their preaching, or desire to attain heavenly bliss through contemplation. The number *sixty* is made up of six and ten. The number six (*senarius*) denotes the completion of work, because GOD finished His work in six days. The number ten (*denarius*, the Vulgate word for a *penny*) signifies the wages and reward which shall be given to the elect at the end: wherefore they who came into the vineyard are said to have received a *denarius.* Moreover, these Doctors who guard the Church are not only called *valiant,* but *of the valiant of Israel,* that is, of all who believe in CHRIST and love Him, Who is Israel, that is, Seeing GOD." They are *threescore* for yet another reason. The chosen guard of David consisted of thirty warriors, and David's kingdom denotes only the Jewish Church. But our Solomon rules over Jews and Gentiles together, and therefore His guard must needs be double that of His FATHER'S Saints of the old Law.
S. Just. Org. Ps. cxxxii. 14.	The Church is the bed of CHRIST, observes another, because He rests there, as it is written: "The LORD hath chosen Sion to be an habitation for Himself: He hath longed for her. This shall be My rest for ever; here will I dwell, for I have a delight therein." The
Beda.	bed of Solomon is, in this life, remarks a third in nearly the same spirit, the peaceful conversation of the Saints, withdrawn from worldly noises, which, by checking or lulling the strife of sin, is a type of the happiness of
S. Greg. M. Philo Carp.	unending peace. Or you may take it, with S. Gregory the Great and various others, to be the devout soul, in which CHRIST is pleased to repose, when it is prepared for Him by the removal of all worldly things, and guarded by the teaching and example of those mighty men who, fulfilling the ten precepts of the moral law in the six days of their earthly labour, are symbolized by the number *threescore.* And this title of Solomon's
Avrillon.	bed especially fits the soul after sacramental reception

of the Body and Blood of CHRIST in the Holy Eucharist, when He is pleased to dwell for a time with His guest. The sixty valiant men who then guard the soul, are holy thoughts and resolutions armed with the sword of the Spirit. They are sixty, because the five senses, ruled and guided by reason, added as a sixth and a supreme sense, are trained in obedience to the ten precepts of the Law, so as to resist all snares and terrors of the evil one. Yet again, the *bed* on which our Wise King lay down to His rest was the Cross, the bride-bed of the Church, where is the true repose of the Saints, which is also the standard of the battle, round which the most valiant men are ranged as a guard. The poet will tell us what are the tokens of these valiant men whom the Wise King chooses as His companions: *Tres Patr.* *Corn. à Lap.*

> A glorious company, the flower of men, *Tennyson,*
> To serve as model for the mighty world, *Guenevere.*
> And be the fair beginning of a truce.
> I made them lay their hands in mine and swear
> To reverence the King as if he were
> Their conscience, and their conscience as their King,
> To break the heathen and uphold the CHRIST,
> To ride abroad redressing human wrongs,
> To speak no slander, no, nor listen to it,
> To lead sweet lives in purest chastity,
> To love one Maiden only, cleave to her,
> And worship her by years of noble deeds.

Another and especial bed of our Solomon was that wherein He was first cradled, the hallowed womb of His Virgin Mother, who was fenced about by the Patriarchs, Kings and Prophets of her race, as one tells us, and by a special guard of Angels, as another comments, who did in truth watch around the manger where He first lay after His Nativity. *Aponius. Rupert. Dion. Carth.*

And, to pass rapidly over such interpretations as those which take the bed to be Holy Writ, or the Manhood of the WORD, or prayer, wherein the tried soul reposes with CHRIST, or the sepulchre round which the Jews posted an armed guard, we may dwell for a little on that last bed of which they tell us, the eternal peace and bliss of heaven. That rest is called a bed, because therein is repose from all the unrest and toil of this life. They who toiled here for GOD, repose in that rest, for "there" (as is read in Job,) "the weary be at rest, the prisoners rest together." *Theodoret. Parez. Corn. à Lap. Philo Carp.* *Beda. Ric. Vict.* *Job iii. 18.*

There eternal quiet refreshes and rewards those whom toil here in GOD'S precepts and progress in virtue wearied, and they who here were bound in the chains of human infirmity, there breaking their bonds asunder, sacrifice to GOD the offering of praise.

8 They all hold swords, being expert in war: every man hath his sword upon his thigh because of fear in the night.

<small>Ric. Vict.</small> Richard of S. Victor, in his comment on the preceding verse, bids us observe that the valiant men who compass Solomon's bed in desire, do not ascend it, nor sleep there, and that even to compass it in guard is not for those who must still mourn for their sins and wash the bed of sorrow with tears of repentance, for their bed is a troubled one, and not the peaceful couch of Solomon. But when they have been cleansed from their sins by true repentance, and have been freed, by daily combat, from evil passions, and have been strengthened by grace, passing from fear and hope to perfect love, then they may take their stand, and hope one day to mount the bed themselves, and contemplate the bliss of heaven. And their weapons, he adds when discussing this verse, are Holy Scripture and psalmody. Observe first, that it is not said, They all *have* swords, but They all *hold* swords, because it is no very wonderful thing to know GOD's Word, but <small>S. Greg. M. Moral. xix. 29.</small> it is so to do it. He who is familiar with the Divine Scriptures has a sword, but if he neglect to live in accordance with it, he does not *hold* the sword, and is therefore not *expert in war*, because he knows not <small>Serm. in Cant. xvi.</small> how to wield his weapon or resist temptation. "Why puttest thou thy hand to valiant deeds who art not of the valiant men?" asks Gilbert of Hoyland, addressing ignorant, dull, and worldly preachers: "Why undertakest thou a guard, who shakest not off thy sloth? Why dost thou compass the bed, who hast no sword, or if thou hast the sword of the Word, hast it in the scabbard, not on thy tongue? Thou holdest not in the hands of thy tongue the turning sword of the Word of GOD. The Word runneth very swiftly, the Spirit is fiery, but I know not how it is that it, contrary to its nature, becomes dull in thy hand. That which is sharper and more piercing than any two-edged sword is blunted and weakened in thy grasp. The Word

is not swift in thy mouth, it runs not swiftly, it turns not readily in thy hand according to varying needs, though it is more than enough for all the wants of spiritual combat. Why undertakest thou an office of which thou hast no experience? *All holding swords, and expert in war.* Thou with no reason carriest a sword who hast no adequate acquaintance with warfare, or if thou hast learnt to combat, engagest thyself in preference with worldly tasks rather than with those of CHRIST . . . Thou who art an Evangelical,[1] speak altogether evangelically. Let thy sermon savour of the Law, the Prophets, the Apostles; sharpen thy tongue with their words. Borrow from them the weapons of GOD, mighty to the pulling down of strongholds, casting down imaginations, and every high thing that exalteth itself against the knowledge of GOD? Let the sword of the SPIRIT turn in thine hands, that it may serve thee for every need, nor let the power of sacred eloquence forsake thee when a casual and sudden occasion demands it. Let the powerful and effectual word be on thy lips, and not in the leaves of a book. 'For the Priest's lips,—not his leaves—should keep knowledge.' Take thy purse of money with thee. Let thy sword be at thy side, not out of sight, let it be close to thee. Gird thyself with it upon thy thigh, that thou mayest be mighty and ready, both to exhort in sound doctrine, and to convince the gainsayers." Observe in the second place, that the words seem, though not necessarily, to imply the possession of *two* swords by each warrior. In Japan, at the present day, two swords borne by one person are a mark of superior rank; in the later middle ages the usual weapons of a noble were a sword and a long dagger, almost a sword in dimensions, which was used, instead of a target, to parry, while the sword was employed for attack. So in explaining this passage, we shall do well to recall that saying of the Gospel: "He that hath no sword, let him sell his garment, and buy one. And they said, LORD, behold, here are two swords. And He said unto them, It is enough." And if we take the two swords, as the commentators so often do, to denote spiritual and temporal rule, then the sword in the hand will denote the active strife of the soul against evil spirits, or zeal for passion and martyrdom, and that upon the thigh the passive restraint of our

2 Cor. x. 4.

Mal. ii. 7.

S. Luke xxii. 36, 38.

Dion. Carth. in S. Luc. xxii.
S. Greg. M.
S. Just. Org.

---

[1] "Vir evangelicus."

carnal passions, kept in check by temperance and modesty. Or, rather, as Richard of S. Victor wisely tells us, by the love of GOD, the only sufficient weapon against the assaults of the flesh. So wearing the sword, the valiant men are conformed to their Leader, of Whom is written, "Gird Thee with Thy sword upon Thy thigh, O Thou most mighty, according to Thy worship and renown." Psellus gives a quaint explanation of the verse, saying that the swords denote the sign of the Cross, which Christians employ against the evil one. And it may be added, in illustration of this view, that the Cross *fitchée*, (that is, with the lower limb ending in a point) borne still on so many shields, is traditionally said to denote the cross-handled sword of a Crusader, when set up in the ground before his eyes as he lay wounded on the battle-field, to bring the emblem of his salvation to his mind. *Because of fear in the night.* That is, because of all the snares of the devil, all the darkness and terror of adversity, of ignorance, of the world's gloom. One sword might be sufficient, did we fight in the day, and not against powers of darkness; but as we know not on which side the attack will be made, there must be a sword ready on the thigh as well as one in the hand.

9 King Solomon made himself a chariot of the wood of Lebanon.

10 He made the pillars thereof of silver, the bottom thereof of gold, the covering of it of purple, the midst thereof being paved with love, for the daughters of Jerusalem.

The word אַפִּרְיוֹן, *appirion*, here translated *chariot*, ought rather to be *litter* (LXX. φορεῖον, Vulg. *ferculum*.) The Chaldee takes this, as well as the *bed* of the previous verse, to be the Temple, in the midst of which was the Ark of the Covenant, wherein lay the stone tables of the Law, more precious than fine silver and than the purest gold, overlaid with a veil of blue and purple. And whereas the bed denotes night and rest, the *litter* implies the royal pomp of a procession by day, a notion partly borne out by the Arabic version, which here reads *throne*. So, with the Christian interpretation that the Church is here described, we see it less as the refuge for the weary than as the triumphal car of the Saints. As CHRIST made His own human Body first to be the *litter* in which the Godhead is borne, so He made the Church to be that vehicle in which He, the Man-GOD, should be borne in procession among the people to whom He comes as King and Conqueror. The woodwork of this litter is of the *wood of Lebanon,* of incorruptible cedar from the "white" mountain, denoting the holiness, incorrupt truth, and steadfast perseverance of the Saints; though one of themselves reminds us, not inaptly, that as Lebanon is taken often to denote fierceness and pride, so that it is written, "The LORD breaketh the cedars of Libanus," we are to understand here that the very framework of the Church is made up of sinners and idolaters whom GOD has converted to the faith. And one of the very earliest Christian comments on the Song leads in the same direction, pointing out that the LORD took His flesh from Gentiles as well as from Judah, and that the *wood of Lebanon,* lying outside the Holy Land, in an idolatrous region, typifies Ruth the Moabitess, from whom He sprang: and similarly, that we, who spiritually carry Him in our souls, are of Lebanon too, for we were once the wood of the gainsayer, but have been cut down by the axe of the WORD to be made a chariot for our Master. *The pillars of silver* are generally taken to denote the Apostles and other principal Saints, as the stays and props of the Church. So we read of "James, Cephas, and John, who seemed to be pillars." They are *silver,* not only to denote their purity of life and conversation, but also because to them was intrusted the ministry of that Word whereof is said, "The words of the LORD are pure words, even as the silver, which from the earth is tried, and purified seven times in the fire." *The bottom thereof of gold.* The LXX. reading ἀνάκλιτον, the Vulgate, *reclinatorium,* come nearer to the meaning of the Hebrew, רְפִידָה, *rephidah,* which seems to denote the sloping *back* of the litter, against which the rider leaned in a half-reclining posture. They differ as to this. Philo of Carpasia, holding that as one class of Saints is denoted by the cedar-wood, and a second by the silver pillars, takes the golden back to be a third, and to mean the Martyrs. Till they came, the Son of Man had not where to lay His head, but now He has these, of whom is written, "As gold in the furnace

Philo Carp.

Hugo Victorin.

S. Greg. Nyss.

Ps. xxix. 5.

S. Theophil. Antioch.
† circ. A.D. 190.

Polychronius.

Gal. ii. 9.

Ps. xii. 7.

Rosenmüller.
De Wette.
Hitzig.

Philo Carp.

S. Luke ix. 58.

hath He tried them, and received them as a burnt-offering." Cassiodorus, however, will have it that this *reclining-place* denotes the everlasting rest promised to the Saints in the Church, while S. Gregory in his comment here takes it to be Divine contemplation; and in another place, that rest in charity which the devout find even on earth. *The covering of it of purple.* Here again the LXX. and Vulgate differ from the A. V. reading, *The going-up* (ἐπίβασιν, *ascensum,*) while modern critics take it to be the *seat*, with a purple cushion or carpet laid upon it. *The going-up* is *purple*, tersely writes S. Beda, because no one can enter the Church save by means of those Sacraments which derive their power from the LORD's Passion, and are purpled with His Blood. Aponius bids us see in the litter the Cross of Calvary bearing the Crucified Redeemer, being itself that Cedar of Lebanon which is the stateliest of trees, and carrying on it the silver pillar of His most pure and spotless Body, which shows the gold of His perfect Godhead, while the purple denotes the precious tide which flowed there for us. And we have all these tersely expressed in the world-famous processional hymn :

> O Tree of beauty, Tree of Light,
> O Tree with royal purple dight,
> Elect, on whose triumphal breast
> Those holy limbs should find their rest.

Tree of Lebanon, having the *beauty* of fine silver, the rich *glow* of pure gold, and decked in its midst with kingly *purple*. O most happy litter of the Cross, wherein CHRIST descended to our basest depths, that He might draw us to His majestic height! He made this litter *for Himself*, because He voluntarily underwent death for us. He made it of the wood of Lebanon, a Gentile mountain, because He elected to die by a Roman punishment, and not a Jewish one. He *paved* it with love, because He gave Himself to be rejected, and as it were, trampled under foot. Akin to this is the interpretation, already indicated, which takes the litter to be CHRIST's human nature, whereby He was borne into the world. The silver pillars are the gifts of the HOLY GHOST wherewith He was endued, according to that saying, "Wisdom hath builded her house, she hath hewn out her seven pillars." The golden slope is His most pure and holy soul. The purple, as before, is His Passion, and His Heart is full of love, and that for the daughters of Jerusalem, the Vision of Peace, because He gives to holy souls those graces and virtues which bring the peace which passeth all understanding. Now the holy soul is borne on this litter unto GOD, this same litter whereby Elias was taken up to heaven. This is the ladder of sinners by which CHRIST drew all things to Himself, as He foretold. We too may have our spiritual Cross, gemmed with love at its summit, with obedience on the right, patience on the left, and humility below. The Cross of our body will be abstinence, even from things lawful; watchfulness; and diligence in toil. The Cross of our heart, the fear of GOD; sorrow for sin; compassion on our neighbour; and the Passion of CHRIST. The Cross of our soul, perpetual clinging to Divine love; ardent humiliation of self; sincere affection for enemies; and perfect forgiveness of injuries. But a more frequent explanation of the *litter* than either of these two, is that which takes it to be the CHRIST-bearing soul. The *litter* of Solomon, writes Hugh of S. Victor, is a heart trained in the practice of virtue. It must needs be, in the first place, of the *wood of Lebanon*, by purity, and incorrupt truth; of *silver* in precepts and promises. In the whiteness of the silver is seen stainless conversation, in its musical sound the sweet promise of GOD. It has *gold*, too, by reason of heavenly wisdom, which rusteth not for evermore, but is ruddy in love. It has *purple*, when it preaches the Passion, and a *going-up* to glory. *In the midst* there is *spread love for the daughters of Jerusalem*, love set before the feeble and infirm, that they may win salvation. For who is so feeble that he cannot love? If thou canst do nothing else, at any rate thou canst love, and so belong to Solomon's litter. Others limit the reference somewhat by seeing here the Doctors of the Church, by whom CHRIST is borne, as in a litter, in their preaching. Their silver pillars are the words of the LORD, their golden slope the calmness of a peaceful mind, the purple ascent that Heavenly Country where CHRIST robes the victor in kingly raiment. And such a litter was Saint Paul, that stately cedar cast to the ground and broken by GOD, silver in his preaching of CHRIST, golden in his constancy and meekness, purple in his sufferings and martyrdom. Taking the true sense of מֶרְכָּב, *merkab*,

Hugo Vict. Erud.Theol. i. 60.

Tres Patr.

Theodoret. Ghislerius.

to be *seat*, and not *ascent*, as the Vulgate, nor *covering*, or *curtain*, as A.V., Syriac, and Arabic, we get the meaning that for all the Saints, as for CHRIST Himself, the Passion is the only road to the throne of glory. That seat is covered with purple, and with no other tint. And then you may take the Saints of GOD to be that central pavement, costly stones now laid low on the ground, in the humiliation of the Church Militant, but soon, in the Church Triumphant, to be "as the stones of a crown, lifted up as an ensign upon His land." The most glorious Virgin, too, is aptly called the litter, that is, the throne or royal seat of Solomon, the SAVIOUR. He made it of the wood of Lebanon, holy and uncorrupt in body and soul. He gave it silver pillars, those seven pillars of the gifts of the HOLY GHOST which support the House wherein Eternal Wisdom dwells. So S. Peter Damiani:

Cocceius.

S. Epiphan.

Zech. ix. 16.

*Hugo Card.
Dion. Carth.
Cantacuzene.*

*The Hymn,
Gaudium
mundi.*

Aula cœlestis speciosa Regis,
Fulta septenis sophiæ columnis,
Quem totus nequit cohibere mundus
    Claudis in alvo.

Beautiful palace of the King of Heaven,
Reared on the pillars sevenfold of Wisdom,
Him Whom the whole world faileth to encompass,
    Thou art enshrining.

The golden slope was that most ardent love which prepared her for the Conception of her Divine Son; or, as another hymn will have it, that holy breast on which the Infant SAVIOUR lay reclined:

*The Hymn,
Gaude Virgo
principalis.*

Gaude sacrum pectus aureum
Vere reclinatorium
Salomonis.

Joy, O sacred golden breast,
Truest Pillow, where in rest
Solomon is lying.

And the purple ascent was her sorrowful union in the Passion of JESUS, wherein she was more than Martyr, crying, like her royal forefather, "O my Son, would GOD I had died for Thee, my Son, my Son."

2 Sam. xviii. 33.

*J. Beaumont,
Psyche,
xiii. 343.*

O Heavenly Mother, never agony
Was more heroic than was this of thine;
Excepting that of thy great Son, when He
His humble patience did prove divine.
  Fitting it was that thou shouldst tread alone
  The hardest steps of glory next thy Son.

Also her heart, in the *midst* of her body, was *strewed* *with tender love for all weak and suffering souls, daughters of Jerusalem,* but in Babylonian exile below. Cardinal Hugo bids us note the contrast between the chariot of Pharaoh, touching earth always, and borne along with rattling speed, and the silent litter of Solomon, raised far from the ground, proceeding noiselessly, types of the carnal and holy soul. There is another explanation given of this passage by more than one author of mark, by mistaking the force of the Vulgate *ferculum,* which is often used in classical Latin to denote a *dinner-tray* or a *dish of meat.* This dish is, one tells us, Holy Writ. The woodwork of its frame are the inspired Seers and Apostles and Evangelists, cedars of Lebanon, who have composed its several books. The silver is the outer form of their words; the gold the inner sense; the purple is the royal cloth of CHRIST's Passion which covers the whole, and on which the food is served up. That food is mingled of rare and costly ingredients, peace, patience, long-suffering, joy in the HOLY GHOST, and the like, and the name of the dainty so compounded is Love. Hugo Card.

Ricard. Vict.
Rupert.
S. Bernard.
de Grad.
Hum.

The midst thereof being paved with love for the daughters of Jerusalem. The extreme difficulty of this passage calls for separate consideration, rather than for treatment with the remainder of the verse. First, then, let us look at the various renderings of importance. The LXX. has [He made] *a stone pavement within it, love from* (ἀπὸ) *the daughters of Jerusalem.* The Vulgate, He *spread* (or, *carpeted, constravit*) *the midst of it with love because of the daughters of Jerusalem.* The Arabic reading is, *And the interior of it incrusted with jewels, and that for the daughters of Jerusalem.* Some of the older critics translate, *The midst of it kindled with love for,* &c.; the later ones, *The midst of it beautifully covered* (sc. with tapestry) *by the daughters of Jerusalem.* The general meaning is plain, that the very innermost core of the Church's being is not purity, nor beauty, nor preaching, nor even the Passion itself; but the love of CHRIST for us, and our love for Him. And now let us see what they tell us, obscure though most of their comments be. S. Gregory Nyssen holds that dedicated virginity, the special offering of the *daughters of Jerusalem* to the Bridegroom, is set, as a tesselation of jewels, in the midst of the Church. Others say that S. Greg.
Nyssen.

Tres Patr.

CHRIST makes, with His example and teaching, a tesselation, which is love, in the hearts of the faithful, beginning with His work in the souls of His first Hebrew converts, here called Daughters of Jerusalem. And the LXX. version, λιθόστρωτον, *pavement*, applied here to the love on which the throne of our righteous Judge is reared, recalls that other Pavement of earthly power, the Gabbatha where the unjust judge Pilate set his tribunal. Turning to the Vulgate reading, we find the common explanation to be that CHRIST fills the hearts of His faithful people with love for Him, in return for the love which made Him lay down His life for us. And on this S. Gregory the Great remarks, "What shall we do, who have no merit, who see that we have no place amongst the Doctors, or amongst the Martyrs? It follows: *He spread the midst of it with love.* Let us then have love, wherewith the midst of this litter is spread, which is therefore called a 'commandment exceeding broad,' because it procures eternal salvation for all who observe it. Let us hold effectually to this, and we shall be saved by it, and that *because of the daughters of Jerusalem*, for simple souls, knowing themselves to have no strength; which, the more conscious they are of their own weakness, the more eagerly desire to love their SAVIOUR and Redeemer." Another tells us that there are many actions of our lives which are *middling*, neither very bad nor very good in themselves, but which, if done in a loving spirit, become part of the ornaments of CHRIST'S own car. Aponius gives two lovely meanings here. Love was the mean, the mid part of union between the Godhead and Manhood of CHRIST, between GOD and Man through CHRIST. And He spread the *midst* of the Cross with love by hastening the time of His Resurrection for the elect's sake, keeping the letter of the prophecy of His three days' sojourn in the grave, but rising in little more than thirty hours from the Nones of Good Friday. This, he says, is that love put under our feet, which "beareth all things," and though trodden, yields not, but by the example of its holiness, uplifts the fallen. The Abbat Gillebert, preaching to Cistercian nuns, explains the whole verse of the Religious Life. He bids them remember first, how CHRIST provides delights for them even on the journey, and next that, precious as the litter is for its material, it is yet dearer for its Maker's sake. It is but the vehicle to the bridal bed, and if the Bride be carried on her way with such royal pomp, what will her reception in the King's own palace be? Here, in the toil of earth, He gives His Bride a golden reclining-place to rest her weary frame, what then must be the glory and the utter tranquillity of Heaven? Virginity is the *wood of Lebanon*, incorrupt, perennial, fragrant, from the Mount of whiteness. The *pillars* of the claustral life are knowledge and memory of the divine law, faith and steadfastness. They are *silver* pillars if trained in holy discourse, if not only at the seven Hours of prayer Religious sing and make melody in their hearts, but if their tongues speak often of CHRIST in the words of Holy Writ. Let your tongues, he says, be silver. Let no mass of lead be cast into your mouth. That mouth is leaden which utters nothing refined, nothing keen, nothing of heavenly things; but is altogether relaxed, feeble, busy with the meanest and, perchance, the most ungodly things. For wickedness sitteth in the talent of lead. Zech. v. 7. The third grade, after purity of body and gravity of speech, is the *golden slope*, where the unveiled Face of the LORD is seen in kingly and golden majesty, and this is a purified and bridled spirit. No need now to cite that saying of the Gospel, "The Son of Man hath not where to lay His head." Seest Thou not, O LORD JESU, how many resting-places Thou hast here? Nowhere does Thy majestic Head more gladly lie than on the golden bosom of virginity. Behold these virgin breasts, breasts free for Thee. Here Thou reposest oft, and restest at noon, in the golden stillness of Thy radiance. Foxes have here no holes, nor do the birds of the air make here their nests. These things are hidden from the wise and prudent, and revealed unto babes, who follow the lowly ascent, the purple ascent, and advance in the traces of the Passion of CHRIST. Then come the *purple steps*. If thou scornest, or fearest these steps, remember that they are purple. Lowliness accepted for CHRIST, bestows royal dignity. Tread then, Bride of CHRIST, these purple steps with innocent foot. The path whereon thy Beloved first advanced is noble. How beautiful are those purple steps, which CHRIST first marked out with His snowy feet, with the track of His precious Blood! Follow then with eager zeal. Loose the fleshly shoe from off thy feet, for this is holy ground where thou essayest

S. Luke ix. 58.

to go up. Tread in these steps with bare and rapid foot, that it may be dipped in the Blood of CHRIST. And not thy foot alone, but dip thou thy hands and thy head too, that thou mayst go up altogether purple, altogether royal, and ennobled with the Passion of CHRIST. And there is something more. The gold and purple would be dull and cold without love, and therefore, while coveting earnestly the best gifts, seek the more excellent way. That is, *Love in the midst for the daughters of Jerusalem*, the sisterly bond of the cloister, the banishment of all spiritual envy, the desire for mutual help, encouragement, affection, which train the soul in that love which casteth out fear, so that CHRIST is to it the source of gladness, and not of dread. This is the wedding-garment which even a priest must wear, and how much more the Bride!

11 Go forth, O ye daughters of Zion, and behold king Solomon with the crown wherewith his mother crowned him in the day of his espousals, and in the day of the gladness of his heart.

Cassiodor.

The *daughters of Sion* are the same as the daughters of Jerusalem, children of the Church, holy souls, citizens of that city on high who with the angels enjoy perpetual peace, and by contemplation behold the glory of GOD. *Go forth*, the Bride says, *O ye daughters of Sion*, that is, pass out from the troublous conversation of this world, that you may with unburdened soul look on Him Whom ye love. *And behold King Solomon*, that is, CHRIST, the truly Peaceful One, *with the crown wherewith His Mother crowned Him*. As though she said: Consider CHRIST, clothed for you in flesh, which flesh He took from the flesh of His Virgin Mother. For she calls that flesh which CHRIST assumed for us a *crown*, wherein dying He destroyed the empire of death, in which rising again He bestowed on us the hope of Resurrection. Of this crown

Heb. ii. 9.

the Apostle saith: "We see JESUS, by the suffering of death, crowned with glory and honour." And *His Mother* is said to have *crowned Him*, because the Virgin Mary gave Him the substance of His flesh from her own. *In the day of His espousals*. That is, in the time of His Incarnation, when He united the

Church to Himself, not having spot or wrinkle, or when GOD was united to Man. *And in the day of the gladness of His heart.* For the joy and gladness of CHRIST is the salvation and redemption of mankind, according to His own saying in the Gospel when He saw many flocking to the Faith. "At that time JESUS answered and said, I thank Thee, O FATHER, LORD of Heaven and earth, because Thou hast hid these things from the wise and prudent, and revealed them unto babes." And in the Gospel parable, when the sheep was found, He gathered His friends together, saying, "Rejoice with Me." S. Gregory the Great, giving exactly the same explanation, notices the objection that a crown is the mark of glory and honour, whereas the Incarnation of CHRIST was His humiliation. And he replies by saying that the crown and glory are ours, because He is our Head, and that which was His humbling is our boast, and pride, and exaltation. S. Mat. xi. 25.
S. Luke xv. 6.
S. Greg. M.

Next, to cite Cassiodorus again, all this verse may simply and literally be referred to the Passion of CHRIST. For Solomon foreseeing in the spirit that Passion, warned long before the daughters of Sion, that is, the people of Israel, saying, *Go forth, and behold King Solomon,* that is, CHRIST, *with the crown,* the wreath of thorns, *wherewith His mother* the Synagogue *crowned Him in the day of His espousals,* that is, when He wedded the Church to Himself, *and in the day of the gladness of His heart,* when He rejoiced that the world was redeemed by His Passion out of the power of the devil. *Go forth,* then, that is, pass out from the shades of unbelief, and *behold,* that is, understand in soul, that He Who suffers as Man, is Very GOD: or even *go forth* beyond the gates of your city, that ye may see Him crucified on Mount Golgotha. And in this sense more than one hymn takes it, as thus: Cassiod.

> Daughters of Sion, see your King!
>   Go forth, go forth, to meet Him!
> Your Solomon is hastening
>   Where that dear flock shall greet Him!
> The sceptre and the crown by right
> He wears, in robe of purple dight.
>
> It glitters fair, His diadem,
>   But thorns are there entwining,

The Hymn, *Exite, Sion filiæ.*

> And from the Red Sea comes each gem
> That in its wreath is shining:
> Their radiance glows like stars at night,
> With precious blood-drops are they bright.

Eusebius.
Gen. xii. 1.

Hugo Card.

Ricard. Vict.

Go forth from fleshly thoughts, and behold the crown of living stones which is the Church itself, set on the head of CHRIST by love. Like Abraham, "Get thee out of thy country, and from thy kindred, and from thy father's house, unto a Land that I will show thee." Others take the days of the espousals and gladness to be different, and expound the latter of the Resurrection or the Ascension. Go forth, O ye daughters of Sion, from carnal desire, from evil habits, from blindness of heart, and behold the Glory of our King, the bliss of His celestial gladness, that ye may be drawn on by its sweetness and delight, and advance so far, as to go forth from your very selves. When ye suffer adversities, go forth from your imperfection and impatience, so as to bear readily the sorrows laid upon you, and behold your King suffering for you, and by His Passion crowned with glory and honour. Think on that which is eternal, and cheerfully bear that which is momentary; think on the exceeding weight of glory, and then the affliction will be light, which is accompanied by so great a reward. When ye suffer, look upon that crown, and it will become a diadem for you, wherewith you shall be crowned in the day of festival when you go forth from the body, or when ye pass from the bridal of the Church Militant to the bridal of the Church Triumphant. Therefore, O ye daughters of Sion, O ye wise Virgins, get your lamps ready, prepare the oil of good works, and the flame of love, and so go forth to meet the Bridegroom and the Bride.

Isa. lxii. 3.

S. Ambros. in Ps. cxix.
S. Greg. Nyss.
Theodoret.
Hugo Vict.
Erud. Theol.

Then shall ye be "a crown of glory in the hand of the LORD, and a royal diadem in the hand of your GOD." And thus comes His last bridal crown, that glorious diadem made up of Saints, living jewels, set in purest gold, which the Church still places on the head of JESUS at the marriage-supper of the Lamb, more perfect than the crown of Love which Judea, unawares, gave Him in His martyrdom, or than that of righteousness, gemmed with joy, love, fear, and sorrow, which Mary placed upon the brow of her Son.

CHAPTER IV.

1 Behold, thou art fair, my love; behold, thou art fair; thou hast doves' eyes within thy locks: thy hair is as a flock of goats, that appear from mount Gilead.

The Bridegroom here begins the praise of His Bride's beauty, and, as has been aptly observed, not like the maidens in Ps. xlv., by dwelling on the richness of her attire, but on the graces of her person. And thus the mystical import is the enumeration of those special tokens of perfection and holiness which are to be sought in every pure Church and every faithful soul. Corn. à Lap.

Doubly *fair* is she, in faith and in works; doubly fair in body and soul, in knowledge of GOD and knowledge of herself; fair in passive abstention from evil, fair in active performance of good. Fair in that contemplation of divine glory which is *claritas*; fair in that zeal for GOD's honour, the good of her neighbour, and her own humiliation, which is *charitas*. Fair by nature, fair in grace, fair in the practice of holiness, fair in preaching the Word. And the *doves' eyes* denote, as we saw before, purity, simplicity, the enlightenment of the HOLY GHOST, steadfast contemplation of things divine. But now comes a difficulty. The A.V. adds *within thy locks*, or tresses arranged over the face, which is also the view of Kimchi. And if we take this rendering, we shall find its mystical sense by noting that loosened and uncovered hair was a token of mourning and captivity. But the Bride, freed by her Spouse from the dominion of sin, has her tresses orderly disposed and bound, in token of peace and of subjection to Him. Her calm, pure eyes are in keeping with the rest of her external mien, and look happily and peacefully on Him. But this is not the interpretation given by the old versions, nor yet that of several modern critics. The literal sense of מִבַּעַד לְצַמָּתֵךְ *mibbaad letzammathek*, seems to be *out from within thy binding*, or, *restraint*, from the root צָמַם, *tzamam*,

Philo Carp.
S. Just. Org.
Hugo Card.

Dion. Carth.
Beda.

R. Kimchi.
Hengsten-
berg.
Ainsworth.
Isa. xlvii. 2.

"he tied up;" and the LXX. translate, *without* [making mention of] *thy silence;* while the Arabic, a little more full, is *besides the beauty of thy silence.* That is, as they variously explain, devout silence is an additional grace, which increases the beauty of holiness. It is said of the holy soul, remarks S. Ambrose, *Thou hast doves' eyes, besides thy silence,* because she sees spiritually, and also knows the time to speak and the time to be silent, that she may utter her discourse in due season, and not incur the risk of sinning by importunate speech. I would, says Thomas à Kempis, that I had oftener been silent, and not been in company. Why are we so ready to speak and talk with one another, when we so rarely return to silence without some wound on our conscience? And again: No man speaks safely, unless he who is silent gladly. The Three Fathers go deeper than this, and explain the phrase of the silent and hidden meditation of the soul on those divine mysteries which are unspeakable, but which she beholds with her dove-like eyes. And Philo takes us yet further, reminding us of that secret and unspoken prayer which goes up from every soul which is rapt in contemplation and kindled with longing after GOD. And of every such soul may be said in the words of a modern poet, but with deeper meaning:

> Her eyes are homes of silent prayer,
> Nor other thought her mind admits
> But, He was dead, and there He sits,
> And He that brought Him back is there.

The Vulgate, however, is quite different. It reads, *without that which lies hid within.* That is, without the glory of that heavenly reward which thou shalt receive at the end of the world; which lies hid within, though thou contemplatest it now by faith; for it cannot be seen in this world, but shall be perfected in that which is to come. It is a noble and beautiful thing, observes another, to dwell in simplicity amongst men, to feel no wish for any of those temporal things which she sees before her eyes. But it is far nobler and more beautiful that she is striving to keep her heart's desire unspotted, and that she shares in her soul the glory of everlasting bliss. The outer beauty of the soul may be seen, comments Richard of S. Victor, by moderation in food and dress, by rejection of superfluities, by repose in demeanour and language, by friendliness, courtesy, harmlessness, honesty, sympathy, and helpfulness; by a cheerful face, ears which do not itch, eyes not boldly lifted nor prying, an instructed tongue, checked from light and useless talk, uttering good and wholesome words. Further ornaments are freedom from anger, impatience, and spite; aversion from quarrels, detraction, or judgment of others, and even from listening to those so engaged. The soul is fair also when fervent in good works, in GOD's service, in brotherly love: when active, zealous, and discreet in all her doings. Yet there is an inner beauty which surpasses all this; which is purity of intention, lowliness of mind, and that spirit which ever prompts her to do great things and yet look down upon herself, that perfect humility which walks hand in hand with the love of CHRIST. But the true meaning of the passage appears to be, *Thine eyes are like doves' eyes, from behind thy veil.* The very word which is translated *silence* here by the LXX., is rendered by them *veil* in Isaiah xlvii. 2, where the A. V. again reads "locks." The *veil* may be, as many will have it, that of the Bride's flowing tresses, but it seems better to take it of that covering which maidens put on when in the presence of their betrothed husbands, as did Rebecca: "What man is this that walketh in the field to meet us? And the servant said, It is my master; therefore she took a veil, and covered herself." The wearing of the veil, then, denotes not merely that modesty and reserve which Tertullian urges as the fittest graces of Christian maidens, but is a token of the Spouse's submission to her Bridegroom, and further implies the duty of keeping herself for and to Him alone, because "He is to thee a covering of the eyes, unto all that are with thee, and with all other." Not unfitly, then, shall we see here a special reference to the delight of CHRIST in the purity of the Religious Life, the doves' eyes behind that veil which consecrated Virgins have worn since the infancy of the Church. And thus runs the ancient English form for bestowal of this veil at the profession of a nun: "Receive, Virgin of CHRIST, the veil, a token of virginity and chastity, whereby may the HOLY GHOST come upon thee, and the power of the Highest overshadow thee against the heat of evil temptations, through the help of the same our LORD JESUS CHRIST." And the

R. Jona.
Rosenmüller.
Hitzig.

1 Cor. xi. 15.

Gen. xxiv. 65.

De Veland. Virgin.
Coccelus.

Gen. xx. 16.

S. Ambros. de Laps. Virg.

Pontif. Exon.

response was from the office of S. Agnes: "The LORD hath clad me in a robe wrought with gold, and hath decked me with priceless jewels."

Thy hair is as a flock of goats. As the *eyes* of the Church are sometimes taken to denote her greatest teachers, Prophets, Apostles, and Doctors, who give light to the rest of the body, so too the *hair*, close to the head, and its most comely ornament, is explained of those more perfect members of the Church who are nearest to CHRIST their Head. And as hair in itself is insensible and dead, so too those who have come nearest to CHRIST by following His counsels of perfection, and by adopting the Religious Life, are dead to the world and its desires. Moreover, the Saints are compared to a *flock of goats,* because of their love for ascending to lofty heights. "Let not these animals seem vile to thee," observes a Saint; "thou seest that this flock feeds in lofty places, to wit, on a mount. Therefore, where there are precipices for others, there is no peril for the goats; there is the food of this flock, there their provender is sweeter, their pasture choicer. They are seen by their herdsmen, hanging from the wooded cliff, where can be no attacks by wolves, where the fruitful trees minister abundant produce. There they may be seen bending anxiously with milk-laden udders over their tender young: and therefore the SPIRIT chose them as a comparison for the assembly of Holy Church. And, that you may hear the mystical import, the *hair* denotes the exaltation of the WORD, and a certain loftiness of righteous souls, because the understanding of a wise man is in his head. For wisdom, no doubt, lies in the exaltation of human thought. And whereas goats are shorn that they may cast off their superfluous covering, so too Holy Church has her flock of shorn souls, that is, the virtues of many such souls, in which flock you can find nothing insensible, nothing superfluous; because faith hath made them wise, and spiritual grace hath purged them from all taint of superfluity. Fitly then are the souls of the righteous *revealed* (LXX.,) and revealed from *Mount Gilead,* that is, from the 'passing over of witness,' because the Heavenly Witness hath passed from the Synagogue to the Church. In this mountain spring frankincense, balm, and other perfumes. These perfumes, which merchants, gathered by faith and devotion from the Gentiles, have brought, the Church possesses." And similarly another Western Doctor _{S. Greg. M.} comments: "The hair of the Bride is said to be as a flock of goats, because the peoples of the Church, while chewing the cud of the Law's commandments, contemplate heavenly things in faith, are clean animals, and feed on high. And Gilead is interpreted, 'The heap of witness,' denoting the Martyrs, who, holding steadfastly to the faith of CHRIST, maintained the witness of the truth even by their death. Thus the flock of goats *ascends* (Vulg.) from Mount Gilead, because the people of the Church go up with readier faith towards eternal things according as they know that the holy Martyrs have more boldly borne witness to that same faith." A Greek Father bids us extend _{Philo Carp.} the meaning of Gilead further, so as to include all the Prophets and Apostles who, by word and deed, have borne faithful witness to CHRIST.

A second view of the passage, looking rather to the multitude of hairs in the tresses of the Bride than to their height from the ground, sees denoted here the whole body of professing Christians, rather than the more eminent Saints. For thus saith the Apostle, "If _{Philo Carp.} a woman have long hair, it is a glory to her, for her _{1 Cor. xi. 15.} hair is given her for a covering." Wherefore the hairs of the Bride of CHRIST are assemblies, gatherings, and congregations of peoples who worship the One GOD, the true ornament of the Bride herself, and the joy of JESUS CHRIST, Who is the Head of the Bride and the Creator and Redeemer of all mankind, according to that saying of the Prophet, "As I live, saith the LORD, _{Isa. xlix. 18.} thou shalt surely clothe thee with them all, as with an ornament, and bind them on thee, as a bride doth." And then they are called a flock of *goats*, because the _{Theodoret.} bulk of the Church is made up of converted sinners, who feed on Mount Gilead to obtain there wholesome herbs which may cure all the disorders of sin. Or again, the whole body of the laity is implied, as busied _{Beda.} in worldly cares and occupations, with which sin is, for the most part, mixed up. CHRIST Himself is the Heap of Witness on which the multitude of the faithful rests, themselves living stones, clinging to that True Stone, of which Peter saith, "To Whom coming, as unto a _{1 S. Pet.} living stone, disallowed indeed of men, but chosen of _{ii. 4.} GOD, and precious, ye also, as lively stones, are built up." Therefore the flocks of goats go up from Mount Gilead, because the multitudes of the Saints ascend to the heights of holiness, and aim to follow CHRIST'S teaching and commandments in all things.

 Again, as the hair is a superfluity of the body, lifeless, and not essential to life, it may be taken to denote all those purely human cares and occupations in which the Church cannot help being engaged, which are no help to her spiritual life, but in which she can so demean herself as to make them a grace and beauty, and a proof of loftiness of soul. And somewhat in this sense Aponius takes the phrase to denote wealthy Christians, surrounded by luxury, and not self-denying enough to adopt Apostolic simplicity of living, but yet useful and ornamental to the Church by reason of their faith and almsdeeds.

<small>Theodoret.</small>

<small>Aponius.</small>

 Yet another explanation is that which sees in the hair, springing out of the head, a type of the holy thoughts and words of the devout soul, dead to the world and the flesh, and brought out of the darkness of sin, ignorance, and ungodliness, to truth, knowledge, and piety, by means of the Gospel, revealed from Mount Gilead, the invisible hill of Divine testimony. The thoughts of the Saints are like *goats*, because they never rest from climbing higher and higher even in those very temporal things to which bodily necessity compels their attention. They go up from Mount Gilead which is CHRIST, that Mount of GOD, that fat mountain, where are the richest pastures, because every holy meditation comes from Him as its true source. He nourishes them in our hearts, makes them arise, and ascend, and that by the way of prayer.

<small>Tres Patr.</small>

<small>Cassiod.</small>

<small>Ricard. Vict.
Ps. lxviii. 15,
LXX. and
Vulg.</small>

2 Thy teeth are like a flock of sheep that are even shorn, which came up from the washing; whereof every one bear twins, and none is barren among them.

<small>Targum.</small>

 The Targum, while explaining the hair, as many Christian expositors do, to be the whole congregation of GOD'S people, takes the *teeth* to denote the Priests, who eat of the hallowed flesh, tithes, and first-fruits, who are white, and pure from violence and rapine. And the general scope of patristic comment is nearly the same. Thus S. Gregory Nyssen, followed by many others, inclusive of S. Augustine, explains these teeth to be the Doctors of the Church, who grind, as it were,

<small>S. Greg. Nyss.
S. Greg. M.
Cassiodor.</small>

the hard sayings and dogmas of the Faith down so as to fit them for reception by the body of Christians; and who are themselves, as it were, *shorn,* that is, bare of all clogging matter, *come up from the washing* of conscience, clean from all pollution of the flesh and spirit, and advancing ever in holiness, *bearing,* as *twins,* calmness of soul, and purity of bodily life, and never *barren* in producing virtues. S. Augustine's comment is nearly the same, except that he refers also to the teachers of the Church cutting away their converts from their former superstitions, as the teeth separate a piece of food from the whole bulk, that he takes the washing to denote Holy Baptism, and the *twins* to be the love of GOD, and of one's neighbour. And the upper and lower rows of teeth wherewith this work of incorporating sinners into the body of the Church is effected, are, says Aponius, the books of the Old and New Testament. The righteous preachers of the Church, comments S. Albert, who are the teeth whereby men are incorporated into her body, should not decay through luxury, but be white with innocence, joined in charity, even in justice, firm in constancy, bony in vigour, biting into sin with doctrine and truth. Of such is written, "Thy teeth are as a flock of sheep that are even shorn, which come up from the washing." S. Bernard accommodates the metaphor of teeth with much boldness and ingenuity to the Religious life. As the teeth are whiter than the rest of the white body, so Religious are the purest members of the Church, because of their more self-denying and devout life. Teeth have no flesh, like other bones; and Religious, while in the flesh, have forgotten it, hearing the Apostle say, "Ye are not in the flesh, but in the spirit." They have no skin; and so true monks do not suffer even a trifling scandal or obstacle to abide amongst them. They are cloistered by the lips, as Religious are by the walls of their convent. They should not be seen, save in occasional mirth, and so Religious ought only to appear when intending to do some deed of charity, which will bring a smile of cheerfulness to the sad. They have to masticate food for the whole body, and Religious are bound to pray for the whole estate of the Church, both for the living and dead. The teeth taste no savour from the dainties they chew, and so, true Religious take no glory to themselves for any good thing they effect. Teeth do not easily con-

De Doct. Christian. xx. 6.

Aponius.

S. Alb. M. in Ps. iii. 7.

S. Bernard. Serm. 63, de parvis.

Rom. viii. 9.

sume away, and perseverance is a quality of the cloistered life. They are ranked in fixed and even order, and nowhere is there so much orderliness of rule and life as in the convent. They are upper and lower, as monasteries have their dignitaries and ordinary members, united in harmonious toil. And even when the lower ones are moved, the upper remain still, denoting the calmness with which Superiors should rule, even when there are disturbances in the lower ranks of their community.

Again; the teeth are explained to denote the operations of the soul, whereby it gradually assimilates divine truth, or discerns the spirits, to ascertain whether they be good or evil. While the devout mind ponders and discusses all matters, notes the Prior of S. Victor, it does as it were crush and grind them with the teeth of discernment. These are the teeth of the Bride, which are likened to flocks of shorn sheep, for the shearings are innocent meditations, which cut away outer things, that is, the love of earth, and the desire of possessing worldly wisdom. Shorn in this wise, they more readily take hold of spiritual things and discern them. They come up from the washing, to wit, that of compunction and penitential tears. They are *even*, not because every Christian is equally given to practising every virtue alike, but because all virtues spring from one common source, which is charity, so that each merit that can be observed is this same charity under one form or other. They produce *twins*, as one tells us, because they develop both contemplation and action; or, as another will have it, because they teach others by precept and example.

Ric. Vict.

Theodoret.
S. Bernard.

3 Thy lips are like a thread of scarlet, and thy speech is comely: thy temples are like a piece of a pomegranate within thy locks.

By the *thread of scarlet* He reminds the Bride of Rahab, the harlot, who was a type of her in the Old Testament. The Bridegroom beholds this sign in the mouth of the Bride, as in a window, and saith, *Thy lips are like a thread of scarlet, and thy speech is comely*, for it hath received its tint from My Blood, and brings forth the words of truth, wherewith the hearers are caught and bound, as with a cord; for thy comely speech soothes, and persuades them, nor suffers them to depart, but compels them to abide by thy lips. The

S. Epiphanius.
Theodoret.
Josh. ii. 8.

scarlet colour denotes preaching of the Passion, but the thread is love. Scarlet is also the colour of fire, and thus the words denote that ardent preaching of the Apostles which they derived from the tongues of flame which came down upon them at Pentecost. It denotes the blood of Martyrs too, as well as that of CHRIST, and therefore preachers persuade their doubting hearers by the example of those who died for the Faith, showing what must have been the prize for which they so strove. The Latin commentators dwell much on the Vulgate word *vitta*, which means properly a *fillet* or *head-band*. For the Doctors of the Church, by their eloquent preaching, bind the multitude of the faithful, like the tresses of a head, into one orderly body in the Church. And the holy soul, too, binds and restrains her many thoughts with the discipline of the fear of GOD. She does more, for she practises silence, which the cord on the lips denotes, though she can speak too, when needful, in comely fashion. Therefore the lips of the Bride are not compared to every sort of fillet, but to one of scarlet, which is more precious, because her restraint of her speech is the higher and nobler, since it comes not from human wisdom, nor natural temperament, but from divine love. *Thy speech is comely*, is pleasant, and edifying, because it springs from charity, and flows out of the fount of grace, for it tastes how sweet the LORD is, and gives out again that sweetness which it experiences, and breathes that fulness which it enjoys. Its words are sweet also, because the conscience is cleansed from the bitterness of sin, and the dregs of fleshliness. And thus they have no savour of rancour, indignation, wrath, envy, or any hurtful thing, but only of kindliness, meekness, patience, humility.

Thy temples are like a piece of pomegranate. The old versions, taking the word רַקָּה *rakkah* in its widest meaning, translate *Thy cheeks*. And these, as the seat of blushes, resembling the ruddy tint of the pomegranate, denote the modest shamefastness of the Bride, and that, as before with her gentle eyes, *from within her veil.* Therefore this praise denotes the Virgins of the Church, imitators of the ruddy Passion of CHRIST the Virgin-born, white, like the grains of that fruit, in purity, and that in a life as hard and austere as the rind of the pomegranate. Some, however, less happily, see here as in the preceding verse, a reference to preachers of the Word, and others, somewhat better,

Cassiod.
Beda.
S. Ambros.
Aponius.
Cassiodor.
Ric. Vict.
Psellus.
Ric. Vict.
Theodoret.
Psellus.
Aponius.
S. Greg. Nyss.
Philo Carp.
S. Greg. M.
S. Just. Org.
Beda.

prefer to take it as applying to the Martyrs, reddened with their own life-blood without, and white within, like the Virgins, in their purity. The penitent soul, which blushes for its sins, and guards all the good things it contains with the rind of humility, is lovely in the eyes of GOD. And it is not said to be like a whole pomegranate, but a *piece* of one, because as a piece of the fruit partly discloses and partly hides its grains, so the Saints try to hide their virtues so that only GOD may know them, but cannot altogether conceal them from men. When the rind is torn open by adversity, the virtues appear; patience in peaceful endurance of wrong, humility in cheerful acceptance of contempt; obedience, charity, with love of GOD. A *piece*, too, because the most suffering amongst them has never borne the like of CHRIST's sorrow. Rupert, who explained the previous verse of the burning love which made the lips of the Blessed Virgin break out in the *Magnificat*, so that the words, "Full of grace are thy lips," are especially true of her, takes this one to denote the perfection of her modesty, and the yet higher graces that *lay hid within*. (Vulg.) S. John Chrysostom, dwelling on the LXX. translation, *besides thy silence*, singularly explains this whole passage of secret almsgiving, doubtless because the pomegranate, embracing many grains in one fold, is typical of charity.

4 Thy neck is like the tower of David builded for an armoury, whereon there hang a thousand bucklers, all shields of mighty men.

They agree, for the most part, in explaining the *neck* of the Church to denote her Prelates and Doctors, but differ widely in the reasons assigned for this view. The most obvious one, that the prelacy occupies the highest place, under the Head, in the body of the Church, and is the link of union between CHRIST and the corporate assembly of the faithful, is given by only a few expositors. The other reasons alleged for the simile, are that the neck transmits food to the body, just as preachers are the channel of the Word, and that as the neck is stretched out when we are on the watch against enemies, and see them coming from a distance, so the Doctors are the sentinels of the Church, posted on high to keep a look-out against our spiritual foes. They are

like the tower of David, first, by reason of their strength, <small>Cassiodor.
Beda.</small>
because they are stablished in CHRIST; next, by reason <small>Ric. Vict.</small>
of their height, because they soar upward in their aim
after heavenly things; and thirdly, because they are
foremost in the brunt of battle. They are no common
tower, but *David's,* for the strength they possess is not
their own, but derived from CHRIST, of Whom David
is but the type. When the tower falls, observes Car- <small>Hugo Card.</small>
dinal Hugo, it is not for its own ruin alone, but for
that of the entire city; for if the tower be taken or
razed, the whole city is easily stormed. So, when the
assembly of the Doctors falls into sin, the city of the
Church lies exposed and defenceless before its enemies.
That they may be the better guarded against any such
peril, it is added, *builded for an armoury.* Truly so,
says Aponius, (taking for the moment the true sense of <small>Aponius.</small>
the passage, though following the Vulgate,) for as King
David built his tower in the citadel of Sion for his
armoury and guard, so the true David, the WORD of
the FATHER, when He ascended into heaven, stored up
for us in our Sion, the Church Militant, our true supplies and weapons, the strength of our souls, His Cross,
His Body, and His Blood. But the Vulgate reading <small>Cassiodor.</small>
is, *builded with its outworks (propugnaculis.)* And <small>S. Greg. M.
Aponius.</small>
these outworks or bastions are variously interpreted. <small>S.Ans.Laud.</small>
One explains them of the mysteries of Holy Scripture; <small>Ric. Vict.</small>
another, of the gift of miracles; a third, more happily,
takes them to be the examples given us of love, mercy,
patience, and other virtues, in the life of CHRIST; and
the view that chosen sentences of Scripture are intended is maintained by more than one. The LXX.
rendering is different. It simply transliterates the
Hebrew word for *armoury,* and reads *builded to Thalpioth.* The Greek Fathers, accordingly, have fallen
back on the reading of Aquila, ἐπάλξεις, which is practically the same as the Vulgate; or upon that of Symmachus, which is ὕψη, *heights.* The *tower of David,*
observes one of them, to which the holy Doctors are
likened, is CHRIST, sprung from David according to
the flesh. And if any one desire to know the *height* of
that tower, he must not look at it only in its human <small>Philo Carp.</small>
building in Mary, the Mother of GOD, but pray that
he may likewise behold it above the heavens, set on
the right hand of the FATHER.

Whereon there hang a thousand bucklers. That <small>Ezek. xxvii.
11.</small>
shields were hung in this wise as ornaments on the

outer walls of fortresses, we have learnt from the bas-reliefs of Nineveh. And a similar custom existed many ages later, when the sides of the war-galleys of the Norse Sea-kings were adorned in the like manner. These *bucklers*, high in air, are taken by S. Gregory Nyssen to denote the Angel-guards of the Church, a view which he believes enforced by the succeeding words, *all darts* (LXX.) *of the mighty ones.* And he cites the Psalmist, "The Angel of the LORD shall camp round about them that fear Him, and shall deliver them." A commoner opinion is, that Christian virtues are intended, the fences of the soul against assaults of sin. These are a *thousand* in number, to denote universality and perfection, and they are supplemented by all the *armour of the mighty;* every example of holiness given us by Saints of old. And we may not unreasonably assume the blazoning of some device on each such shield, by which its owner may be known, his own especial bearing and motto, as a rallying-point for his followers in the battle. The keys of S. Peter, the sword of S. Paul, the various instruments of torture by which the Martyrs went to their crown, mottoes such as *Humilitas*, the chosen badge of S. Carlo Borromeo, and the like, recall the valiant deeds of these captains in GOD's host to the thoughts of the mere rank and file in that great army, nerving them to similar daring. But of all the glorious escutcheons hanging on that tower which rises from the valley of weeping up to the Mount of Paradise, there is none like the King's own shield, on which the Cross is blazoned. "Safe under the shelter of that buckler, the Saints fear no darts of the evil spirits, but say, as Paul did with smiling pride, 'Let no man trouble me: for I bear in my body the marks of the LORD JESUS.' And again; 'GOD forbid that I should glory, save in the Cross of the LORD JESUS CHRIST, by Whom the world is crucified to me, and I unto the world.' These are those true and strongest arms which can keep CHRIST's soldier unhurt as he fights against the cohorts of the powers of the air, which war daily with the faithful, hurling at them the missiles of sins. But a soldier of this kind is valiant, to whom a glorious life of victory is promised by the Prophet, saying, 'A thousand shall fall beside thee, and ten thousand at thy right hand.' This is the armour wherewith all the world was rescued, with which the Martyrs routed the kings and princes of the earth, and all the legions of evil spirits." And so a poet of our own:

> And on his brest a bloodie Crosse he bore,
> The deare remembrance of his dying LORD,
> For Whose sweete sake that glorious badge he wore,
> And dead, as living, ever Him adored:
> Upon his shield the like was also scored,
> For soveraine hope, which in His help he had.

Spenser, Faery Queene, i. 1, 2.

Again, some take the towering neck of the Church to be Holy Scripture, hung round with the bucklers of testimony. And, not dissimilarly, it has also been explained of preaching the Gospel, as the neck is the channel whence the voice comes from the chest to the lips. Upon this neck of the Church, that is, in her preaching of Holy Writ, which for strength and height is likened to the tower of David, hang a thousand bucklers, because as many as are the precepts therein, so many are the fences for our breasts. For, behold, as we hasten bravely to the fight against the powers of the air, we find in this tower the arms of our soul, that we may take thence the commandments of our Maker, the examples of our forerunners, whereby we can be invincibly equipped against our adversaries. And note, that it is said to be built with its outworks, for the outworks are of the same use as the shields, because both shelter the combatant: but there is this difference between them, that we can move the shield at our pleasure for defence, while we cannot move the outworks, though we may be defended by them. The shield is in our hand, but we do not lay hold of the bastion. What is then the difference between these two, save that in Holy Writ we read both of the wonderful deeds of our forerunners, and of the power of good works? How truly they spake of GOD, their miracles testify; for they could not have done such things through Him, unless they spake truth concerning Him. And their works testify how gentle, how lowly, how kindly they were. What then are their miracles, save our bastions? since we can be guarded by them, and yet have them not in the hand of our will, because we have no power to do the like. But the shield is in our hand, and defends us, because the virtue of patience, the virtue of mercy, through forestalling grace, is in the power of our will, and guards us from peril of adversity.

Eucherius. S. Just. Org.

S. Greg. M. Hom. 15 in Ezek.

> S. Ambros. Hom. 4, in Ps. cxix.

The holy soul has her tower-like neck too, lifted up to GOD, and fitted for the yoke of CHRIST, bent by no curve towards the allurements of earth, as it is the royal tower of CHRIST, on which Nebuchadnezzar cannot impose his yoke, for David, strong in battle, built that tower, and set battlements upon its walls for a defence and a glory, for a defence, because it discovers and repels the enemy; for a glory because it soars up not only amongst lowly buildings, but even amongst lofty ones. And it is thus for a defence or a glory if it have in it the doctrines of the Word, as though its jewelled necklets, and also have the darts of the mighty prophets, which are hurled with the sinews of faith against every high thing that lifteth itself up.

> Corn. à Lap.

Again, not only constancy, as here, but prayer, may be taken as the neck of the Church, through which her voice goes up in petition, and wherein, as in a tower, are stored her surest weapons against all her enemies.

> Rupert.

A third will have it that humble obedience is intended, since the neck is the part which bears the yoke.

> Hugo Card. Joann. Carmel.

And others again hold that charity, which is our true link of union with our Divine Head, is denoted by the neck. It is a tower, because the loftiest of all virtues, and the strongest too. Its *bastions* are the Evangelical counsels of chastity, poverty, and obedience; its *shields*, humility and patience, multiplied a thousand-fold.

5 Thy two breasts are like two young roes that are twins, which feed among the lilies,

6 Until the day break and the shadows flee away.

The *two breasts* of the Church, whereat her children are fed with milk, are the two Testaments, and the Prophets and Doctors of the Circumcision and the uncircumcision, who teach the faithful, who are likened to *two young roes* because of their clear vision in divine mysteries and their swift speeding in their daily course to reach their LORD, and which *feed among the lilies* of a pure conscience and holy life, until, when the day breaks and the shadows flee away, they attain the prize which He has prepared for them. They are *twin* roes, because of the perfect accord between the Old and New Testament, the one being rich in

> Philo Carp.

> Theodoret.

> S. Greg. M.

type, and the other in fulfilment. Another view sees in the two breasts the precepts of love to GOD and love to our neighbour, while Psellus stands alone in his explanation that they denote the Blood and Water which flowed from the crucified SAVIOUR. The outer and inner man, united in one sentient being, visible and invisible, is, S. Gregory Nyssen alleges, the basis of the comparison here, whether applied to the whole Church or to the individual soul, but no other Father has followed him. Richard of S. Victor, after assenting to the view that the teachers of the Church are designated by her breasts, and dwelling on the tests of motherly tenderness, proceeds to distinguish the two breasts into the contemplative and active, both yielding the same spiritual nutriment. Again, the two breasts denote the building up of faith, and the training in holiness; the shunning of evil and the practice of good. They are twins, because they are born at one time, that is, the time of grace, of one and the same Father, which is CHRIST, and one Mother, the Church. They feed among the lilies, in the flowery pastures of the Scriptures, until the day break which has no evening. They feed therefore among the lilies until the day break and the shadows flee away, because the preaching and doctrine of holy teachers is needful only in the present life, for in the life to come, so soon as the everlasting day has appeared and the night of this world has ended, there will be no need to teach any one, for all shall with open face behold the glory of the LORD. Therefore the LORD saith also by the prophet Jeremiah, "And they shall teach no more every man his neighbour, and every man his brother, saying, Know the LORD, for they shall all know Me, from the least of them unto the greatest of them, saith the LORD."

Aponius.
Psellus.
S. Greg. Nyss. Hom. 7.
Ricard. Vict.
Hugo Card.
Cassiodor.
2 Cor. iii. 18.
Jer. xxxi. 34.

There is also a moral exposition, according to which the breasts of the Bride are her fellowship in joy and sorrow with those who rejoice and those who mourn. These are likened to young roes, because in compassion there should be quickness and cheerfulness of help, and in congratulation there should be clear-sighted acuteness to guide us aright in knowing what things ought to be subject of rejoicing.

Henr. Harphius.

6 Until the day break, and the shadows flee

away, I will get me to the mountain of myrrh, and the hill of frankincense.

The majority of the commentators take the first clause of this verse with the preceding words, as denoting the time during which the young roes feed amongst the lilies. But the Masoretic pointing reads it with the succeeding clause, and it will be convenient to consider it in this connection. And it is no marvel that the great mass of comment on the verse sets before us the Passion of CHRIST as the mystery hidden under the types here set down. "The Bridegroom," comments Theodoret, "having eulogized the beauties of His Spouse, saith, 'I will go for Myself (LXX.) to the mountain of myrrh and to the hill of frankincense.' Seeing thou art so fair, so lovely, so bright in comeliness, and so wounded with love of Me, I accept death for thy sake, and will go of Myself to the *mountain of myrrh*. But I will rise again, and return to the *hill of frankincense*. We said above that myrrh denotes death, and frankincense the Divine nature. There is need therefore to ask why He speaks of a mountain, when referring to His death, and of a hill, when to His Divinity. And the reason is, because it is so great, unspeakable, and unsearchable a thing that He Who was in the form of GOD, and thought it not robbery to be equal with GOD, should have humbled Himself, and taken the form of a servant, and be found in fashion as a man, and be obedient unto death, even the death of the Cross. But for Him to return to His own glory, and to be glorified with that glory which He had before the world was made, was no great or toilsome thing, rather it was most easy. Wherefore He saith, a *mountain* of myrrh and a *hill* of frankincense, showing thereby that one of these things was light for Him, but the other very hard because of His Manhood. So, when He draws near to His Passion, He saith, 'Now is My soul troubled,' and 'FATHER, if it be possible, let this cup pass from Me.' And yet again He added, 'And what shall I say? FATHER, save Me from this hour, but for this cause came I unto this hour.' This is what He means here in saying, *I will get Me to the mountain of myrrh and the hill of frankincense*. For I do both willingly, not constrained nor compelled by aught. 'Because I lay down

My life, that I might take it again. No man taketh it from Me, but I lay it down of Myself. I have power to lay it down, and I have power to take it again.'" Or by the mountain of myrrh may not inaptly be understood the human Body of the Bridegroom, which He offered voluntarily to death. For that is the *mountain* of which is read: "A stone was cut out without hands, and smote the image, and became a great mountain." It is of *myrrh*, because of that Joseph by whom the mountain was anointed and laid in the tomb. To this mountain of myrrh and hill of frankincense the Bridegroom willingly came, not only that He might die and be buried for the Bride, but that He might rise again immortal, and therefore His Flesh is likened to a *hill of frankincense*, because after His Resurrection it was to give forth living tongues, that is, Saints. And it is to be noticed that the Chaldee suggests a connection of ideas between this mountain of *myrrh*, הַר הַמוֹר, *har hamor*, and that Mount *Moriah*, הַר הַמּוֹרִיָה, *har ha-Moriah*,[1] whereon the typical sacrifice of Isaac took place, and whereon Solomon built that Temple which foreshadowed the true Tabernacle wherein the WORD of GOD tarried amongst men. Thither the Bridegroom betook Himself till the dawn of the Resurrection morning, till the shadows and types of the Law vanished along with the dark cloud of sorrow which had settled upon the mourning hearts of His Mother and His Apostles. And still, evermore, till the dawning of the Great Day, when all the shadows and unrealities of earth shall flee from the rays of the Sun of Righteousness, or, for each soul, till the evening of life close in, the Bridegroom comes to the mountain of myrrh and the hill of frankincense. For myrrh denotes mortification of the flesh or endurance of suffering for CHRIST's sake, and frankincense implies the devotion of holy souls. The mount and hill, then, are the souls of the Saints, lofty in contemplation. The Bridegroom there-

Philo Carp.

Dan. ii. 34, 35.

Targum.

Cassiodor.

---

[1] The Targum therefore takes these latter words as if meaning, *Mount of the myrrh of the Lord*. There is a similar play of words in גִּבְעַת הַלְּבוֹנָה, *gibeath ha-lebonah*, "hill of frankincense," which suggests the name of Mount Lebanon, לְבָנוֹן, the "white" hill. And so, as will be seen presently, it has been taken by an old commentator.

fore promises that He will come to this mountain of myrrh and hill of frankincense, because He vouchsafes to bless with His visitation those souls which mortify their members with their affections and lusts, and which offer themselves a sacrifice acceptable unto GOD by zeal in devout prayer. One expositor, admitting the truth of this view, differs so far as to suppose the Bridegroom to speak, not to the Bride, but to Himself, because of the delight He takes in what He is about to do. *I will go for Myself.* He goes for Himself, because His singular love admits no partner of its secret. He goes for Himself, because He will have no companion in His journey, any more than He suffers any one to share His love. *Myrrh,* which is bitter to the taste, and preserves the bodies of the dead from corruption, signifies mortification of the flesh, *Libanus,*[1] which name is by interpretation "whiteness," signifies purity of the flesh. This then is the way by which the Bridegroom comes to the Bride, the mount of myrrh and the hills of Lebanon, because He first slays concupiscence by abstinence of the flesh, and then cleanses the ignorance of the soul by purifying the heart. And observe too, that we know in another way that such must be the preparation of the Bride before she is ready for the King, for it is written, "Now when every maid's turn was come to go in to King Ahasuerus, after that she had been twelve months, according to the manner of the women, (for so were the days of their purifications accomplished, to wit, six months with oil of myrrh, and six months with sweet odours, and with other things for the purifying of the women;) then thus came every maiden unto the King." And note, says Cardinal Hugo, that He calls the bitterness of repentance a *mountain,* and the devotion of prayer a *hill,* because penitential sorrow surpasses devout prayer as a mountain does a hill. Not without cause does Wisdom say, "I yielded a pleasant odour like the best myrrh," which perfumes not only the Church, but all Paradise. Whence is written, "Joy shall be in heaven over one sinner that repenteth, more than over ninety and nine just persons which need no repentance." And it should be known that there is a valley of myrrh, and also a plain, a hill, and a mountain of myrrh. The valley of myrrh is repent-

---

[1] He reads, "hills of Libanus."

ance for sins, which are a deep valley; whence the Psalmist, "Out of the deep have I called unto Thee, O LORD." The plain of myrrh is the endurance of bitterness in defence of one's country, and in zeal for justice, which is compared to a plain because of the level of equity. The hill of myrrh is the endurance of bitterness for the protection of one's own innocence. The mountain of myrrh is the endurance of bitterness through longing for the Heavenly Country. And to all these the Bridegroom promises to go when He says, *I will get Me to the mountain of myrrh.* For there is no getting to a mountain save by the valley, the plain, and the hill. So too there is a valley of frankincense, and also a plain, a hill, and a mountain of it. The valley of incense is prayer for the remission of sin, as, "Forgive us our trespasses." The plain is prayer for the bestowal of grace, "Give us this day our daily bread." The hill is prayer for the gift of perseverance, "Lead us not into temptation." And the mountain of frankincense is prayer for the bestowal of glory, which is, "Thy kingdom come." And He significantly says, *I will get Me to the hill,* not to the mountain, *of frankincense,* because the LORD gives us the three first by coming to us in this present life, but He will give the fourth in the next world to those who come to Him. Wherefore He will say, "Come, ye blessed of My FATHER, inherit the Kingdom." _{Ps. cxxx. 1.} _{S. Mat. xxv. 34.}

Another interpretation sees here the calling of the Jews and Gentiles. *I will go,* in the person of My preachers, and therefore they *must* go. *To the mountain of myrrh,* that is, to nations in bitterness, salted with no salt of doctrine. *And to the hill of frankincense,* to the Jews who keep to the incensings of the Law. And in the Church, I will go to the Martyrs, who endure the bitterness of death, and to the Confessors, who offer devout prayers; bestowing patience on the first, and perseverance on the second. _{Gloss.} _{S. Ans. Laud.}

It is to be noted that some commentators ascribe the words to the Bride, but the mystical meaning is the same, whether she gets to the mountain, there to meet her LORD in prayer, or He comes to it, because He knows He will find her waiting for Him. "O happy is the mountain to which Thou goest, good JESU, to which Thou comest, which Thou traversest, wherein Thou dwellest, yea, and inhabitest for ever, wherein Thou dwellest alone, and that to its utmost bounds. _{Gillebert. Serm. 28.}

Come, JESU, begin to possess this mountain. Let no man question Thee, let no man say, Wilt Thou dwell in this mountain alone? A fertile mountain, a great mountain, an abundant mountain, a mountain flowing with unguents. These unguents cannot be exhausted, for great is the plenty of them in the mountain of myrrh. They will not fail therein, and therefore he who goes to the mountain of myrrh will lack no unguents, nor shall he lack perfumes who goes to the hills of Lebanon. For the frankincense of Lebanon will not fail. Come, good JESU, to these hills, that the incense may flow down before Thy Face. O what smoke of incense goes up from these hills, when kindled with Thy fire, yea, with Thyself. Thy fire hath abundant matter to feed on, and great fuel of incense. This incense will not be quickly consumed, its smoke will not readily vanish. Its plenteous abundance cannot be grasped in the hand, nor held in a censer, no vessel can contain it, it knows not measure, because it knows not intermission. Come then, good JESU, to the hills of frankincense, for the mountains which Thou touchest, send up the copious incense of prayer."

7 Thou art all fair, my love; there is no spot in thee.

Beda.

These words cannot, in the fullest sense, be spoken of the Church Militant here on earth, compassed with weakness, and stained with the sins of her children. But they hold good of the Church Triumphant, that "glorious Church, not having spot or wrinkle, or any such thing,"

Eph. v. 27.

Phineas Fletcher, Purple Island, xii. 69.

  The fair Eclecta,[1] who with widowed brow,
   Her absent LORD long mourned in sad array,
  Now silken linen clothed as white as snow,
   Whose silver spanglets sparkle 'gainst the day;
  This shining robe her LORD Himself had wrought,
  While He her love with thousand presents sought,
And it with many a wound, and many a torment bought!

Rev. xxi. 11.

  And thus arrayed, her heavenly beauties shined,
   (Drawing their beams from His most glorious face,)
  Like to a precious jasper, pure refined,
   Which, with a crystal mixed, increase his grace;
  The golden stars a garland fair did frame,
  To crown her head; the sun lay hid for shame
And yielded all his beams to her more glorious flame.

[1] The poet is referring to the "Elect Lady" of the Second Epistle of S. John, by whom many commentators understand the Church.

But even the Church Militant is *all fair* in her Bride-groom's sight, fair in all the ranks and orders of her Saints, great and small; not only in her Martyrs, Confessors, and Virgins, but in her temperate, alms-giving, and penitent members. There is *no spot* in her, because she keeps herself free from mortal sin, and washes away with daily penitence those stains of venial guilt which she has contracted through her frailty. She is all fair, remarks a later commentator, fair with the beauty of the Gospel Law; fair with the knowledge of GOD, and of true faith and worship; fair in the outward beauty of her Sacraments and stately rites; fair in the grace and righteousness of her members; fair in the holy deeds of her Saints. S. Just. Org.
Philo Carp.
Corn. à Lap.

And spoken of the holy soul, it is true that the words cannot have their highest and noblest application during her probation here, but only when she has come close to her Bridegroom, and so has received the blaze of all His splendours, being made radiant by Light itself. Still she may be all fair even on earth, in mind, and soul, and flesh. In flesh, because purged by action from all passions, and adorned with the practice of holiness; in soul, as parted from all evil concupiscence, and decked with the words of the Commandments; and in mind because set free from frivolous thoughts, and made glorious and Godlike by grace in the HOLY GHOST. There is no perfect beauty without colour, observes Richard of S. Victor, and a pale face lessens the charm of lovely features, and the fairness of the Bride is completed by the blush of penitence for her sins, as she washes away those sins by daily confession and contrition. And it is especially true, observes S. Ambrose, of those who live a life of virginal consecration. For what greater loveliness can one fancy than her beauty who is loved by the King, approved by the Judge, dedicated to the LORD, consecrated to GOD? Ever a bride, ever unwedded, so that love has no ending and modesty no peril. This is true loveliness, which lacks nothing, which alone merits to hear from the LORD, *Thou art all fair, My love; there is no spot in thee.* And, above all, it is true of her, of whom the Church exclaims in the Greater Antiphons of Advent, "O Virgin of Virgins, how shall this be? For neither before thee was any like thee: nor shall there be any after;" of whom the Doctor of Grace, when dwelling on man's universal sinfulness, Theodoret.
Tres Patr.
Ric. Vict.
S. Greg. M.
S. Ambros. de Virgin. lib. i.
Brev. Sarisb.

observes, "Excepting the Holy Virgin Mary, touching whom I would raise no question, for the honour of GOD, when treating of sins. For we know that abundant grace was given to her to overcome sin in every wise: to her, who merited to conceive and bear Him, Who, it is certain, had no sin;"

<small>S. August. De Nat. Grat. 36.</small>

For from that sin which could not touch Himself, He kept His Virgin Mother undefiled.

<small>S. Joh. Dam. Canon for Christ. Day, Ode vi.</small>

And so the Holy Eastern Church heaps up all epithets of purity in her praise: "Stainless, immaculate, spotless, unblemished, holy Virgin, Bride of GOD, Our Lady." Thou art *all fair*, exclaims Hugh of S. Victor, preaching on the Feast of the Conception of the Blessed Virgin, fair without and within, in heart and body. Ruddy with charity, white with purity, graceful with humility; fair by nature, fairer by grace, fairest of all by glory. *There is no spot in thee*, for, as we read,

<small>Horologion. Little Comp.</small>

<small>Hugo Vict. Instit. Mon. Serm. ix.</small>

In that, O Queen of queens, thy birth was free
From that which others doth of grace bereave,
When in their mother's womb they life receive,
GOD, as His sole-born daughter, loved thee.

<small>Donne, *Divine Poems*.</small>

Nor does her praise cease down the centuries, as poet after poet hands the torch on to a successor in the race. Let us hearken again:

Mother! whose virgin bosom was uncrost
With the least shade of thought to sin allied;
Woman! above all women glorified,
Our tainted nature's solitary boast;
Purer than foam on central ocean tost;
Brighter than eastern skies at daybreak strewn
With fancied roses, than the unblemished noon
Before her wane begins on heaven's blue coast.

<small>Wordsworth, *Eccl. Sonnets*.</small>

8 Come with me from Lebanon, my spouse, with me from Lebanon: look from the top of Amana, from the top of Shenir and Hermon, from the lions' dens, from the mountains of the leopards.

"CHRIST, in the person of Solomon, summons the Bride to Himself, by the calling of the Gentiles. For thou hast read, *Come, My spouse, from Lebanon.* The name of Mount Lebanon is appropriately introduced, for the word is in use amongst the Greeks to denote incense. For He will betroth the Church to Himself

<small>Tertull. c. Marcion. iv. 11.</small>

from idolatry." So wrote an ancient Father, when three of the Ten Persecutions had yet to run their terrible course, and when Paganism still ruled with all but undisputed sway in every province of the Empire. The LXX. reads instead of, *Look from the top of Amana,* thus, *Thou shalt pass over from the beginning of faith*.¹ On this Theodoret observes that the verse accords with that passage in the Psalms, " Hearken, O daughter, and consider, incline thine ear: forget also thine own people, and thy father's house. So shall the King have pleasure in thy beauty, for He is thy LORD GOD, and worship thou Him." He calls her then from *Lebanon,* which, lying outside the Land of Promise, typifies Gentile idolatry, and also from *Shenir* and *Hermon,* which denote the Law. *Shenir,* observes Theodoret, means the " path of lanterns,"² and denotes that light which illuminated the night-season, before

<small>S. Athan. Synops.</small>

<small>Theodoret. Ps. xlv. 11, 12.</small>

---

¹ This curious variant, whereby the mystical sense is denoted, requires some explanation. In the first place, though the wording of the A. V. implies that *Amana* is a mountain, yet the Chaldee takes it to be a river, and the "top" is therefore its fountain-head, and *beginning.* Next; the word אֲמָנָה (derived from the root אָמַן, "he stablished," "he was faithful," and akin to *Amen,* " verily,") is used twice as a common noun in Nehemiah, in x. 1, (ix. 38, A. V.) to denote a "covenant," and in xi. 23, a "sure ordinance" (A.V. marg.) The meaning given by the LXX. is thus tenable, but it seems better to explain it as a summons to the Church to pass not only from Gentilism, but from Judaism, the Old Covenant, as is practically done by some of the commentators.

² Theodoret apparently derived שְׂנִיר from the root שָׁנָה, *splenduit,* but the etymon now accepted is שָׁנֵי *he clashed,* spoken of the sound of weapons, and the name *Shenir* is diversely explained as "cataract," from the noise of falling water, or as "breastplate," from its form and glittering appearance. *Hermon,* חֶרְמוֹן, a part of the same range, and sometimes used for the same mountain (Deut. iii. 9,) is also variously explained as meaning simply "lofty hills," or else as the "devoted" or "accursed" place, akin to *Hormah* (Numb. xxi. 3,) from the Hiphil הֶחֱרִים (" devoted by curse to destruction,") of the root חָרַם, *he shut up* from common use, or *dedicated.* The mystical force will then be a summons to pass from the earthly Jerusalem, a bondwoman, encompassed with strife and the clash of arms, and doomed to utter overthrow, unto the heavenly Jerusalem, the " Vision of Peace," free, tranquil, and eternal, which the Bride beholds spread out before her view as she stands on the summit of those mountains which she is called on to abandon, seeing it as Moses beheld Canaan from Pisgah.

the Sun of Righteousness arose with the glory of day. And *Hermon* is the mountain of which the Psalmist speaks, mentioning "the dew of Hermon which fell upon the hill of Zion," denoting the precepts of the Law. From these, and from the *lions' dens* of fierce and persecuting Jews, as well as from the *mountains of the leopards*, the subtle and deceitful sophists of the Gentiles, the Bride is urged to hasten away. She must come *from the beginning of faith*, observes one Father, because her earliest training was in the rudiments of the Law, from which she is to pass into the fuller light of the Gospel; she must come thence in another sense, remarks a second, because faith must be her own beginning ere she can undertake the work of converting the world; then she will *pass over*, as the Chariot of GOD, amidst rejoicing thousands, out of this world to the FATHER, that her Bridegroom's words may be fulfilled in her: "I will that they also, whom Thou hast given Me, be with Me where I am." The Latin Fathers take *Lebanon*, "whiteness," to be the laver of Baptism, as the starting point of the Church's career. Besides the occurrence of the title *Spouse* here first in the Song, the Vulgate has two peculiarities to be noticed. First, the invitation to *come* is thrice repeated, thus, *Come from Lebanon, My Spouse, come from Lebanon, come.*[1] Next, the following clause runs: *Thou shalt be crowned from the head of Amana.* This triple calling is variously explained. It denotes, says one, that the Bride must be perfect in thought, word, and deed. *Come*, first, by faith; *come*, freed from the body, to receive a heavenly reward; *come*, at the general Resurrection, taking that body again, to be crowned with double glory. *Come*, another takes it, in faith, hope, and charity. *Come*, from merit to reward, from faith to sight, from the chariot to rest, from time to eternity, from the struggle to the prize, from the way to the country, from peril to safety, from misery to salvation. *Come*, renouncing the devil, *come*, renouncing the world, *come*, renouncing thyself. *Come*, in the Name of the FATHER, Who made thee, *come*, in the Name of the SON, Who redeemed thee, *come*, in the Name of the HOLY GHOST, Who sanctifieth thee. *Come*, to the crown of that blessedness which is three-

---

[1] Reading אֲתִי, the fem. imper. from אָתָה, *he came*, instead of אִתִּי, *with me.*

fold, in vision, in fruition, in perpetual security. Not only so, but come and be crowned in this world too, by the conversion of kings and rulers, of persecutors and heretics, typified by the mountains and the wild beasts, now become thy children and thy crown, according to that saying of the Wise Man, "Children's children are the crown of old men." Not less does the verse apply to the devout soul, which is summoned from *Lebanon*, and from Shenir and Hermon, whence the Jordan flows, to pass on from the baptismal flood wherein she was cleansed, away from the sins and passions of her unregenerate life. Go forth, cries S. Ambrose, go forth from the body, and strip thyself completely, for thou must not be with Me, until thou art a pilgrim from the body, because they who are in the flesh, are pilgrims from the kingdom of GOD. *Come,* He saith, *Come,* fitly repeating it, because whether present or absent, thou shouldest be at hand and please the LORD thy GOD. Come present, come absent, though thou be still in the body, for all are present with Me whose faith is unto Me. He is with Me, who goes forth from the world. He is with Me, who thinks of Me, looks at Me, hopes in Me, whose portion I am. He is with Me who is absent from himself; he is with Me who denies himself. He is with Me who is not within himself, for he who is in the flesh is not in the spirit. He is with Me who goes forth of himself. He is close to Me, who is without himself. He is safe and sound with Me, who for My sake hath lost his life. Therefore, come, My Spouse, thou shalt pass over, and throughly pass over from the beginning of faith. She passes over and throughly passes over others who arrives at CHRIST. She passes over by the merit of faith and brightness of works, who shines like Shenir and Hermon, that is, who passes by the way of the lantern, conquering the temptations of the world, and overcoming spiritual wickedness, seeking the crown of a lawful contest, and therefore attains the glory of praise from CHRIST the Judge. She comes from the *lions' dens,* from the palaces of earthly kings, all the temptations of rank, power, and wealth; she comes from the *mountains of the leopards,* from her variegated and powerful sins, to the poverty of CHRIST, to the snowy pureness of a holy life. And as "a man is not crowned, except he strive lawfully," so the crown promised to the Bride must be won by victory over the world, and over all

Philo Carp.
Beda.

Prov. xvii. 6.

S. Greg. Nyss.

S. Ambros. de Isaac 5.

S. Epiph.

2 Tim. ii. 5.
Gillebert.
Ric. Vict.

<small>Dion. Carth.</small> evil spirits and bad passions, denoted by Shenir, the place of strife, and Hermon, the place accursed, and by the lions and leopards. And this crown of life promised to them who are faithful unto death, is of twelve stars. They are the twelve joys of heavenly bliss, to wit, radiance, surety, sweetness, calm, brightness, impassibility, subtilization, swiftness, renewal unspeakable, loving fellowship, gladness in the Manhood of CHRIST, joy ineffable in the goodness of GOD. On all these Henry Harphius dilates with deep fervour, but at too great a length for citation. What he has said in the terms of mystical theology, has been said before him by a Christian poet in the more acceptable form of verse.

<small>Rev. xii. 1.</small>

<small>Henr. Harph.</small>

<small>S. Pet. Dam. TheRhythm, Ad perennis vitæ fontem.</small>
To their first estate return they, freed from every mortal sore,
And the Truth, for ever present, ever lovely, they adore,
Drawing from that living Fountain, living sweetness evermore.

And they drink in changeless being as they taste those waters clear,
Bright are they, and swift, and gladsome, no more perils need they fear,
There the youth can know no ageing, never cometh sickness near.

Thence they draw their life unending, passingness hath passed away,
Thence they grow and bloom, and flourish, freed for ever from decay,
Now that deathlessness hath swallowed up the might of death for aye.

They know Him Who knoweth all things, nothing from their ken may flee,
And the thoughts of one another in the inmost heart they see,
One in choosing and refusing, one are they in unity.

<small>S. Ambros. de Virgin. lib. 3.</small> This summons, and this crown, belong especially to virgin souls. And therefore one, who trained many such, speaks to them: "Dedicate the first-fruits of thy vigils to CHRIST, sacrifice to CHRIST the first-fruits of thine actions. Thou hast heard that He called thee, saying, Come from *Lebanon, My Spouse, come from Lebanon, thou shalt pass over: and throughly pass over from the beginning of faith.* Thou shalt pass over as a creature into the world: thou shalt throughly pass over to CHRIST, triumphing over the world. Thou hast heard that He hath parted thee from the attacks of lions and leopards, that is, from all spiritual wickednesses." And finally, the verse has been applied to the

<small>Rupert.</small> Assumption of the Blessed Virgin, and is used as an

Antiphon on that feast in some French Breviaries. *Brev. Ambianens.* "I will open my mouth," exclaims the Eastern Church *S. Johan.* on the same festival, "and will breathe a word to the *Damasc.* Mother Queen. And I shall be seen praising her glo- *Menæa, Aug. 15.* riously, and will sing with exultation her Repose. O youthful virgins, with Miriam the prophetess, uplift now the Song of Exodus, for the Virgin, the only Mother of GOD, passes unto her celestial heritage. The divine tabernacle fitly received thee, all-holy One, thyself a living heaven; and thou tookest thy stand, gloriously adorned, as a spotless Bride, beside thy GOD and King." She is thrice called, says Vieyra, the FATHER calls *Vieyra,* His Daughter, the SON calls His Mother, the HOLY *Serm. 2, de N. S. de* GHOST calls His Spouse, to her crown. Thrice was she *Graça.* crowned even on earth; in the Incarnation of her SON, in His Passion, and in His Resurrection.

9 Thou hast ravished my heart, my sister, my spouse; thou hast ravished my heart with one of thine eyes, with one chain of thy neck.

Ravished. That is, as the margin reads, *taken away mine heart.* The LORD'S words are more true of Himself than of any other, that where a man's treasure *S. Mat. vi.* is, there will his heart be also, that while His bodily *21.* Presence is in Heaven, the longings and affections of His human Heart are on earth amongst His kindred. And the especial way in which the constraining force of His love compels Him to abide within the faithful soul, is beautifully typified in the legend of a Virgin Saint, of whom is told that He appeared to her once in vision, and took her heart from out of her side, replacing it *Vit. S. Cath. Senens.* with His own: so that she, whose daily prayer there- *Acta Sanc-* tofore had been, "My LORD, I commit my heart to *torum,* Thee," thenceforward said, "My Spouse, I pray Thee *Apr. 30.* to guard Thine own Heart:" in accordance with the prophecy, "And it shall be at that day, saith the LORD, *Hos. ii. 16.* that thou shalt call Me Ishi (my Husband) and shalt call Me no more Baali (my Lord.)" But the Vulgate, agreeing substantially with the Chaldee, reads, *Thou hast wounded my heart.* They refer it, generally, not only to the love which CHRIST bears to the Church, but to the proof of that love which He gave by suffering Himself to be pierced upon the Cross. "Hence," observes the Illuminate Doctor, "appears CHRIST'S boundless love to us, in that He gave Himself wholly for us. What more could He do than He has done? He unlocked His Heart for us as His most secret chamber, to bring us in thither as His elect Spouse. For His delight is to be with us, and to rest with us in silent calm, in peaceful silence. He gave us His Heart, sorely wounded, that we might abide there, until, thoroughly purged, cleansed, and conformed to that Heart, we might be fit and worthy to be drawn, together with Him, into the Divine Heart of the Eternal FATHER. He gives us then His Heart, that it may be our dwelling, and asks for ours in turn, that it may be His abode. He bestows His Heart on us as a bed decked with the ruddy roses of His purple Blood; and requires instead our heart, a bed adorned for Himself with the white lilies of good works." There is yet another sense of the word לִבַּבְתִּנִי *libbabtini*, which is simply "to hearten," exactly represented by the word here coined by the LXX., ἐκαρδίωσας, (although most Greek Fathers accept the idea of wounding) and turned by the Syriac *strengthened, made confident*, as though giving a double heart, or as denoting the trust and reliance CHRIST has in the love and fidelity of the Church to Him, asking her, as it were, in the words of Jehu to Jonadab, "Is thine heart right, as My Heart is with thy heart?"

My sister, My spouse. Wherefore does He call her both spouse and sister? A bridegroom generally does not give the name sister to his spouse. That name, however, He bestows here, in order to show that it is before no carnal bridechamber that the marriage-song is here being chanted. In calling her *spouse*, He means that the WORD has wedded to Himself the human soul; in styling her also *sister*, He witnesses that He Himself has worn our flesh. Again, as kings and queens entitle one another brothers and sisters, so here the Bridegroom uses the name *sister* to denote the royal station of His Bride, that she is no mere inferior companion, but one decked, as Esther was, with the crown and title of a queen. *Thou hast wounded My heart.* It is said twice, of the Jewish Church, because she wounded Him living with the nails, and dead with the spear. It is said of evil Christians, because they wound Him daily with their sins; it is said of the faithful Church, for whose sake He was wounded in His Passion and in His compassion. Every wound, every blow He suffered was twofold, for hate smote Him in His Body, and love in His Heart. *With one of thine eyes, with one chain of thy neck.* The Targum explains the *eye* to be even one of the least amongst the righteous, the *chain* or tress of the neck to be one of the princes of the House of Judah, wearing the kingly diadem. And the Christian interpretation of this will be the direct personal love which CHRIST bears to each faithful soul in particular, as well as to the whole Church corporately. But the commentators adopt a different view. The eye whose glance has attracted the Bridegroom is, as the Greek Fathers allege, the faculty of Divine contemplation, the tress lying on that neck which bears the yoke of GOD's commandments, is active performance. The right eye is that which looks at heavenly things, the left that which is fixed on earth, and therefore the spiritual Nahash (by interpretation "serpent,") the enemy of our souls, desires to pluck out our right eye, even if we voluntarily yield ourselves as his slaves. But the LORD, on the other hand, tells us, "If thine eye be single, thy whole body shall be full of light." With this single eye, that is, with the sole and undivided contemplation of thy salvation, of My love, and of its fruition, thou woundest My Heart, and also with one tress of thy neck. The neck joins the head and members. Thou art a neck to Me, when thou strivest to convert souls and unite them unto Me. The one tress of thy neck is the single thought and fixed intention wherewith thou toilest for this end. In this twofold care, that for thine own salvation and for the salvation of others, thou winnest My peculiar love for thyself, and makest thy way unto the depths of My Heart. S. Jerome takes the two eyes to denote the virginal and the married lives. "I reject not marriage, thou hast a left eye, which I have given thee because of their weakness who see not aright; but the right eye of virginity is dearer to Me, which, if blinded, leaves the whole body in darkness." Spare not, O Bride, to aim at thy spouse with such weapons as these. Use thy loving glances as darts. Be not slack in this matter, be not content to wound thy Beloved once only, but smite Him with wound on wound. Happy art thou, if thy shafts be fixed in Him, if thy love wars in CHRIST, if thine eyes be steadfastly fastened

Vieyra, Serm. de las Chagas de S.Francisco.

Targum.

Theodoret. Tres Patr.

S. Ambros. 1 Sam. xi. 2. Luc. Abb.

S. Mat. vi. 22.

Ricard. Vict.

S. Hieron. in Jovin. lib. i.

Gillebert.

upon Him. Good is the wound out of which power goes. A woman touched the hem of His garment, and CHRIST perceived that power had gone out of Him. How much more, when His Heart is not lightly touched, but wounded, does He cause grace to flow from Him! That wound is not insensible. Therefore aim the darts of a pure glance at Him, count Him as a mark set up for such arrows. He receives them gladly, because He hurls the like Himself. He looked on Peter, and smote his heart, and pierced him to repentance. Tears give signs of a wounded heart. And then with His merciful glance He wounds the heart which He urges to any holy affection. Would that He might multiply such wounds in me, from the sole of my feet to the crown of my head, that there might be no soundness in me. For that is an evil soundness where are none of those wounds which the loving glance of CHRIST inflicts.

The commoner explanation, however, of the Latin Fathers, is that the eye denotes the Doctors and preachers of the Church, and the tress, bound together, and not left dishevelled, the multitude of the laity. One eye, because of unity of doctrine; one tress, because of unity of fellowship, in the Catholic Church, for which Church the Bridegroom was content to be wounded unto death.

10 How fair is thy love, my sister, my spouse! how much better is thy love than wine! and the smell of thine ointments than all spices!

For *love* the LXX. and Vulgate read *breasts*. But the LXX., reading the second clause, *Thy breasts are fair from wine*, give rise to a peculiar treatment of the verse by the Greek Fathers. Explaining the breasts to be the doctrine of the Church, they for the most part agree in saying that these breasts no longer yield milk for babes and imperfect believers, but the immortal wine of the Saints, the fuller teaching which is reserved for those of full growth. Philo of Carpasia, however, gives a better interpretation of the same reading, by saying that it is wine which the Bride has drunk which makes her breasts fair and plenteous, and that wine is the Blood of CHRIST, which fills the two breasts of the love of GOD and the love of man with the milk of charity, the gift of the HOLY GHOST. The Three Fathers, also taking the wine to be the efficient cause of the loveliness of the breasts, explain them to be the active and contemplative states in the Church. But the Vulgate reading is more consonant with the Hebrew, and implies comparison. The more usual Western interpretation is that the breasts are the Doctors of the Church, who supply spiritual nourishment to her children, giving them in the form of milk that which they themselves have received in the form of heavenly Bread. And this milk is better than the wine of the ceremonial Law, which wine failed at the mystical marriage of the Church, and was replaced by CHRIST with a more generous vintage. Richard of S. Victor, applying the words to the faithful soul, takes the two breasts to be spiritual and corporal compassion, whereby the sufferings of all, whether in soul or body, are shared by the true follower of CHRIST. And He is better pleased in this manner than with the *wine* of rigorous judgment, because it is written: "Mercy rejoiceth against judgment;" and mercy flows from the breasts of heavenly wisdom and knowledge of GOD, the fairest ornament of the Bride. They note further that the Vulgate uses two distinct words in this verse to represent breasts, *mammæ* and *ubera*. The former is used of mothers, feeding their children at the breasts; the latter word is of general application. *Mammæ*, then, observes Aponius, denotes the blessing of fruitfulness, *ubera* the glory of virginity. With these the Church is shown to be fair at the time of CHRIST'S appearing, in that she daily conceives, daily brings forth, daily suckles, and is yet a virgin. And that is an unhappy man who does not believe that GOD does by the Church what He did by the Virgin Mary.

And the smell of thine ointments than all spices. So the Vulgate, but the LXX. read *the smell of thy garments.* And these garments they take to be the works of mercy wrought by the Church, or the graces with which she is decked, under the Gospel, as sacrifices to GOD, more pleasing to Him than the incensed oblations of the Law, because they are perfumed with CHRIST Himself, Who is, indeed, according to Theodoret, not merely the fragrance of these garments, but Himself the raiment of the Church, which saith of

S. Greg. M.
Tres Patr.
Cassiodor.
Beda.
Ricard. Vict.
S. James ii. 13.
Dion. Carth.
Henr. Harphius.
Luc. Abb.
S. Greg. Nyss.
Tres Patr.
Theodoret.

Him, "He hath clothed me with the garments of salvation, He hath covered me with the robe of righteousness." The Western expositors differ little from this, taking, as they do generally, the words to denote the grateful perfume of the virtues and good deeds of the Church, spread over the world by the preaching of the Gospel, and superior in diffusion, number and fragrance, to the observances of the Law, the lore of philosophy, and the vanities of the world. And that because they spring out of charity, which is lacking in mere earthly virtues, but which gives them that especial odour which is a sweet savour unto GOD. They are called *ointments*, moreover, because they are derived from the unction of the HOLY GHOST, and they were typified under the Law by the compound "oil of holy ointment" made of four principal spices mingled with olive-oil, and designed for the consecration of the priests and the furniture of the Sanctuary.

Isa. lxi. 10.
Cassiodor.
Beda.
S. Just. Org.
S. Greg. M.
Ricard. Vict.
Aponius.
Hugo Card.
Ex. xxx. 23.

11 Thy lips, O my spouse, drop as the honeycomb: honey and milk are under thy tongue; and the smell of thy garments is like the smell of Lebanon.

Theodoret.

As the honeycomb. This denotes the Doctors of the Church, who bring forth her holy teaching, and have as it were the combs of bees upon their lips, which drop honey. And they have not only honey, but milk also, providing for each his proper food, as well that which suits infants, as that which befits the perfect. And the honeycombs which are borne on the lips of teachers are the Divine Scriptures, containing bees which make wax as well as honey, that is, the sacred Prophets and Apostles, who, flitting over the meadows of the HOLY GHOST, and, as it were, framing the cells of Holy Writ for us and filling them with the honey of instruction, confer their benefit on us. The letter is like wax, and the meaning hidden in it like honey. This *drops*, because as the honey drips from the comb when it is too plentiful to be retained in the cells, so Holy Scripture has manifold senses, and is diversely explained, sometimes literally, sometimes allegorically, sometimes morally, and sometimes by anagoge, which is the highest sense of all. And these four senses are exemplified in the fourfold

Cassiodor.

Beda.

meaning which Jerusalem bears in Scripture. Literally, it is the earthly city in Judæa; allegorically, it is the Church throughout the world; morally, it is any Christian soul which has become the city of GOD; anagogically, it is the heavenly Jerusalem, the Church Triumphant. The preachers of the Church are compared to honeycombs also for another reason, because the sweet doctrines of the Gospel come from men themselves weak and frail as the waxen cells of the bee, according to that saying of the Apostle, "We have this treasure in earthen vessels, that the excellency of the power may be of GOD, and not of men." This honeycomb the soul gathers from divers flowers of Scripture; she seeks them out, settles on them, and draws from them the sweetness of spiritual delights. She puts aside and despises the knowledge that puffeth up, and seeks rather for edification; she chooses fragrant texts, not ornate eloquence. She searches also for the examples of the Saints and their spiritual sayings, and ponders them in her mind, for the Saints were flowers too, and flourished like the palm-tree. And as their life was holy, so what they produced or taught was sweet and pleasant. She flies then to these flowers, and draws from them spiritual honey, but above all from that especial flower which came forth from the stem of Jesse, the flower of the plain and not of the garden. And the perfume of this flower is as the smell of a field which the LORD hath blessed. This is the field wherein the fulness of the Godhead dwells, wherein are all the treasures of wisdom and knowledge, wherein the righteous flourish and bring forth fruit in sanctity of life as well as in holiness of knowledge. This is that flowery field wherein are as many blossoms as there are righteous ones bringing forth fruit in good works, and outside which there is no flowering, but only withering. To this flowery and abundant field the Bride flies like the prudent bee: she runs after the perfume of this Flower, speeds to It longingly, clings to It in love and faith, sucks the honey of grace from It with the importunity of prayer, receives graces from its plenteousness, grace so diffused upon her lips that they breathe forth the savour of heavenly sweetness, and offer it to others that they too may quaff. And there is no inconsistency between the epithet here applied to the lips of the Church, and that a little before, when they were compared to a scarlet thread.

S. Greg. M.

2 Cor. iv. 7.

Ric. Vict.

Beda.

For the same teachers are cords in salutary precepts and honeycombs in heavenly promises : cords, when they bridle us from giving way to the glow of carnal pleasures ; honeycombs, when they offer us the gifts of celestial joys. They are cords also when they teach openly what has to be done or avoided ; honeycombs, when they disclose the majesty and salvation which *Hugo Card.* lie hid in typical words and action. And observe that they are said to *drop,* not to pour, because the teaching of the Doctors and preachers of the Church should be carefully proportioned to the capacity of their hearers, and not all poured out at once, according *Prov. xxv.* to that warning of the Wise Man : "Hast thou found *16.* honey? eat so much as is sufficient for thee, lest thou *Philo Carp.* be filled therewith, and vomit it." Philo reminds us that honey is food, and wax gives light, and both are to be found in Holy Scripture. Another most beau- *Hugo Vict.* tiful interpretation is that which sees in the honey- *Erud. Theol.* *i. 15.* comb dropping from the lips of the Church, Him Whose Name is ever in her mouth in prayer and praise, in the pure virgin wax of Whose most pure Body, taken of the Blessed Mary, is stored the golden honey of the Godhead, ever pouring forth its grace and giving to each according to the measure of that grace.

Ric. Vict. *Honey and milk are under thy tongue.* That is, refreshment for the robust, and comfort for the little ones, solid food for the perfect, and the milk of easy doctrine for the weak. For she had a foretaste of the sweetness of the life to come, where souls are refreshed with the fruition of CHRIST's Godhead, and with the milk of His Manhood. She had a foretaste of that *Job xx. 17.* blessedness, because she is refreshed with "the rivers, the floods, the brooks, of honey and butter," which the wicked and the hypocrite shall not see, that is, understand or taste. This twofold sweetness, as the rivers *Ps. xlvi. 4.* of a flood, makes glad the City of GOD on high, but it visits with its brooks the righteous who are still exiles and pilgrims, and gently bathes and refreshes them. *Beda.* *Under thy lips,* not merely *on* them, but coming from the depth of the heart. For false preachers carry honey on their tongue which they have not under their tongue, who preach of heavenly joys, while they are yearning after mere temporal benefits with all their might. But not so they who imitate the Great Teacher, Whose inner love was as perfect as His outward words and deeds, and of Whom His own Virgin

Martyr said, "I have received honey and milk from His mouth, and His Blood hath adorned my cheeks." And it is not only the Doctors of the Church who can have the honey and milk under their tongues, but every faithful soul which utters prayers and praises to GOD in simplicity and sweetness of heart, with devout affection, and with meditation on the simple doctrines of the Faith. Say then evermore most earnestly, "Thou shalt open my lips, O LORD, and my mouth shall show Thy praise." It is to but little or no profit for me to open wide the lips of my mouth, unless Thou open these lips of my heart. Open these lips of mine, O LORD, and then they shall drop, like the honeycomb, Thy sweet praise. Open these lips of mine, O LORD, and then honey and milk shall be under my tongue. So that becomes true which the heathen poet said: ^{Mart. S.} ^{Agnetis ap. S. Ambros.} ^{S. Ambros. de Virgin. lib. 1.} ^{Ps. li. 15.}

τὸ στόμα δ' ἦν πακτᾶς γλυκερώτερον· ἐκ στομάτων δὲ
ἔρρεέ μοι φωνὰ γλυκερωτέρα ἢ μέλι κηρῷ.

^{Theocrit. Idyll. xx. 26.}

Sweeter than milk-curd is my mouth, and from my mouth there wells
A voice more sweet than honey is from out the waxen cells.

That is but a feigned sweetness which does but sound on the tongue, and is not felt under it. That is but scanty, which is all on the lips and tongue, and not the greater part of it underneath. Some have only honey under the tongue, and no milk; others have only milk, and no honey. But both honey and milk are under the tongue of the Bride. Nor does the honey flow, but rather drops. For she does not commonly and recklessly pour forth the august and hidden meanings of the heavenly secrets and mysteries of the Godhead, nor offer milk when there is no pleasure in the draught. She, under whose tongue are honey and milk, is ready to speak sweet things. Blessed is the tongue which drops as the honeycomb, and is full of milk like the breast given to babes. All crying, and bitterness, and blasphemy is banished far from lips like these. Nor is there ungodliness and vanity under this tongue, but honey and milk. "The lips of a strange woman drop as an honeycomb, and her mouth is smoother than oil." But there is no honey and milk under her tongue, nor in her heart, nor yet in her last end, for "her end is bitter as wormwood, sharp as a two-edged sword." But of a virtuous woman is said also in Proverbs, ^{Gillebert. Serm. 34.} ^{Ps. x. 7.} ^{Prov. v. 3.}

Prov. xxxi. 25.

"Strength and honour are her clothing, and she shall rejoice in time to come. She openeth her mouth with wisdom, and in her tongue is the law of kindness." Her mouth is even now bringing forth that spiritual and blessed rejoicing, and its sweetness is lying hid under her tongue. And the honey and milk now there shall burst forth in full exultation at the last day.

And the smell of thy garments is like the smell of Lebanon. So the LXX., but the Greek Fathers practically agree with the Vulgate in taking the last word to be *incense.* That is, as S. Gregory Nyssen observes, the holy acts of the Church in the devout soul imitate the divine blessedness itself, and their fragrance is like that of the frankincense burnt in honour of GOD. And he dwells at some length on the fitness of *garments* as a simile for a holy life, because the cloth of which they are made is composed of countless threads crossing and re-crossing each other, and so holiness of life does not consist in a single virtue or a single good deed, but in the union of a multitude of them woven together in the daily course of existence. Theodoret, as noticed already, declares that CHRIST Himself is the only true covering and vesture of His Church, and that the incense denotes His Godhead. The garments of the Church, says a Western Father, are the ornaments of good works, as S. John saith in the Apocalypse, "the pure linen is the righteousness of Saints;" and it is said in Job, "I put on righteousness, and it clothed me; my judgment was as a robe and diadem." And by incense the beauty of holy prayer is denoted. Therefore the garments of the Church are compared to incense, because all her works are of the nature of prayer. And observe: that good works are called garments for three reasons: first, they cover sins, as it is written, "Love covereth all sins;" and again, "Charity shall cover the multitude of sins;" next, they give spiritual heat, when done to help others; thirdly, they are marks of honour and distinction, and so it is said, "Let Thy priests be clothed with righteousness." He who does not bring forth fruits meet for repentance does not clothe himself as he ought, and of this is said, "Blessed is he that watcheth and keepeth his garments, lest he walk naked." Of the second, when there is no true charity, we read, "They covered him with clothes, but he gat no heat." And of the third is written, "He that is the High Priest

S. Greg. Nyss.

Theodoret.

Cassiodor.

Rev. xix. 8.
Job xxix. 14.

Hugo Card.
Prov. x. 12.
1 S. Pet. iv. 8.

Ps. cxxxii. 9.

Rev. xvi. 15.

1 Kings i. 1.

Lev. xxi. 10.

shall not rend his clothes." These good works, acutely observes Beda, as being external and done by men, are compared to incense, itself made of spices; but of the inner anointing of the HOLY GHOST, whereby the will to do these works is given us, is said, "How much better is the smell of thine ointments than all spices!" The incense smells sweetly in the garment of outward abstinence. And that is in truth a seemly garment, when the soul is not so much clothed with flesh as with fasting from carnal things and restraint in pleasures. Virginal purity is a seemly garment, and sends forth a pleasant odour of incense as well to the Beloved as to her who loves Him. For it cannot be that what is offered with love should not yield delight to her who offers it. What then is the perfume of these garments. Is it not incense? So the heavens are clad in radiant light, but the heavens declare, not their own glory, but the glory of GOD. O happy me, if but one or other of my garments could give forth the pure fragrance of incense, not marred by any foreign admixture! For I hold that none hath yet attained to this measure, that every garment should smell like incense, who hath not yet merited to be ranked in the bridal lot by the LORD JESUS, the Bridegroom of the Brides. *[margin: Beda. ver. 10. Gillebert. Serm. 34.]*

It is enough to say of the A. V. reading, that it seems to denote two things, the perfume of the incorrupt cedars of Lebanon, and that of the wine produced from the mountain grapes, strong and fragrant, denoting the mingled purity and zeal, the contemplative and active states, which are the "vesture of gold wrought about with divers colours," that decks the queenly Bride. *[margin: Hos. xiv. 7. Ps. xlv. 10.]*

12 A garden inclosed is my sister, my spouse; a spring shut up, a fountain sealed.

Inclosed, that Satan may not enter, but ever open to the Bridegroom. The Church, once His handmaid, now His *sister*, and betrothed to Him as His *Spouse* with the dower of the HOLY GHOST, is a *garden*, because she brings forth the buds of spiritual virtues, which, in a subsequent passage, are called by the name of spices. This garden is *inclosed*, because the Holy Church, fortified by the protection of her LORD and Redeemer, and fenced by the guard of the angelic hosts, lies not open to the snares of evil spirits. This same Church is also a *fountain sealed*. A *fountain*, be- *[margin: S. Epiphanius. Cassiodor.]*

cause she flows with the streams of heavenly doctrine, wherewith she washes all believers in CHRIST from their sins, and gives them the knowledge of truth to quaff. This fountain is *sealed*, because the word of the Gospel creed is protected with the seal of truth, so that neither heretics nor evil spirits may be able to violate or break in upon the Catholic Faith. And so the Apostle saith, "I planted, Apollos watered, but GOD giveth the increase." I planted the spices of virtues, as in the garden of GOD, Apollos watered, as from the sealed fountain of heavenly teaching, but the LORD helped His labourers, lest they should toil in vain. Others severally take the flowers of the garden to be various orders of Saints, and the wall which incloses the garden to be charity, or the union of faith and works, or, again, the discipline of the Church. And whereas the A. V. translates in the second clause, *A spring shut up*, following the received text גַּל, *gal*, all the old versions with one voice accept the variant גַּן, *gan*, (found in more than fifty MSS.) and repeat, *A garden inclosed*. It is said twice, as one will have it, because the garden of the Church was first made of the Jews, and then of the Gentiles. It is, remarks another, because of its faith and works, and its division into the active and contemplative lives. A fountain is *sealed* when covered with a stone, and that stone marked with the signet of the owner, that no stranger may approach to draw water from it, but that it may be kept for its lord alone, as the water of the Choaspes was for the kings of Persia.[1]

The seal of this fountain is said by some Fathers to be the sign of the Cross impressed at Holy Baptism, but S. Augustine, writing against the Donatists, combats this view on the ground that the fountain is within the one inclosed garden of the Church, whereas Baptism is common to heretics as well as Catholics, and observes: "To this peculiar fountain, of which no

---

[1] I know not why Mr. Thrupp defines a sealed fountain to mean one diverted by a subterranean channel to a place different from that in which it springs. Such is the case, no doubt, with Solomon's pools near Bethlehem, to which he refers, following Maundrell and Hasselquist, but he does not add that there is a local tradition that they were literally closed by the king's signet, and that Maundrell states that the very small size of the opening makes it quite possible that they were so closed.

stranger partakes, to this sealed fountain, that is, to the gift of the HOLY GHOST, whereby the love of GOD is shed abroad in our hearts, none of them draws near, unless changed, so to be throughly cleansed, that he may be no more a stranger, but thus a sharer in heavenly peace, a partner in holy unity, and, full of undivided love, a citizen of the City of the Angels."

The holy soul is a garden inclosed, because in putting forth virtues, it gives birth to flowers, and in refreshing itself with the gladness which those virtues yield, it guards the fruits it has produced. The garden is called *inclosed*, because it hedges itself round with holy resolve, as it hides its own good things with that resolve for eternal life, and altogether despises the praise of men, so that the ancient enemy cannot break in to plunder its hidden treasures. It is also called a fountain, because while constantly pondering heavenly things, and ever gathering knowledge of Scripture in the storehouse of memory, the holy soul ceases not to produce living waters within itself, to give to its thirsty neighbours for their refreshment. Whence it is written that the LORD said, " Whosoever shall drink of the water that I shall give him, shall never thirst; but the water that I shall give him shall be in him a well of water springing up into everlasting life." Yet why is that fountain said to be *sealed*, save because the spiritual sense is hidden from unworthy souls? But in the case of a faithful man the LORD saith, " The SPIRIT bloweth where He listeth, and thou hearest the sound thereof, but canst not tell whence He cometh and whither He goeth." S. Greg. M.

S. John iv. 14.

Theodoret.

S. John iii. 8.

The soul is a garden wherein the plants of virtue and the seedlings of spiritual pursuits are cultivated. This garden is dug, when vices are rooted up in it, and the habits of life are turned over. And it is dug yet deeper when a man strives to learn the nature and cause of his sins. For no lukewarm labourer, ignorant of the nature of sins, can successfully mortify his vices. It must then be dug with the memory of the LORD'S Passion, and those nails wherewith the ungodly pierced His hands and feet pierce it too, when we remember those things, and sorrow with His sorrow. This garden is inclosed with the lock of silence, and with bars set to both sight and hearing, lest aught evil should enter by them. It is inclosed even from praise, and it is a fountain sealed with the signet of the HOLY Ricard. Vict.

GHOST, and the precepts of Scripture, and walled with the examples of the Saints.

And it may well be asked, Who can be a fitting gardener for such a garden as this? S. Mary Magdalene gives us the answer, "She, supposing Him to be the Gardener." And He had one peculiar garden, wherein He abode, inclosed for Him alone, sealed with His own signet, and fenced by the overshadowing SPIRIT, His own most blessed Mother. In the first garden He planted He put a Virgin, yet sin entered, and she fell; but into this garden none entered save Himself:

<small>S. John xx. 15.</small>

<small>Rupert.
S. Just. Org.
Philipp.
Harveng.</small>

<small>J. Beaumont,
Psyche, vii. 103.</small>

O Paradise, how poor a soil art thou
  To the rare richness of this virgin bed!
That Tree of Life which in thy heart did grow,
  Itself but as the shade of this was spread:
Here is the Garden where the noble Tree
Of everlasting Life would planted be.

<small>Dion. Carth.</small> That princely Lady is the sweetest, most blooming, and most fruitful Garden of the LORD, wherein are planted all manner of spiritual trees, wherein rested the Tree of Knowledge, wherein all virtues were planted, all divine graces blossomed; where the Sun of Wisdom poured His brightest rays, wherein no winds, nor rains, nor floods of sin could ever find a place, which brought forth Him Who is the Maker of all things, and bare the SAVIOUR of the world; and which was inclosed and sealed evermore with the signet of inviolable virginity; which is the fountain of grace, and, after GOD Himself, the source and author of all blessings bestowed on us. Accordingly, this verse formed the Antiphon at the First Vespers of feasts of the B.V.M. in the old English Use. And what holds of the Virgin of virgins, holds also, in its degree, of the maidens of her court, which be her fellows. So, following the clear leading of the Targum, many of the Fathers have delighted to tell us. For the Chaldee paraphrase runs thus: "And thy women, who are wedded to husbands, are honourable spouses, and as a pleasant garden, to which no man hath entrance save the righteous whose souls are sent thither by the hands of the Angels. And thy virgins are hidden, and clustered within, and sealed like a fountain of living waters, which springs beneath a tree, and is divided into four river-heads, and unless it were sealed in the great and holy Name, it would go forth, and flow, and inundate

<small>Brev. Sarisb.</small>

<small>Ps. xlv. 15.</small>

<small>Targum.</small>

the world." And similarly that great Saint who ruled the convents of Milan: "Thou, O virgin, art a garden inclosed, preserve thy fruits, let no thorns arise in thee, but let thy grapes flourish, let not any take from thee the fence of thy modesty, for it is written, 'Whoso breaketh a hedge, a serpent shall bite him.' Thou art a sealed fountain, O virgin, let no one defile or trouble thy waters." And again, the same Saint observes: "A virgin is as a garden inaccessible to thieves; she has the perfume of the vine, the fragrance of the olive, the glowing beauty of the rose; as religion grows in the vine, peace in the olive, and the modesty of holy virginity in the rose. Gird thyself then, O virgin, and if thou desire that thy garden should yield thee such odours, inclose it with the counsels of the prophets. Set a watch before thy mouth, and keep the door of thy lips." So too, S. Jerome, writing to the Abbess S. Eustochium, tells her that consecrated virgins ought to be shut up and sealed, not given to leave their home and wander, not even to seek their Bridegroom in the streets, lest they fall like Dinah, though she had patriarchs for her brothers and Israel himself for her father.

S. Ambros. de Inst. Virg. c. 8.

Eccles. x. 8.

S. Ambros. de Virg. 1.

S. Hieron. Ep. 22, ad S. Eustoch. de Cust. Virg.

That all this is no mere fanciful treatment of the words appears from the exact coincidence of idea in a heathen poet, by no means of an ascetic turn. Hear Catullus:

Ut flos in septis secretus nascitur hortis,
Ignotus pecori, nullo contusus aratro,
Quem mulcent auræ, firmat sol, educat imber,
Multi illum pueri, multæ optavere puellæ.
Idem quum tenui carptus defloruit ungui
Nulli illum pueri, nullæ optavere puellæ,
Sic Virgo, dum intacta manet, tum cara suis est,
Quum castum amisit polluto corpore florem,
Nec pueris jucunda manet, nec grata puellis.

Catull. lxii. 39.

As a hid flower within closed gardens grows,
By plough uninjured, and by herds unknown,
And fed by winds, sun, rain, in beauty blows,
Till youths and damsels wish it for their own:
And yet, if it be lightly plucked, and fade,
No youths nor damsels wish for it again;
So, dear and honoured is a spotless maid,
But if she lose her virgin bloom through stain,
On her no youths are bent, for her no damsels fain.

13 Thy plants are an orchard of pomegra-

nates, with pleasant fruits; camphire, with spikenard.

14 Spikenard and saffron; calamus and cinnamon, with all trees of frankincense; myrrh and aloes, with all the chief spices.

Thy plants. More exactly, *thy shoots,* and accordingly the LXX. and Vulgate read *thy sendings-forth* (ἀποστολαί, *emissiones*.) Further, the word translated
Cassiodor. *orchard* in the A. V. is פַּרְדֵּס, *paradise,* and is rightly
Corn. à Lap. so rendered by the old versions. The apostolates, then, or emissions of the Bride, are her augments of faith and spreading of preaching, that is, her planting local Churches throughout the world, each of which is a *paradise,* resembling that first and central one which is their source and model. Or you may take them to
Philo Carp. be the Apostles themselves, ruddy, like the pomegranates, with the blood of martyrdom, and bringing forth many spiritual children to CHRIST by their toils and sufferings, answering to the grains within that fruit.
S. Greg. M.
Luc. Abb. S. Gregory takes the *sendings-forth* to be the holy words and works of the Church, whereby she produces offspring, and trains up some for martyrdom, and others for holy continuance in life. And another view, which takes the emissions to denote the flow of irrigating water, sees here all the devout baptized. However the word be explained, there is much depth in the thought of some Greek Fathers, that this sending-forth
Origen.
Theodoret.
Hugo Vict.
S. Greg.
Nyss.
S. Ambros.
Beda. does not barely denote emissions, but the gifts and offerings which the Bride sends to her Spouse at the time of her betrothal, in token of her love and faith, and especially the Saints she presents to Him.

Spoken of the holy soul, they take, for the most part, her *sendings-forth* to be all the words she utters for GOD's glory. But a fuller interpretation is that of
Ricard. Vict. Richard of S. Victor, who sees here all the virtues of devotion, putting forth their shoots and sending up their fragrance to Heaven, and that especially in the case of her who was that Paradise wherein GOD put
Rupert.
R. Ishaki. the Man Whom He had formed to dress it by His labours and to keep it by His grace and power. The
Gillebert.
Serm. 34. words of Gilbert of Hoyland, who follows some Rabbins and also Aponius in taking the word *emissiones* to denote irrigating waters, merit citation. After

dwelling on the sealing of the fountain as denoting the partial concealment of Divine mysteries even from those who dwell in the garden, he adds: "That fountain is sealed indeed, but not dried up, whose sendings-forth are so gracious. The fountain of wisdom is sealed, but you may know it by its sendings-forth. 'In that day there shall be a fountain opened to the house of David and to the inhabitants of Jerusalem for sin and for uncleanness.' The one is open, the other sealed; the one washes, the other waters; the one cleanses sins, the other produces pleasant things; the one belongs to many, the other is the Bride's alone. There are remissions, here emissions. Yes, good JESU, yes, it is even so. Her sendings-out are Thy sendings-in, sent in by Thy good Angels. She would never send forth such pleasant things unless Thou sentest forth within her the delightsome waters of life. Thou hast both,—a paradise inclosed, and a paradise sent forth. The one is in pure affection, the other in loving actions. The one is inward, the other comes forth from it, and proves its existence." Zech. xiii. 1.

So much, in brief, for the general scope of interpretations. But the various fruits and spices enumerated have given rise to a garden, not less various, of mystical exposition, and it will therefore be needful to enter into somewhat fuller detail.

Pomegranates. Spoken of the Church, these, as observed before, denote martyred Apostles, containing in them the seeds of many faithful souls won to GOD by their toils, or other martyrs endowed with many inner virtues. Again, the pomegranate, with its thorny branches, and the hard and bitter rind in which its fruit is inclosed, that fruit itself being red with white seeds, denotes an austere and mortified life, ruddy with suffering, white with purity and good works. Or, once more, it signifies, as noted previously, charity, because uniting many seeds in one receptacle. Especially does it signify the fraternal union of the members of one Religious order or house. Would, exclaims a Cistercian Abbat, that we imitated these seeds, agreeing together in unity of heart, as though in the inclosure of an Order. The seeds of this fruit cling to one another with a nearly unbroken surface, and their difference is rather that of separate number than of aspect. Let us in turn learn to differ from one another in number, not in mind. These seeds do not quarrel with each Philo Carp.
S. Greg. M.
S. Greg. Nyss.
Ricard. Vict.
Theodoret.
Hugo Card.
Gillebert.

other, they do not murmur against the rind, they do not strive to break through it, they patiently bear being inclosed within it, so that they almost seem to say, "Behold, how good and joyful a thing it is, brethren, to dwell together in unity." And does not the ruddy colour glow in this our Order, brethren, through imitation of CHRIST, as within the rind of the pomegranate? And they are like the seeds of this fruit, who think it natural to be restrained by the outer discipline of the Rule, and count themselves not oppressed thereby, but protected.

Pleasant fruits. Here the LXX. and Vulgate are directly at variance. The former reads μετὰ καρποῦ ἀκροδρύων, *shelly fruits* or *nuts;* the latter has *cum fructibus pomorum,* which properly denotes all fruit with a soft rind, though it may sometimes be used more widely. The Greek Fathers pass lightly over the phrase, but from coupling it, as they do, with the pomegranates, they show that their view is that the *nuts* denote souls guarded by rigid external discipline, which shelters them from all outward troubles, and keeps them safe till they are fully ripened by the Sun of Righteousness. The Latins take the fruits as something of less note than the pomegranates, sweet, indeed, and fragrant, but not ranking with the Martyrs, and rather denoting the less exalted Saints who busy themselves in good works. Or again, the slightly acid and astringent flavour of the pomegranates, contrasted with the sweeter taste of apples, denotes the austerer Christian virtues of justice and temperance, compared with the softer and gentler ones, mercy and loving-kindness. Another, and the truest, way of regarding the latter clause, *pleasant fruits,* is that it is meant to include all the productions of the garden, and that the catalogue which follows is not additional, but explanatory of what these divers fruits are, denoting either various classes of Saints, or various spiritual graces.

Coming from the fruits to the spices, the LXX. and Vulgate, both reading *Lebanon* where the A. V. has *frankincense,* count up exactly seven aromatic plants, the mystical number. And accordingly, the Fathers see here the seven gifts of the HOLY GHOST, the seven Sacraments, the seven virtues, three of them theological, faith, hope, and charity, and four cardinal, justice, prudence, fortitude, and temperance, and the seven orders of Saints in the Church.

Of *camphire*, or *henna*, it has been already observed that it denotes propitiation or atonement (chap. i. 14,) but this is not a view put forward here by any of the elder commentators. Cassiodorus, stating that the plant has seeds like coriander, white and semi-transparent, takes it as a type of the manna, and thus as denoting heavenly grace, the more that it was used in the chrism for anointing kings. For this latter cause another writer sees here those Saints who bring forth good works wherewith GOD is, as it were, anointed; while a third understands it of the gift of ruling, and therefore as denoting all Prelates and rulers in the Church. Philo, who takes it to signify faith, rests on the lowliness of the plant and its white clustering blossoms as bearing out his view. And others hold this whiteness to denote purity, as the first of graces, especially as manifested in the Religious life. Cassiod.
Exod. xvi. 31.
S. Ans. Laud.

Hugo Card.

Philo Carp.
Hugo Card.
Nic. Argent.
Honor. Aug.

Spikenard. Because this was the chief ingredient of the ointment wherewith CHRIST was anointed just before His Passion, the plant in the garden of the Church denotes thankful remembrance of that Passion, and all it has obtained for us. Another, referring to the same anointing, draws the different conclusion that the spikenard signifies the unction of GOD's love in the heart, whereby we are refreshed, and strengthened for the combat. Philo takes it to be hope, because it is warm, fragrant, and medicinal, and it is twice mentioned, coupled first with camphire and then with saffron, because hope is the link between faith and charity. S. John xii. 3.
Cassiod.

Ric. Vict.
Philo Carp.
Luc. Abb.

Saffron, because of its golden hue, denotes charity, for charity is among the virtues what gold is amongst metals. And others dwell on its elasticity when trampled under foot (a cause assigned by some for calling it humility,) and the custom of mingling it with wine as additional arguments for the sense. And as the golden stamens of the plant, which alone are used for flavour and perfume, are three in number, they signify the threefold love of the devout soul for the Persons of the Blessed Trinity, and the fulfilment of its triple duty to GOD, to its neighbours, and to itself. One more circumstance, on which they do not dwell, may be added, that it was an ancient custom to sprinkle a bridal couch with saffron wine, or with the flowers of the plant. Cassiodor.
Joann. Carm.
Philo Carp.

Corn. à Lap.
Philo Carp.

Tryphiodorus.

> Conscia jam Veneris nova serta parate Napææ,
> Crocumque lecto spargite. Martianus Capella.

> Prepare fresh wreaths that know the Lesbian queen,
> And strew the couch with saffron.

And, as is more familiarly known, the bridal veil of ancient Rome was of saffron hue. Wherefore we may add that the mutual love of the Bridegroom and Bride *[Tres Patr. Theodoret. Cassiod.]* is denoted in this place. Finally, several dwell on the real or supposed effects of saffron as a cooling febrifuge, and take it to be justice, or the Divine grace whereby the desires of the flesh are quenched.

[Isa. xliii. 24.] *Calamus*, the "sweet cane" of another book of Holy Writ, from being the same word as the reed or pen in *[Ps. xlv. 2.]* the verse, "My tongue is the pen of a ready writer," *[Theodoret.]* is taken by Theodoret to denote the Doctors of the Church, whose writings are full of sweet instruction. Other Greek divines dwell on the slenderness and lofti- *[Tres Patr.]* ness of the reed, as a type of the virtue of temperance, which lightens the soul of much of the burden of the body, and uplifts it to spiritual things. Again, the straight uprightness of the reed, and its use as the sceptre of CHRIST, make it a type of justice. The hard bark and inner sweetness of the calamus have led also to its being taken here as a type of religious *[Nic. Argent.]* poverty, or of the contemplative claustral life. Cassiodorus and some others, mistakenly identifying calamus with cassia, a totally different plant, give further explanations which need not be detailed.

Cinnamon, because of its outer ashen-grey bark which incloses the inner brown spice, denotes those *[Cassiod. Ricard. Vict.]* Saints who are lowly and penitential in their outward conversation, while warm within through the heat of *[Tres Patr.]* Divine love. Others in this same warmth see forti- *[Cosm. Dam.]* tude, and also loving-kindness, because of the fragrant and penetrating odour of the plant. And the ashy tint *[Nic. Argent.]* is also explained of obedience, whereby the self-will *[Gillebert.]* of man is consumed into dust and ashes. Gillebert, contrasting the tall calamus with the lowlier cinnamon, observes, applying the whole verse to CHRIST, Who suffered as our propitiation in the camphire, was buried with the spikenard, rose again in golden beauty like the crocus, and ascended like the reed, that the cinnamon when broken gives forth a gush of fragrance. That, he says, was JESUS, when He took bread, brake, and gave it. The Bride is like the calamus when she goes up towards GOD in prayer from the waters of weeping; she is like the cinnamon, when she humbles herself for the sake of man. The ascension is beautiful, but take care that the descent be like to cinnamon; when any reasonable cause calls thee back and restrains thee from that ascension and going forth, be like the cinnamon. Let thy conversation, thine ordinary life breathe grace. If thou be sometimes turned aside from thine own will and resolve, and that will be bent, and as it were broken at the bidding of an elder, let there be no murmuring, no complaint. Be cinnamon, give forth a breath of grace, not a complaint of injury. Gillebert. Serm. 36.

With all trees of frankincense. That is, since incense is offered to GOD only, all those Saints who in every part of their lives aim at likeness to Him and conformity to His will. Others, dwelling on the stately trees of Lebanon, explain it of the more eminent Saints, compared to the cedars for strength and beauty. Or, remembering that Lebanon means whiteness, you may take it of the Virgins, pure in snowy chastity and rising boldly up towards heaven. S. Greg. Nyss.
Cassiodor. S.Ans.Laud.
Hugo Victorin.

Myrrh and aloes. At once we recall that "mixture of myrrh and aloes, about an hundred pound weight," which Nicodemus brought for the burial of the LORD, and are taught hereby the need of being conformed to the likeness of His death, before we can share in His Resurrection and glory. Myrrh, as noted before, is mortification; aloes, yet more bitter, the pain of trial and temptation. Others see two degrees of suffering, as martyrdom and confessorship, or two degrees of temperance, as continence and abstinence. S. Greg. Nyss.
S. John xix. 39.

Theodoret.
S.Ans.Laud. Cassiodor.
Hugo Victorin.

With all the chief spices. That is, as they for the most part explain, the spiritual gifts of the HOLY GHOST. Or, with S. Gregory Nyssen, all the great doctrines of the Church, pure from any heresy or adulteration. Or, yet again, as Cassiodorus aptly puts it: "After myrrh and aloes fitly come the chief spices, because after continence of the flesh comes that true love which is GOD Himself, and whereby GOD is loved above all things. For they who are changed by the love of the world, that is, who still delight in pleasures and allurements, cannot be partakers of this love." Tres Patr. Ricard. Vict. Hugo Victorin.

Cassiod.

And having gone through the list of the chief plants in that Paradise of GOD, let us hear how S. Bernard applies the whole parable to the Religious Life: "Count not this paradise of inner delight to be any tangible place. Not the feet, but the affections enter here. It is no orchard of earthly trees which is set before thee, but S. Bernard. de Convers. ad Clericos, cap. 13.

a sweet and lovely park of spiritual virtues. A garden inclosed, where the sealed fountain is parted into four heads, and from one source of wisdom virtue goes forth in a fourfold stream. There the glittering lilies bloom, and when the flowers appear, the voice of the turtle is heard. There the spikenard of the Bride sendeth forth its most fragrant smell, and the other spices flow out, as the south wind breathes, when the north has fled away. There, in the midst, is the Tree of Life, that apple-tree of the Canticles, fairer than all the trees of the wood, whose shadow refreshes the Bride, whose fruit is sweet to her taste. There the whiteness of continence and the gaze on truth undefiled irradiate the eyes of the heart, and the soft voice of inward consolation gives joy and gladness to the hearing. There the pleasant odour of that rich field which the LORD hath blessed reaches the nostrils of hope. There the peerless cates of love are eagerly tasted, and there the soul, anointed with the unction of mercy, rests happily with a clean conscience, when the briars and thorns, which once pricked her, have been cut down." And in the same spirit runs that mystical old Dutch hymn, written by one of those Brethren of the Common Life who sat at the feet of Thomas à Kempis.

The Hymn, Heer Jesus heeft een Hofken.

Our Master hath a garden which fair flowers adorn,
There will I go and gather both at eve and morn;
   Nought's heard therein but Angel-hymns with harp and lute,
   Loud trumpets, and bright clarions, and the gentle soothing flute.

The lily white that bloometh there is Purity,
The fragrant violet is surnamed Humility.

The lovely damask rose is there called Patience,
The rich and cheerful marigold Obedience.

One plant is there with crown bedight, the rest above,
With crown imperial, and this plant is Holy Love;

But still of all the flowers the fairest and the best
Is JESUS CHRIST, the LORD Himself, His Name be blest;

O JESU, my chief good and sole felicity,
Thy little garden make my ready heart to be;
   So may I once hear Angel-hymns with harp and lute,
   Loud trumpets, and bright clarions, and the gentle soothing flute.

15 A fountain of gardens, a well of living waters, and streams from Lebanon.

They agree, for the most part, in explaining this *fountain* to denote, first, either Holy Scripture itself, or the Church as the preacher and expounder thereof. It is a fountain of *gardens*, because it irrigates not only the various local Churches which are derived from the one centre, but also all holy souls, which are God's pleasures. It is a fountain, again, by reason of its ready accessibility, because its stream of love breaks out so freely that man can drink of it as he stoops, or can turn its fertilizing channels among the beds of his garden to water his fruits. But it is also a *well*, because of its profound depth and the hidden mysteries it contains, which have to be searched out with toil, and drawn forth with humility. For Holy Writ is a stormy sea to the proud, and a fordable river to the humble, and sometimes appears as the tiniest rill to water the unlearned and simple, while it is, nevertheless, deepest in the spots which seem to mark the easiest fords; so, as a Saint has truly said, an elephant needs to swim where a lamb can ford easily. It is a fountain of *living waters*, because it flows from the perennial source of Divine wisdom, not like the teaching of heretics, stored in tanks of human construction, and sure to dry up when the sun is hot. Of these the Prophet saith, "They have forsaken Me the fountain of living waters, and hewed them out cisterns, broken cisterns, that can hold no water." But of him who hearkens to the voice of the Lord Jesus is said: "Whosoever drinketh of the water that I shall give him shall never thirst; but the water that I shall give him shall be in him a well of water springing up into everlasting life." This is He of whom the Psalmist saith: "Thou shalt give them drink of Thy pleasures, as out of the river. For with Thee is the well of life: and in Thy light shall we see light." And as He, the Eternal Wisdom, is the Source of both well and fountain, they are rightly called *streams from Lebanon*. He is Lebanon, the mountain which fills the earth, the stone cut out without hands, "whiteness" in His absolute holiness and purity, "incense" in His atoning Sacrifice and perpetual intercession. His Bride is Lebanon too, washed white by Him in His own Blood, and from her pour down those waters of Baptismal grace and Apostolic teaching, which descended with irresistible power upon the earth, so that the rivers of the flood thereof make glad

S. Ambros. de Isaac. 4.

Philo Carp.

S. Greg. M.

Cassiodor.

Jer. ii. 13.

Beda.

S. John iv. 14.

Ps. xxxvi. 8.

Luc. Abb.
Ricard. Vict.

Cassiodor.

S. Greg. M.
Beda.
Ps. xlvi. 4.

the city of GOD. And observe the gradual magnifying of the one idea, how the *fountain* deepens into a *well*, and the well widens into *streams*, denoting the continual growth and advance of GOD's grace in the Church and in the soul, so that the latter things are greater than the former. And so it is written, "I also came out as a brook from a river, and as a conduit into a garden. I said, I will water my best garden, and will water abundantly my garden bed: and lo, my brook became a river, and my river became a sea." This is what Ezekiel beheld in vision, when the waters issued from the temple eastward and grew into a mighty torrent swarming with fish, and bordered with green and fruitful trees.

The devout soul is a fountain which glides and flows, and which ever springs up anew, because it is renewed in GOD. It never ceases to bubble forth, and break out in love for Him, to swell for its own needs, and to expand itself in affection for its neighbour. It is also a well of living waters, because it contains the deep grace and knowledge of the HOLY SPIRIT, enough to supply itself and to pour forth again for others. This is the third well which Isaac dug, and which he called "Room," because the LORD has spread it over the earth. For man is spread over the earth when he arrives at the perfection of grace, and having passed over servile fear, ascends from the beginning of love to the affection of a son. Man digs the first well when he casts earth, that is, earthly sins, out of himself through fear of punishment. He digs the second when he avoids sin not only through fear, but also through love of good. He digs the third when he abandons evil and does good from love alone. And while digging the two former ones, he endures the slanders and enmity of the herdsmen of Gerar, that is, the evil spirits who behold our "sojournings," while we are strangers and pilgrims on earth, and who strive to encourage carnal passions in us. But when we attain to perfect charity and spiritual fervour, the inner struggle and the outer attack of evil spirits cease, because they are no longer a match for us in the fight. Then the soul expands so much in love and grace, and is so enriched with their fulness, that it can pour forth its streams on others also.

They take the Religious Life also to be the fountain, watering the garden of many a famous Order, Benedictines, Cistercians, Dominicans, Franciscans, and the like. And each such Order in its turn is a fountain watering the gardens of the various devout souls gathered in them. Each Society is one garden, because of its unanimity, many gardens by reason of the varying gifts and graces of its members. And note, that before any one member can be truly called a garden, he must cultivate more than one grace or virtue, for that is no garden which contains but one flower, however lovely. "Follow, then, after the wells of heavenly delights, the wells of faithful and of living waters which pour in a flood from Lebanon. Be a flower in the garden, and that garden inclosed, that thou be not plucked, and thou shalt see how the LORD will make fountains and streams spring up for thee. Dwell in the garden, that thou too mayest perchance become a well, and out of thy belly living waters may flow. O that one would give me these waters for my little garden, the well of gladness to my heart. 'Cleanse me, O LORD, from my secret faults, keep Thy servant also from presumptuous sins.' Make me to be Lebanon, 'Wash me, and I shall be whiter than snow.' 'So shall I be undefiled and innocent from the great offence. Let the words of my mouth and the meditation of my heart be alway acceptable in Thy sight.' Make me Lebanon, and I shall ever pour these streams forth to Thee." *Gillebert. Serm. 37.* *Ps. xix. 12.* *Ps. li. 7.* *Ps. xix. 13.*

And finally, they take the verse to denote the Blessed Virgin, as the earthly source or fountain, whence the Divine River of Mercy (as the Holy Eastern Church calls her Eternal Son,) went forth to water the earth, parted into the four sacramental channels of His Incarnation, Passion, Resurrection, and Ascension, without the confession of which our paradise cannot exist, without which the world cannot be saved. And yet she is not the first source of these sacred waters. They flow from a height far above her lowly garden, from Lebanon itself, the mysterious height of Godhead, pure, majestic, awful, clothed in shadowy darkness. *Rupert. Alanus. Ord. Ol. Sanct. Guiliel. Parv. Cantacuzene.*

16 Awake, O north wind; and come, thou south; blow upon my garden, that the spices thereof may flow out. Let my beloved come into his garden, and eat his pleasant fruits.

Theodoret.	Throughout Holy Scripture, the north, as the region of darkness and cold, is typical of the powers of evil,
Isa. xiv. 13.	according as it is written of Lucifer, "Thou hast said in thine heart, I will ascend into heaven, I will exalt my throne above the stars of GOD, I will sit also upon the mount of the congregation, in the sides of the
Jer. 1. 14; iv. 6.	north." And twice in Jeremiah, "Out of the north an evil shall break forth upon the inhabitants of the land;" and again, "I will bring evil from the north, and a great destruction." So too, when the LORD
Joel ii. 20.	promises mercy, He saith, "I will remove far off from you the northern army." And accordingly a frequent exposition of this verse by the Fathers is that it is a summons to the powers of evil to begone from the garden, and a prayer to the HOLY SPIRIT, denoted by the moist and warm south wind, to enter in instead.
Hab. iii. 3.	For it is said in Habakkuk, "GOD came from Teman,"
S. Greg. Nyss. Hom. 10.	which is "the south." S. Gregory Nyssen reminds us also that the north is on the right hand of him whose back is towards the east, and who is journeying westward, and so Satan is friendly to those only who turn away from the Day-spring from on high, and set themselves towards the sunset, where the powers of darkness prevail. Also, the second clause, the prayer which was answered when the rushing mighty wind came down on the disciples at Pentecost, notes the great change which then passed over the Church of GOD, when the prophetic streams of waters of the Old Testa-
Ps. cxlvii. 18.	ment, of which we read, "He bloweth with His wind, and the waters flow," were changed into the more glorious streams of fragrant spices, diffused throughout the world in such channels as the mighty S. Paul, or the Evangelist S. John, both of them a good odour of CHRIST.
S. Paulin. S. Just. Org.	Others, however, take both winds to be diverse operations of the same HOLY SPIRIT, the north bringing coolness to the fevered, the south softening the hard and frozen. And because these two are but one Spirit,
S. Ambros. in Ps. cxix.	the verb is singular, not plural. Again, the north and south may be taken to denote the nations of different parts of the earth, alike invited to enter the garden inclosed, and the north, signifying the more distant lands, is therefore bidden to *awake* from its sleep, to arise from the dead, that CHRIST may give it light. Further, they take the two winds to be various forms of trial, for which the Church prays, that she may be

tested for her LORD. For when the virtues of the Church have been counted up under the name of spices; the LORD, Who is the Bridegroom and Redeemer of His Church, knowing that it would be increased by persecution, afterwards, as it were, directs that persecution to come, not enjoining, but permitting it. The north and south winds signify troubles and persecutions raging against the Church. The north is a very cold wind, the south a warm one, and therefore terrors and threats are denoted by the north, and guileful flatteries by the south, by both which kinds of trial the Church is proved. And in saying, *Awake, O north wind, and come, thou south,* He does not command nor urge wicked men to do evil, but permits them, and gives them power to rage against the Church, that it may be tested by their malice, and they be the more severely punished. For the more cruelly the Church is smitten, the greater fragrance of holiness does she give forth. Cassiodor.

Others differ so far as to see the bane and antidote summoned together, the north wind of sorrow and trial, the south wind of grace and comfort to refresh and restore the Church or soul wearied with its combat. But the north wind is not suffered to stay long. When it has sufficiently exercised its chilly power, then the south comes, and not only blows, but *blows through* (so, correctly, LXX. and Vulg.) the garden, occupying the whole of it, so that no sorrow can abide there, but all the spices flow out together in abundance and gladness. And in this sense S. Anselm tersely comments: "The north wind, shaking the trees, makes them bud, that the south which follows may cause them to bear fruit. And so persecution, followed by the fervour of charity, makes the Church bear fruit through the grace of the HOLY GHOST." Luc. Abb.
Ric. Vict.
S.Ans.Laud.

Rupert, diversely, following the view which identifies the north wind with Satan, holds that the verse is a challenge to him to arise from his secret ambush, and to advance to do battle with the south wind of the HOLY SPIRIT for possession of the garden. And it has been taken, not only of the Pagan persecutions, and of the struggles of heretics to overthrow the Faith, but also of the last great effort of Antichrist, when GOD will permit him to awake against the Church, but will ere long send His refreshing and warm wind to restore the lapsed, and to give new strength and beauty Rupert.
Honorius.

to His enfeebled and mourning garden. It should be observed that while the majority of the Fathers take the words to be the Bridegroom's, dealing with the garden and the winds as their absolute LORD, some few, amongst whom are Theodoret and S. Gregory Nyssen, will have it, that it is the prayer of the Bride.

Corn. à Lap. The application of the verse to the Blessed Virgin is twofold; first, that she was guarded from evil, repelled from her by the grace of her perfect obedience and purity, and that she was filled with the Holy Spirit, whereby not only her virtues flowed forth in beauty, but He came forth from her, Who is the source of all beauty and holiness. And so runs the hymn:

The Hymn, Imperatrix gloriosa.

Auster levis te perflavit,
Et perflando fecundavit,
Aquilonem qui fugavit,
  Sua cum potentiâ;
Florem ergo genuisti,
Ex quo fructum protulisti,
Gabrieli dum fuisti
  Paranympho credula.

That soft south-wind, through thee going,
And thus fruitfulness bestowing,
Put to flight the north-wind's blowing,
  With his breath of greater might;
Therefore thou hast borne the Flower,
Yielding fruit within thy bower,
When to Gabriel, in that hour,
  Thou didst hearken with delight.

And again; no life ever so mingled joy and sorrow as hers did, none ever felt such woe and desolation, nor yet such consolation and rejoicing, as she who knelt by the cradle of the Most High, and who stood later by His Cross.

Keble, Christian Year.

Thou wept'st, meek Maiden, Mother mild,
Thou wept'st upon thy sinless Child,
  Thy very heart was riven,
And yet, what mourning matron here
Could deem thy sorrows bought too dear
  By all on this side heaven?

Philipp. Harveng. Even against her, His Mother, He permitted the evil one to rage, to threaten, to storm, either through the means of the evil Jews, or through the sufferings which she could not but share with her Son, but He knew well what would be her victory and her crown, what will yet be the triumph and the reward of those who take her for their pattern, and bear the chilling blast with patience, knowing that, cold as it is, it will clear the sky, and drive away the clouds which hide the sun, and then the warm breeze will spring up, and the heart be gladdened to its inmost core. *Coccelus.*

Let my Beloved come into His garden, and eat His pleasant fruits. These words of the Bride are assigned by the present copies of LXX. and Vulgate to the following chapter, with which they have a closer connection. But the juxtaposition of the A. V. is also that which some Greek Fathers and not a few Westerns have accepted. And the first thing to be observed is that one phrase in this address of the Bride seems to prove that all the earlier part of the verse is uttered by the Bridegroom. She says, "Let my Beloved come into *His* garden." She does not say *my* garden, as the previous speaker does, because she knows that she herself and all that she has are utterly and entirely His, and not her own. On the other hand; if the words be taken as the Bride's, this variation of language will denote that in her humility she calls the garden hers, so long as the bleak, dry, nipping north wind is blowing, and no sign of fertility is visible, but the moment that endurance has been crowned, and the spices begin to flow out, then, because the garden is productive and beautiful, she calls it His. Next; the LXX. and Arabic version read, Let my Beloved come *down* into His garden, which the Syriac amplifies further, Let Him come through my garden into His garden. And on the LXX. rendering, S. Gregory Nyssen observes, that as the Bride cannot reach the Most High unless He condescend to her lowliness; she, while soaring to the utmost limit of her power, intreats Him to meet her, by coming down from His majesty to earth. She calls Him all the more, because hearing that He is going to try her by persecution, she cannot rest till He is in the midst of her, to support her in her struggle, and to be the glad spectacle of the holy deeds she means to do for love of Him. The Church invites Him also to see the children she has brought up for Him, the newly-baptized converts won to Him from unbelief. These are, according to the LXX. rendering, *fruits of nuts,* because safely closed in by the strong shell of His commandments. Or, as S. Ambrose, writing of and to Virgins, says, following the same text, the WORD of GOD is *Philo Carp.* *S. Greg. Nyss.* *Cassiodor.* *S. Ambros. de Sacram. v. 3.*

invited into the garden of nuts, wherein is the fruit of the study of prophecy, and the grace of the priestly office, compared to a nut, because bitter at first with trial and sorrows, then hardened by toil, and finally fruitful in hidden virtues. And this verse is more directly applied to the virginal life by another, following the Western rendering, *apples.* The Bride invites CHRIST to hallow for Himself, as the firstlings of good works, the produce of the fruits of virginity, that He, Who proceeded from a Virgin, may taste thereof, and may send by the hands of angels into heaven that fruit of penitential joy which He receives from the Church. He hath said of Himself, " My meat is to do the will of Him that sent Me, and to finish His work;" and therefore He tastes His pleasant fruits whenever He visits and enters any holy soul to see its progress in sanctity. And He was especially invited by S. Mary, when she said, " Behold the handmaid of the LORD, be it unto me according to thy word." Eve offered her bridegroom an apple which was none of hers to give, nor of his to accept, but Mary called her GOD to eat His own fruits, that is, to unite and incorporate His elect with Himself, calling Him into herself, His garden, because while fields or plains often lie fallow or barren as the seasons change, a garden has always some fruit or flower to please its master's eye, and she was not merely a Saint as others, but full of grace. And whereas Rupert goes on to represent the words as those of the Virgin Mother desiring her Son to call her from the world to Himself; so too some of the commentators have seen here the cry of every soul which longs to flee away and be at rest, to be dissolved and be with CHRIST, that He may enter the garden, and bear its fruit away with Him to Paradise. And it is all summed up in the one petition of the Our FATHER, "Thy kingdom come." Let Him come then. Why does He invite the south wind to come? Let Him come to me Himself, and it is enough. He is my south wind, He is my fragrance. He is my south wind, He is my Love. GOD cometh from the south, and the south wind comes with Him. And then He is full of grace and truth. Truly He is my south wind, Who brightly shines, Who softly glides upon me. My CHRIST is my south wind, He blows through my garden, He eats my fruit.

CHAPTER V.

1 I am come into my garden, my sister, my spouse; I have gathered my myrrh with my spice; I have eaten my honeycomb with my honey; I have drunk my wine with my milk: eat, O friends; drink, yea, drink abundantly, O beloved.

The Bride has scarcely formed her wish, scarcely uttered her prayer, before it is heard and answered, according to that saying, "Thou shalt call, and the LORD shall answer; thou shalt cry, and He shall say, Here I am." For GOD did come into His garden, the creature, took flesh of the Virgin, and was made man. The Body He took was mortal, but united with the fragrance of the All-Holiest WORD. They dwell, too, in another way on the *myrrh*, as denoting suffering, and say with S. Cyril of Jerusalem, as he tells his catechumens of the place where the LORD was crucified, " Of this garden I sang long ago in the Canticles to My Bride, and I said thus to her, *I have come into My garden, My sister, My spouse.* ' Now in the place where He was crucified there was a garden.' And what thence drawest thou? *I have gathered My myrrh*, when He drank the wine and vinegar mingled with myrrh, and having received it, said, ' It is finished.' " And on this a Spanish writer says very well: As Adam committed his sin in the garden of Paradise, so CHRIST, the Atoner for that guilt, willed to enter the garden of Gethsemane, and there He prayed for Adam and all his posterity, there too He willed to be taken, bound, dragged away, and smitten by the servants of the chief priests. Also, as Adam stretched out his hands to the tree and seized the forbidden fruit, therefore CHRIST stretched out His hands and arms on the Tree of the Cross, and there was nailed by hands and feet, and pierced with a spear. Moreover Adam ate the fruit which was sweet to the taste, but CHRIST drank the bitter vinegar mingled with myrrh on the Cross.

S. Greg. Nyss.
Isa. lviii. 9.
S. Athan.
Cat. Myst. xii. 32.
S. John xix. 41.
S. John xix. 30.
Parez.

And though that Passion was as the bitterest myrrh to CHRIST, to us it was as the sweetest honey in effect, and fragrant as all restorative spices, intoxicating as wine, nourishing as milk. Yet, as one of our own poets has taught us, the first interpretation is deeper than the second one.

<small>Keble, *Lyra Innocent.*</small>

And surely not in folds so bright the spotless winding-sheet
Inwrapt Him, nor such fragrance poured the myrrh and aloes sweet,
As when in that chaste bosom, His awful bed, He lay,
And Mary's prayer around Him rose, like incense, night and day.

<small>Luc. Abb.</small>
<small>Philo Carp.</small>
<small>S. Just. Org.</small>
<small>Rupert.</small>
<small>Cassiodor.</small>
<small>Beda.</small>
<small>Theodoret.</small>
<small>Delrio.</small>
<small>Ricard. Vict.</small>
<small>Dion. Carth.</small>

He gathered His myrrh too in another fashion, by converting the fierce thief upon the cross, as He had gathered His spices a little before when He drew the sinful woman to Him. He gathered His myrrh and His spice when He was borne dead into the garden where Joseph's new tomb was, and when they wrapped Him in fine linen with myrrh and aloes. He gathered myrrh indeed in His death, but when He went into that other garden of His, in Hades, He gathered thence His spice, when He brought back into the light of Paradise the spirits that were in prison. And this coming is not all past and over. Daily He comes still into His garden, daily does He visit His Church and every soul that loves Him, to gather fruits for Himself. He gathers myrrh in His martyrs, spice in His other Saints, myrrh in all who mortify their carnal passion, spice in all who yield the odour of devotion and good works. Myrrh denotes the Baptism whereby we are buried with Him, spice the graces of the HOLY SPIRIT which He breathes on His disciples. And thus He speaks to the soul unto whose garden He comes: "Thou hast borne, O My spouse, the sorrow of penance; the strife, the trial, the toil of correction, and thou hast come to the harvest of perfection in virtue, from the life of toil to the calmer state of contemplation. Therefore have I gathered in the myrrh with spice, because the spices of virtue have been prepared and perfected in thee with the bitterness of toil, and wisdom hath made progress through keeping the commandments. For when fleshliness and self-will have been mortified, then the spices of holiness flow out, and by the fulfilment and triumph of this toil the summit of perfection is reached." And why is He said to gather His myrrh, instead of letting it grow still in the garden? Why, but that He may give it as a posy to His Bride, that bunch which lies all night between her breasts, for her delight and refreshment.

I have eaten My honeycomb with My honey. And this He did when He stored the golden sweetness of His Godhead in the frail, pure shrine of His human Body. He hath *eaten* the honeycomb, that is, taken it to Himself, in raising it to Heaven by His Ascension. And in precisely the same sense is it added, *I have drunk My wine with My milk,* wherein the hypostatic union of the Two Natures in His Person is similarly shadowed forth. But as the phrases *eating* and *drinking* denote bodily refreshment, they are more usually explained of the pleasure which CHRIST derives from the holiness of His Saints. By the *honeycomb* and *wine*, comments Cassiodorus, holy preachers are figured, and by *honey* and *milk* devout hearers. For preachers are honeycombs who bring forth the secret and hidden mysteries of Scripture like honey out of the comb, when they disclose them to others by preaching. And devout hearers are the *honey*, because they delight to receive eagerly and to be fed pleasantly with the sweetness of GOD's Word. The same preachers who are honeycomb are also *wine*, because they declare the mighty Sacraments of the Scriptures. The hearers, as weaker, are *milk*, in that they need the mysteries to be explained and simplified for them. And whereas all these spend their lives in different ways, the Redeemer is fed and gladdened with the holy resolutions of them all, and thus does, as it were, eat His honeycomb with His honey, and drink His wine with His milk. And we may refer it also to the death of the elect, whom the LORD eats, when He calls them by death to eternal life, and unites them to His Body, that is, to the fellowship of the elect who already rejoice in that heavenly bliss. And if we do so take it of the death of the Saints, we should understand them by *wine* whose souls now are exulting in heavenly bliss, and by *honeycomb* those who rejoice both in body and soul in that blessedness, such as they who arose together with the LORD. Again, He accepts all kinds of holiness,—that which is solid, denoted by the comb; that which is sweet, signified by the honey; that which is strong and vigorous, typified by wine; that which comes from weak and imperfect Christians, shadowed forth by milk. Another will have it that the honey-comb with its honey fitly signifies those Saints who delight in the study of Holy Writ, and who make their hearts and memories the cells wherein they, like bees, store up the sweet food drawn from all the flowers of Law and Prophet, Psalm and Gospel. And another writer reminds us that we too may eat and drink in this wise in imitation of our LORD, when we digest not merely the outward letter of Holy Scripture, which is the comb, but its inner spiritual sense, which is the honey; when we drink not only the stinging and powerful wine of compunction, but the soothing milk of trust in the mercy of GOD. He drinks His *wine* too in another manner, the new wine of His kingdom, in His delight in those of His Saints who have kept the faith and finished their course, and come to Him where He no longer weeps for Lazarus, where He is no more sorrowful unto death, where He drinks not vinegar and gall again. He drinks His *milk* in His love for His Saints yet militant and imperfect, who are still in the way, and need daily refreshment and food. He eats His honeycomb when He delights in the inner capacities of the soul for good. He adds His honey to that feast when those capacities develope into action, like the comb pouring out its golden streams. He drinks wine and milk when He looks on a soul delightedly contemplating Him in His double aspect of perfect Godhead and glorified Manhood. And the soul too eats and drinks in its turn, nay, in the same order. For amended ways and good works must come before the grace of contemplation is bestowed. A various reading of the LXX. and Arabic, *bread* for *honeycomb*, has pointed more directly a further sense also latent here, and thus some of the Fathers have bidden us see here a prophecy of the Holy Eucharist, that Food which is all sweetness and strength. And Cornelius aptly notes that it was the custom of the primitive Church to give the Blessed Sacrament to the newly-baptized, and immediately thereafter, honey and milk, typical of the gentleness, sweetness, and simplicity of the Law of CHRIST. And as He is not only LORD of the feast spread upon His Altar daily, but fellow-guest, in that His own members are they who feed there, He is said to share in the repast, as He did on that first Maundy Thursday amongst His Apostles.

Eat, O friends,[1] *drink, yea, drink abundantly, O beloved.* The first question they ask here is, Who are these friends? And the Targum helps us to the answer. As it takes the invitation of the Bride to be the invocation of GOD unto His Temple, and His reply to denote His sending down fire to consume the oblations, so it explains this clause of His summons to the priests to draw near in order to eat their share of the sacrifices, which He leaves for them. And thus we shall see here CHRIST's invitation to those Apostles whom He then called no more servants, but friends, saying, "Come, eat of My Bread, and drink of the Wine which I have mingled." And not only they, but all Christians of whatever degree, who are in a sense His priests, are called to that same banquet. *Drink abundantly.* The marginal reading, more exactly, with LXX. and Vulgate, *Be drunken.* For, as a great Saint and Martyr teaches us, the intoxication of the LORD's Chalice and Blood is not like that of this world's wine, therefore the HOLY GHOST when saying in the Psalm, "My inebriating chalice," addeth, "How good it is!"[2] because, no doubt, the LORD's Chalice in such wise inebriates those who drink of it, as to make them sober, and recall their souls to spiritual wisdom, so that each may turn from the savour of the world to taste the knowledge of GOD : and just as the mind is relaxed, the soul loosened, and all sorrow cast aside by means of ordinary wine ; so when we drink the Blood of the LORD and the Cup of Salvation, the memory of the old man is laid aside, forgetfulness of our former conversation comes upon us, and the sad and mourning heart, which just now was oppressed with torturing sins, is freed by the gladness of GOD's merciful pardon. Accordingly that ancient morning hymn, once daily used in the Western Church, but now for many centuries restricted to the Lauds of Monday, runs:

_{Targum.}

_{S. Greg. Nyssen. S. Ambros. S. John xv. 15. Prov. ix. 5.}

_{S. Cyprian. Ep. 63 ad Cæcilium.}

---

[1] The word רֵעִים, *friends,* is the same which is translated in the A. V. of Ps. cxxxix. 17, as "thoughts," and in the Prayer Book as "counsels," whereby the force of its ancient use and beautiful Antiphon, as employed in the Common of Apostles, "How dear are Thy *friends* unto me, O GOD," is lost.

[2] This is the LXX. and Vulgate reading of Ps. xxiii. 5, where the A. V. translates (as do modern critics) "my cup runneth over."

S. Ambros. The Hymn, *Splendor Paternæ Gloriæ*.	And CHRIST shall be our daily Food, Our daily drink His Precious Blood, And thus the SPIRIT's calm excess[1] Shall fill our souls with holiness.

Cassiod.

But this is only one out of a variety of expositions. One Father tells us that it is an invitation to all GOD's faithful and loving servants to behold and imitate the examples of His Saints, and that if we interpret the passage of Saints departed, then the *friends* called on to rejoice are the angelic spirits, delighting in seeing the elect translated from this life to the rest of everlasting blessedness, according to that parable of the Gospel, "Rejoice with Me, for I have found My sheep which was lost." Another sees in the friends called on to eat, the Patriarchs and Prophets, summoned to share in the Word of Life and in the Passion of the LORD, and in the stream of the HOLY GHOST; and the beloved, called to drunkenness, the Apostles, so inebriated with the torrent of the HOLY GHOST poured on them from heaven, that they were thought to be full of new wine, while preaching the wonderful works of GOD. S. Anselm of Laon tells us that preachers are called on to *eat*, that is, to incorporate sinners into the body of the Church with pains and care, by converting their hearers, and to *drink*, in the case of those who are more readily won over and quickly give in adhesion, while the term *be drunken* denotes their zealous pleasure in their work, and their heedlessness of all temporal things so long as they may carry it on. Not very dissimilarly, S. Gregory the Great, taking the banquet to be Holy Scripture, says that they eat of it and are CHRIST's friends, who, though not attaining perfection, do yet strive after holiness in their degree; but His beloved, who are drunken with its delights, are those who have cast away all thoughts of earth in their eagerness to quaff His cup. And this is true also of divine contemplation, wherein GOD feeds His friends, but more abundantly refreshes His beloved, though both receive in that banquet spiritual consolation, as they are fed with the love of CHRIST, are enlightened in faith, comforted in hope, kindled in charity, gladdened with righteousness, truth, purity, and all other graces. And finally, they take it of the summons to the un-

S. Luke xv. 6.

Philo Carp.

S. Ans. Laud.

S. Greg. M.

Ric. Vict.

---

[1] "Sobriam ebrietatem."

ending festival of heaven. There, exclaims Gilbert of Hoyland, there all are friends, all beloved. All drink, and all are inebriated. Not so in this vale of tears, not so, but there are many friends, few beloved; many drink, not all are inebriated, and they who are so, become sober again. For a moment they pass forth in ecstasy, and then return again to the wonted soberness. There it is different: Gilbert. Serm. 41.

Ever full, yet ever craving, they desire, and yet possess,
But their fulness brings no loathing, and their hunger no distress,
Eagerly they eat for ever, ever eat in joyfulness. S. Pet. Dam. The Hymn, *Ad perennis*.

And with this last interpretation we may couple that other version of the clause, *Be drunken with love,* with all the unspeakable gladness of the Home of eternal joy.

2 I sleep, but my heart waketh: it is the voice of my beloved that knocketh, saying, Open to me, my sister, my love, my dove, my undefiled; for my head is filled with dew, and my locks with the drops of the night.

Here begins another main division of the song, the fourth in order, and marking the central time of the action. It typifies, as some of the commentators tell us, the trials of the Bride after her union with the Bridegroom; her failure, yearning, and search for Him after He had again withdrawn Himself for her better probation. It is thus taken of the Church after she relaxed in her first love and zeal, after the days of Pagan tyranny were over, and of the soul which yields to spiritual negligence even after true conversion to GOD. The Chaldee paraphrase is quite in keeping with this view, in that it explains the sleep of the Bride to be the seventy years' captivity in Babylon, whence Israel was wakened by the voice of the HOLY GHOST, warning them by the Prophets, and rousing them from the slumber of their heart. And similarly one or two are found who explain this sleep of the Bride to denote a season of negligence and indevotion, soon to be shaken off, and prevented from working fatal results because her *Heart*, her Love, her Bridegroom, is watching over her slumbers, and guarding her from all fear of the enemy, according to that saying, " Behold, He that Hon. Aug.

Targum.

S. Greg. Nyssen.

Ps. cxxi. 4.

keepeth Israel shall neither slumber nor sleep." But the great majority take the words in a good sense. Her LORD has just given her His inebriating chalice, which closes her eyes to all earthly cares and anxieties, and she now slumbers in the deep repose of perfect trust, and divine contemplation, while her heart is waking in eagerness of love for Him. She sleeps, because sleep is a type of death, and she has learnt to die to the world and its affections, whilst she wakes in contemplation of heavenly things. And therefore S. Ambrose thus addresses a Virgin, "Let thy flesh sleep, let thy faith wake, let the allurements of the body slumber, let the prudence of the heart keep watch, let thy members breathe the odour of CHRIST's Cross and grave, that slumber bring no heat, and arouse no passions." And this mingled condition of sleep and wakefulness involves, S. Gregory warns us, a perpetual struggle, that contemplation may not sink into torpor, nor evil passions take possession of the soul whence secular occupations have been banished. How this struggle is to be carried on, another Saint will tell us: What means, *I sleep, but my heart waketh*, save that I so rest that I may hear? My repose is not devoted to encouraging sloth, but to acquiring wisdom. I sleep and my heart waketh, I have time for thought, and I see that Thou art the LORD, for "the wisdom of a learned man cometh by opportunity of leisure; and he that hath little business shall become wise." I sleep, and my heart waketh; I rest from the cares of business, and my mind is busy with divine affection, but while the Church is peacefully delighting in them who thus sweetly and humbly rest, behold One knocketh Who saith, "What I tell you in darkness, that speak ye in light: and what ye hear in the ear, that preach ye upon the housetops."

And in this sense of peaceful contemplation of the pure and untrammelled soul, they delight to recall her who "kept all these things and pondered them in her heart." Desire for sleep came not on her, says a great Saint, before its need, and yet when her body was at rest, her mind was waking, busy even in dreams in recalling what she had read, continuing in sleep what had been interrupted, or carrying out plans, or else declaring what should be carried out. And in imitation of her the ancient English Church prays in one of her Compline hymns and antiphons:

> O let our eyes due slumber take,
> Our hearts to Thee for ever wake!

The Hymn, CHRISTE, *Qui lux es et dies.*

And again; "Save us watching, O LORD, and guard us sleeping, that we may watch with CHRIST, and sleep in peace." This we may do, observes S. Cyprian, by being earnest in prayer, for he who recites prayer carelessly, wakes with his body, but sleeps with his heart. Cassiodorus tells us that the words are those of the Church, saying that she sleeps, because she is enjoying comparative peace, and not suffering the persecutions endured by the primitive Church, and therefore her heart waketh because she is able to devote herself to the love of her Bridegroom in greater security than before. But as she errs in supposing this time to be one of peace, rather than of toil and strife, she is quickly roused by His voice, calling her to labour and striving to spread His kingdom. Again; the words have been taken to denote the condition of the faithful departed, sleeping indeed bodily in the grave, but with the affections alive and active in worship of GOD and intercession for the loved on earth. And in this sense they form the noble motto over the tombs of the kings of Spain in the Escorial.

S. Cypr. de Orat. Dom.

Cassiod.

There is a further interpretation of the words, ascribing them to the Bridegroom. And first; they take it of His sleep in the grave, where His Body rested, but His Godhead was ever wakeful, and, as another adds, His soul was even then engaged in harrowing hell, and spoiling it of its prey. Again; He sleeps in the sense of His perfect rest in the bosom of His FATHER, and yet labours there that all who love Him may come to Him. And thus He, as it were, sleeps in bodily absence, while He watches over us in ever-present and loving Godhead. Once more, He sleeps, so far as all outward sign of life is concerned, in the great Sacrament of His love, where He is hidden under the forms of Bread and Wine, but His heart waketh there in the love wherewith He gives Himself to be our Food.

Hugo Vict. Psellus.

Philo Carp.

S. Greg. M.

Luc. Abb.

Vieyra.

> I rise from dreams of time,
>   And an Angel guides my feet,
> To the sacred Altar-throne,
>   Where JESUS' heart doth beat.
>
> The lone lamp softly burns,
>   And a wondrous silence reigns,

> Only, with a low still voice,
> The Holy One complains:
>
> "Long, long I've waited here,
> And though thou heed'st not Me,
> The Heart of GOD's own SON
> Beats ever on for thee."
>
> In the womb of Mary meek,
> In the cradle, on the Tree;
> Heart of pure, undying love,
> It lived, loved, bled for me.
>
> Ever pleading, day and night,
> Thou canst not from us part,
> O veiled and wondrous SON,
> O love of the Sacred Heart!

<small>S. August. Tract. 57 in S. Joann.</small>

It is the voice of my Beloved that knocketh. And this knocking, as S. Augustine told us but just now, is that the Church may rise to the life of action from that of contemplation, may understand that it is her duty to go forth and compel the multitude of the Gen-

<small>Cassiodor.</small>

tiles to come in. The words, observes a Western divine of a later age, denote CHRIST's anxiety for the neglectful and erring, that they may be corrected by spiritual

<small>Honorius Augustod.</small>

persons, and imply at the same time the eagerness of the Church in contemplation, and the irksomeness to her of external activity. The Voice of CHRIST knocking at the door of the faithful is this: O Church, *My sister,* because through Me co-heir of My kingdom, *My friend* (Vulg.) because through Me versed in heavenly mysteries; *My dove,* filled by Me with the HOLY GHOST; *My undefiled,* because cleansed by Me from sin; *Open to Me* by exhortation the door of their hearts, who have fastened it with the bar of wicked works, and who have become like the *drops of the night,* that is, members of the evil spirits, and thou shalt be My sister, if thou make those now disinherited through sin, My fellow-heirs through grace; thou shalt be My friend, if thou make them, now Mine enemies through unbelief, My friends in steadfastness of faith; thou shalt be My dove, if thou make the double-hearted simple; and thou shalt be My undefiled, if thou make those stained with guilt undefiled through virtues. For

<small>S. August. loc. cit.</small>

how, (as S. Augustine puts it,) shall I enter into them who have shut the door against Me, unless there be some one to open? And how shall they hear without a preacher? He knows full well that He is setting her a task which seems hard to her; that He is, for once, telling Mary to leave His feet and her own better part, and go forth to help Martha in her service, and therefore He heaps up all loving epithets, that she may be well assured that it is from no slackening of His affection that she is summoned from her secret converse to the troubles of the world. She would fain say with Peter on Mount Tabor, "LORD, it is good to be here," but she must go down to the plain, from the glory of the Transfiguration to the group around the struggling demoniac, from the vision of GOD to the strife with Satan. And she, who had barred herself in lest the prowling wolf should enter the fold, hearing the words of love, each title of affection being a fresh knock at the door of her heart, knows the Voice of the Good Shepherd, and exclaims, even before she sees Him, "My LORD and my GOD," for she is aware that He only can call her *sister*, who is her Brother by His Incarnation, His *love*, Who gave Himself for her; His *dove*, to whom He gave the seven-fold gifts of the SPIRIT; His *undefiled*, whom He washed in the waters of Baptism. One writer suggests that the unsheltered condition of the Bridegroom tells us of His rejection by the Jews, and that this is an appeal to the Gentile Church to receive and house Him. Philo Carp.
Corn. à Lap.

S. Just. Org.

And as He is still in truth despised and rejected of men, as too often He wanders in this world not finding where to lay His head, so in the chill night of spiritual coldness and darkness, He knocks at the door of the faithful soul, asking that there at least He may be sheltered. Open, He says, My sister, thy heart to Me, Who have opened My side for thee by My Passion, and heaven by My Ascension. And on this S. Gregory Nyssen comments at much length, bidding us notice four points in particular. First: GOD presents Himself to him who sleeps to the world and watches to GOD, heeding that saying of the Gospel, "Be ye yourselves like unto men that wait for their LORD, when He returns from the wedding; that when He cometh and knocketh, they may open to Him immediately." Next; although GOD has often opened to the Bride, yet as she never can arrive at full knowledge of Him, she delights in every fresh opportunity of gaining some fresh knowledge, of beholding some new manifestation, and therefore she exults in hearing His voice asking for admittance. Thirdly; that this longing of hers makes Gillebert.

Henr.
Harphius.

S. Greg.
Nyss.
Hom. 11.

S. Luke xii.
36.

P

her advance both in knowledge and love of GOD, for she first hears merely the knock, but does not recognize it, till she is informed by the tones of His voice. Fourthly; that the door which He calls her to open is that of inquiring search after divine mysteries, and contemplation of them; and as she has no power to open this of herself, He gives her four keys, signified by the four titles He bestows on her, as though saying, If thou desire that thy door should be opened and thy gates lifted up, that the King of Glory may come in, thou must first become My *sister*, by doing the will of My FATHER Which is in heaven; thou must draw near the truth, and thus be so exactly My *nearest* (LXX.) that there may be no interval or barrier between us; thou must have in thy nature the perfectness of a *dove*, and be full of all innocence and purity. Again; you may take the door to be devotion, as S. Ambrose teaches: "Even though thou be sleeping, yet if CHRIST do but know the devotion of thy soul, He comes and knocks at its door, and saith: Open to Me, My Sister, for the spiritual bridal of the WORD and the Soul is come. Open to Me, but shut the door to strangers, shut it to the world; nor yet come forth thyself to those earthly concerns, nor quit thine own light to seek another's. Open thyself to Me, be not straitened, but expanded, and I will fill thee." And the same Saint tells us elsewhere that the soul has other doors too, at any of which her LORD may knock. He may choose the door of prayer, and desire to have it opened that He may hear her voice uttering His praise in a psalm, or confessing His grace and Passion in the Creed. Or He comes in by the door of faith, or by that of righteousness. A Greek Father tells us, truly enough, that our bodily senses are doors of the soul, and by these we may admit CHRIST, just as we may also admit His foe, if we keep them not barred with due custody. However it be taken, at any rate, we can be sure of this, that the knock, whenever and wherever given, is a call to greater exertion, contemplative or active. Whoso obeys GOD and zealously keeps His commandments, feels himself daily summoned to the door of his heart, and ever urged to accomplish better and loftier works of charity, which the very knocks denote. And He knocks in another fashion, at the hour of death, when He calls on the faithful soul to arise and follow Him. Then we open at once to Him, if we accept death gladly, and fear not to be led before His judgment-seat, because we remember that we have striven to please Him, and have ever had Him in honour. And, as S. Gregory aptly tells us, every sickness which tells us that the hour of death is drawing near, is one of these knocks of the Bridegroom at the door. *S. Greg. M. Hom. 13, in Evang.*

S. Bernard, preaching on the Incarnation, tells us that the words may well denote the call made to the Blessed Virgin to signify her assent to that mystery when revealed to her by the Archangel, whom the Saint represents as saying in effect: "Open, O Blessed Virgin, thy heart to faith, thy lips to confession, thy womb to the Creator. Behold, the Desire of all nations knocks without at thy door. O, if He should pass by through thy delay, and thou shouldest again begin with sorrow to seek for Him whom thy soul loveth! Arise, haste, open. Arise by faith, haste by devotion, open by confession." Another writer, keeping more closely to the first explanation given, takes this as an appeal to the Mother of GOD after her Son's Resurrection not to withdraw, as her own desires would prompt her, into secret retirement and contemplation, where only the Angels would be her companions, but to remember that He was still shelterless, rejected by the Synagogue, and not yet accepted by the Gentiles, and that she therefore should open her mouth to confirm the teaching of the Gospel, and thus help to find Him a home in the hearts of men. But it is not to His Church alone, nor to His Saints, nor yet to His Mother only that He thus speaks. To all, even to sinners, He addresses these words: "Behold, I stand at the door, and knock; if any man hear My voice, and open the door, I will come in to him, and will sup with him, and he with Me." When CHRIST, the Lover of all souls, sees any soul at ease, busied with carnal pleasures, allowing entrance for the devil at the heart, and being fenced round with the snares of the enemy; then He comes back in the dead of the night, that is, by hidden compunction, and knocks at the door of her understanding, that, roused from her fatal sleep, she may see that she is beset with perils, and implore His aid. And the doors by which He then seeks entrance are repentance and faith, as He came into the heart of S. Thomas, when he doubted concerning the Resurrection. So He calls to us in the night, that we may *S. Bernard. Serm. 4, sup. Missus.* *Rupert.* *Rev. iii. 20.* *Luc. Abb.* *Cassiodor.* *Philo Carp.*

open and take Him in ere the dawning of the Great Day.

Kynaston.

The night is far spent, and the day is at hand,
There are signs in the heaven, and signs on the land,
In the wavering earth, and the drouth of the sea—
But He stands and He knocks, sinner, nearer to thee.

His night-winds but whisper until the day break
To the Bride, for in slumber her heart is awake :
He must knock at the sleep where the revellers toss,
With the dint of the nails and the shock of the Cross.

Look out at the casement; see how He appears,
Still weeping for thee all Gethsemane's tears,
Ere they plait Him earth's thorns, in its solitude crowned,
With the drops of the night and the dews of the ground.

Will you wait? Will you slumber until He is gone,
Till the beam of the timber cry out to the stone,
Till He shout at thy sepulchre, tear it apart,
And knock at thy dust, Who would speak to thy heart?

For My head is filled with dew, and My locks with the drops of the night. This is the reason which the Bridegroom gives why the door should be quickly opened to Him; and it may therefore be taken diversely, according as it is understood to be an appeal to the Bride's compassion for His forlorn state, or a promise of the reward which her compliance will bring to her. There is no reason why both interpretations may not hold, for the LORD JESUS blessed those who wrought a good work on Him during His earthly life in ministering to His bodily needs. The woman of Samaria who gave Him drink, the sinful woman who anointed Him, the publican who made Him a feast, all obtained from Him rich payment for their care. Let us then take first the Man of sorrows, before we kneel to the rewarding King. He saith then : Open to Me, My sister, My spouse, My dove, My undefiled, for My head is full of dew, and My locks with the drops of the night, as though He implied, Thou art at ease, and the door is shut against Me, thou art careful for the repose of a few, and because iniquity prevails, the love of many waxes cold. For *night* denotes iniquity, and its *dew* and *drops* are they who grow cold and fall, and chill the Head of CHRIST, that is, cause that GOD, Who is CHRIST's head, should not be loved. And these are carried in the *locks,* that is, they are admitted to outer Sacraments, but they do not reach the inward meaning. He knocks, therefore, that He

S. August. Tract. 57 in S. Joan.

may rouse the restful Saints from their repose, and cries, Open to Me, preach Me. Cassiodorus, agreeing with nearly all this exposition, differs on one point. He takes the *locks* adorning CHRIST the Head to be His Saints, filled with the drops of the night when persecuted by cold and unloving and unbelieving souls. Or again; the locks adhering to the head, yet full of dew, may well denote those who yield a partial obedience to CHRIST, who believe in His Godhead, and have faith so far, but not love, in that they are full of darkness and iniquity. And in this sense other writers have limited the phrase more particularly to careless and ignorant bishops and clergy, who do not preach CHRIST of sincerity. On this there is a legend recorded by S. Thomas of Cantipré, that a Cistercian monk in Brabant once saw the LORD JESUS in the form of a little child shivering in the snow, and crying with cold and pain. When asked the cause, He replied, trembling all over, "Alas, alas, why should I not weep? why should I not wail? Lo, thou seest that I sit needy, alone, and in the cold, and there is no one to take Me in, and give Me shelter." Hereupon the monk took Him up, and set Him on his horse, but the Child, leaping from his arms, suddenly disappeared, darting a great pang of suffering and love into his heart. This quaint legend (and indeed the whole verse) receives a curious illustration from a poem of a heathen bard:

<small>Cassiodor.</small>

<small>S. Greg. M.</small>

<small>S. Just. Org.
S. Ans. Laud.</small>

<small>S. Thomas Cantip. Apum ii. 1, 13.</small>

> Once at the midnight tide,
> While swept along the Bear
> Boötes' hand beside,
> And when, worn out with care,
> Lay all the tribes of men:
> Love reached my door, and there
> He plied the knocker then.
>
> Who knocks so loud, I said,
> And drives my dreams away?
> "A child, be not afraid,
> But ope the door, I pray,
> For I am wet in plight,
> And I have lost my way
> In this dark moonless night."
>
> With pity at his cry,
> I light my lamp, and so
> I open, and descry
> A winged child with a bow
> And quiver, near me stands:
> Close by my fire's glow,
> I seat him, chafe his hands,

<small>Pseudo-Anacreon.
Μεσονυκτίοις ποθ' ὥραις.</small>

And from his hair the rain
  In dewy drops I wring,
But he, when warm again,
  Cries, "Let us try the string,
Lest wet have hurt my bow."
He drew it, and the sting
Sent through my heart its blow.

He laughed with merry voice,
  And, leaping with a bound,
Cried, "Host, with me rejoice,
  My bow is safe and sound,
No harm its horn hath ta'en,
  But, as for thee, thy wound
Will give thy heartstrings pain."

<small>S. Ambros. de Isaac. 6.
Id. Serm. 12, in Ps. cxix.</small>
Again, the dew and drops of the night typify sorrow and trouble, which the LORD endures even still throughout the world, finding no place of rest. But it is just then, when His Body is suffering in this wise, and when He, as the Head, shares its affliction, that He knocks at the door to visit those who are in distress, lest they should faint and yield, if not sustained by His Presence.

But it is now time to turn to the other school of interpreters, who see here the blessings which the Bridegroom brings with Him as He enters. First, taking the locks <small>S. Greg. Nyssen. Luc. Abb. Tres Patr.</small> of His head to denote His chief Saints, whether Angels, Apostles, or Prophets, they explain the drops of dew to be the holy doctrines which they possess and impart to men, lofty and glorious indeed, as being on the head, and seeming to us very rivers and seas of knowledge, yet only drops when compared with the abysmal ocean of Divine wisdom. Then, the dew may be explained <small>S. Ambros. de Virgin. 3.</small> of heavenly grace, moistening the dry heart during the darkness of the world, to make it glad and fertile. <small>Ric. Vict. Targum.</small> Or, again, it is mercy falling on the darkness of human sin and blindness. And this may be coupled with the view of the Targum, that the drops in the locks of the <small>S. Paulinus, Ep. 4, ad Severum.</small> LORD are the tears of repentant sinners. And another, reminding us how the dew-drops glitter in a clear night, says that these shining drops amidst the locks of the Bridegroom denote the starry virtues with which His Saints were decked, when the full moon of the Church shone down on the conversion of the Gentiles. Finally, the Bridegroom's Head filled with dew, typifies His Resurrection very early in the morning, while those locks of His, wet with the drops of night, signify the souls of His redeemed and the nations won over to the

Faith, but still in the cold of their sins and the darkness of imperfect knowledge, soon to be lightened and warmed by the life and teaching of their pastors, through the grace of the HOLY GHOST.

<small>Philo Carp.</small>

3 I have put off my coat; how shall I put it on? I have washed my feet; how shall I defile them?

On this verse also there is a great discrepancy of exposition. That which is the most obvious meaning also has on its side the names of highest authority, to wit, that the Bride, lately so eager for her Bridegroom's presence, has now relaxed in her zeal, is resting in ease and comfort, and is reluctant to put herself to the inconvenience of rising, dressing, and opening the door. In the spirit of the man asked at midnight for the loan of three loaves, she answers her LORD, "Trouble me not; the door is now shut: I cannot rise and give Thee." She has, of course, some excuse to put forward as a cloak for her ingratitude and sloth, and she pleads the difficulty and unpleasantness of compliance. She says, "*I* have washed my feet," not knowing that her LORD saith, "If I wash thee not, thou hast no part in Me," much less asking Him, as S. Peter did, to wash her hands and her head also. The *coat* she had put off, is, as some will have it, the very bridal robe given her but now as a marriage present, whose smell was like Lebanon, denoting the love of GOD, which, as involving self-denial, she now postpones to love of self. And then we know what must follow,—that terrible warning to a once faithful and toiling Church, "I have somewhat against thee, because thou hast left thy first love. Remember therefore from whence thou art fallen, and repent, and do the first works; or else I will come unto thee quickly, and will remove thy candlestick out of his place, except thou repent." S. Augustine, taking the words to denote the lull in the missionary zeal and vigilance of discipline which overtook the Church after its establishment under Constantine, represents her excusing herself in this fashion: "O CHRIST, Thou biddest me, Thy Church, to soften and open for Thee the hearts of men, harder than rock, and I would gladly do it, but I have no fit workmen; at any rate, I do not yet clearly know what they can endure, and what they will refuse. The former ones, whom I knew

<small>S. Luke xi. 7.

Sanchez.
Luc. Abb.
S. Greg. M.
Hom. 38 in Evang.

Rev. ii. 4.

S. August.
Tract. 57 in S. Joan.</small>

to be competent, whom I sent boldly into the fight, the late storm of hostile wrath, the past violence of Maximian, Maxentius, Diocletian, and the almost ceaseless cruel persecution by Licinius, have swept away. These my warriors, closely united to me, hemmed me in, sheltered me, and veiled me like an inner robe; and, whilst obeying Thee, and sparing not my champions, I have been, and remain, all but stripped and naked. Of those who remain, some are broken down by age and toil, others by wounds and tortures, and the youthful residue, by whose zeal Thou willest that I should speed, as on feet, through the world, being but lately washed [in baptism,] are yet but tender, and I therefore fear lest they faint under the burden, or lest they should again be soiled, and I be thus once more defiled in my feet." Or it may, as several others represent, denote an undue exaltation of the contemplative life over the active, when the Church, or any individual soul, pleads its own spiritual advantage as a reason for refraining from the task of converting others. Thus Cassiodorus says: "I have stripped myself of the cares and occupations of this world, without which the task of preaching can scarcely or not at all be carried on, and how can it be that I should return again to what I have abandoned? For he who sets himself to undertake the office of preaching, must also see to the temporal needs of those placed under him, which cannot be done without much anxiety. And that the *coat* does signify the anxiety and cares of the world, the LORD shows in the Gospel, saying, 'Neither let him that is in the field return back to take his clothes,' which means, that he is not again to be entangled in the things of the world. Therefore the Church or any faithful soul, which has stripped off this coat, fears, when resting in contemplation of its Creator, lest it should be clad in it again, and busied in secular concerns." But GOD is not willing that souls should perish for any such cause as this, and therefore He compels His Bride to bestir herself, and to act on that saying of a Saint, "It is needful that even religious hearts should be defiled with earthly dust." And therefore, though she has washed her feet, those affections of her heart which guide its path, with penitential tears, and dreads to soil them again, she must needs leave her bed, and tread the floor a second time. There is, however, a good sense in which the Bride may utter these words, and that sense is pressed by many of the Fathers. They take it to be a resolution against any relapse into sin, that having put off the old man and his deeds, and washed herself in the Blood of the Lamb, she determines that nothing shall draw her back to her former conversation. She casts off that coat of skins, type of dead works, which clothed Adam after his fall, and she puts on CHRIST Himself for her raiment. She will not keep both together, for she remembers the precept given to the Apostles, "Neither two coats;" nor will she endeavour to blend them into one, for the LORD hath also said, "No man seweth a piece of new cloth on an old garment." And she has washed her feet, too, in the laver of Baptism and the grace of the HOLY GHOST, from the defilement of earth, loosing from them those shoes of dead hides that she may do so. So Moses put off his shoes at the burning bush, and Holy Scripture nowhere tells that he resumed them; so, in all the elaborate vesture of the High Priest, there is no mention of shoes; so too, the Apostles were directed to provide no shoes for their journey. And that because there is neither dust nor mire on the Way to our Country, paved as it is with portions of the Rock, according to that saying, "He brought me out of the horrible pit, out of the mire and clay, and set my feet upon the Rock, and ordered my goings." And again, the words are taken of that voluntary poverty in spirit and body, when the Bride is eager to strip herself of everything which may entangle her in her race and delay her approach to the goal where the Bridegroom awaits her with the first of His beatitudes. For they who imitate by voluntary poverty His suffering life are intrusted with the special privilege of judicial power, as saith the LORD to them who had forsaken all, "Ye which have followed Me, in the regeneration when the Son of Man shall sit in the throne of His glory, ye also shall sit upon twelve thrones, judging the twelve tribes of Israel." And that because in being conformed and united to Him Who is Truth and Righteousness, there is nothing left in their judgment to swerve from justice, and thus they are fitted for the office. The Targum, taking the words *I have put off my coat* as spoken by the congregation of Israel, doubtful how to repent and clothe itself again with the garment of obedience to GOD's Law, ascribes the second clause to GOD Himself,

Margin notes: Col. iii. 9. S. Greg. Nyss. Gen. iii. 21. S. Mat. x. 10. S. Mark ii. 21. Tres Patr. Ps. xl. 2. Hen. Harph. S. Mat. xix. 28. Targum.

Who asks the guilty nations in turn how He can defile His feet by walking amongst them as of yore. And one *Philo Carp.* Christian writer applies the whole verse to the Bridegroom, when He stripped off the mortality and passibility of His Flesh, and passed in His Ascension from the narrow limits of earth to the boundless regions of heaven, where death hath no more dominion over Him. There too, where the Body follows the Head, and has attained the "blessed necessity of sinlessness," she may say in thankful adoration, *I have put off my coat* of *Rev. xxi.* corruption, *how shall I put it on?* for here is no more *4, 5.* death and all things are new. *I have washed my feet*, *Irimbert.* which stand now on the golden pavement of the heavenly Jerusalem, *and how shall I defile them?* seeing *Rev. xxi. 27.* that "there shall in no wise enter into it anything that defileth."

4 My beloved put in his hand by the hole of the door, and my bowels were moved for him.

Although the words *of the door* are not in the Hebrew text, nor in the early versions, yet this gloss is supplied by several Rabbinical authorities, and many commentators. This hole is variously taken to be the orifice left for raising the latch from the outside, whether with the hand or a key, or else as a grille or wicket in the door, designed as a look-out, and for the transmission of small articles without opening the whole gate. Else, it may be taken, as by S. Ambrose and by some modern critics, to denote a window in the wall of the cottage of the Bride. This seems somewhat less probable, as we should in that case find one of the several words denoting *window* or *lattice*, instead of a term not elsewhere employed in this *Eusebius.* sense.[1] Coming to the mystical import, the *hand* is the *Theodoret.* symbol of power in operation, and the *hole*, contrasted with the wide opening of the entire door, denotes the partial and imperfect glimpse which the soul can obtain of GOD when she puts any barrier between herself and Him. So we read that when He came to His own

---

[1] The reference to this opening as a definite and familiar one, *the* hole, is alone enough to dispose of Bishop Wordsworth's theory, that the Bridegroom, refused admittance at the door, miraculously causes a breach in the wall, through which He shows His hand, in warning to the Bride that it is impossible to exclude Him if He wills to enter.

country, Nazareth, typically the house of His sister, "He did not many mighty works there, because of their unbelief." Some works He did, but not many. He showed them His hand, so to speak, but not His face.

^{S. Mat. xiii. 58.}

The Incarnation, whereby the Eternal WORD, the Right Hand of the FATHER, was revealed to mankind, is denoted, as more than one ancient commentator urges, in this place. He is said to be manifested through the *hole*, just as in another part of Holy Writ we are said to see Him "in a glass darkly," because He emptied Himself of His glory, and though incomprehensible, narrowed Himself within the bounds of a human body; nay, passed through the yet narrower strait of His Passion, making in the Rock that hole where His dove should have her nest. In this same body too He stretched out His hand in a series of miracles, all performed within the narrow area of Palestine. And this manifestation of His power is intended to encourage His Bride to rise, as knowing that He is strong enough to help her in all perils, nay, that even in peace there is no safety unless He be near. In this manner He usually arouses a slumbering Church or soul. It is not by any startling display of His might, any full disclosure of His presence, that He commonly operates, but by secretly moving the understanding and will, by the secret mission of the HOLY SPIRIT. The hole through which He does this, according to one, is our outward sense, whereby we perceive the working of His power; or as another takes it, the memory of His Passion endured for our sakes; or, yet again, the lower creation, testifying His goodness and power. And it may be also taken of the partial measure of grace vouchsafed to stir the soul up to more vigorous action. So Richard of S. Victor explains it: When the holy soul dreads to be entangled in worldly concerns if she undertake the burdensome care of her neighbours, and devote herself to promoting their salvation, then the Beloved, Who had urged her to the task, comforts her, and visits her heart, penetrating it with additional grace. Which visitation of grace the Bride describes as the putting of His hand through the hole, because CHRIST infuses grace as through a fissure, when He does not flood the entire soul, but visits with a certain measure of grace, and does not, when so visiting, fully illuminate. And

S. Greg. Nyss.
Cassiodor.
1 Cor. xiii. 12.

Hugo Card.

S. Greg. M.
Philo Carp.

Tres Patr.

Theodoret.

Cassiodor.
S. Greg. Nyss.

Ric. Vict.

S. Ans. Laud.

there is much force in that suggestion of Honorius, that He gives this grace by showing His hand, that is, the finished work of His own obedience,—how finished, the scar in its wounded palm may tell—that she may be roused to like zeal for accomplishing the work assigned her. He stretches His hand through the hole in yet another way when He makes His Bride pass through trouble and persecution. If she will not open to Him when He knocks, He will punish her by means of suffering, calling her back to Himself by famine, and pestilence, and war, letting her feel, but not see, His corrective hand. Philo would have us remember how He drew the doubting and incredulous to Himself through the hole, when He spoke to Thomas, "Reach hither thy hand, and thrust it into My side, and be not faithless, but believing."

And my bowels were moved for Him. Here they all substantially agree that the mingled awe and delight of the Bride's heart are described; awe at His presence, because of her own unworthiness and sense of recent failure, and delight, because where His right hand is, there pleasures must be. And accordingly the holy Abbat of Deutz recounts a vision granted to a nameless person, supposed to have been himself, telling us: "The Beloved appeared plainly in a vision of the night, and wondrously put His hand, as through a hole, into the man's breast, and laid hold of his heart within, and held it for some time, pressing it gently, and that heart rejoiced with gladness unspeakable, leaping and bounding within the clasp of that Hand." Lastly, the passage is explained of the rejoicing of the hallowed womb of the Virgin Mother when He, the Right Hand of GOD, came to her at the Annunciation in secret and mysterious wise, finding her all pure, free from every garment of sin, resolute in her spotless maidenhood, with no speck of the earth on which she dwelt defiling her feet.

5 I rose up to open to my beloved; and my hands dropped with myrrh, and my fingers with sweet smelling myrrh, upon the handles of the lock.

We open to the Beloved not merely when we receive Him coming, but when we preach Him to others, and cause them, who had formerly barred their breast with sin, now converted by our preaching, to open the door of their heart to CHRIST. And it is well said in the first place *I rose up*, and afterwards *to open to my Beloved*. For he who wishes to open the hearts of others to CHRIST by preaching, must first rise up, that is, be alert in zeal for good works, and fulfil in deed what he preaches, lest perchance when he has preached to others, he himself should " be a castaway." Wherefore also Luke saith of the LORD, " All that JESUS began both to do and to teach." He mentions *do* first, and then *teach.* And *I rose up* to a more toilsome and holy task, that by many a labour, and by mortification of the flesh, I might *open* a wider door of meditation, and so take in the Bridegroom Whom I could not receive before. *I rose up* to strive after Divine contemplation, roused by the touch of His hand, that I might be ready for the full bestowal of celestial grace. For if His touch moved me, what will His embrace be ? if a drop from His hand had such effect, what will be the overflowing of His bounty ? if His whisper was sweet, what will be His open speech ? So then, the Bride rises up to open to her Beloved when, having obtained some grace, she is the more fired to win it again, to love more fervently, and to devote herself more earnestly to the care and the salvation of her neighbours. For even ere she had opened to her Beloved, she is more eager for Him, and for toiling in works of charity. She trains herself then in the love of GOD, or in contemplation; she labours in works of mercy for the profit of her neighbours according as their need requires and the occasion demands. She prays for some, she comforts others, she gives wholesome counsel to some more, and she prepares herself to undertake the task of ruling or of preaching, if the occasion demand it, when she is thus visited with grace, and endeavours to answer the call of that grace, and to conform herself to it. It is no labour to open the door for CHRIST, when once the Bride is erect and ready, but it may be toilsome enough to rise and make the needful preparation, shaking off slumber, and removing any obstacles that lie between her and the door.

And my hands dropped with myrrh, and my fingers with sweet-smelling myrrh, upon the handles of the lock. This is the order of the sentence, according to the Masoretic pointing, the Syriac, Arabic, and LXX. The Vulgate, on the other hand, stops at the second *myrrh*, and begins a new sentence, *I opened the bolt of the door for my Beloved.* The first question they ask is, Whence came this myrrh? And various answers are suggested. Some urge that the Bride had anointed herself for the reception of her Bridegroom, to which it is very reasonably objected that she makes no mention of this herself, and that it is inconsistent to suppose her to have so prepared, and then refuse to open the door. Others suppose that she may have carried with her to the door a box of unguent ready to anoint the dank tresses of the Bridegroom, and broken it in her haste, so as to spill the contents. Thirdly, and best, the myrrh comes from the Bridegroom, and is the trace of His recent presence and of His touch when He put in His hand through the hole, and tried the lock. And so Lucretius may tell us:

At lacrymans exclusus amator limina sæpe
Floribus et sertis operit, postesque superbos
Unguit amaracino.

The tearful lover, shut without, oft clothes
With blooms and wreaths the threshold, and anoints
The stately jambs with marjoram.

They agree in taking myrrh to be, as usual in Scripture, the type of repentance and voluntary mortification, though supposing it to flow spontaneously from the Bride herself, as a result of that sudden yearning produced in her by the apparition of the Bridegroom's hand. But it is better, on all accounts, to take this motion of grace as proximately derived from Himself, and that, by recalling His Passion. Moreover, it accords exactly with His own words a little before, "I have gathered My myrrh," and He now gives her of that which He has so collected. Observe next that not only the *hands* of the Bride, but her separate *fingers* are said to drop with myrrh. That is, the effect produced upon her was not merely general, but particular. Each virtue of her soul was separately affected, each detail of her conversation, and not merely the general scope of her life, was influenced. For as several fingers exist separately in one hand, so in one holy life or conversation divers virtues are independently discerned. For liberality is one kind of virtue, frugality another. Humility is one task, frank rebuke another. We practise one when we speak for our neighbour's advantage; another, when we keep silence for our own edification. And the fingers are said to be full of the choicest (Vulg. *probatissima*) myrrh, because it is essential in all our actions that mortification of fleshliness hold a place. The myrrh is rightly called choicest, when in the case of every prompting of the Enemy, carnal pleasure is kept from admission. When this is so, all the hardness of the soul is melted, and an ingress is provided that the Bridegroom may enter the heart. The myrrh is twofold, an ordinary kind, and *sweet-smelling*, or rather, with the margin of A. V. *passing*, that is *fluid* myrrh (LXX. πλήρη) dropping naturally from the tree, and not forced out by incision or other artificial means. And this denotes the progress of the soul in grace. The first and inferior myrrh, is that penitence which comes from fear of punishment, or after actual chastisement at GOD's hand. The second, and more acceptable, is the overflowing of a softened heart, melted by the love of GOD, and streaming forth its tears naturally and easily under the rays of the Sun of Righteousness. And observe too that it is the hands and fingers of the Bride, not her mouth, which is said to drop myrrh, teaching us thereby that an austere and self-denying life, carried out in all details of action, is more important than eloquent preaching on the part of those who are engaged in the conversion of sinners. The myrrh drops *upon the handles of the lock.* That is, the repentance of the Bride is first directed to the particular act, habit, or temper of mind which is *the* barrier, the besetting sin which keeps the Bridegroom out. And the myrrh, falling on the stiff or rusted bolt, makes it easy to draw it back, showing that amendment of life and the reception of divine grace must be preceded by contrition. A further sense is well put by Cocceius: "The *lock,* whereby our heart is opened to CHRIST, or by which CHRIST is shut up within the heart, is faith. Its bolt is withdrawn when our heart is expanded, so that CHRIST can always come to us, with all His retinue, and in every array. The bolt of this lock is shot by fulness and pleasure. And it is very properly shot against other desires, but not against the kingdom of CHRIST, to prevent it from flowing into us wholly. The fulness which shuts out everything save CHRIST,

Guilielmus.

Tres Patr.

Cocceius.

is from the HOLY GHOST, but that which checks any desire for Him is of the flesh. Besides, the Bride hints that she found the myrrh on the lock, that is, the effectual working of the HOLY GHOST when she desired to open her heart. And if we desire to press the parable further, she finds this fragrant ointment on her hands and fingers, that is in her toil and action, which she has begun in the fear of GOD."

6 I opened to my beloved; but my beloved had withdrawn himself, and was gone; my soul failed when he spake: I sought him, but I could not find him; I called him, but he gave me no answer.

Cassiodor.
S. Greg. M.
Beda.

The Latin Fathers, reading in the first clause of this verse (as noted above) *I opened the bolt of the door for my Beloved*, discuss here the nature of this bar or bolt. And first, they take it to denote worldly pleasure, which shuts GOD out of the heart. S. Anselm of Laon, looking at the verse as descriptive of the Church's missionary work, takes it to be ignorance and blindness, which preachers remove when they proclaim the Gospel to their hearers. And Richard of S. Victor aptly points out that a lock is but small, though it keep a great door fast, and its bolt is but a small part even of it, whence he draws the conclusion that in the spiritual life it is small negligences and defects which are the surest barriers between the soul and grace, so that it is needful to amend and withdraw them before the Beloved can enter in to the soul. And Parez, according to his wont, treating the Canticles as the history of the Church under both the Old and New Covenants, remarks that after the Bridegroom's Incarnation, the Bride withdrew the bolt of ceremonial usages, and threw open those doors of the Law which hid the sanctuary of CHRIST from sight, and barred the access of the Gentiles. *I opened.* Fitly do anointed hands open the door for CHRIST, Who takes His title from anointing. It may be that He cannot enter save through an anointed door. Wherefore in the Temple there were little doors (Vulg. *ostiola*) made of olive-tree, through which was the entrance into the Holy of holies. For this is the kind of tree which yields the anointing fluid. They are called little doors, and

S.Ans.Laud.

Ric. Vict.

Parez.

Gillebert. Serm. 44.

1 Kings vi. 31.

the olive-wood entrance is narrow, but thou canst glide in easily in the fatness of grace, where the understanding is subtilized, and the mystery secret. Ingress will not be toilsome, if thou wilt but use the oil of devotion and charity as a door. And it seems to me that a suitable testimony is produced as to the temple. 'For the Temple of GOD is holy, which temple ye are.' 1 Cor. iii. 17. Have therefore in thy temple doors through which the High Priest alone may enter the inmost chamber of thine heart. Shut the door, draw the bolt, save when thy Beloved knocks, desiring to enter. If there be no door, there will be free entrance for every passer-by. If the door be shut, but not secured with a bolt, it will readily yield, and give way to pressure, having no surer fastening. Have both, the door of watchfulness, and the bar of firmness. Keep a watchful look-out, resist firmly. Let not forgetfulness and ignorance creep in, let not wickedness break in. And if thou wantest a more precise definition, let anxious forethought be the door, and prayer its bolt. Fastened with such a bar, thy door will yield to no hostile push. 'He hath made fast,' saith the Psalmist, 'the bars of thy gates.' Ps. cxlvii. 13. In the bars and gates dost not thou think that thou hearest of the *door* and *bolt*? Both are needful, but only against the enemy. When thou hearest the voice and knock of the Beloved, when thou feelest the light touch of His hand through the hole, draw back the bolt, open the door, let every barrier give way; if it may be, pull down the whole mid-wall, that thy Beloved may pour Himself freely upon thee. Let thy carefulness against the snares of evil spirits be turned into security, and at the presence of the Bridegroom change caution in keeping off the foe into plenteousness of enjoying the Beloved. He knew that he had opened the door, who said, 'O GOD, my heart is ready, my heart is ready.' Ps. cviii. 1. But how is it that JESUS needs a door, Who saith in the Gospel, 'I am the door?' S. John x. 9. It is a strange thing. He is the Door, and yet He knocks at the door. He, by Whom 'if any man enter in, he shall be saved, and shall go in and out and find pasture,' Himself desires to enter. There is a great diversity of doors. There is the door of natural religion, the door of Church Sacraments, the door of experimental grace. In that first door of natural religion, wisdom becomes known to us by reasoning on it as it operates in the works of creation, and we gain access to a certain measure of truth, we gather some knowledge of the Deity, but not of the personal character of GOD. At this door there is no distinction of persons, no bestowal of grace. And therefore no one ought to be a very frequent or eager knocker at this door. By the second, through which we are initiated into the Sacraments of salvation, we enter into the unity of the Church, the Communion of Saints. At the second door, men are in such wise within as to be in fact without, until they come to the third; which we explain to be familiar access, by the emotions of love, to a certain abundant fruition and contemplation of the Beloved. This secret and innermost door is not open to all, but yields entrance to the Bride alone. It makes but little difference whether thou enter in to Him, or He to thee, save that thou seemest as the entering one when thou art as it were the first to come, and to petition Him; and He comes first to thee when He anticipates thee, knocks at thine affections, glides in unexpectedly, and raises thee looking for no such thing, with His touch of undefiled sweetness."

But my Beloved had withdrawn Himself and was gone. And very often, when we are anxious to handle spiritual things, the more acutely we essay them, the more the heart's edge is beaten back and blunted, whence Solomon observes: "I said, I will be wise, but it was far from me." For the more one lifts up his heart by purification of the flesh to divine contemplation, the more unattainable does he find that which he seeks to be. The Bridegroom withdraws and goes away from His Spouse, not removing to a distance, but merely turning aside. For He is at her right hand, that she may not be removed from her good beginning, but He does not show her His face. "He is nigh unto all them that call upon Him faithfully." She desires to look on Him, and to talk with Him face to face, as a man talketh with his friend. But He hides His face, while abiding with her, and in her, though she perceives not His presence. And in this wise, though He hath truly taken up His lodging with her, He withdraws from her, and goes away, lest she become uplifted, and ascribe the fulfilment of her wishes to her own merit. Even when she has shown herself more worthy of receiving Him, He does not give Himself to her as she desires, but withdraws from her, to keep her in humility, to whet her desire more sharply, to gratify it more fully. How brief too were the Lord's appearances after His Resurrection, how sudden, how soon cut short! Scarcely was He recognized by a few of His disciples, when He vanished. Some He does not suffer to touch Him. He glides in amongst others through closed doors, needing no opening of the valves. When we think that we hold Him, He robs us, as it were, of His dear presence, coming secretly and going secretly. For the joy of contemplation is but an instant. It swiftly departs, and utterly surpasses all the power of human understanding, and where it goes, we cannot, in this flesh, follow it with equal step. Yes, adds a devout commentator, so that there is silence for but half an hour in the heaven of the pious heart. He withdrew Himself also, when He departed out of the world to His FATHER, though He hath not abandoned His Spouse, nor left her children orphans, but comes again and again in Sacraments and inspiration to visit and console her. And whereas the Vulgate instead of *gone* reads *passed through* (*transierat*), they dwell on the special meaning of the Latin word as conveying fresh lessons. "He passed through me, through all my powers, through myself. For the WORD of GOD is a sword, JESUS is a sword of fire, passing without delay or difficulty, through the soul, which melts at His passage, and cannot bar His way." And so, as another and earlier writer reminds us, He was Himself that sword which pierced the heart of His own dear Mother, that the secrets of many hearts should be revealed. Whence, as they explain her rising up to denote the alacrity of her service, and the droppings of myrrh in her case to be her incorruption, humility and self-denial, so they take the withdrawal of the bolt to be her breaking her wonted silence that she might preach her Son; though Honorius will have it that the bolt denotes sin, and that we are hereby taught that she opposed no obstacle of the kind to the Most Holy when He would enter in.

My soul failed when He spake. The Vulgate reads, *My soul melted,* while the LXX., closer to the original, has, *My soul went forth.* That is, remarks S. Ambrose, it followed the WORD of GOD, and went forth from the body, lifting itself out of its tabernacle, and makes, as the same Saint observes in another place, a good exit, when, coming to Him, it

[margin notes: Gillebert. Hugo Card. Philo Carp. Gillebert. S. Ambros. in Ps. cxix. Id. de Isaac, cap. 6. Guilielmus. Rupert. Honorius. S. Ambros. de Isaac, 6. Id. de Virgin. 3.]

passes from sin to holiness, and, despising earthly
things, melts with the love of heaven. Whatever is
hard and frozen in the heart softens and melts under
the fire of GOD's love, and pours out in a stream of
penitence and longing. The Beloved passed by, but
He did not therefore abandon the soul, but rather
drew her to Himself, and that by His word. O happy
going forth! "The LORD preserve thy going out and
thy coming in." The going out is from that wherein
we are now placed; the coming in is to those good
things which are above us. She goes forth to the
WORD, because the Bridegroom saith, "I am the
door, by Me if any man enter in, he shall go in and
out," so as never to cease going in and out, but ever
go in to greater things, and go out from lesser ones.
And taking the reading of the A. V., *My soul failed*,
let us hear a Western Doctor: "Did she not feel herself exhausted in her strength who said, *My soul
melted*, because when the mind, in its strongest condition, is touched with the inspiration of secret speech,
it melts with the very desire in which it is swallowed
up, whence it finds itself utterly wearied out, because
it sees the height to which it would fain ascend beyond its strength. Hence the Prophet, when he tells
how he saw the vision of GOD, adds, 'I fainted, and
was sick certain days.'" And Philo, uniting all the
ideas together, notes, The Bride declares that she went
forth and fainted at the speech of the Bridegroom,
because she cannot, while still prisoned in the body,
long endure the power of JESUS CHRIST's love, Who
pours Himself into the longing soul by the HOLY
GHOST, "For the corruptible body presseth down the
soul, and the earthly tabernacle weigheth down the
mind that museth upon many things," and the soul
fired with divine love is often caught up in contemplation to those eternal joys, but cannot abide there
long, because laden with the burden of the flesh, but
falls back after going forth, drowned in tears, and yet
in gladness. And so the Cluniac:

> Jerusalem the only,
>   That look'st from heaven below,
> In thee is all my glory,
>   In me is all my woe.
> And though my body may not,
>   My spirit seeks thee fain,
> Till flesh and earth return me
>   To earth and flesh again.

Wherefore it fitly follows: *I sought Him, but I could not find Him; I called Him, but He gave me no answer.* For although the soul have passed out of her own nature, so as not to be hindered by anything in her consciousness, yet she still seeks, still calls, and finds not. How could she find that which nothing that is known can show us? She sought Him by reasonings and meditations, but He is beyond them all, evading the grasp of the mind. She called, that is, she devised countless phrases to denote His goodness unspeakable, it surpassed them all. So David, after he had said, "Thou, O LORD GOD, art full of compassion and mercy, longsuffering, plenteous in goodness and truth, my strength, the horn of my salvation," and so forth, at length confesses that he is at a loss for words, and marvelling cries out, "How excellent is Thy Name!" But why is it that GOD seeks when He is not sought, that He comes when He is not called, and that when He is sought He withdraws, and flees when He is called? If He does not love, why does He come? and if He does love, why does He flee? He does love, and therefore He comes; but He does not love here, and therefore He flees. What do I mean by saying that He does not love *here?* I mean in this world, in this land, in this country, in this exile. But He calls us to His own Land, for such love as His befits not a land like ours, and the pleasantness of His Country is a bulwark to our love. A happy love seeks a pleasant spot, and therefore He praises His Land to us, saying, " The flowers appear on the earth, the vines with the tender grape give a good smell, the voice of the turtle is heard in our land," that we may desire such a region, long for such a country, and follow Him. There He loves us; there He desires to enjoy our love; there He asks for our embrace; there He no longer flees from them who follow Him, but awaits them as they come.

But the words are also spoken in terrible warning to the Church or soul which neglects to hear and obey the call of the LORD, so that He, the Eternal Wisdom, cries in the streets, "Because I have called, and ye refused; I have stretched out My hand, and no man regarded; but ye have set at nought all My counsel, and would none of My reproof; I also will mock at your calamity. Then shall they call upon Me, but I will not answer; they shall seek Me early, but

S. Greg. Nyss.

Ps. lxxxvi. 15; xviii. 1.

Ps. viii. 1.
Hugo Vict. de Arcâ Morali, iv. 4.

Cant. ii. 12.

Luc. Abb.

Prov. i. 24, 28.

they shall not find Me." And what He spake thus aforetime in prophecy, He said again to the Jews who rejected Him. "Ye shall seek Me, and not find Me, and where I am, thither ye cannot come." Again and again has it been true in Christian history, in that slackness of zeal which preceded the outbreak of Arianism, which left the East a prey to Mohammed, which caused the great schism of Europe three centuries ago. Again and again is it true of souls which GOD has invited, and which, turning away to their farm or their merchandise, or their domestic pleasures, are finally excluded from the marriage-supper of the Lamb. And one commentator points his note with the homely old saw:

S. John vii. 34.

Ghislerius. Delrio.

Corn. à Lap.

> He who will not when he may,
> When he will, he shall have nay.

Luc. Abb.

Ps. cxix. 145.

For even that will is imperfect, because the careless soul cannot say with David, even when it does call for the passing Bridegroom, "I call with my whole heart," since if it did, He could not choose but answer.

7 The watchmen that went about the city found me, they smote me, they wounded me; the keepers of the walls took away my veil from me.

Theodoret.

Whence we may learn to what mischief sloth gives birth, and what toil comes of indolence. For whereas the Bride excuses herself, and is not willing to open at once to the Bridegroom, she is forced a little later not merely to go as far as the door, but even to traverse the city, and to go about the streets, and to fall in with the watchmen, by whom she is wounded, and even so scarcely finds her desired Spouse. But if she had obeyed at once, she would have escaped all this trouble. The meaning of the verse differs according to the interpretation given to the word *city*, whether it be Babylon or Sion, the world or the Church. The Targum, explaining these watchmen to be the Chaldean besiegers of Jerusalem who took it in the reign of Zedekiah, so far blends the two ideas as to take the city in a good, and the watchmen in a bad sense. But the Christian expositors keep the ideas distinct. Thus, Theodoret will have it that the watchmen of the city

Targum.

Theodoret.

are the magistrates, rulers, and tyrants of the Pagan Roman Empire, who persecuted the Church, and stripped the Martyrs of that outer veil of flesh which covered their souls, and that in the streets, because of the bold and public preaching whereby the early missionaries of the Faith exposed themselves to peril. Or, as S. Justus comments, the veil denotes all the external helps of religion, taken away, when the priests were imprisoned, the altars levelled, and the Scriptures burnt. Another, taking the *city* in a yet wider sense, as the whole world, explains the watchmen to be the evil spirits, who prowl about the earth, seeking whom they may devour, wound, and strip of their faith, smiting them with words of false doctrine, and tearing from their souls its baptismal purity. Whence S. Jerome draws the practical lesson that it is wise for Christian virgins to remain sheltered in their home, of domestic or Religious life, and not to go forth even to search for CHRIST. Could he have looked down the ages at the history of that Common Life whose infancy he aided in fostering, he would have seen the world and the cloister engaged in perpetual strife. Again and again would he have observed the spirit of laxity and secularity, fostered by evil rulers within the Church, untrustworthy watchmen of her walls, forcing its way into Houses of the strictest rule, stripping them of the true religious character, and needing the strenuous efforts of reformers such as S. Coletta, S. Teresa, and Angelique Arnauld, to restore it as before. Or he would have seen the civil power in one country after another, laying unhallowed hands on the patrimony of the poor, and driving Religious forth, bare of everything save their faith, from the cloister into the streets and highways. And a yet more literal fulfilment of the type would have presented itself in the many glorious martyrdoms which the convent yielded in its passive resistance to the sword of unbelief, as in those English nuns who disfigured their faces with terrible scars a thousand years ago during the invasion of Inguar and Hubba, that they might not be a prey to the evil passions of the heathen, who then massacred them in rage and disappointment; or in their French sisters nine centuries later, who went to the scaffold singing the *Te Deum*, continuing it with undiminished numbers as each consecrated head fell, until the Abbess died last, with the closing words of the

S. Just. Org.

Luc. Abb.

S. Hieron. Ep. 22, ad Eustoch. Ep. 7, ad Lætan.

Titelman.

Gloria in excelsis on her lips. In the other interpretation there is a diversity, according as the Angels or the great earthly Saints and teachers are regarded as the watchmen of the city. S. Gregory Nyssen and S. Ambrose are in agreement in taking the verse to denote the share of the Guardian Angels in the conversion and salvation of the soul entrusted to their care. They smite her with the sword of the Word of GOD, and with tribulations, after she has come out of the dwelling of her old conversation, and wound her with increased love for divine things, and taking from her the veil, (be it a token of widowhood or a type of bodily thoughts and habits obscuring the free vision of the mind, or else an emblem of mere human reason, impeding faith,) that her beauty may be more perfectly discerned, and that she may see more clearly the mysteries they present to her view.

<small>S. Greg. Nyss.
S. Ambros. de Isaac, 6, de Virg. iii.

Tres Patr.

Psellus.</small>

<small>Henry Vaughan, *Cock-crowing*.</small>

> Only this veil which Thou hast broke,
> And must be broken yet in me,
> This veil, I say, is all the cloak
> And cloud which shadows me from Thee.
>   This veil Thy full-eyed love denies,
>   And only gleams and fractions spies.
>
> O take it off! make no delay;
> But brush me with Thy light, that I
> May shine unto a perfect day,
> And warm me at Thy glorious eye!
>   O take it off! or till it flee,
>   Though with no lily, stay with me!

S. Gregory Nyssen draws a further corollary from the verse, that it betokens progress in grace. The Bride had laid aside her tunic or *coat*, she had no thought of removing her veil also, but the Angels take even this from her, because the soul, as it advances, divests itself by degrees of all that checks its speed in the race of salvation. A more widely accepted interpretation, however, is that which sees here the task of the preachers of the Gospel in the conversion of sinners. And first, the Apostles and Evangelists found the Jewish Church seeking vainly for CHRIST, *smote* their hearers with powerful words, and *wounded* them, so that they were "pricked and cut to the heart," and took away from them that veil of the ceremonial law which lay upon their hearts and hid the light of GOD's countenance from them. Of which veil the Apostle

<small>Acts ii. 37; vii. 54.

Parez.</small>

writes, saying, "Not as Moses, which put a vail over his face, that the children of Israel could not steadfastly look to the end of that which is abolished. But their minds were blinded: for until this day remaineth the same vail untaken away in the reading of the Old Testament; which vail is done away in CHRIST. But even unto this day, when Moses is read, the vail is upon their heart. Nevertheless, when it shall turn to the LORD, the vail shall be taken away."[1] 2 Cor. iii. 13.

Next, applying the words to the individual soul, they tell us that the Church's watchmen, those watchmen set upon the walls of Jerusalem, be they Apostles, Martyrs, Prelates, or preachers, are said to find her, because they seek her out for instruction, they smite and wound her with the arrows of divine love, with their counsels of mortification, with their injunctions to repentance, with their wholesome discipline, and take from her the veil of ignorance and blindness, by teaching her how she may abandon her evil habits, and serve GOD truly. Their sword, wherewith they inflict the wound, is the Word of GOD, and her veil of earthly thoughts and affections is taken from her for her own good, as Joseph left his mantle behind when he fled away from sin, and Elijah cast his to earth when he ascended in the chariot of fire. It is not singular, therefore, that some should here see an exact type of the Sacrament of Penance. The watchmen of the city, who know that they must needs give account for the souls therein, find one such soul wan- Philo Carp.
Cassiod.
Beda.
Gillebert.

---

[1] The force of this argument of the Apostle is somewhat obscured to English readers, by an error of the A.V. in Exodus xxxiv. 33, which reads, "And *till* Moses had done speaking with them, he put a vail on his face." This, taken in conjunction with verse 35, is commonly understood to mean that the veil was intended to prevent the Israelites from being dazzled with the radiance. The LXX. and Vulgate, more correctly, have "*When* he had done speaking," &c. That is, the light was gradually fading from his face after he left GOD's presence, and the veil was merely intended to hide that fact from the people. On returning to GOD's presence, he withdrew the veil, that his face might again be illuminated. Hence S. Paul's reasoning is, that the outer ceremonial Law, as practised by the Jews in his day, only served to conceal from the people the loss of true spiritual enlightenment on the part of the priests, and to prevent the rays of GOD's grace from shining on them; so that the abolition of that Law was now a necessary preliminary to any true knowledge of divine things.

dering in error and darkness. They smite with the warnings and threats of GOD's Word, they wound, by enjoining sharp, but needful penances, they take away the veil, when they urge the sinner to full confession of hidden guilt; and when, by wise ghostly counsel, they show the true deformity of sin to a conscience which had lost the power of seeing it as it is. Thus Cardinal Frederick Borromeo, the worthy successor of his kinsman, S. Charles, when urging his clergy in Milan to careful discharge of the duties of the Confessional, told them of a noble and wealthy lady, living in sin, who made a merely formal confession, and was met by the priest with a stern injunction to abandon her evil habits, and all occasions which might lead to their repetition, before daring to approach the altar. She, who had been accustomed to a laxer discipline, angrily exclaimed: "Sir, if you had been wise enough to do as I asked you, there is not a stone of yon church I would not have covered with gold and silver." To which he replied, in the words of the Prince of the Apostles, "Miserable sinner, 'thy money perish with thee, because thou hast thought that the gift of GOD may be purchased with money.'" Happy, exclaims the great Cardinal, happy is the church or convent which has such a faithful pastor as this was, not afraid to strike where a blow was needed. And that too remembering the saying of the Wise Man, "If thou beatest him with the rod, he shall not die. Thou shalt beat him with the rod, and shalt deliver his soul from hell." And we may learn from another place the deadly peril of those priests who, from sloth or unbelief, are slack to use the Power of the Keys for penitents who seek them. "And a certain man of the sons of the prophets said unto his neighbour in the word of the LORD, Smite me, I pray thee. And the man refused to smite him. Then said he unto him, Because thou hast not obeyed the voice of the LORD, behold, as soon as thou art departed from me, a lion shall slay thee. And as soon as he was departed from him, a lion found him, and slew him. Then he found another man, and said, Smite me, I pray thee. And the man smote him, so that in smiting he wounded him."

Van Neercassel, Amor Pœnitens, 2, xix., 1.

De Ponte. Prov. xxiii. 13.

1 Kings xx. 35—37.

8 I charge you, O daughters of Jerusalem,

if ye find my beloved, that ye tell him that I am sick of love.

Here we have set before us the Communion of Saints in the bond of intercessory prayer. Great is the confidence, observes Philo, of the Bride, be she Church or faithful soul, in the purity of her life and works, when she is bold to declare to her Spouse CHRIST JESUS, by the hand of her chaste and holy daughters, as herself their honoured mother, how she glows with love of Him. For she calls upon the Apostles, Prophets, and Martyrs (to whom their mother the Church ceases not to commend herself) that as they were, next after CHRIST, the authors of her faith and salvation, she may have them also as her defenders, continual guardians, and perfectors of her hope with the same Heavenly Spouse, beside Whom those happy spirits now stand in bliss as watchmen of the heavenly Jerusalem, and intercede for the Bride militant here, still veiled in mortal flesh, but eagerly longing to reach her divine Bridegroom. And therefore burning with love and devotion, she does not merely ask the Apostles and her other most faithful patrons for their prayers on her behalf with GOD, but binds them, as it were, with an oath. So too an old English poet takes the passage: [Philo Carp.]

> Ye holy virgins, that so oft surround
>   The City's sapphire walls; whose snowy feet
> Measure the pearly paths of sacred ground,
>   And trace the New Jerusalem's jasper street;
> Ah! you whose care-forsaken hearts are crowned
>   With your best wishes; that enjoy the sweet
> Of all your hopes; if e'er you chance to spy
> My absent Love, O tell them that I lie,
> Deep wounded with the flames that furnaced from His eye.
>
> I charge you, virgins, as you hope to hear
>   The heavenly music of your Lover's voice;
> I charge you, by the solemn faith you bear
>   To plighted vows, and to that loyal choice
> Of your affections, or if aught more dear
>   You hold, by Hymen, by your marriage joys;
> I charge you, tell Him that a flaming dart
> Shot from His eye, hath pierced my bleeding heart,
> And I am sick of love, and languish in my smart.

[Francis Quarles, *Emblems*, v. 1.]

And the Bride is fitly said to be *sick of love*, when smitten and wounded with the sword of the Spirit, she [Beda.]

strips off the veil of fleshly desire, because, in proportion as the holy soul grows strong in GOD, so she becomes feeble and weak in worldly affection. Nor is it any marvel if the perfect soul be called sick to worldly things, seeing that the Apostle does not hesitate to call those dead who have fully abandoned the world, "For ye are dead, and your life is hid with CHRIST in GOD," and of himself he says, "The world is crucified to me, and I unto the world." The *daughters of Jerusalem* are the citizens of the heavenly country, who are partly in their pilgrimage on earth, and partly now reigning in heaven. But here, when saying, *If ye find my Beloved*, she seems rather to address that part which is still on earth, and has not yet attained to the full vision of the LORD, but which nevertheless often finds Him, when receiving Him in the heart by love. And we make this adjuration whenever we reveal our thoughts to GOD's Saints, either by asking their prayers on our behalf, or by disclosing to them our hidden longings after divine grace. And it is the usual order of devout persons, advancing in holiness, first to seek GOD themselves, and to busy themselves in purging their heart, and then to consult skilful advisers as to their condition and their hidden dangers, to ask the prayers and seek the intimacy of the godly. Note too, the brevity of her message. She does not say, "Tell Him to come to me, to visit me, to heal me." She knows all that may be safely left to Him, to His wisdom and love. She asks only that He may know that she is sick. So too His Mother, when at Cana, said to Him, "They have no wine," but did not say, Work a miracle for them. So Martha and Mary, when weeping for their dead brother, said to their Master, "LORD, come and see;" they did not say, Raise up Lazarus. And yet He answered in each case the unspoken prayer. *Tell Him*, then, *that I am sick of love*. My love is not sick, but I, who love, am sick. Where love is strong, there sickness is strong too, if the loved one be absent. What is this sickness, but a yearning for the absent Beloved, slaying the lover? Tell Him, then, that I am sick with love, through my great longing to see His face, now that He is gone from me, that I am weary of life, and scarcely endure the lingering of my exile here. Some take the words as specially applying to the Blessed Virgin's yearning for the presence of her

Divine Son after His Ascension into Heaven, and that not as implying that He needed to be told of her love, but that she might ease her longing by giving expression to it. In us, alas, there are many other sicknesses,—the sickness of fear, of weariness, of sorrow, because of past sins, possible relapses, and the toil of pilgrimage. Speak the word only, O LORD, and we shall be healed of these disorders. But whereas such ailments as these are told to the physician, that He may heal them, that of love is told to the Beloved, not that He may remove, but that He may renew and increase it, for though it is begotten by His absence, yet it is made far stronger by His presence, which is the one thing for which the fainting Bride yearns and strives, the one thing she cherishes in her bosom, the one thing she fears to lose, saying as she does to Him, "My soul hath longed for Thy salvation." Philipp. Harveng. Cantacuzene. Dion. Carth.

Gillebert.

S. Ambros. in Ps. cxix. xi. 1.

9 What is thy beloved more than another beloved, O thou fairest among women? what is thy beloved more than another beloved, that thou dost so charge us?

This question is asked whenever any believer converses with a believing brother, and they mutually suggest words of heavenly desires, to increase their affection for things above. Tell me, who now long and desire to arrive at the vision of my Creator, *what is thy Beloved*, that is, how CHRIST ought to be loved. Long since I have begun to fear Him, but now that love is casting out fear, I wish to hear words whereby I may be kindled to His love. Thou, who art even now seeking Him in love and art sick with that love, tell me, *what is thy Beloved*. They who take the daughters of Jerusalem to be the Saints, glorified or militant, see in this address of theirs to the Bride, only their desire to increase her love for the absent Bridegroom by giving her an opportunity of dwelling on all His graces. But they who, with Theodoret, suppose that the weaker and yet untried believers in the Faith are meant, hold that the question is asked in real desire to be instructed, to be told, when so many false Christs are to be found, what are the marks whereby the true one may be known, lest if they know Him not here, He may refuse to know them in the Day of Cassiodor.

Beda.

Corn. à Lap.

Ainsworth. Cocceius.

Philo Carp.

Judgment. And if the words be ascribed to the Angels, they ask the Bride to tell them how much she has been able to learn of her Spouse, so as to love Him so tenderly, seeing that even they, who behold Him face to face, cannot fathom the depths of His glory, nor know Him as He is. Further; as they do not know Him at all by sympathy, but only by love and worship, since He is not of their nature, they are eager to learn from her who suffers with and for Him somewhat of that mystery of sorrow which is one of those "things which the Angels desire to look into."

The literal Hebrew of the first clause is, *What is thy Beloved before a beloved?* and the LXX. and Vulgate, endeavouring to keep as closely as may be to this, read, *thy Beloved from a beloved*. And the commentators dwell much and variously on this repetition. It denotes, says the Scholastic Doctor, the twofold nature of CHRIST, beloved in His Manhood, and beloved in His Godhead too. It means, remark several others, His eternal generation from His FATHER, in that He is GOD of GOD, Light of Light, Very GOD of Very GOD, and he who loveth the SON loveth the FATHER also, even as he who seeth the SON seeth the FATHER also. They ask her this question because she is the *fairest among women*, and they gather that the chosen Bridegroom of one so lovely must be Himself a marvel to look upon. That is, it is only by superior holiness of life and conversation that the Church, thereby rising above all schools of philosophy and all sects of heresy, can so attract seekers after GOD as to make them inquire from her, rather than from any other, where and how to find Him. And that precisely because she is *fairest* only because of her nearness to Him, whereby His beauty is reflected in her face. They ask her, therefore, By what signs shall we know Him in contemplation, lest, taking falsehood for truth, we should instead of Him, receive that one who pretends to be light, when he is darkness itself? How, too, is He to be known in action, lest we should take evil for good here also, carried away by excitement in well-meant zeal, and deceived by the prospering of our plans? All this we ask of thee, because, having adjured us, thou hast kindled in us the fire of love towards Him, and forced us to seek until we find Him.

10 My beloved is white and ruddy, the chiefest among ten thousand.

"A strange mingling of colours,"—these are the last words of teaching spoken by Gilbert of Hoyland ere he died—"which are found blended in one by divine operation only in the Person of the LORD JESUS, not so as to be themselves one, but to be together in one. O gracious and lovely Bridegroom, in Whom shines divine, and blushes human generation! For He is the brightness of eternal light, and He, though not born of blood, nor of the will of the flesh, nor of the will of man, yet was sprung from His Mother's blood, and there is in Him nought of that ruddiness whereof Isaiah saith: 'Though your sins are red like crimson, yet shall they be as wool.' The whiteness of wool and the redness of crimson agree not together, nor can unite. But there is another redness which is found together with whiteness in the raiment of JESUS. 'Wherefore,' asks Isaiah, 'art Thou red in Thine apparel?' The apparel of the LORD JESUS, naturally white by reason of His Virgin birth, shining with purity and the innocence of holiness, is yet more beautiful with the ruddy hue of His voluntary Passion, whereby He glows in the affections of His faithful. What is that redness which lacks not the power of whitening? 'They have washed their robes,' saith He, 'and made them white in the Blood of the Lamb.' This ruddiness found the whiteness already in my JESUS; it creates it in us, and does not find it. This ruddiness, laid upon the tint of our blood-stained nativity and personal sin, turns its redness into whiteness, purifying our hearts by faith. For we are justified by faith in the Blood of JESUS. Happy for thee is the ruddy glow of His out-poured Blood, if it kindle in thy mind a longing for a change. Happy is its glow for thee, if the mighty love of GOD shines for thee in the Blood shed for thy sake. For JESUS so loved His Bride as to wash her in His own Blood. Love is like flame, and this makes the LORD JESUS ruddy to me. In Him truth is white to me and love is red. *My Beloved is white and ruddy.* Why should He not be white? For GOD is light, and in Him is no darkness at all. Why should He not be ruddy? For GOD is a fire, and He hath come to send fire upon the earth. If He bestow on thee the light of under-

Gillebert. Serm. 48.
Tres Patr. Cassiodor. Beda.
S. John i. 13.
Isa. i. 18.
Isa. lxiii. 2.
Rev. vii. 14.

standing, He is white to thee, but unless He kindle thy soul with love, thou dost not feel Him to be ruddy. He is both in Himself, but He is not so unto thee, unless thou feelest the working of both within thee. If thou be His Bride, strive after this blending of the twin colours; ask it of thy Bridegroom, that thou too mayest be white and ruddy, that is, sincere and fervent. For as He hath the power of calming, so also hath He that of kindling, and whoso draweth nigh unto Him, draweth nigh to the fire." So too, He gave us a type of this His twofold character, when He suffered Himself to be arrayed by Herod in a white robe, and by Pilate in a purple one. So, in His Passion itself, both blood and water issued together from His side. So, again, He showed Himself to the beloved Disciple, clothed in the sweeping alb of His everlasting Priesthood, and also in the "vesture dipped in blood," which pertains to His victorious royalty. And He was white not only in His Nativity, but also in His Resurrection, when He was indeed *the chiefest among ten thousand*, as the First-born from the dead. And note, further, how our Beloved keeps this twofold nature of His, Godhead and Manhood, Virginity and Passion, purity and love, light and fervour, before our eyes in that most dear pledge wherein He gives Himself to us under the Sacramental veils, white in the form of hallowed Bread, ruddy in the chalice of mystic wine. And so runs an old Eucharistic hymn:

Hugo Card.
S. Luke xxiii. 11.
Psellus.

Rev. i. 13.

Rev. xix. 13.

S. Hieron. in Esa. lxiii.

> Ave CHRISTI corpus verum,
> Ave dulce rubens merum,
> Caro cibus, sanguis potus,
> Et ubique CHRISTUS totus.
>
> Hic est Sponsus candidatus,
> Dilectus et rubricatus,
> Castus ortus hunc albavit,
> Sanguis fluens rubricavit.
>
> Hail, O Flesh of CHRIST divine,
> Hail, O sweet and ruddy wine,
> Blood the cup, and Flesh the meat,
> And in each is CHRIST complete.
>
> This is He, the Bridegroom, dight
> In His vesture red and white:
> White, for Him a Virgin bore,
> Red, for He His Blood did pour.

S. Hieron. Epit. Paulæ. White and ruddy is He too, because He gives the prizes of peace as well as those of war to the conquerors. White in His love and gentleness to Saints and penitents, ruddy in His terrible anger against the ungodly and reprobate. White and ruddy is He Who is girt round with the roses of Sharon and the lilies of the valleys, the choirs of Virgins and of Martyrs, Himself the Virgin of Virgins and Martyr of Martyrs in their midst. Dion. Carth.
S. Bernard.
Serm. 28, in Cant.

> O, what are these roses bright,
>   That in Thy garland blow?
> These roses red as blood,
>   These roses white as snow?
>
> These blood-red roses grew
>   On a field with battle dyed;
> These snow-white roses strew
>   A path that is not wide;
> None seek that path but they who seek
>   Him Who was crucified!

Dora Greenwell. *Carmina Crucis.*

And note this, further, that He only is perfect and unchangeable in His whiteness and ruddiness. Others have been white and ruddy too, whether local Churches, Religious Orders, or individual souls, but they have failed in the grace of perseverance, and have lost their beauty through sin. And accordingly it is written by the Prophet, "Her Nazarites were purer than snow; they were whiter than milk, they were more ruddy in body than rubies, their polishing was of sapphire. Their visage is blacker than a coal; they are not known in the streets; their skin cleaveth to their bones, it is withered, it is become like a stick." Thus the only white in which we can trust is the fine linen of His righteousness, the only redness which will abide in our cheeks is that which He bestows from His own Blood. And observe herein, that a further mystery lies hid under the word *ruddy*, which is אָדֹם, *adom*, denoting the same thing as *Adam*, so that He Who is the Brightness of the FATHER's glory, Whose countenance is as the sun shineth in his strength, is also the Second Adam, the Man from heaven, Who hath come to repair the loss we sustained by the fall of the first Adam. And, therefore, too, because He hid that shining of His celestial garments, "exceeding white as snow, so as no fuller on earth can white them," under those robes which tell of the conflict and suffering of our human nature, the Prophet asks in wonder, "Who is this that cometh from Edom with dyed garments?" For Edom,

Gillebert. Serm. 47.
Lam. iv. 7.
Ricard. Vict.
Cocceius.
Heb. i. 3.
Rev. i. 16.
S. Mark ix. 3.
Isa. lxiii. 1.

which is *red*, denotes also that first-born Who lost His birth-right, and became an exile from His home, that His younger brother might have the inheritance.

The chiefest among ten thousand. The LXX. and Vulgate, differing slightly in phrase, but not in meaning, from this version, read severally *elect from ten thousands*, and *elect from thousands.* There is but little diversity in the expositions, as they all dwell on CHRIST being the Only-begotten SON of the FATHER, the only Virgin-born Son of a mother, as alone without sin, as the single High Priest of GOD, and as the One SAVIOUR of mankind, fairer than the children of men, and excelling those thousand thousands who minister unto Him, and the ten thousand times ten thousand that stand before Him. Philo gives two mystical reasons for the number ten thousand; one, that He Who is perfection (denoted by a thousand,) came after the ten precepts of the Law, or that He came into the world, after passing over the nine choirs of the Angelic hierarchy, from the womb of the Virgin, as a bridegroom from his chamber. The margin of the A. V., translating "standard-bearer," is hardly accurate, for though the word דָּגוּל, *dagul*, here used, is connected with דֶּגֶל, *degel*, a standard, yet it is a passive participle, and means not standard-bearer, but *lifted up like a standard*, and therefore conspicuous. It is a prophecy of Him concerning whom Isaiah foretold, "In that day there shall be a Root of Jesse, which shall stand for an ensign of the people: to it shall the Gentiles seek;" because, as He Himself hath said, "I, if I be lifted up from the earth, will draw all men unto Me."

Marginal references: S. Just. Org. Ric. Vict. — Dan. vii. 10. — Philo Carp. — Gesenius. Weissbach. — Isa. xi. 10. — S. John xii. 32.

11 His head is as the most fine gold, his locks are bushy and black as a raven.

"The Head of CHRIST is GOD." So speaks the Apostle, and the Fathers agree, for the most part, in explaining this clause of the verse, dwelling on the purity and costliness of gold, the king of metals, as a faint type of the pre-eminence of the LORD Almighty. And the Godhead of the Eternal WORD is also the Head of the Man CHRIST JESUS, in Whom shone the brightness of Deity. GOD alone, says a Western divine, is to be loved above all things of which we can

Marginal references: 1 Cor. xi. 3. Philo Carp. Cassiodor. S. Greg. M. — Luc. Abb.

think, with all the heart, with all the soul, and with all the strength, even as the head is more cared for than the other members; and as gold is known to be loved by covetous princes, who fear not to die for its sake. And the thinner the sheets are into which gold is drawn out, the more it shines and increases in ductility. Just so, the more searchingly we endeavour to investigate the majesty of divine power, so much the more boundlessly does the ocean spread. And as the substance of gold, by reason of its softness, is ductile in any direction that you draw it; so the unchanging goodness of GOD's majesty, however mocked by the ungodly, is never broken. S. Gregory Nyssen, however, refers the verse to CHRIST's Humanity alone, in that He is Head of the Church; golden indeed, as sinless, and because in Him dwelt all the fulness of the Godhead bodily. Whereon another observes, "His head is as *paz*, that is, pure gold, for this gold is the form of the Saints, who shine as lights in the head of the body, and are gold tried in fire by GOD, because He, having tested them by suffering when melted in the furnace of this world, found them, as it is written, worthy of Him, and stamped upon them the sacred impress of His image, printing the word of His truth on their hearts and lips, and making them His moneyers, that they might stamp, according to His pattern, sterling coins for the LORD, and having defaced the image of Cæsar in us, should mint the living medal of the everlasting King, that we, inscribed with the spirit of redemption, with necks freed from the yoke, and with foreheads guarded by the superscription of salvation, might sing 'The light of Thy countenance is signed upon us.' Let us strive, then, with all our might so to prepare ourselves, that we may attain to be the locks and gold of our Divine Head, which, by GOD's grace, CHRIST is to us."

S. Greg. Nyss.

S. Paulin. Ep. iv. ad Severum.

Ps. iv. 7, Vulg.

The Hebrew term here for *fine gold* is כֶּתֶם פָּז *kethem paz*, and the existing copies of the LXX. read, by a curious error, *gold of Cephaz*, χρυσίον κέφαζ.[1] It would be unnecessary to refer to the erroneous reading, were it not that it has led to a singular interpretation, that of Philo, who, taking the *head* of CHRIST's mystical Body, the Church, to be the most eminent Saints, supposes this text to denote S. Peter, as Prince of the

Philo Carp.

---

[1] The text Theodoret and the Three Fathers used, had ὀφάζ.

Apostles, and eminent in wisdom; a view which had not long to wait for refutation, as it called up S. Jerome in defence of the truer interpretation, which sees here CHRIST, and Him only. The contemplative writers see in the golden head an emblem of the inexhaustible treasures of divine illumination, vouchsafed to the Saints who strive after perfect knowledge of GOD; and therefore, too, some take it of that unsearchable wisdom of CHRIST, whereof He saith in the Proverbs, "My fruit is better than gold, yea, than fine gold;" while a further explanation is that the faith, and still better, the love of the Church, as her principal grace, is symbolically this head, as being that which is most like her true Head and Spouse.

His locks are bushy. Rather, as in margin, *curling*. The older versions translate, *like palm-buds*,[1] which cluster like a bunch of grapes. This has been accepted as the true rendering by Rosenmüller, De Wette, and Gesenius; and the former aptly cites an ancient Arab love-song in illustration. "The tresses which adorn her back are black, like a coal, thick, twining like the clusters of the palm." Hitzig and Weissbach, however, demur, and translate, with no practical difference of result, *grape-clusters*, and like *hills upon hills*. These locks, as before, are taken to denote the Saints who are nearest to the Head, such as the Angels, Apostles, Martyrs, and others eminent in holiness. S. Gregory Nyssen, who however prefers to translate *like pines*, takes the simile to denote the stately height attained by the Apostles, and the manner in which they increase the Bridegroom's beauty when they are moved, like foliage or tresses, by the wind of the HOLY SPIRIT. S. Ambrose, taking the same meaning, draws from it the further simile that the Saints are like the pine-built ships of Tarshish, floating over the waves of the world, and providing a sure life-boat (*tutum remigium salutis*) for all mankind. And another Saint works out the idea more fully still, commenting thus: "The Saints are like flowering palms, and branching cedars, and

---

[1] ἐλάται, *elatæ palmarum*. The Greek word is more commonly used of the *pine*, and thence is sometimes taken to denote an oar, or even a ship, made of that tree. The root is ἐλαύνω, used in the case of the tree in the sense of "shooting upwards," and in that of the buds of "pushing forth" out of the sheath. All these ideas will be found dwelt on by the earlier commentators cited in the text.

they are also like pines, black and good, because they are conspicuous on the heights of their merits in the Church, the mount of GOD, like pines upon the mountains, and as those trees are suited for ship-building, so too these princes of the people, cut down from the Mount of the Law, as from Lebanon, framed the Ark or ship of the LORD,—that is, the Church, intended to sail over this world's floods,—from the Gentiles, hewn with the Word of GOD, and taught therein, closely knit together in the framework of charity by the bond of faith, to plough their way in safety over the billows of this world." The *elatæ* of palm-trees are, notes Cassiodorus, their longer and more prominent branches, sometimes of a golden hue, curling, always tending upwards, and never losing their verdure. And some allege that the words mean an aromatic pine, used for making unguents, but not the great tree employed as timber for ships and houses. To these *elatæ*, then, the locks of the Bridegroom are compared, because the company of the faithful rejoice in their evergreen faith, are lifted up to a longing for eternal things, and taste the sweetness of heavenly bliss. The palm, observes another, is rough near the ground, and confined within a very narrow bark, but above it is beautiful and spreading to the sight, and abundant in fruit. So the members of CHRIST in lower things fare hardly, and suffer tribulation, whilst above they are fair and fruitful in the eyes of GOD; for they purify themselves through bodily hardships, and shoot upwards into beauty of soul and spiritual loftiness, and attain, by the grace of GOD, to that victory whereof the palm is an emblem. The close bark below denotes the many troubles whereby they are straitened here, the green and spreading foliage above the abundant reward which awaits them on high. Again, they take these locks of the Bridegroom to be the Divine graces and attributes wherewith He is adorned, and as it were, clothed; or else as the lofty truths contained in Holy Scripture. <small>Cassiodor.</small> <small>Ricard. Vict.</small> <small>Theodoret. Cassiodor. Tres Patr. Thom. Verc. Rupert.</small>

And black as a raven. The literal sense here is to denote the youthful vigour and prime of the Bridegroom, Who is untouched by age or weakness, and thus has no sprinkling of white hairs upon His head. The mystical interpretations are various. Taking the locks, as before, to denote the Saints, they are called *black*, say many of the Fathers, to denote their hu- <small>Delrio.</small> <small>Cassiodor. Philo Carp. S. Greg. M.</small>

mility. The blackness of good men, remarks one of themselves, is that they count themselves to be sinners, and carry in their faces that shame for their sins, for they choose contempt, they cheerfully endure to be despised, they desire menial tasks, and poor apparel, knowing that in their lowliness lies hid the precious treasure of CHRIST. Or, as another puts it, the very Angels and Saints are black and sinful in comparison with the golden glory of the Head whence they depend. And, confining the reference to the Person of CHRIST Himself, we are struck at once with the contrast between this verse and that of the Apocalypse, where we read, " His head and His hairs were white like wool, as white as snow," even as Daniel beheld six centuries before. And they explain it very well, saying that the vision in Patmos describes Him in the pure holiness of His virgin life, whereas He was black in His Passion, when His flesh was scorched with the fire of pain and suffering in the furnace of the Cross, so that there was no form or comeliness left in Him. And, finally, if we see here either the Divine attributes or the mysteries of Holy Scripture implied, they are called black, because hidden from us in impenetrable darkness, according to that saying of the Psalmist, " He made darkness His secret place, His pavilion round about Him with dark waters, and thick clouds to cover Him."

12 His eyes are as the eyes of doves by the rivers of waters, washed with milk, and fitly set.

His eyes under the Old Testament were the Prophets, or Seers. His eyes now are the Prelates and Doctors of His Church, ἐπίσκοποι, or Overseers. Or, as another will have it, the contemplative Saints who are ever looking to GOD. They are compared to *doves* because of the graces of innocence and simplicity which should characterize them, and they abide *by the rivers of waters,* both as having been cleansed in the laver of Baptism, and as dwelling close to those streams of Holy Scripture whence they ever drink, and mirrored in which they can see themselves and any hawk or other enemy which approaches them. They are *washed with milk,* because, as one Saint observes, the LORD baptizes in milk, that is, in sincerity. And they

are truly baptized in milk who believe without guile
and maintain a pure faith and put on unspotted
grace, so that the Bride ascends in white robes to
CHRIST. S. Gregory Nyssen dwells on the plural S. Greg.
form, *rivers of waters*, and sees in them the divers Nyss.
virtues of holiness, whereby the contrary vices of the
soul must be washed away. Again, as the Saints are Philo Carp.
like doves' eyes by reason of the gifts of the HOLY
SPIRIT, so the words may be taken of CHRIST alone,
as possessed of all His gifts in their fulness, as it is
written: "I beheld, and lo, in the midst of the throne Rev. v. 6.
and of the four living creatures, and in the midst of
the elders, stood a Lamb as it had been slain, having
seven horns and seven eyes, which are the seven Spirits
of GOD sent forth into all the earth." These gifts and Cassiod.
graces are fitly said to dwell by the rivers of waters,
because the HOLY GHOST delights in pure and sincere
hearts. And they are *washed with milk*, because those
heavenly graces are not kept for the strong and vigorous alone, but are freely given to the Church's little
ones, as milk to babes. The literal reference is to the Gene-
clear white of the eye-ball, which contrasts with, and brardus.
sets off, the more beautiful and coloured pupil, whence
we gather that the passive graces of purity and innocence are insufficient of themselves for the perfection of
the holy soul, but are meant as the frame in which the
active powers of saintliness must be set. And in that
they are said to dwell by *rivers*, not by lakes or ponds,
we are led back in thought to the Source, hidden and ex- Beda.
haustless, whence these waters ever flow, not stagnant,
nor collected by the work of any human skill. Again,
following the clue given by the Chaldee paraphrast, Targum.
who sees here the unceasing watch of GOD's providence Dion. Carth.
over Jerusalem, we too may see here the perfection
of CHRIST's wisdom, human and Divine. For in it
are the eyes of Godhead, according as it is written,
"The eyes of the LORD are over the righteous," and Ps. xxxiv. 15.
in another place, "The eyes of the LORD are ten thou- Ecclus.
sand times brighter than the sun, beholding all the xxiii. 19.
ways of men, and considering the most secret parts."
These eyes are the understanding and wisdom of GOD,
or the glance of His loving-kindness, and they may be
compared to doves' eyes, because of their perfect sin-
gleness and purity, most alien from all evil. And also
the inner eyes of CHRIST's Humanity were the reason
and understanding, wisdom and knowledge poured into

Him, shining with dovelike simplicity and full of all sincerity, testified by the clear, pure, and candid aspect of His bodily eyes also.

And fitly set. Literally, *resting in fulness.* The metaphor is taken from a gem skilfully set in the bezel of a ring, so as to be exactly centred, and to shine most brilliantly. Hence the mystical meaning is that the Saints are fixed in the golden circle of GOD's law and discipline, so as not to vary to the right hand or the left, and thereby they attain greater beauty and value, just as clear and limpid eyes, which are free from all distortion, are the chief beauty of a lovely face, while any irregularity in them is the greatest of deformities. But the Vulgate reading, amplified from the LXX., is *dwelling by the fullest of streams.* Theodoret will have it that the words denote the manner in which CHRIST is, as it were, always waiting anxiously by the waters of Baptism to receive fresh souls into His Church, and that these waters are called *fullest,* to warn us that the bare external rite with no inward correlation of will, cannot satisfy Him, as was shown in the case of Simon Magus, who came to that Sacrament unrepentant and unconverted. Others take these fullest streams to be the Holy Scriptures, abundantly supplying the spiritual thirst of the soul, and overflowing with heavenly mysteries. Here it is, then, observes a Saint, that we must sit, and not by the waters of Babylon, where our eyes will be dim with weeping, rather than washed in that milk which, as it reflects no image nor shadow, denotes the perfect truth which suggests no deceitful phantasm to the eyes of the soul. Or again, Love is the fulfilling of the Law, and it is on this fulness of love in the multitudes of the Church, who are the waters in that channel, that the Holy Dove vouchsafes to rest. And yet once more, as CHRIST is He in Whom dwells all the fulness of the Godhead bodily, so it was upon Him that the mystic Dove hovered at the streams of Jordan, upon Him Who is the perennial River of the mercy of GOD. And so the Prophet foretold, "The SPIRIT of the LORD shall rest upon Him, the Spirit of wisdom and understanding, the Spirit of counsel and might, the Spirit of knowledge and of the fear of the LORD."

13 His cheeks are as a bed of spices, as sweet flowers: his lips like lilies, dropping sweet smelling myrrh.

The LXX., Vulgate, and modern critics all vary in the interpretation of the earlier part of this verse so widely, that it is necessary to give their several versions before proceeding to comment on them. In the first place, the LXX. has *His cheeks are as vials of spice giving out unguents.* That is, observes Theodoret, [Theodoret.] the doctrine of CHRIST supplies the preachers of His Word with all the arguments and counsels which they need for making that salve which they prepare for the benefit of wounded and sin-sick hearts. Philo, differ- [Philo Carp.] ing a little in the version he follows, (reading, as he does, the text of Symmachus, which is πρασιαί, *beds*,) takes nearly the same view, that Holy Writ is the [Targum.] store-house of those wholesome medicines which drive away all spiritual diseases; herein agreeing substantially with the Targum, which explains the cheeks as the two tables of the Law. The Vulgate reads *His cheeks are like beds of spices planted by the ointment-makers.* And these cheeks some will have to be the [S. Greg. M.] Martyrs, because as the ruddiness of the cheeks is [Ric. Vict.] an especial beauty of the face, so the blood of the Martyrs, shed for CHRIST, is a glory to His Name. They are *planted by the ointment-makers*, in that the earlier Martyrs were cheered on to their conflict by the counsels of holy preachers, and the later ones by the examples of their predecessors, brought before them by preachers too. And they are *beds of spices* because the sweet and restorative fragrance of their lives and deaths perfumes the garden of GOD. Again, [S. Greg.] some will have it that not the Martyrs but the Doctors [Nyss.] and teachers of the Church are intended, as the cheeks [Psellus.] clothe the jaws which prepare food for the stomach; and these are *beds*, carefully tilled ground, bringing forth the *spices* of prayer and good works, *planted by* [S.Ans.Laud.] those skilled ointment-makers, the Apostles and Prophets of GOD. Or, if you will, you may take these spice-beds to be individual Churches, rich in Saints and in good works, planted by the missionary zeal of [S. Just. Org.] the Apostles and their successors. And, turning to a different class of exposition, several Fathers take the cheeks of the Bridegroom to be the outward bearing [Cassiod. Beda.] and demeanour of the LORD JESUS, according as He [Rupert.] showed Himself gentle, stern, or sad. One will have it that the union of the Two Natures in One Person, bringing GOD and man together, is here intended. [Philipp.] Wherefore, he says, these cheeks are compared to [Harveng.]

beds, that is, to little gardens, whence aromatic herbs and spices are produced, cultivated with benevolent skill by those ointment-makers who are learned and busied in the art of medicine for healing the sick. For after GOD had borne with the world for thousands of years as it was perishing in sin, and no man nor Angel was strong enough to drive sin out, at length the Ointment-Makers chose out in wisdom certain beds, whence they gathered aromatic medicines and healing spices. For they joined together the Divine and human natures, to which, in mysterious counsel, they added a certain joint power of cure; and on them, united in One Person, as cheeks are joined in one face, they concentrated spices, and restored the fainting world with the blessing of health. Nor were these Ointment-Makers other than the FATHER, SON, and HOLY GHOST. The view of modern critics is to be found in their explanation of the literal Hebrew of that clause where the A. V. reads, *as sweet flowers.*

Rosenmüller.
De Wette.
Weissbach. The margin, more exactly, is *towers of perfumes.* And this is explained as most probably meaning pyramidal or conical flower-beds in a garden, so planted as to present to the eye a rising and unbroken mound of sweet flowering shrubs. The metaphor seems to denote the growth of beard upon the cheeks of the

Cocceius. Bridegroom, and therefore, as they tell us, the Saints who draw all their life and being from Him are here designated, towering upward in their aim at heavenly things, and planted so closely together in unity of spirit and doctrine, as to leave no void space where weeds may spring.

His lips like lilies, dropping sweet-smelling myrrh. The lips of the wise, who toil in the Law, says the

Targum. Chaldee paraphrast, flow with decision on all points, and the words of their mouth are like choice myrrh.

S. Ambros.
S. Greg. M.
S. Greg.
Nyss.
S. Just. Org. And this is very nearly the sense given by most Christian expositors, taking the verse, as they do, to denote the preachers of CHRIST's Gospel, pure in life, fragrant in doctrine, and proclaiming first of all the LORD's death, then the passions of His Martyrs, and finally the duty of mortification, patience in suffering, and readiness to endure death for the LORD's sake. Or, with a more restricted application, it may be taken

Luc. Abb. of those Confessors who exercise the power of the keys in binding and loosing, righteously binding the impenitent by condemnation, loosing righteously the penitent from the bond of condemnation by reconciling them to GOD. To the wise they are *lilies* in fragrance, bringing them gladness and healing, to the foolish they have the bitter savour of *myrrh;* but even these, when healed, themselves praise the remedy which has brought them cure of present suffering, and protection from future corruption. Theodoret, looking to the Master, and not to His servants, says that His lips may well be compared to lilies, because the Divine sayings have their own glorious beauty, though devoid of human ornament. For as the LORD Himself teaches, the lilies toil not, neither do they spin, yet the Heavenly FATHER clothes them. Since then the Divine sayings are destitute of all human wisdom, and have only their own Divine beauty, it is well said *His lips are like lilies dropping full myrrh*, for they teach mortification in this present life. For such as these is that teaching of the LORD: "If any man come to Me, and hate not his father, and mother, and wife, and children, and brethren, and sisters, yea, and his own life also, he cannot be My disciple. And whosoever doth not bear his cross, and come after Me, cannot be My disciple." And again: "If thou wilt be perfect, go and sell that thou hast, and give to the poor." Therefore His lips drop full myrrh. And others, also explaining the words of CHRIST's sayings, tell us that the comparison to lilies denotes His promise of eternal brightness, and His counsels of purity and cleanness, both typified by the white flower. There are not wanting some who remind us that we are not to understand here the white lily or narcissus, but the purple one, as better figuring the ruddiness of the lips; but there is one most true sense in which we may prefer to keep the snowy flower in our minds, thinking of Him in His dying hour, when with pale and bloodless lips He dropped that sweet-smelling myrrh of the Seven Words, which has since healed many and many a sorely-wounded heart, for, as our own poet says:

Theodoret.

S. Luke xiv. 26.

S. Mat. xix. 21.

Ghislerius.

Tauler, De Passione.

> The nails and bleeding brows,
> The pale and dying lips, are the portion of the Spouse.

Keble, Lyra Innocent.

14 His hands are as gold rings set with the beryl; his belly is as bright ivory overlaid with sapphires.

Here again in the first clause the ancient translations are utterly at variance with the A. V. The LXX. and Vulgate read in the first clause, *His hands are cylindrical* (τορνευταί, *tornatiles*, literally, *turned in a lathe*) *golden, full of Tharsis* (LXX.) or *of jacinths*, (Symmachus and Vulgate.) And modern critics are divided, some accepting the interpretation of the A. V. and then explaining with Cocceius that the hand, when curved to grasp anything, resembles a ring; and others preferring the Vulgate reading, on the ground that the specific word כף *caph*, always employed in Hebrew for the closed or hollowed hand, is not that found in the text here. They differ, too, as to the phrase, *set with the beryl;* agreeing that the word does not imply that the stone is set in the gold, but that the gold is fixed in the stone. And they give two equally ingenious explanations,—one that the finger-nails, in which the hand terminates, are the beryl, chrysolite, topaz, jacinth, or Tarshish stone, (so variously is the gem described) referred to,—compare the Greek name for one well-known jewel, *onyx*, "a nail,"—the other argued with much ingenuity by Weissbach, that the hand itself is intended, being the costly socket in which those slender golden pillars, the fingers, are firmly rooted, illustrating the argument with a reference to the rich tesselated pavement in which stood the pillars for the hangings in the palace of Ahasuerus. The hands, then, of CHRIST's mystical Body are the stewards and dispensers of His grace, *golden*, even as their Head is of gold, *turned in a lathe*, because rid of everything external and superfluous, *full of Tharsis-stone*, because the outer crust of sin which hid the jewel has been cut away by the lapidary's skill, and thus only the clear radiance remains. The hands of the Beloved, says the Prior of S. Victor, are the works of the godly, which are *turned*, because they are regular and perfect. For as turners' work is regularly and smoothly circular, and admits of no interruption or inequality, so the godly do nothing blameworthy, nor aught whereby their neighbour may be offended or weakened. The energy of the godly is therefore regular and polished, because they seek only heavenly things, swerving neither to right nor left, but keeping to the King's highway. Wherefore it is said that they are *golden* because they shine with divine wisdom, and are not darkened by sin or ignorance. And these works shine before men unto the glory of their FATHER Which is in heaven, unclouded with sins or lack of judgment, and are all performed for GOD's sake and with a single mind. Therefore it is added that they are *full of ja-* Cassiodor. *cinths*, because they are done from pure hope and longing for heavenly things, for the jacinth is a stone of the colour of the sky, with a greenish shade in it. Again, the hands of the Beloved, when referred to the Theodoret. Person of CHRIST Himself, denote His works and miracles, *turned*, because of the ease and rapidity of His operation, *golden*, by reason of the manifestation of Divine power, *full of jacinths*, because arousing Cassiodor. men to hope of heavenly things. They were turned, too, because of their completeness and perfection. And Philo Carp. His bodily hands were turned in yet another sense, when fastened on that cruel lathe of the Cross, there to be fashioned for us into an instrument of salvation; *full of jacinths*, truly, when gemmed with the ruddy Beda. drops of His most Precious Blood. Others are found to take the word *tornatiles* in an active sense, and to explain it as the *hands of a turner*. And then the Nic. Argent. whole clause is taken of the creative power of GOD, shaping all things, as a turner does, with no pattern before Him, but only by force of will and steadiness of hand. And as a cup or a sphere is potentially hidden within the block out of which it is to be turned, so all things, say they, pre-existed in the mind of GOD, and they had no independent being or place till He, so to speak, put them outside Himself, removing from them all that was not of their essence. And it is added that these hands are *golden*, because "GOD saw Gen. i. 31. everything that He had made, and behold, it was very good."

Passing now to the A. V. reading, it remains to be seen what its mystical import is. And first, it is to be noted that the verse in no case can imply that the hands of the Bridegroom are adorned with rings, but that they themselves are in some way like rings, possibly, as suggested above, when curved, and with henna-dyed nails for jewels. The ring, under the Law, as containing the signet, is the token of authority, and is so given by Pharaoh to Joseph, and by Aha- Gen. xli. 42. suerus to Haman. Under the Gospel the ring is the Esth. iii. 10. symbol of marriage. Thus the Bride sees in CHRIST at once her King and her Bridegroom. Here on earth and under the Old Covenant, when the fear of Him is the beginning of her wisdom, He is *Baali*, "My Lord," to her. Under the Law of Grace in our Country, when perfect love hath cast out fear, He will be called by her, *Ishi*, "My Husband." Into His hands she commends herself, by those hands she confesses that she is made and fashioned, for the operations of those hands she rejoices in giving praise. If those hands seem to press hardly on her at times, she recognises that it is only that the imprint of the Everlasting Name may be set upon her forehead, and when they support her in time of weariness and sorrow, she feels in them the loving clasp of her Bridegroom. They are *set with the beryl*. And it is enough to say briefly that in the great vagueness of all translators in explaining the Hebrew names of precious stones, no trust can usually be given to their versions. But as to this stone, the *tarshish*, first in the fourth row of the High Priest's breastplate, it is now for the most part agreed that the Oriental topaz, the stone called by the ancients *chrysolite*,[1] the seventh foundation of the Heavenly City, is intended. And on this let us hear the mystic comment of Marbod of Rennes:

The Hymn, Cives cœlestis patriæ.

The golden-coloured chrysolite
Flashes forth sparkles in the night:
Its mystic hues the life reflect
Of men with perfect wisdom decked,
Who shine in this dark world like gold,
Through that blest SPIRIT sevenfold.

Or, as the great Carmelite writer on the Psalms alleges, "The chrysolite shines as gold in the day; as fire in the night. By the *day*, the good; by the *gold*, their crown, are represented; by the *night*, the wicked; and by the *fire*, their punishment." Hence the stone typifies their final separation, and thus the seventh article of the Creed, "From thence He shall come to judge the quick and the dead." And thus the jewels which adorn the hands of the King and Bridegroom are His Wisdom and Justice. Here too may fitly be cited a vision, which helps to explain the meaning of the ring: "And she saw the most Blessed Virgin standing at her right hand, giving her a golden ring, which she at once offered to the LORD, and the LORD,

---

[1] By a curious interchange, modern lapidaries call chrysolite, the stone anciently known as topaz.

graciously accepting it, placed it on His finger. Then, pondering within herself, she said, O if it might but be that He would give me His ring in token of betrothal! And it seemed to her that it would be enough if the LORD would vouchsafe to send her a pain in the ring-finger, that she might bear it all the days of her life in memory that she was betrothed to CHRIST. To whom the LORD: I give thee a ring, gemmed with seven stones, which thou canst recall in the seven joints of thy finger. In the first joint, thou mayest remember that divine love, which bowing Me down from the FATHER's bosom, made Me serve in many toils for thirty-three years, seeking thee. And when the marriage-time drew nigh, I was sold, by the love in My own heart, to obtain the price of the bridal-feast, and I gave Myself for Bread, and Flesh, and Chalice. And at that feast I was harp too, and organ, by the sweet words of My mouth. In the second joint, remember how I in My beauty led forth the bridal throng to the martial dance after that banquet, and thrice leaping, I fell thrice to the ground, and shed forth drops of bloody sweat. And I clothed My fellow-soldiers in the dance with triple robes, when I granted them remission of sins, sanctification of their souls, and My own divine glory. Thirdly, recollect the love of My humility for the Bride's kiss, when the traitor drew near and kissed Me; in which kiss My Heart felt such love, that had his soul repented, I should have taken him, by that kiss, into the person of the Bride. In the fourth, recall what were the marriage-songs My ears heard from the Bride's love, when I stood before the Judge and so many false testimonies were adduced. In the fifth, remember how beauteously I clothed Myself for love of thee, when I so often changed My vesture, white, red, purple, and wore a garland of roses, to wit, the crown of thorns. In the sixth, be mindful how I embraced thee when I was bound to the pillar, and there took on Myself for thee all the darts of thine enemies. In the seventh, be mindful how I entered the bridal chamber of the Cross. And then I stretched out My hands by those hard nails for thy sweet embraces, singing in that chamber of love seven songs of marvellous sweetness. And then I opened My Heart that thou mightest enter in, when dying on the Cross, I slept the sleep of love with thee."

His belly is as bright ivory overlaid with sapphires. Here it is necessary to premise that the word עֶשֶׁת *esheth,* translated *bright* in the A. V., is passed over by the Vulgate, is explained by *box* or a *tablet* (πυξίον) in the LXX., and is held by modern critics to mean *a work of art.* There is this further difference, that the Vulgate agrees with the A. V. in taking the sapphires as set in the ivory, while the LXX. reverses this notion, reading *an ivory box* (or *tablet*) *on a sapphire stone.* Theodoret, taking πυξίον to be a box or vessel, comments thus : The depth of His mysteries, and the storehouse of His knowledge, where are hid all the treasures of His wisdom, are an *ivory box* to those who are worthy of His revelation. They are naturally incomprehensible, and therefore they are said to be *upon a sapphire stone,* which signifies the hidden depth of divine things. Philo explains the belly of the Bridegroom to be the Law, wherein the oracles, prophecies, and types of CHRIST were inclosed, as in a box, like the records of princes. This box was ivory on sapphire, because as ivory is opaque and of trifling cost compared with the transparent and precious sapphire, dyed with the hue of heaven, so the Old Covenant is altogether inferior to the Gospel of CHRIST, just as a picture or a flower ranks below a fruit or a living creature. Or, as the same Father adds, we may understand here the choir of the Saints, pure and shining, like an ivory box, having no spot or defilement. In this spiritual box lie the documents of wisdom and the title-deeds which will confer no earthly possession, but a heavenly kingdom. And this rests upon a sapphire stone, which may be referred to the Communion of the Saints, their love, and their glory. Taking πυξίον to be a *tablet* for writing, the Three Fathers beautifully interpret it of the Book of Nature, the visible creation, firm and lovely, and written by the hand of GOD, resting on that which is yet firmer and lovelier, His unseen Almightiness and heavenly wisdom, figured by the sapphire stone. And S. Gregory Nyssen takes the tablet to be any pure human heart on which GOD writes "not with ink, but with the SPIRIT of the living GOD; not in tables of stone, but in fleshy tables of the heart." It is white with holiness, it rests on sapphire, because its whole longing is bent on heavenly things. Turning to the Latin Fathers, we read first

"In the members of the human body nothing is weaker or more delicate than the belly, and therefore the frailty of CHRIST'S assumed Humanity is thereby denoted. It was *ivory*, because it had no spot or corruption, for 'He did no sin, neither was guile found in His mouth.' It was *studded with sapphires*, because of the heavenly graces and powers with which CHRIST'S Manhood was endowed, since the sapphire, having the colour of a clear sky, signifies GOD'S Majesty, as it is written, 'And they saw the GOD of Israel, and there was under His feet as it were a paved work of a sapphire stone, and as it were the body of heaven in his clearness.'" Another, applying the words to CHRIST'S mystical Body, says that the belly denotes those who bring forth spiritual children in faith; nay, that the ivory belly itself may not unfitly denote the baptismal font, as the pure white ivory is taken from a dead animal, for the Apostle saith, "Know ye not that so many of us as were baptized into JESUS CHRIST were baptized into His death? Wherefore we are buried with Him in baptism unto death, that like as CHRIST was raised up from the dead by the glory of the FATHER, even so we also should walk in newness of life." And this font is *studded with sapphires* because of the great Saints, glorious in their confession, who have issued from it. A third takes it of the contemplative Saints, not actively busy in external work, like hands and feet, nor yet employed, like the lips, in preaching the Word, but silently receiving into themselves the food of the HOLY GHOST, and adorned with tokens of true holiness, and thereby profiting the whole body to which they belong. There is yet another sense, applying the words to the human Person of CHRIST. His Body, in its perfect purity and beauty, is ivory, the stripes and weals inflicted on Him in His Passion, studded it with sapphires. Even yet the mysteries of the sapphire are not exhausted. It, like the beryl, gleamed on Aaron's breastplate; it is the promised foundation of the afflicted Church; it is the second jewel in the base of the New Jerusalem.

Cassiodor.

1 S. Pet. ii. 22.

Exod. xxiv. 10.

S. Just. Org.

Rom. vi. 3.

Luc. Abb.
Thom. Vercell.

Cocceius.

Exod. xxviii. 18.
Isa. liv. 11.
Rev. xxi. 19.

> The azure light of Sapphire stone
> Resembles that celestial Throne:
> A symbol of each simple heart
> That grasps in hope the better part:
> Whose life each holy deed combines,
> And in the light of virtue shines.

Marbod.
The Hymn,
Cives cœlestis patriæ.

And therefore the blue of sky and sea, typifying the height and depth, and length and breadth of the wisdom and love of GOD, was reproduced mystically in the Temple of old, and in the robes of Aaron, along with the purple of CHRIST's royalty and the scarlet of His Blood, while the sacred ephod was all of blue. Therefore too, the children of Israel were enjoined to put a "ribband of blue" upon the fringe that bordered their garments, to remind them of GOD's commandments; and it was this blue ribbon which formed the hem of that white robe of CHRIST, whose touch healed the woman with an issue of blood.

Exod. xxv. 4; xxvi. 1; xxviii. 5; xxviii. 31.
Numb. xv. 38.
S. Mat. ix. 20.

15 His legs are as pillars of marble, set upon sockets of fine gold : his countenance is as Lebanon, excellent as the cedars.

By reason of the title "pillars" given to SS. Peter, James and John, by their colleague S. Paul, several of the Fathers take the legs here to mean the Apostles in general. They are *marble*, because of their firmness and solidity, especially S. Peter, whose own name denotes a rock; they are set on *golden sockets*, because they rest on the base of which is written, "Other foundation can no man lay than that is laid, which is JESUS CHRIST." And the Apostles are in a sense the legs of CHRIST, not merely because they bore at first the whole weight of His mystical Body the Church, but because CHRIST Himself passed in and on them into the whole world to proclaim the Faith to the Gentiles, when He commanded them, "Go ye into all the world, and preach the Gospel to every creature." The words are applied to other Saints also, besides those chief and earliest ones. All the righteous who support others by their charity, and prop them with the consolations of Scripture, are such, as the Apostle writes: "We that are strong ought to bear the infirmities of the weak, and not to please ourselves." And the bases on which such Saints rest may well be Holy Writ, for it follows soon after, "Whatsoever things were written aforetime were written for our learning, that we, through patience and comfort of the Scriptures, might have hope." Or, the examples of the great Saints of old are the bases which support later ones, as it is written, "Ye are built upon the foundation of the Apostles and Prophets."

S. Epiphan.
S. Greg. Nyss.
S. Ambros.
Psellus.
1 Cor. iii. 11.
Philo Carp.
S. Mark xvi. 15.
S. Just. Org.
Rom. xv. 1.
Rom. xv. 4.
S. Ans. Laud.
Eph. ii. 20.

Again, applying the words to CHRIST Himself, they give divers explanations. One is that the two precepts of love to GOD and love to our neighbour, firm as marble in their claim on our faith, and based on the golden foundations of GOD's truth and love, are, as it were, the legs wherewith CHRIST enters the building of the faithful soul. Or you may take the Bridegroom's legs to be the journeyings of the SAVIOUR, undertaken for our salvation: His coming down from heaven to become Man, His descent into the grave, His Resurrection and Ascension. They are *marble*, for all the ways of the LORD are straight and strong. Of His strength the Psalmist saith, "He rejoiceth as a giant to run His course, His going forth is from the uttermost part of the heaven." Of His straightness elsewhere, "All the paths of the LORD are mercy and truth." These legs are *set upon sockets of gold*, because all things which were to be done by CHRIST or in CHRIST, were foreordained and appointed before the foundation of the world. Wherefore the Prophet exclaims, "O LORD, Thou art my GOD; I will exalt Thee, I will praise Thy Name; for Thou hast done wonderful things; Thy counsels of old are faithfulness and truth." And that we might be assured in type how unchangeable these counsels for our salvation are, the LORD did not suffer His legs to be broken upon the Cross, as were those of the malefactors; just as He signified the unity of His Church in preserving the seamless robe from being rent. But if you will have it, that only two journeyings can be signified by the two legs, you may take them to be the first and the second Advent; the first for redemption, the second for judgment and salvation.

<small>S. Greg. Nyss.</small>
<small>Tres Patr.</small>
<small>Cassiodor.</small>
<small>Ps. xix. 5.</small>
<small>Ps. xxv. 19.</small>
<small>Isa. xxv. 1.</small>
<small>Beda.</small>
<small>Hugo Card.</small>

His countenance is as Lebanon, excellent as the cedars. Lebanon, towering and white, is taken as the type of Him Who was fairer and purer than the children of men, and of Whom that first King of Israel was a mystical type, of whom it is written: "There was not among the children of Israel a goodlier person than he; from his shoulders and upward he was higher than any of the people." Theodoret, translating Lebanon by "incense," bids us see in it the Divinity which we worship, and in the *cedars*, the Man Who is incorrupt. And a Western writer, accepting the same idea of incense, explains it that CHRIST is so entitled, as at once Priest and Victim in the One Great Sacri-

<small>1 Sam. ix. 2.</small>
<small>Theodoret.</small>
<small>Luc. Abb.</small>

fice. Others, dwelling on the version "whiteness," see Him who washes away the sins of His people, making them white as snow. And the Virgins of the Church are said to be the countenance of CHRIST, white as Lebanon, for because of the chaste purity of their life, and because they are free from stain of pollution, they are nearest to the spotless Lamb. Rupert reminds us, very aptly, that the great stones whereof the Temple was built were hewn on the slopes of Lebanon, and that as that Temple, to which CHRIST compares Himself, was the head, and glory, and Holy of holies of the earthly Jerusalem, so is CHRIST the Head, and glory, and Holy of holies in the heavenly Jerusalem, and every stone in that building made without hands is a Saint of GOD, part of Lebanon itself, as a member of the Body of CHRIST. *Excellent as the cedars.* Where note, that the same Beloved is compared to Lebanon, which produces mighty trees, and to the cedar which amongst others, Lebanon produces, because He, one and the same, brings forth and carries the trees, and is Himself brought forth and carried amongst the trees by Himself. For our LORD JESUS CHRIST, while bringing forth to life and nourishing by His Divine grace all His elect from the beginning till the end of the world, bears Himself also amongst men, in willing to be made Man, and filled that Man with the grace of His own SPIRIT, albeit far more than all others. The LORD then is *excellent as the cedars*, because He transcends in His sole and singular dignity all the trees of that wood of the Holy Church wherein He was born. *His countenance is as Lebanon,* which produces the cedar also amongst its other noble trees, because, when He willed to become Man, He created Himself as the Tree of Life in the midst of the garden, just as a painter might depict himself with fitting colours, in the midst of a group. He was *elect,* or excellent *as the cedars,* because He bore a likeness to all those great Patriarchs, His forefathers, and united in Himself every virtue and grace which they separately possessed. And as the cedar seems to tower up to the sky, while its roots go deep and firmly into the earth, so the Divinity of CHRIST reaches to the Heaven of heavens where He dwells, and yet His Incarnation binds Him closely to the children of men.

16 His mouth is most sweet: yea, he is al-

together lovely. This is my beloved, and this is my friend, O daughters of Jerusalem.

By the *mouth* of CHRIST they understand, as by His lips, the preachers of His Word, and in especial the first of them, the Baptist Forerunner. Or, applied to Himself, it will denote His own words. For what, asks Theodoret, can be sweeter than the sayings of GOD? Wherefore holy David saith, "O how sweet are Thy words unto my throat: yea, sweeter than honey unto my mouth;" and again, "More to be desired are they than gold, yea, than much fine gold: sweeter also than honey, and the honey-comb." Therefore, also, the officers of the chief priests, who were sent to the LORD, fascinated and attracted by longing for the sweetness of His words, said, "Never man spake like this Man." And, seeing that the whole New Testament is His utterance, we may well understand it by the mouth (or *throat*, as LXX. and Vulgate read) of the Bridegroom, especially by reason of the sweetness of reading and meditating on its heavenly sayings. And S. Anselm of Laon reminds us that as it is not the outer letter, but the inner spirit, which is profitable, so the hidden speaking of CHRIST to the heart is the sweetest of all, by reason of the lovingkindness which is His utterance. And whereas the margin of the A. V. reads *palate*, so there are not wanting those who tell us that here is meant the internal savour of CHRIST and His spiritual consolation, which are so sweet to those who taste them. The more this sweetness is preserved, the more it is longed for. It hath hunger, not satiety, in this life: it hath refreshment, not fulness. It is so sweet as to be ever desired; it is so vast, as never to be fully comprehended. The Bride calls the throat *most sweet*, and we are not told *how* sweet, nor yet what it is like. Some comparison is given us in all the other cases, as that the head is fine gold; the locks like palm-buds; the eyes like doves' eyes by the waters; the cheeks beds of spices; the lips lilies; the hands cylindrical, golden, full of jacinths; the belly, ivory studded with sapphires; the legs pillars of marble with golden sockets. But the Bride calls the throat only *most sweet*, and gives no simile, that thereby you may ponder how unspeakable and priceless is that divine inner sweetness, which eye hath not seen, nor ear heard,

S. Greg.
Nyss.
S. Just. Org.
Psellus.

Theodoret.

Ps. cxix. 103.

Ps. xix. 10.

S. John vii. 46.

Tres Patr.
Philo Carp.

S. Ans. Laud.
Beda

Ricard. Vict.

Rupert.

neither hath entered into the heart of man, but which God hath prepared for them that love Him. *Yea, He is altogether lovely.* Or, as all the ancient versions read, *desirable.*[1] And a heathen philosopher will tell us how desirable, in those marvellous words whereby he forecasts the Beatific Vision as shadowed in trance and communion, and the attractive power of the Incarnation: "We cannot, in mere similitudes here, behold the glory of Righteousness and temperance, and those other things that are precious to our souls; nay, scarce even a very few, reaching with their imperfect organs to the images thereof, beheld what kind of things it is which is pictured. But it was then permitted to gaze on resplendent beauty, when, together with the choir of the blest, we attained, with God, to the blissful vision and contemplation; and others too beheld, and were initiated into that mystery which may well be called the happiest of all; which we celebrated, purely, and free from all the passions which abode in us in the later time.[2] And so initiated, and admitted as beholders, we, pure and spotless, and freed from the body which we bear about with us like a shell, beheld those perfect, simple, unwavering, and blissful visions in light unsullied. And all this is a delight to memory, wherefore has it now been spoken of at length, through longing for it once more. And that beauty, as we have said, shone forth, coming with them,[3] and we, reaching this point, perceived its clearest shining by the clearest of our senses. For sight is the most acute of our bodily senses, and yet wisdom cannot be seen by it, for wisdom would excite the most eager love, if any like image of it could appear, and show itself to sight." So when the Eternal Wisdom, the Beauty uncreated, did show Himself to men, He inspired such passionate yearning in them that they could not but rise up, leave all, and follow Him, to poverty, exile, shame, and death. *Altogether lovely,* because He is lovely as God, and lovely as Man also. He is lovely in Himself, and lovely in His Saints. Lovely was the

---

[1] The Syriac included; with singular poverty, however, it applies the epithet to the raiment of the Bridegroom, not to Himself.

[2] It is not a forced interpretation, using the passage as is done here, to interpret this latter time of the Fall, succeeding that earlier time of man's innocence.

[3] So it is recorded of more than one Saint, that the face, after returning from Communion at the Altar, seemed to shine with supernatural light and beauty.

vision of His Humanity upon earth, but lovelier by far will be His glorified Humanity in heaven; lovely is that Countenance which the whole company of the heavenly citizens desires, most lovely of all the contemplation of His Godhead, to which all that can be desired may not be compared. He is *altogether lovely*, because the mystery of His Humanity kindles such universal longing in the souls of His elect, that not merely the glory of His Resurrection calls them forth, but even the ignominy of His Passion invites them to imitate His example. Altogether lovely, because the more He is possessed, the more He is longed for; we desire to behold Him, and when we behold Him, we desire Him more ardently than before. S. Pet. Dam. Opus. l. 4.
Rupert.

> O JESU, King of wondrous might,   S. Bernard.
> O Victor, glorious from the fight,   Rhythm.
> Sweetness that may not be expressed,   Jubil.
> And altogether loveliest!

This is my Beloved, and this is my Friend, O daughters of Jerusalem. He is *my Beloved*, because I cling to Him by faith and love; He is *my Friend*, because He vouchsafed to redeem me from the bond of sin, to make me His friend, and the sharer of His secrets, and the more each one loves Him, the more worthy does he become of His friendship. And observe that He is called *Beloved* first, and then *Friend*, " because He first loved us," and was united to us by that love even before He came upon earth to speak unto us face to face, as a Man speaketh unto His friend. Cassiodor.
1 S. John iv. 19.
Exod. xxxiii. 11.

> One there is, above all others,   John
>   Well deserves the name of Friend,   Newton.
> His is love beyond a brother's,
>   Costly, free, and knows no end;
> They who once His kindness prove,
>   Find it everlasting love.

CHAPTER VI.

1 Whither is thy beloved gone, O thou fairest among women? whither is thy beloved turned aside? that we may seek him with thee.

The Three Fathers, assuming that the speakers here are the Angels, represent the words as an attempt on their part to penetrate the mystery of the Incarnation, because they did not fully comprehend it until the Ascension, as appears from their question when bid to lift up their gates : "Who is the King of Glory?" But the more general view is, that we have the weaker and less-instructed believers, the *Ecclesia discens*, asking to be taught by the wiser and more perfect, the *Ecclesia docens*, the history, as well as the beauties of the Bridegroom, the place where He may be found, as well as the marks whereby He may be known. Tell us, then, they say, how it is that thou seekest Him as absent, Whom thou preachest as everywhere present? If He be present, how may He be seen ; and if He be absent, how can He be found? And one answer to this part of their inquiry is, that GOD never leaves those whom He has once taken to Himself, that He may go elsewhere to win others, but that the power of the Divine presence is in such wise ubiquitous that it goes, as it were, or turns aside, to attach others to itself, yet so as to keep that grace which has begun in those whom it had already gathered, just as the putting the Spirit on the seventy elders of Israel, took nothing from the grace given to Moses, or as a candle may light many other candles, with no diminution of its flame. They dwell, too, on the double phrase, *gone*, and *turned aside;* the one word denoting a distant journey, the other a mere withdrawal to some place close at hand, as, for instance, passing out of the sun into the shade. CHRIST is *gone* bodily into heaven by His Ascension ; He has *turned aside* spiritually from the Synagogue into the Church. He is *gone*, too, when He altogether refuses to comply with any prayer; He is but *turned aside*, when He delays a little when sought, that He may excite more eager longing in the soul which seeks Him. And the verse may be explained also of days of grievous scandals, coldness, and laxity in the Church, times like those of Arian supremacy, or of Mohammedan conquest, or that dark and sorrowful century of which the historian exclaims that the LORD appeared to be sleeping in the barque of Peter. Then men anxiously inquire where may be found the marks of true piety, where are the Confessors of CHRIST's Name. And once, the answer would have been that He was in the deserts of the

Thebaid, with Paul, and Antony, and Pachomius; at another time that He had passed from the Arian East to His faithful in Gaul, where Hilary and Martin upheld the standard of the Consubstantial; and even in the tenth century itself, great Houses like Cluny, reforming Saints like Dunstan, and missionary triumphs in Norway, Bohemia, Russia, and Pomerania, testified to the presence of CHRIST in the outskirts of His Church, when those who looked for Him in the midst could nowhere see Him. Again; the verse has been explained of all those mysterious journeyings of the LORD, of His passage from heaven to the womb of the Virgin, of His dealings in Hades between His Passion and Resurrection, of the intervals between those sudden and intermittent visits granted to the Apostles during the Great Forty Days, intervals of which Holy Scripture tells us nothing. And, lastly, the question is asked by every devout seeker after CHRIST, that he may know who those true Saints are in whose hearts He rests, that imitating their example, he too may find Him. This seeking must be twofold, in action and in contemplation, in faith also and prayer, and the finding is in holiness of life. Wherefore is added, *That we may seek Him with thee*, because they who seek for CHRIST outside the Church, and without her aid, are scarcely likely to find Him. And remember, after all, what one of those who first sought Him vainly outside the Church, and at last found Him, as few have found so truly and closely, within it, has said, " Let us seek Him while He is yet to be found; let us seek Him even when we have found Him. He is hidden that He may be sought when not yet found, and that He may still be sought when He has been found He is incomprehensible." Card. Hailgrin. Cassiodor. S.Ans.Laud. S. Greg. Nyss. Honorius. Cassiodor. S. August. in S. Joann.

2 My beloved is gone down into his garden, to the beds of spices, to feed in the gardens, and to gather lilies.

The Chaldee paraphrase explains this verse in a very remarkable manner of the Captivity: "The Ruler of the world willingly received their prayer, and descended into Babylon, to the council of the wise men, and gave His people rest, and led them out of their captivity by the hand of Cyrus, and Ezra, and Nehemiah, and Zorobabel son of Salathiel, and the elders Targum.

of the Jews. And they built the House of the Sanctuary, and set priests over the oblations, and Levites over the guardianship of the Word of holiness. And He sent fire from heaven, and willingly received their oblation and the incense of spices, and as a man reareth up his son in pleasant things, so tenderly did He nourish them; and as a man gathereth roses out of the valleys, so did He assemble them together out of Babylon."

<small>Ghislerius.</small> And, not dissimilarly, the Fathers take it of the special aid which CHRIST gives His Church in time of need, going down into it, that it may go up unto Him. And though this time of need may be variously understood, <small>S. Greg. Nyss. Hom. 15.</small> yet there can be little doubt that S. Gregory Nyssen is right in understanding it first and chiefly of the first Advent of CHRIST in the flesh, when the whole creation was groaning and travailing in pain, and looking for the promised Deliverer. He went *down*, for the sake <small>S. Luke x. 30.</small> of that man who going down from Jerusalem to Jericho, fell among thieves; *down* from His unspeakable majesty to our lowly nature. He came into His *garden*, as the True Gardener and Husbandman, to plant it anew; for we men, as saith the Apostle, "are GOD's <small>1 Cor. iii. 9.</small> husbandry." Seeing then that it was He Who tilled in Paradise at the beginning of the world the garden of human nature which the Heavenly FATHER planted, <small>Ps. lxxx. 13.</small> and that the wild boar and singular beast preyed on that garden, to wit, ourselves, and rooted up the field of GOD, He came down to deck that garden once more by planting virtues there, and by sending through it, by the channels of His Word, the pure and holy fount of doctrine, to cherish the plants. He comes not merely to the garden generally, but in especial to the *beds of spices*, in that He seeks in preference those souls where there is no mere desert, barren of virtues, but where the spices and odours of holiness abound. It is said, too, that He comes into His *garden*, which is one, to feed in the *gardens*, which are many; and <small>Theodoret. Philo Carp.</small> that because the Church Universal, which is His garden, contains within it many local and particular Churches, and each such Church many devout souls which He delights to visit; and *to gather lilies*, that is, to take away for Himself out of this world those <small>Cassiod.</small> holy souls which by maturity in sanctification have attained to perfect whiteness, that He may cause them to rejoice evermore with Him in eternal blessedness. And that He might do all this, He went down into

that garden where they laid Him in Joseph's new tomb, and there too, by appearing to Mary Magdalen, He consecrated the first-fruits of the Church. He went also into that other garden of His when He descended into hell, to those *beds of spices*, the holy Fathers and Patriarchs who awaited His coming, to Abel and Noah, Abraham, Isaac, Jacob, Moses, Job, David and other great Saints before and under the Law. He entered Paradise also in triumph after He had pierced down to hell. And GOD Himself is our witness to this fact, in that He mercifully replied to the thief upon the Cross, who devoutly commended himself to Him; "To-day shalt thou be with Me in Paradise;" that is, thou shalt see and behold My Divine glory, Myself, and My garden of delights (for such is the meaning of Paradise,) and there thou shalt feed and rejoice for ever, where no weariness or satiety can come. Hence it is, pursues the Bishop of Carpasia, that in the fragrant gardens of human souls, glowing throughout the world with Christian faith and charity, GOD Himself *feeds;* and thence He gathers, to deck His bridal chamber, the white and perfumed garlands of His *lilies,* the Apostles, Prophets, and Martyrs and all Saints. Had He not first gone down into His garden to overcome the sharpness of death, never could He have delighted Himself with His holy feeding in the gardens, that is, in the many Churches of the faithful throughout the world. And when He was gone and turned aside from the unbelieving Jews, to whom it was necessary that the Word of GOD should first be spoken, He turned to the Gentiles, because those to whom He came judged themselves unworthy of everlasting life. And thus He went down into His garden to the beds of spices. For out of the Gentile nations, and out of the fanes and temples, He made for Himself beds of spices and a fruitful garden, casting out thence the filthiness of idolatry, that He might feed in those gardens and gather thence lilies, Virgins and Martyrs, Confessors and Doctors, and just persons, both men and women; and be fed there with the food of worship, of sacrifice, oblations, and prayer. And He is said to have *gone down* from the Jewish people to the Gentiles, as from the more worthy, which worshipped GOD, to the less worthy, which worshipped idols. He came, in His Incarnation, into His garden the Church, but He came first to the choicest spot of all that garden,

S. John xix. 41.

Philo Carp.

S. Luke xxiii. 43.

Acts xiii. 46.

Parez.

the bed where the most fragrant spices grew, to the spotless Maiden at Nazareth, where He might gather the white lilies of purity and holiness as nowhere else. And there is another garden besides those of the Church and the soul, where He comes to meet His Bride, which is the reading of Holy Scripture, whence He gathers for her lilies, violets, roses, and divers spices, to fill the beds of believing souls, and to pluck thence abundantly lilies of the LORD.

<small>S. Just. Org.</small>

<small>S. Hieron. Com. in Zachar.</small>

<small>Dora Greenwell, *Carmina Crucis*.</small>

"O what are these lilies tipped
  With fire, that sword-like gleam?
O what are these lilies dipped
  As in the pale moon-beam,
That quiver with unsteadfast light,
  And shine as through a dream?"

"These fiery spirits passed
  From earth through sword and flame;
These quiet souls at last
  Through patience overcame;
These shine like stars on high, and these
  Have left no trace nor name;
I bind them in one wreath, because
  Their triumph was the same."

3 I am my beloved's, and my beloved is mine: he feedeth among the lilies.

After her fall, and her repentance, the Bride, returning to her first love, is enabled once more to speak of Him as in the days of her earliest fervour. Her LORD called upon her by the memory of that happy time, saying, "I remember thee, the kindness of thy youth, the love of thine espousals, when thou wentest after Me in the wilderness, in a land that was not sown. Israel was holiness to the LORD, and the first-fruits of His increase." And as it was in the trials and sufferings of the wilderness that she first learnt to know Him, so it is by trials and suffering that He purifies her, and brings her to Him again; as it is written in another place: "Behold, I will allure her, and bring her into the wilderness, and speak comfortably to her. And I will give her her vineyards from thence, and the valley of Achor for a door of hope, and she shall sing there, as in the days of her youth, and as in the day when she came up out of the land of Egypt." Thus, as S. Gregory Nyssen teaches, she has become so like her Beloved by conforming herself absolutely to His will,

<small>Cocceius.</small>

<small>Jer. ii. 2.</small>

<small>Hos. ii. 14.</small>

<small>S. Greg. Nyssen.</small>

that all who behold her feel as the spectators of a skilfully painted portrait, or as those who look on an image reflected in a mirror, that they see not a mere representation, but the very original itself. Nay, the Bride herself, irradiated with the light of GOD's glory, wherein she beholds shadowed His wondrous attributes of beauty, goodness, wisdom, and love, is tranced at the sight, and so absorbed in Him that she has no heed for aught else, and neither sees nor hears anything which pertains to earth. *I for my Beloved,* she says, prepare the food He loves. *My Beloved for me* will provide the grace of perfection, the reward of eternal life. *I for My beloved* prepare a mansion in myself. *My Beloved is mine* because He dwells in me, and makes me dwell in Him, as He says Himself in the Gospel, " Ye in Me, and I in you." S. Thomas Aquinas. Sec. Secund. Q. 175, art. 2.
Cassiodor.
Honorius.
S. John xiv. 20.

> Nor time, nor place, nor chance, nor death can bow
>   My least desires unto the least remove;
> He's firmly mine by oath; I His by vow;
>   He's mine by faith, and I am His by love;
> He's mine by water; I am His by wine;
> Thus I my best Beloved's am, thus He is mine.
>
> He is my Altar, I His holy place;
>   I am His guest, and He my living Food;
> I His by penitence; He mine by grace;
>   I His by purchase; He is mine by Blood;
> He's my supporting elm; and I His vine;
> Thus I my best Beloved's am, thus He is mine.
>
> He gives me wealth, I give Him all my vows;
>   I give Him songs; He gives me length of days;
> With wreaths of grace He crowns my conquering brows;
>   And I His temples with a wreath of praise;
> Which He accepts; an everlasting sign
> That I my best Beloved's am, that He is mine.

Francis Quarles. *Emblems,* v. 3.

And observe the change in the order of the words from that earlier passage where the same Divine truth was enunciated. Before, it was said, " My Beloved is mine, and I am His," " because He first loved us." Now, she has learned to love Him, not as perfectly as He deserves, nor as He loves her, but yet in such wise that she can feel that she is not merely taken possession of by Him, but that she willingly and joyfully gives herself up to Him for ever. This, then, is the full promise of the marriage bond. The Bridegroom has made His vows, and plighted His troth to her already, and now she is asked to plight hers in turn, that as He promises to ii. 16.
1 S. John iv. 19.
Delrio.
Henr. Harphius.

love her, comfort her, honour her, keep her in sickness and in health, and endow her with all His goods, so she in her turn promises loving obedience and steadfast faith to Him. This is the fulfilment of that which He spake unto her by the Prophet, "I will betroth thee unto Me for ever; yea, I will betroth thee unto Me in righteousness, and in judgment, and in loving-kindness, and in mercies. I will even betroth thee unto Me in faithfulness; and thou shalt know the LORD." And as the essence of marriage consists in mutual consent, CHRIST the Bridegroom asks for the heart of His Bride, saying, "Give Me thine heart, and let thine eyes observe My ways." For there is none other to whom she may so profitably, happily, and honourably give it, since it is well to bestow the heart on such a Bridegroom as can alone be sufficient for the heart, as the Bride herself saith with the Psalmist, "GOD is the strength of my heart, and my portion for ever." Only the love of GOD, then, which is the union of a fitting Bridegroom with a suitable Bride, makes spiritual marriage. For charity, which, according to the Apostle, "is the bond of perfectness," makes us agree perfectly with GOD, and therefore establishes perfect marriage between GOD and the soul, binding GOD to the heart and the heart to GOD by a spousal bond, and knitting it so closely to Him, that whoso thus clings to GOD is made one spirit with Him. Consider then, O soul, if thy love is yet to give, where thou canst better fix it than on Him Who is fairer than the children of men, in Whom are all the treasures of wisdom and knowledge hid. If thy love is for sale, does not He buy it at the great price of His own Blood, lovingly forestalling thee, and faithfully ransoming thee? Moreover, this Bridegroom is a Virgin, and the Child of a Virgin, Who desires to have a virgin Bride. And according to the Law, it is ruled that the High Priest "shall take a wife in her virginity;" wherefore the Apostle saith, "I have espoused you to one husband, that I may present you as a chaste virgin to CHRIST." Yet fear not, O soul, for so often as thou art cleansed by grace, thou art counted as a virgin; art freed from the corruption of sin, pure through love, asking, seeking, and desiring one thing, and that the one thing needful. And this is the great difference between earthly and spiritual marriage, that in the former a virgin ceases to be such, but in the latter a soul which has been stained is made a virgin; whence blessed Agnes saith, "Whom when I love, I am pure, when I touch, I am undefiled, when I receive, I am a virgin." The beginning of this bridal is by faith in Baptism, it is confirmed by progress in holiness, it is consummated in glory, when the soul is inseparably joined to CHRIST. And there are three blessings attached to this spiritual marriage, as to all true and loving marriages of earth, mutual faith, offspring, and indissoluble union. The spiritual offspring of the soul and GOD, of Divine grace and free-will, is threefold, active pursuit of good, passive avoidance of evil, patient endurance of suffering; the inseparable bond which shall unite them in glory is also a triple cord, conformity in holiness, identity of will, perfectness of inward love. And as fire melts two masses of metal into one, so the fervour of this love melts the soul, and causes it to flow into GOD, and thus be united with Him, thenceforward to be parted from Him nevermore. Further, as all marriage is sealed with a solemn pledge, so it is in the vows of the Religious Life that this bridal of the soul and GOD is most frequently seen. Not but that countless great Saints in other vocations have been firmly knit to Him, but that nevertheless the saying of the Apostle holds, and must always hold good in the main, "He that is unmarried careth for the things that belong to the LORD, how he may please the LORD; but he that is married careth for the things that are of the world, how he may please his wife. There is a difference also between a wife and a virgin. The unmarried woman careth for the things of the LORD, that she may be holy both in body and spirit: but she that is married careth for the things of the world, that she may please her husband." And as in the discharge of our obligations there is more acceptability in giving that which we are not bound to pay, but which we do pay for love's sake, therefore it is that such especial honour is yielded to the Religious Life. Wherefore a great Saint speaks thus of the Brides of CHRIST, those *lilies* among which the Beloved feeds: "'With joy and gladness shall they be brought, and enter into the King's palace.' Not they who have submitted to virginity by compulsion, not they who have adopted a celibate life from sorrow or necessity, but they who with joy and gladness delight in this good thing, these shall be brought unto the

S. Thomas Aquinas.

1 Cor. vii. 32.

S. Hieron. ad Pollent.

S. Basil. M. in Ps. xlv.

King, and be brought into no common places, but into the King's temple. (LXX.) For the sacred vessels, which no human use has defiled, may be carried into the Holy of holies, and are permitted entrance into that shrine where no profane feet may tread."

J. M. Neale,
The Hymn,
Christ's own
Martyrs.

CHRIST's dear Virgins, glorious lilies,
   Tell us how ye kept unstained
Snowiest petals through the tempest,
   Till eternal spring ye gained :
Snowiest still, albeit with crimson
   Some more precious leaves were stained ?

" In the place where He was buried
   There was found a garden nigh ;
In that garden us He planted,
   Teaching us with Him to die,
Till to Paradise He moved us,
   There to bloom eternally."

4 Thou art beautiful, O my love, as Tirzah, comely as Jerusalem, terrible as an army with banners.

The word *Tirzah*,[1] implying "pleasantness," has not been translated as a proper name by the LXX. and Vulgate, which severally read εὐδοκία and *suavis*. But taking it first as we have it here in the A. V., the mystical import is that the life of the Bride, even as militant in this world, (of which the northern kingdom, with its capital Tirzah, is a type) has a beauty and attractiveness which rivals all earthly bliss, besides that yet greater loveliness which belongs to her in her triumph when she has reached her Country, and attained to the Vision of Peace. And that, because she has now been conformed to her Bridegroom, the Eternal Wisdom, of Whom Solomon elsewhere saith, " Happy is the man that findeth Wisdom .... her ways are ways of pleasantness, and all her paths are peace."

Prov. iii. 13, 17.

[1] The juxtaposition of these two names supplies an item of internal evidence as to the date of the Song of songs. Tirzah became the first capital of the northern kingdom, after the revolution of the ten tribes under Jeroboam I., (1 Kings xiv. 17.) The wars, jealousies, and religious differences which thenceforward divided Israel and Judah, make it all but certain that no southern poet would have praised Tirzah, and no northern one Jerusalem, at least so as to couple them. Thus the actual reign of Solomon is the most probable era of the composition.

Accordingly, the LORD Himself tells His Apostles: "Verily I say unto you, There is no man that hath left house, or brethren, or sisters, or father, or mother, or wife, or children, or lands, for My sake and the Gospel's, but he shall receive an hundred-fold more in this time, houses, and brethren, and sisters, and mothers, and children, and lands, with persecutions; and in the world to come eternal life." Those Fathers, however, who explain the verse of the Church, do not contrast here the Militant and Triumphant divisions of it, but the Gentile and Jewish. The WORD, remarks S. Athanasius, beholding and approving the faith of the Gentiles, saith, *Thou art beautiful, My love, as approval, comely as Jerusalem, terrible as forces in array.* For they who are come from the Gentiles ought not to be unlike Jerusalem, that there may be but one people, for this is so when we honour the Law and believe in CHRIST. For the GOD of the Law and of the Gospels is One, and whoso is not made like to Jerusalem, does not become the Bridegroom's friend. So too S. Gregory the Great: "The Synagogue is called *beautiful,* and *love, sweet,* and *comely as Jerusalem,* because when converted, she will follow the four Holy Gospels as does the Church. Hence she derives beauty of conduct, so as to please, she gathers training in holy action, that she may abide in love; she learns the sweetness of meekness, that she may persevere; she exhibits the comeliness of fair conversation, that she may attract by her example." This Church of the LORD is *terrible* to heretics, unbelievers, and evil spirits, by reason of the number and valour of her warriors, their long training in arms, their loyalty, zeal, and unanimity in battle; because of the alliance of the Angels; and yet more, in that she is aided by the presence of the mightiest of Kings, ready to protect His subjects. And so it is written: "The shout of a king is among them," and as Captain of the LORD's host is He come. *As an army in array,* for in the foremost line is the King Himself with His generals the Apostles; in the second, the army of Martyrs; in the third, the company of the Confessors.

S. Mark x. 29.

S. Athan. Synopsis.

S. Greg. M.

Hugo Card.

Numb. xxiii. 21.
Josh. v. 14.

> Let angelic armies
> Guard us on each side,
> But Thyself as Leader
> First in battle ride;

> Thou Whose Name is Faithful,
> Thou Whose vesture glows
> White with perfect pureness,
> Red with blood of foes.

Again, the Church is *beautiful* in the devout lives of her Saints; she is the Bridegroom's *love* in those to whom by holy love His secrets are disclosed; *sweet* in those who are busied in works of mercy; *comely* in her contemplative and hermit Saints; *terrible as an army in array*, by reason of her Religious Orders, militant under rule, and each company under its own chief, or spiritual Superior. And following that other version, *as an army with banners*, we are reminded by the Targum of the twelvefold array of the children of Israel in their march through the wilderness, every man pitching " by his own standard, with the ensign of their father's house." In the vanguard is the victorious standard of the King Himself:

The Royal Banners forward go,
The Cross shines forth in mystic glow;

even as it is written, "On the east side, toward the rising of the sun, shall they of the standard of the camp of Judah pitch throughout their armies," but behind it clusters many a banner and pennon of the inferior chieftains of the host. There is the ruddy Rose of the Martyrs, the candent Lily of the Virgins, the golden Chain of the Doctors, the starry Crown of the Confessors. There too—as in ancient Rome, where every especial type of military valour had its own appropriate crown, one like the beaks of ships for a naval victory, one like the battlements of a city for him who first scaled the enemy's wall, one like the palisades of a camp for the leader in storming the intrenchments—gleam the ensigns which tell of the armorial bearings won by each champion in his hardest fight. There is the lion which sent Ignatius to his reward; there are the anchor of Clement, the grating of Laurence, the fiery chair of Blandina, the arrowy sheaf of Edmund the King, and countless other tokens of victory in many a well-fought field, once tossed to and fro by the stormy breezes of earth, now hung up for ever in the peaceful calm of heaven, yet not so high but that we may see them still. And all this is true in its degree of every holy soul which makes one in the ranks of that great army, *beautiful*, because of her gentle ways; *sweet*, in pureness of heart; *comely as Jerusalem*, from its love of peace; *terrible*, with the arms of truth and purity. Comely as *Jerusalem*, also Theodoret. because imitating here the life of the Angels, pondering on earth the thoughts of heaven, following after the prize of her high calling, seeking the things which are above, where CHRIST sitteth at the right hand of GOD. And not only comely, but *terrible* to beholders, because of her set *array*, having nothing irregular, uncertain, confused, but all things in due order and judgment. For, as Philo and S. Gregory aptly say, Philo Carp. it is well known to the experienced that soldiers, when S. Greg. M. advancing in array against the enemy, if they march in close order and keep step together, are feared by the foes that come against them, because they see no gap in the ranks whereby they may pierce them. So too, in our war against evil spirits, the unity of faith, the cheerfulness of hope, the bond of charity, are what make us terrible, since, if there be discord and schism in the body, it is no hard task for the enemy to rout it. *In array*, not only because of the orderly regula- Hugo Card. tion of all the faculties, powers, and habits of each soul Cassiod. within itself, but by reason of each soldier in the great Hugo Vict. army of GOD having his own appointed place in its Erud. Theol. ranks, according to his order and calling, and thus by ii. 1. faith and obedience being *sweet* to man, *comely* to the Rupert. Angels, *terrible* to evil spirits. And finally, they apply Alanus. the verse fitly to S. Mary, *beautiful* in her holiness, Guilielmus *sweet* in gentle meekness; *comely as Jerusalem*, be- Parvus. cause in her peace was made between GOD and man, when she became the abode of the Prince of peace, and palace of the King; *terrible as an army in array*, because compassed by the ranks of the Angels.

5 Turn away thine eyes from me, for they have overcome me: thy hair is as a flock of goats that appear from Gilead.

Overcome me. The LXX. and Vulgate, with little Theodoret. difference, *have given me wings*, or *made me fly away*. The beauty of thine eyes, the contemplation of thy vision, and the clearness of thy mental sight have drawn Me to thy love, but gaze not steadfastly on Me beyond measure, lest thou shouldst suffer some harm thence. For I am past searching out, and incomprehensible, not only by men, but by angels; and if thou shouldst pass the bounds, and vainly occupy thyself with matters above thy powers, not only wilt thou fail in thy search, but thou wilt make thine eye dimmer and feebler. For such is the nature of light that just as it illuminates the eye, so it punishes with hurt its insatiability. Therefore *turn away thine eyes from Me;* search not out things that are too hard, seek not that which is too mighty for thee, but ponder evermore upon that which is enjoined thee. I have given thee doves' eyes, wherewith thou mayest behold Me, and penetrate most keenly the hidden things of Scripture, but beware lest thou shouldst direct them to look on Me now, for whilst thou art in this present life, thou canst not, "for there shall no man see Me, and live." But, when freed from the fetters of the body, thou shalt attain to Me, then thou shalt behold Me in open vision, and that shall be fulfilled which is promised in the Gospel, "He that loveth Me shall be loved of My FATHER, and I will love him, and will manifest Myself to him." In that it is said, *for they have made Me fly away,* it is not to be supposed that GOD deserts those who seek Him and departs from them, seeing that He Himself commands, "Seek and ye shall find;" but it is rather to be understood that the more any one aims at searching out GOD's divine majesty, the more clearly he understands how unsearchable and incomprehensible it is. Again, they take the words as denoting fervent love, and not any warning. *Turn away thine eyes* of prayer and meditation from Me for a little, since they have forced Me to so much, have made Me *fly away* from My throne in heaven to the manger on earth, have made Me fly away from the unbelieving Jewish people to the faithful Gentile Church. *Turn away thine eyes* from My bodily presence, not always desiring to see Me in the flesh, Whom thou mayest see better in the Spirit by faith. For therefore I ascended into heaven, that I, Who fill all things with My divine presence, might not always seem to thee tied to place, Who am everywhere, Who contain all things, and am uncontained in any place. *Turn away* not merely *thy* fleshly *eyes* from Me, but eyes clouded with sin, since they make Me fly away, but look on Me with the eyes of holy contemplation, and I will draw near. The marginal reading of A. V., *they have puffed Me up,* is nearly that adopted and commented on by S. Ambrose, as though Christ were saying to the soul, If thou be perfect, yet there are other souls remaining for Me to redeem and prop up, wherefore *turn away thine eyes from Me, for they lift Me up,* but I came down to lift all up. And he explains this somewhat obscure comment more clearly by adding that a teacher who wishes to lecture on a difficult subject to an audience, however learned and eloquent he may be, yet lowers himself to the standard of those who are uninstructed, and uses simple language, that he may be understood. Hence the words are an injunction to preachers and Christian Saints in general to withdraw at times from contemplation and from discussing the darker mysteries of the Faith, that they may teach the babes in Christ, and appeal to them with the simplest language of the Gospel and the plainest object-lessons of good works. S. Ambros. de Isaac. 8.

There is yet another rendering, found both in some ancient writers and in modern critics. *Turn thine eyes towards Me, for they encourage Me.* And then it may be explained of the devotion of those few faithful ones who clung ever to their Lord, even at the Cross itself, as being the one and only help His human nature had in bearing up against all the sorrows of His life and Passion. And especially when His dear Mother stood by His Cross, gazing on Him with sorrowful eyes, the thought that He was dying for her salvation braced Him to endure unto the end. There are not wanting those who, following this version, put the words into the mouth of the Bride, and make her ask that those blessed eyes may look on her, to strengthen her for the battle; or, following in part the other rendering, to give her wings that she may flee away from the world, may direct her flight into the hole of the rock, and there, in the wounded Side, be in safety and at rest. Targum. Psellus. Weissbach. Ainsworth. Psellus.

> I heard the voice of Jesus say,
> "I am this dark world's Light,
> Look unto Me, thy morn shall rise,
> And all thy day be bright."
> I looked to Jesus, and I found
> In Him my Star, my Sun,
> And in that light of life I'll walk
> Till travelling days are done.

Bonar.

Thy hair is as a flock of goats. Here begins a repetition of some of the words of praise with which the fourth chapter opens, on which S. Beda, expanding Cassiodorus, observes, "These verses, as well as the succeeding ones, have occurred before, and have been fully explained so far as we had understanding to do it. But we ought not to be weary of repeating in exposition what the author of the sacred poem was not weary of repeating in composition; either that we may recall to mind what has been said before, or, by the help of divine grace, may produce something fresh and profitable. For when these, and countless other passages in Scripture, already uttered, are repeated, it is a token of firmness, that it is indeed the Word of GOD, and will truly be fulfilled, as the Patriarch Joseph testifies when explaining the dream of the king." We are told, then, of additional reasons for comparing the Saints to goats. The goat was constantly offered in sacrifice, and the devout offer, by penitence for their sins, of which the goat is also a type, their "bodies a living sacrifice, holy, acceptable unto GOD." Goats, preferring steep and rocky places, up which they bound with swift but silent footfall, are types of those who deliberately choose a hard and austere life, and pass their time chiefly in silent ascent of the steep Way of perfection. And in that it is said a *flock* of goats, we are taught the need of union in the Church and in Religious Orders, for as there is no beauty in the hair if it consist of but a few scanty threads, neither is there beauty in that Church or community which is rent asunder by schisms and disputes. And R. Ishaki goes at length into the various sacred uses to which both sheep and goats were put, to enforce the lesson that every act and faculty of a devout soul can be pressed into the service of GOD. The fleece and hairs were woven into curtains for the sanctuary, the flesh was offered in sacrifice, the horns were made into trumpets, the leg-bones were used for flutes, the entrails for stringing harps, the skin for covering drums; whereas no part of the dog could be applied to any holy purpose, just as the entire life of a sinner is displeasing to the LORD.

6 Thy teeth are as a flock of sheep which go up from the washing, whereof every one beareth twins, and there is not one barren among them.

These *teeth*, says Cassiodorus, are the words of the Church, pure and clean, firm and strong; *twins* in uttering the twofold law of love to GOD and to our neighbour. They are the Saints purified by regeneration, which bear *twins*, observes S. Epiphanius, because each soul goes down alone into the font of Baptism, and comes back joined by the HOLY GHOST, so that they two go over on dry ground. They are twins, in the double guard over soul and body, in the arms of righteousness on the right hand and on the left, in the promises of GOD for this life and for that which is to come. Cocceius, agreeing with some others in taking these verses to refer to a later period of the Church's history than the earlier panegyric does, bids us observe the absence of the epithet *even* or *shorn*, which occurs in the parallel passage in the fourth chapter, and thence argues that some inferiority of the Church of the latter days to that of the primitive age is implied, chiefly in the more relaxed discipline, which permits irregularities and errors which would have been sternly repressed in the era of martyrdom. Cassiodor. S. Epiphanius. 2 Kings ii. 8. Beda. Cocceius.

7 As a piece of a pomegranate are thy temples within thy locks.

Here too they have little to add. Aponius takes the cheeks here to be those who have fallen into post-baptismal sin, and who, washed anew with tears of repentance, beautify the face of the Church with the ruddy blush of shame. And they are compared to the *rind of the pomegranates* (Vulg.,) itself not ruddy, which encloses the bright colour, because their example restrains others from falling into like sin, albeit those others know nothing of the roughness and hardness of penance. Philo of Carpasia sees the mingled glow of faith and hope in every holy soul that serves the LORD, *besides that which lies hid within* (LXX.,) the numerous seeds of good works and devout thoughts, hidden within the rough rind of the fruit, but one day to be disclosed by the Bridegroom Who alone knows them now. Cardinal Hugo, explaining the words of the preachers of the Church, likened to pomegranates because of the firm rind and the many seeds, calls their purity and fervour the red and white which vie in the cheeks, and that *without the hidden things* (Vulg.,) meaning either that even their outer life is holy, with- Luc. Abb. Philo Carp. Hugo Card.

out taking into account the more precious inner devotion, or else that their venial sins of ignorance are not enough to mar their spiritual beauty. And these verses are repeated, observes S. Justus of Urgel, because GOD is foretelling, with the fruit of His twofold love, the conversion of both Jews and Gentiles, and describing the glory and merits of the Martyrs in these two portions of His Church.

S. Just. Org.

8 There are threescore queens, and fourscore concubines, and virgins without number.

That these several titles denote three classes of believing souls is the view of most commentators, although there is some diversity in their explanation. The *queens*, according to Origen, are the perfect souls; the *concubines*, wives of the same royal husband, but of inferior rank, and without right of succession to the throne for their children, are those which are progressing, and the *virgins* those only beginning the way of holiness, and still outside the King's palace, though within the royal city. S. Gregory Nyssen and others, not very dissimilarly, take the *queens* to be those who serve GOD for love; the *concubines*, those who do so through fear; the *virgins*, imperfect believers, looking nevertheless for salvation. And S. Justus of Urgel, accepting this view, explains the application of the titles, saying that the first are called *queens*, because they are not the servants of sin, for "where the Spirit of the LORD is, there is liberty;" the *concubines* are those who receive the seed of the Word of GOD, but bring forth carnal, not spiritual fruit; and the *virgins without number* are that great multitude which is always willing enough to listen to good and holy things, but is by no means equally ready to carry what it hears into action, and so has no spiritual offspring as yet. Philo gives a different interpretation, seeing in the *queens* those who led righteous lives before the Law and under it; in the *concubines*, those Gentiles who lived only by the law of nature, and fell into grievous sin of idolatry, but were at last united to CHRIST by conversion; and in the *virgins*, the general mass of Christian believers, not distinguished by any remarkable graces. And S. Epiphanius, agreeing that the *queens* denote the Patriarchs from whom CHRIST

Origen. Hom. 2.

S. Greg. Nyss. Theodoret. Tres Patr. Rupert.

S. Just. Org.

2 Cor. iii. 17.

Luc. Abb.

Philo Carp.

Cont. Hær. lib. iii.

descended, takes the *concubines* to be the heretical sects of Christendom, and the *virgins* to be the countless schools of heathen philosophy. Others will have it that the *queens* are the Doctors of the Church (with which agrees the curious comment of S. Epiphanius in his gloss on the Canticles, that the *threescore* queens are the souls of the *threescore* valiant men who guard Solomon's bed,) admitted to the bed of CHRIST by faith and knowledge, and bringing forth spiritual children for Him; while the *concubines* are those who preach CHRIST indeed, but not of sincerity, and only for temporal gain or popular applause. These too bring forth spiritual children, but are themselves alien from the crown of the everlasting kingdom. And the *virgins* are those souls regenerate in CHRIST, which have laid aside the old man and are renewed, but are not as yet fitted for the nuptials of the King, nor able to preach CHRIST at all. And now, before coming to the mystical explanation of the numbers, the remark of S. Augustine may be referred to, that the discrepancy between this passage and that wherein it is written that Solomon "had seven hundred wives, princesses, and three hundred concubines," gives evidence that the Song of songs dates at an early period of his reign, before the sins of his old age. [Cassiod. Beda. S.Ans.Laud.] [S. August. Cont. Faustum Manichæum.] [1 Kings xi. 3.]

The queens are *threescore*, say they, for these reasons, because they fulfil the ten moral precepts of the Law in the six days of mortal work, or because they govern their five senses by the teaching of the twelve Apostles. Another, and still quainter exposition, is that of Aponius, who sees here the union of the Churches of the Old and New Covenant, the Saints of each being *thirty*, because the number *ten*, denoting fulfilment of GOD's commandments, was multiplied thrice before the coming of CHRIST, by the law of nature, the ordinance of circumcision given to Abraham, and the Law of Moses; while after the preaching of the Gospel this same number ten is found repeated in the baptized, the penitent, and the Martyrs. The concubines are *fourscore*, says Theodoret, because they differ from the queens in their motive for serving GOD. For whereas the queens fulfil GOD's commandments during the six working days, looking to the seventh, which is rest, the concubines think of the eighth day, that awful Day of Judgment, the first of the new creation, and are [Cassiod. Theodoret.] [Luc. Abb.] [Theodoret.]

obedient, only because they fear condemnation.¹ Much less happy than this, because abandoning the recognised mystical meaning of the number eight—the new birth of creation, one more than the seven days of the week, whence the octagonal form of mediæval fonts—is the interpretation which sees here worldly compliance with GOD's Law, eight being supposed to designate the world, ruled by four seasons in its four quarters. Better than this, though not working clearly out, is that other suggestion that here are intended souls striving by obedience to obtain even the smallest blessing of some one of those eight beatitudes which are all granted to the perfect. The virgins are *without number*, because they have not yet been entered on the roll of the elect. For if they were so entered, their number would be known, as the Apostle saith, "The LORD knoweth them that are His;" and as the LORD Himself saith, " I know whom I have chosen." But if they were on the other muster-roll, that of Babylon, their number would be known too, and therefore their lot is not yet fixed, till they hear that saying, " Choose ye this day whom ye will serve," and elect between the LORD and Baal.

marginalia: Cassiod.; Hugo Card.; Luc. Abb. S. Greg. M.; 2 Tim. ii. 19.; S. John xiii. 18.; Guilielmus.; Josh. xxiv. 15; 1 Kings xviii. 21.

9 My dove, my undefiled is but one; she is the only one of her mother, she is the choice one of her that bare her. The daughters saw her, and blessed her; yea, the queens and the concubines, and they praised her.

That is, notes Cassiodorus, there is but one Catholic Church diffused throughout the world, which, though consisting of queens and virgins, has also concubines in it, that is, such as are Christians or teachers in name only. The Church is *one*, because she does not admit of rending and schism, but as there is " One GOD, one faith, one baptism," so there is one Church Universal, which is also rightly called a *dove*, because she is betrothed and hallowed to CHRIST by the dowry of the HOLY SPIRIT, Who appeared in the form of a dove.

marginalia: Cassiod.; Eph. iv. 5.

---

¹ This is a very forcible way of putting that view which was universally held by theologians till the lax days of the sixteenth century, that mere servile dread of hell is no true motive to holiness, and is of the nature of sin.

The Church is *one* before the Law, under the Law, and under grace. *One*, because created for the "one thing needful," that one thing which she hath desired of the LORD; *one*, because the Bride of one Husband. *The only one of her mother.* That is, as some have it, the sole representative on earth of the Heavenly Jerusalem, the Mother of us all; or, as others say, the one true lineal successor of that primitive Apostolic Church from which all local Churches spring. Or, again, they take it of the Synagogue, which has never had any other spiritual offspring than Christianity. A yet deeper view than any of these interprets the *mother* to be divine grace, which bore the Church in the font of regeneration, through the means of Incarnate Wisdom. One Latin Father will have it that the pure and spotless Humanity of CHRIST is here intended, the only offspring of His Virgin Mother, the choice, elect One of His mother the Synagogue, elect as the One Sacrifice, the One Mediator between GOD and man. Spoken of the holy soul, the verse tells of her perfect and steadfast union with GOD, her advance in sanctification of the Spirit, her election from amongst the daughters, hirelings, and servants, to a share, through grace, in the throne of Godhead itself. And she is *one*, because endowed with the spirit of peace and unity, single in heart, and not made up of warring and dissonant elements, but simple, harmonious, and at rest. It is true of Our Lady, notes Psellus, purer than cherubim and seraphim, the only one of earthly Saints who is the true likeness of the Heavenly Jerusalem, the one elect daughter of her mother the ancient Church, of Patriarchs, Kings, and Prophets, the *only* one, for neither before nor since was there, nor can there be any such; His *dove*, because full of grace; *elect*, because not merely saved, but the bringer-forth of salvation.

The daughters saw her and blessed her. In this collocation we have at once the fulfilment of her own prophecy, "For, behold, from henceforth all generations shall call me blessed." But applying the words to the Church, Philo says very well: By *the daughters of Sion* (LXX.) those holy men of old, the souls of the Patriarchs and all the Prophets, are intended who beheld afar off this Bride as yet to come in the Bridegroom Who was to be born, and the Apostles by their preaching united her to the Heavenly Bridegroom.

Side notes: Hugo Card. S. Luke x. 42. Ps. xxvii. 4. Philo Carp. Cassiod. S. Ans. Laud. Luc. Abb. Philo Carp. S. Greg. M. Luc. Abb. Tres Patr. S. Ambros. Psellus. Rupert. S. Luke i. 48. Philo Carp.

And this He Himself plainly declares, when He teaches that they were mindful and thankful for so great a blessing, saying, "Many prophets and righteous men have desired to see those things which ye see, and have not seen them; and to hear those things which ye hear, and have not heard them." And the words may also be applied to Churches and any faithful souls, which look with longing at that Church as they see her triumphing in this mortal life, and are thereby lifted up daily more and more from this militant and pilgrim state unto life everlasting. *And blessed her.* The Vulgate reads, *called her most blessed.* Blessed in her spiritual wealth, more blessed in her numerous children, *most blessed* in the bridal and embraces of the Bridegroom. And note that it is said that the daughters *saw* her and blessed her, whereas it is said of the queens and concubines that they *praised* her, without adding that they saw her. It is because " the King's daughter is all glorious within," and only those holy souls which are truly GOD's children can see that inner beauty, since they look for the Kingdom of GOD, while "the eyes of a fool are in the ends of the earth." The queens and concubines, types now of the outer world, do not *bless* the Church, for they have no desire for her prosperity, but they are compelled, in their own despite, to *praise* her, to extol the valour of her Martyrs and the purity of her Virgins. Aponius, taking the words of CHRIST's Humanity, explains that the heavenly host, citizens of Jerusalem on high, when they saw that holy Body, united to the FATHER's love, born upon earth, wrapped in swaddling clothes, and yet resplendent with glorious majesty, called Him most blessed, bursting out with their song, " Glory to GOD in the highest." Most blessed, truly, for only in that One Person did all the Beatitudes meet, one of which alone is enough to make others blessed in their degree.

10 Who is she that looketh forth as the morning, fair as the moon, clear as the sun, and terrible as an army with banners?

Here is set forth for us the gradual progress of the Church or of the holy soul, as it goes on in holiness, advancing to the perfect day. Honorius of Autun, recognizing the identity of the Church of GOD through all the phases of its existence, tells us that the *morning* signifies the Patriarchal dispensation; the *moon* the Mosaic Law, drawing its light from the unseen sun, and gradually crescent to the full, while the *sun* denotes the full light of the Gospel revelation. Or, if the words be limited to the Christian Church, they may be taken of its small beginnings in Judea, when it was hidden from the world at large, and then was fair as the moon, indeed, but pale with the light of suffering, terror, and martyrdom during the Ten Persecutions, till under Constantine it became like the sun, visible in faith and glory through the world, and *terrible as an army*, because then began its active career against heresy and Paganism, which it had combated before only with the passive weapons of endurance. Another view, but partially different from this one, is accepted by several Fathers, who put these words into the mouth of the repentant Synagogue at the end of the world, or else into that of the Angels who attend the Bridegroom. The Church *looketh forth as the morning*, in passing from the clouds of darkness, and beginning to shine with the light of truth; she is *fair as the moon* in this life, borrowing all her brightness from the Sun of Righteousness, and crescent or waning according as she is in prosperity or adversity; *clear as the sun*, in the world to come, when radiant with the open vision of her Creator. And the words may be taken not only of the Church Universal at three epochs of her existence, but of the three classes of beginners, who are leaving their sins behind and making their first steps towards light; of progressing Christians, setting a good example to sinners, like the *moon* shining in the night; and of Saints, who serve as patterns even for the good, and are therefore like the *sun*, shining in broad day. And S. Bernard, limiting the reference further to the Religious Life, sees here the three principal virtues which befit a community; humility, which is the *dawn* or *morning*, driving away the darkness and heralding the light, because it is the line of distinction between the righteous and the sinner; chastity, denoted by the *moon*, and charity, which resembles the *sun*, and makes the Common Life the terror of evil spirits.

Corn. à Lap.

Cassiodor.
Theodoret.

S. Ambros.
Hexaëm.
iv. 8.

Philo Carp.

S. Greg. M.

S. Bernard.
Serm. 60,
ex parvis.

Spoken of the faithful soul during the progress of her sanctification, Philo notes that she is fitly compared to the dawn, because as the dawn brings a slight chill with it, and the arising of the light of heaven, so too every faithful soul and spouse that turns to righteousness from an evil life, begins to contemplate the first rays of the light of Salvation, and to feel the restful lowering of the heat of sin by that cold which checks it. And there are some, moreover, who when carefully pondering what punishments and grievous torments are prepared for the ungodly, and those everlasting, begin to examine their lives and habits strictly, and so minutely to review themselves, and all their words and deeds, as to cast away at once the works of darkness and put on the armour of light, making themselves radiant with acts of righteousness and holiness, and thus are said to arise as the dawn from the darkness. Not as He arises, Who is the Dayspring from on high, for of Him it is written, "He shall be as the light of the morning, when the sun ariseth, even a morning without clouds." She has to make her way slowly and painfully through the mists of error and clouds of temptation, and her first turning to GOD will appear sombre and chill enough, for it has been usually true of GOD's greatest Saints that a time of struggle and comparative darkness preceded their fuller knowledge of Him, that—

> morning fair,
> Comes forth with pilgrim steps in amice grey.

But, as the advancing sun turns the black clouds into purple, and the white into gold, so the very trials and difficulties of the soul become, through GOD's grace, new beauties, royal apparel for her, His Bride.

Fair as the moon is she too, because whatever divine light she possesses she receives from the Sun of Righteousness, steadfast and divine, what time she places herself meekly before Him; and, like the moon, she now seems to decrease and wane through temptation and sufferings, and again to become new and crescent when her cruel enemies have been routed. Or else because she will one day fail altogether in bodily death, and at the last arise again with all the righteous to everlasting glory, never more to pass through phases of change, but to abide immortal and most blessed. Thus the second comparison exhibits progress, but two things are yet lacking, the steadfastness which knows no change, the light which is not merely clear, but warm and quickening. Faith has broken through the clouds of night; Hope, even in the night of this world, yields a calm radiance, telling of something more glo- *Dion. Carth.* rious and genial, teaching the world what must be that splendour of which she is but the faint shadow:

> Soon as the evening shades prevail,   Addison,
> The moon takes up the wondrous tale,   The Hymn,
> And nightly to the listening earth   *The spacious*
> Repeats the story of her birth.   *firmament.*

And S. Gregory dilates on this theme as follows: The *S. Greg. M.* moon, as she illuminates the earth, shows to clouded eyes the path by which man should go. So the soul which parts the clouds, and puts itself forth to holy activity, sheds light on darkened eyes while setting its neighbours an example of good work. For while sinners see any good thing done and set themselves to do the same, they are like wanderers in the night returning to the road by the light of the moon. There is another *Dion. Carth.* cause of likeness too, for if the moon suffer aught to come between her and the sun, she is straightway eclipsed and darkened. Last comes that perfect like- *Philo Carp.* ness to CHRIST Himself, attained by conformity to His Passion and His will, and perfect trust looking to Him alone, which make the soul, now flooded with divine light, and glowing with the fervour of the SPIRIT, *clear as the sun.* Then, too, as it is written of the wild beasts, "The lions roaring after their prey, do seek *Ps. civ. 21.* their meat from GOD: the sun ariseth, and they get them away together, and lay them down in their dens;" so when the glory of holiness is visible in any Christian soul, and it arises to resist the devil, he must needs flee, for then she is *terrible as an army with banners,* and that because she comes not to the battle alone, but with the examples and miracles of the Saints, and the alliance of the Angels, on her side, so that she may say with the Prophet to all timid wa- verers: "Fear not, for they that be with us are more *2 Kings vi.* than they that be with them." Rupert explains the *Rupert.* verse of the Mother of GOD, saying, "When thou wast born, O Blessed Virgin, then the true Dawn arose on us, the Dawn which heralds the eternal Day; for as each day's dawn is the end of the past night and the beginning of the following day, so thy nativity, of the seed of Abraham, from the illustrious race of David, to whom GOD made with an oath the promise of blessing, was the end of sorrows, and the beginning of consolation, the end of sadness and the beginning of our joy. Then we pass from dawn to morn. For when the HOLY GHOST came upon thee, and thou, a Virgin, didst conceive a Son, and bring Him forth in Virgin-birth, then, and thenceforward thou wast fair with divine fairness; *fair*, I say, not in any wise, but *as the moon;* for as the moon shines and illuminates with light which is not her own, but derived from the sun, so thou, O most blessed one, hast not of thyself, that thou art so bright, but of grace divine, that thou art full of grace. Lastly, we pass from the moon to the sun. For when thou wast taken up out of this world, and translated to the heavenly hall, then, and thenceforward thou wast *elect as the sun*, elect, I say, for us, for as we adore and worship the SON of GOD, sprung from thee, the True Sun, the eternal Sun, as Very GOD; so we honour and venerate thee, as the Mother of Very GOD, knowing that all honour paid to the Mother, doubtless redounds to the honour of the Son."

Keble.

What glory thou above hast won,
By special grace of thy dear Son,
We see not yet, nor dare espy
Thy crownèd form with open eye:
Rather beside the manger meek,
Thee bending with veiled brow we seek,
Or where the Angel in the thrice great Name
Hailed thee, and JESUS to thy bosom came.

Henceforth, Whom thousand worlds adore,
He calls thee Mother evermore;
Angel nor Saint His face may see
Apart from what He took of thee;
How may we choose but name thy name,
Echoing below their high acclaim,
In holy creeds? since earthly song and prayer
Must keep faint time to the dread anthem there.

And she is *terrible as an army with banners.* How an *army*, one of the sweetest of English poets tells us in his quaint anagram of the name *Mary*,

George Herbert.

How well her name an *army* doth present,
In whom the LORD of Hosts did pitch His tent!

With banners; since where the King's pavilion is, there will be the royal standard. And accordingly S. Ambrose says:

> The LORD a Maiden's womb doth fill,
> But keeps her stainless Maiden still,
> The banners there of virtue shine,
> Where GOD is present in His shrine.

S. Ambros. The Hymn, Veni, Redemptor Gentium.

Aponius, continuing his reference to CHRIST'S Humanity, says that JESUS came as the *dawning* after the darkness of ignorance to His Baptism in Jordan, that He advanced as the *moon* by His miraculous works, and shone as the *Sun* after His Resurrection. And He will appear on the Judgment Day to the righteous with the calm beauty of the moon, to the Angels in the fuller glory of Divine majesty, whilst to sinners, doomed to eternal fires, He will be *terrible as an army with banners*.

Luc. Abb.

11 I went down into the garden of nuts to see the fruits of the valley, and to see whether the vine flourished, and the pomegranates budded.

There is some variance here as to the speaker. The Targum, followed by the great majority of the Fathers, ascribes the words to the Bridegroom; while a small minority, agreeing with some later critics, puts them into the mouth of the Bride. Taking the former view, and interpreting, as several have done, the *garden of nuts* to be the Synagogue, Philo says, Behold, the Heavenly Bridegroom first *went down* into the Synagogue of the Jews, to the priests and Scribes, by the Manhood which He took on Him of their seed, according to the oath and promise which He had sworn to Abraham and David. By the *garden of nuts* Jerusalem and the priesthood are rightly signified. For the rod of Aaron held the dignity of royal priesthood. And the nut is an apt symbol of the Mosaic Law, for as the nut-tree has bitter and trifoliated leaves, and produces its fruit covered with an exceedingly bitter rind called the hull, and a yet harder dry shell, within which is contained a pleasant kernel divided fourwise by a wooden cartilage, or a thin membrane while it is green; so that Law, written by the finger of GOD, seemed to consist of those carnal sacrifices and ceremonies, as the nut-tree with its bitter leaves, though mystically signifying the Triune GOD. And the Law was covered over with a meaning hard to be understood, and mys-

Philo Carp.

S. Epiphanius.

Philo Carp.

tical, like a harsh rind, and yet held veiled within it that sweetest and most wholesome fruit CHRIST JESUS Himself, Who should come down from heaven, to be made openly known through the four quarters of the globe by the fourfold sense of the Gospel, and yet only for those who could take Him fitly and reverently out of that shell, and eat Him in the holiest manner. Down to this garden came the Bridegroom *to look into the plants of the torrent* (LXX.)[1] that is, at the time appointed for His death (of which I hold that David was thinking when he said, "He shall drink of the torrent in the way;" and again, "Our soul had passed through the torrent," that is, had endured most cruel scourges, painful tortures, and death,) *to see if* the nut itself and *the vine flourished.* O wondrous mercy of GOD! O unspeakable goodness! It was not enough for Thee to have given the Law, to have sent so many eminent Prophets and Kings, famous in learning and holiness, but Thou wouldest come Thyself to see and act for Thy garden of nuts and Thy vineyard, and that in the *plants of the torrent,* that is, in the mortality and death of our flesh which Thou didst take, that Thou mightest gather some fruit thence. But, alas, an ungrateful and wretched Hebrew people, after slaying the servants and messengers of the LORD's vineyard, dared to cast the heir, His Only SON, shamefully out of the vineyard (that is, Jerusalem and the Synagogue,) and to slay Him most cruelly. So when He came first to the garden of nuts He gathered no fruit there, but only thorns; wherefore He passed to the Gentiles, for whom He made ready faithful Churches for Himself, and let out His vineyard to them, having ruined and destroyed those former vinedressers whom He had graciously called out of Egypt. He found that the *vine* did not *flourish* with them, for He Himself saith, "He looked that it should bring forth grapes, and it brought forth wild grapes." Nor had *the pomegranates budded,* but now they blossom in the Christian Church, where the

Ps. cx. 7.
Ps. cxxiv. 3, LXX.

Isa. v. 2.

---

[1] So too the Arabic version. The meaning is the same as the A.V., because commonly in the Semitic languages, and notably in Arabic, the same word stands for "valley" and "river," or rather "watercourse," a deep cleft in the hills, dry in summer, and a rapid stream in winter. The second of these meanings has left its mark in Spanish, where the Arabic *wady* enters into the names of several rivers, as Guadiana, Guadalquivir, Guadalavier.

multitudes of the people of GOD lie enclosed as pure white seeds in the mystical body, washed and ruddy with the Blood of JESUS CHRIST, and full of the goodness of divine grace and the juice given by the heavenly SPIRIT; and with these fruits the Spouse gives holy gladness daily to the Bridegroom. Aponius varies somewhat from the latter portion of this exposition of Philo, taking the valley to be this world, the *fruits* of the valley to be the tears of the righteous, shed because of their exile and prison, and for the sins of men, and the visit as intended to see whether in Israel the *vine* of devout thought, leading to repentance, *flourished*, whether the *pomegranates*, the mystical teaching of the Prophets, *budded*, in producing other Saints besides that one Baptist Forerunner. Luc. Abb.

They also explain the *garden of nuts* to be that garden inclosed of which we have already heard, the hallowed womb of the Virgin Mother, into which the LORD went down, she who kept her sweet purity sheltered in firm resolve, where the Bridegroom found *fruits of the valley* in her lovely humility, and saw that vine which bore Him, the True Vine, flourishing in beauty, as it conceived Him, and the pomegranates of her charity to all men, as they were budding forth. Honorius. Alanus. Hugo Card.

A further sense for the *pomegranates* is suggested by the fact that this fruit was embroidered on the hem of the High Priest's robe, thus typifying the inferior priests or Levites, who derived their office from him. And therefore the words will here denote the visitation of the Christian Church, to see whether the prelates and clergy, vicars of the One High Priest, are fulfilling their duties, and bringing forth fruits to GOD. Lyranus. Exod. xxviii. 33.

And, applying the words to CHRIST's visitation of souls, S. Gregory tells us that the *garden of nuts* signifies the hearts of the Saints, who retain divine wisdom in their bodies, like a kernel in a fruit-shell, for there are many in the Church, constantly busied in the study of Holy Writ, tasting how sweet the LORD is, desiring to taste Him more, chewing the cud of sacred joy in their heart, and thereby growing ever stronger; and yet to those without, who know them not, they seem valueless, because that sweet food which they bear within them is unknown. But why is He said to come to the garden of nuts, not to see *nuts* but *apples?* (*poma*, Vulg.) Because He comes first to His perfect Saints, that He may visit the weaker S. Greg. M.

ones through their ministry, and so be manifested to them.

The *vines flourish* when children are brought up in the Church in faith, and are trained to a holy life as to firmness of fruit. The *pomegranates bud* when the perfect edify their neighbours by their example, and invite them to new and holy conversation by preaching and the exhibition of good works. Or, as another takes it, the *vines flourish* when local Churches and congregations are healthy and abundant in holy meditations and prayers, the *pomegranates bud* when prelates and contemplative Religious, who should be ruddiest with charity and zeal, give forth beauty and fragrance to adorn the Church. Cassiodorus and Beda, albeit ascribing the verse to the Bride, vary little from the interpretation of S. Gregory, representing her as watching the progress of the various classes of Saints in this life. Happier than this is the explanation of S. Athanasius, followed by S. Justus of Urgel, that the garden of nuts is Holy Scripture, which exhibits one thing in the outer letter or rind, and another in the inner spirit or kernel; though the latter agrees with the authors already cited in seeing lowly Saints figured in the *fruits of the valley*, and Martyrs in the pruned vines and ruddy pomegranates. What the especial nut is which the Bride seeks there S. Augustine will tell us: The nut has three substances united in itself, the hull, the shell, and the kernel. In the hull the flesh, in the shell the bones, in the kernel the inner soul, have their types. The hull of the nut denotes the flesh of the SAVIOUR, which had in itself the harshness and roughness of the Passion. The kernel denotes the inner sweetness of His Godhead, which made the covenant with us, and gives us the help of light.[1] The shell signifies the transverse wood of the Cross, which did not separate that which was within from that without, but by the interposition of its mediating wood allied earthly things and heavenly, as the blessed Apostle saith, "Having made peace by the Blood of His Cross, by Him to reconcile all things to Himself, by Him, whether they be things in earth or things in heaven." Similarly, with his wonderful knowledge of Scripture and of theology, sings Adam:

---

[1] The Saint is referring to the nut-oil, anciently used for lamps.

> Nux est CHRISTUS, cortex nucis
> Circa carnem pœna crucis,
> Testa corpus osseum,
> Carne tecta Deitas
> Et CHRISTI suavitas
> Signatur per nucleum.
>
> Adam. Vict.
The Sequence,
Splendor Patris et figura.
>
> CHRIST the nut, the hull His Passion
> Closing round His human fashion,
>   And His bones and frame the shell:
> Hid in flesh, Divine completeness
> And CHRIST JESUS' perfect sweetness,
>   In the kernel mark ye well.

Seeking Him, then, in the time of His utter humiliation, when He was in truth the *fruit of the valley*, she desires to know if that True *Vine* can possibly be *flourishing* after the beast of the field and the wild boar have done their worst upon it, if the ruddy *pomegranate* of the Passion shows any promise of succeeding produce. So too, each soul has to go down into the garden of its own heart, where the LORD is hidden in the shell of reticent affection, to see if the vine-branch He has planted be thriving, if the graces which spring from His Passion are showing signs of spiritual fruit to come. And she need be at no loss what to do with these fruits and flowers when she finds them. She will say, as once said a faithful Bride of CHRIST, "And now, O only Beloved of my soul, I offer Thee my heart, as a blooming rose, whose beauty may daily attract Thine eyes, and its fragrance delight Thy Heart. And I also offer Thee my heart, that Thou mayest use it as a cup, to drink Thine own sweetness with all Thou hast done to-day for me. Further, I offer Thee my heart, as a pomegranate of choice flavour, fit for Thy royal banquet, that eating it, Thou mayest so take it unto Thyself, that it may rejoice in feeling itself thenceforth within Thee." [S. Mechthildis Revel. iii. 6.]

12 Or ever I was aware, my soul made me [*like*] the chariots of Ammi-nadib.[1]

The LXX. and Vulgate, in the first clause, read correctly, with the margin of A. V., *I knew not.* The

---

[1] The italic *like*, unnecessarily inserted after "me" in the A. V., is superfluous and misleading, and is therefore bracketed.

ancient versions, for the most part, oscillate in the second clause between the rendering of the A. V., as given above, and its marginal reading: *My soul set me on the chariots of my willing* [or *princely*] *people.* Symmachus and the Vulgate, however, read *My soul troubled me,* [or, *was perplexed*] *because of the chariots,* &c. This most difficult verse has given rise to a great variety of interpretations, and there is no more agreement as to the speaker, whether it be Solomon, the Bride, or one of the queens and concubines acting as mouthpiece to the rest. The latest view of modern critics is that the words are an exclamation of wonder at the dazzling beauty of the Bride. She had been compared, a little before, to an *army with banners,* and now the speaker declares that she is stately and ornate as the war-chariot of the king, so that to be near her is like being set upon it. And it is easy to see the mystical force of such an interpretation, if we put the speech into the mouth of the Gentile world, noting the progress of the Church. It had already recognized her beauty, as Solomon's *litter* (iii. 9, 10,) in her peaceful holiness and passive endurance of suffering, saying, "See how these Christians love one another." Now it was to see her as the *war-chariot* of the Great King, to confess the resistless might of her conquering advance, and to exclaim, in the words of Elisha, echoed later by Joash, "My father, my father, the chariot of Israel, and the horsemen thereof." And this comes very near to the explanation of several Fathers, who ascribe the verse to the Synagogue. Thus Cassiodorus comments: *I knew not,* O Bride of CHRIST, that such grace and such gifts of spiritual power had been given thee by thy Bridegroom, and I am troubled with great anxiety of soul because of this sudden preaching of the Gospel. For I knew that the Law and the Prophets were divinely given, and therefore when all of a sudden I saw the Gospel preached, *I was troubled because of the chariots of Amminadab.* Amminadab was great grandson of Judah, through whom CHRIST's genealogy is derived. And the name is interpreted "The willing one of my people," and consequently denotes CHRIST, Who was the willing One of His people, because, being GOD, He voluntarily was made Man, and being Creator and Maker of the world, of His loving-kindness alone He was made a part of His people. And the sense is this: I am troubled because of the sudden preaching of the Gospel, which has suddenly sped through the whole world like a very swift chariot. Rupert dwells on the phrase, *My soul troubled me*, as meaning something different from *I was troubled*, and explains it that the Chief Priests, Scribes, and Pharisees, who were the *soul* of the Jewish people, guiding them in their religious and social matters, did nothing but perplex and trouble them, instead of giving them wise counsel, when the preaching of the Gospel began. The Latin Fathers also lay stress on the Vulgate word here used for chariots, *quadrigas*, or four-horse cars, and interpret it for the most part as mystically referring to the Four Gospels; though Rupert gives the further explanation that the four principal mysteries of the Gospel itself, the Incarnation, Passion, Resurrection, and Ascension, are indicated. Of this chariot CHRIST Himself is the Charioteer, and He is most fitly designated, as the Abbat of Deutz continues, by the name of Amminadab, because it was from that descendant of Judah that the royal and priestly lines were both derived, inasmuch as his daughter Elisheba was wife of Aaron, and mother of Nadab, Abihu, Eleazar, and Ithamar, from whom all the High Priests were sprung, while Amminadab himself was ancestor in the direct line of David, and thereby of Him Who is King of Israel and a High Priest for ever after the order of Melchizedek. There is also an ancient Jewish tradition that when the Israelites reached the Red Sea, all the tribes hung back, till Amminadab, prince of the house of Judah, seizing his standard, advanced boldly between the walls of water, and won thereby the immediate honour of leading the vanguard of the march, and the later one of the kingdom for his posterity. It is needless to dwell on the type this yields of CHRIST as the Leader and Standard-bearer of His people in their pilgrimage and warfare. Cassiodor.
S. Greg. M.
Beda.

Rupert.

Dion. Carth.

De Lyrâ, also ascribing the verse to the Synagogue, explains it very differently. He interprets Amminadab to mean *My ruling people*, and thus paraphrases: *I knew not* GOD's LAW, but was ignorant and as a beast before Him. My own self-will led me into the sin of idolatry, and thereupon I was punished by the Captivity, which made me like the mere chariot of the conquering Assyrians and Babylonians, who became my ruling people, with power to drive me whither- Lyranus.

soever they pleased. Applied to the devout soul, the earliest interpretation we meet is closely akin to one already given; saying that every faithful soul is borne by the four steeds of the Four Gospels, swift and strong, throughout the world, as they are driven by the HOLY SPIRIT. And this in order that the Bride may be happily borne in this chariot of fire, which she has ascended in faith, to heaven itself. It is to be carefully noted, too, that the Bride and faithful souls are not merely said to be set on the chariots, but that the Church herself is *made* these chariots, that she may understand herself to be the holy car whereby multitudes are to be borne to their country. For as they who are conveyed in chariots, cars, and carts are lifted up above the inconveniences of the road, such as mire, ruts, stones, and the like, and are often quite free from them, so Christians, borne in the heavenly chariot of faith, and cherished in the holy bosom of their loving mother the Church, are preserved safely for the kingdom of heaven. And thus she is made the chariot of the Prince of the people, that she may bear Him, by means of her preachers, into the hearts of men. He so deals with her when she has gone down from the heights of mystic contemplation into the garden of active work, to see if she could find Him in the lives and hearts of His people, but failing to see Him there, she says, *I knew not*, and her zeal at once hurries her into missionary toils. If the soul be His chariot, comments S. Ambrose, beware lest the flesh be the horse, but let vigour of mind be the driver, to guide and check the flesh and its passions, like steeds, with the reins of wisdom. But, as he says more forcibly in another place, CHRIST, the true Amminadab, drives the soul of the righteous like a chariot, and guides it from His seat with the reins of the Word, lest it should be hurried down the steep by the violence of untamed steeds. For its four passions are its horses, anger, desire, pleasure, and fear, and when these run away, the soul, as she begins to be hurried along, does not know herself. There is another interpretation, akin to that of De Lyrâ, explaining Amminadab as the prince of this world, oppressing the Church and enslaving her, returning evil for good, and interfering with the freedom of her operations. Or again, the soul says, *I knew not*, I was ignorant and blind, and so I became the mere chariot of my own unrestrained will, which hurried me away at its pleasure, until GOD called me to return.

The view which takes the Bridegroom as the speaker has the authority of the Chaldee paraphrase on its side, which interprets the verse of GOD promising to change His dealings with His people, now repentant, and instead of chastening them further, to set them as on the chariot of a king. Very few Christian expositors have followed in this track, and the only noteworthy comment is far-fetched and strained. The evil spirits, says Aponius, as created by GOD to test the endurance of the Saints, are, in a sense, His people. They are His *free-willing* people, because they have refused His service, and have chosen to follow their own wicked devices. These spirits sit like drivers on the necks of sinners, forcing them to accomplish crimes. And they made Pilate, Herod, Caiaphas, and their companions, *chariots* on which CHRIST was carried to His death with shouts of "Crucify Him, crucify Him," wherefore He was *troubled*, as He Himself has said, "My soul is exceeding sorrowful, even unto death." And He begins the sentence by protesting His innocence, saying, *I knew not*, for in truth He knew no sin.

<small>Targum.</small>

<small>Luc. Abb.</small>

<small>S. Mat. xxvi. 38.</small>
<small>S. Just. Org.</small>

13 Return, return, O Shulamite; return, return, that we may look upon thee. What will ye see in the Shulamite? As it were the company of two armies.

The first question to be settled here is the meaning of the name *Shulamite*. One literalist view is that it is a local appellation from a supposed place *Shulem*, formed by the same analogy as Shunammite from Shunem. And in fact the LXX. does read *Sunamitis*, and the Vulgate did read it, so that a reference to Abishag has been seen here by some ancient writers, and Abishag herself by some modern ones. Another opinion is that the name is strictly a proper one, the personal name of the Bride, akin, perhaps, to *Shelomith*, the feminine form of the name Solomon. And this brings us closer to the mystical view, which takes the word as an adjective, and explains it variously as "belonging to Solomon," or "daughter of Salem," or "perfect;" or again, most satisfactorily, as "Peaceful," which last is supported by the authority of Aquila, who

<small>S. Just. Org. Rupert. Dion. Carth.</small>

<small>Smith's Dict.</small>

<small>Rosenmüller.</small>

translates it εἰρηνεύουσα. One other suggested meaning is that of Symmachus, who, deriving the epithet from שָׁלַל, *shalal, spoliavit,* views it as equivalent to "plundered," or "captive," ἐσκυλευμένη. Either of these last-given meanings will suit the Synagogue, to which the Targum applies the verse, paraphrasing thus: "*Return* to Me, O congregation of Israel, *return* to Jerusalem, *return* to the House of My Law, *return* to receive prophecy from the Prophets who prophesy in the Name of the Word of the LORD. Israel heard and obeyed the call, notes De Lyrâ, and returned at four several times after the Captivity; first, under Zorobabel and Ezra, in the reign of Cyrus; secondly, in the next migration headed by Ezra in the seventh year of Artaxerxes; thirdly, under Nehemiah; and, fourthly, when Judas Maccabeus cleansed and restored the profaned sanctuary. The *We,* then, Who desire to look upon the Shulamite, and therefore call her back, may best be taken, as many of the Fathers do take it, of the Most HOLY TRINITY, calling the wandering Church, Jewish or Christian, or the soul which has gone astray, back to its true home, to the presence of the Divine Countenance. It is, notes Rupert, the Voice of Amminadab Himself as He sits upon His chariot, saying, Thou, *O Shulamite,* that is, captive or depised, thou, O faith, O dignity of the true Priesthood (wellnigh given up to oblivion through carnal ceremonies, so that the Synagogue knows not, and thinks not that her father Abraham was justified by thee, and not by the Law, as it is written, "Abraham believed GOD, and it was counted unto him for righteousness,") *return,* and again I say, *return,* and a third time I say, *return,* and a fourth time I say, *return,* one call for each horse of My chariot. For I was born and I suffered to this end, that thou mightest return, and rise again, and ascend into heaven to Me, and therefore till thou dost return I cease not My calling upon thee.

Aponius, closely agreeing with this view, adds that our merciful LORD calls the Synagogue daily to repentance by the four voices of the four Gospels, and that, in order that *We may look on thee,* that the Image of GOD may be reflected in thee, as in a mirror, when thou art cleansed by penitence and Baptism, and confessest the Trinity. *Return* to the true faith, *return* to brotherly peace, *return* to acknowledgment of thy Redeemer, *return* to perfection in good works. *Return*, too, from the four quarters of the world, whither thou hast been scattered, for thy sins, among the Gentiles. And the call will continue till that happier cry is raised, [S. Greg. M. Dion. Carth.]

> Rise, Sion, rise, and looking forth,
> Behold thy children round thee,
> From east and west, and south and north,
> Thy scattered sons have found thee!
> And in thy bosom CHRIST adore,
> For ever and for evermore!

[S. John Dam. *Golden Canon*, Ode viii.]

There is less beauty and force in the common interpretation, which ascribes the words to the Christian Church, typified by the daughters of Jerusalem, and makes her, not GOD, address the Synagogue. *That we may look on thee*, standing to do penance for thy sins, and acknowledging thy crime in slaying and crucifying thy King, as one will have it; that we may see thy beauty and purity, as others, more gently, interpret. Spoken of the soul, the words may be variously taken. If addressed to a perfect one, then it may be the voice of GOD calling the preacher back from peaceful contemplation to the harder task of converting sinners, promising His aid in all time of weakness, but not the less summoning him to descend from the Mount of Transfiguration to the plain of the demoniac, or it may be a cry for help from weaker Christians, asking to be taught how to bridle the four passions of their souls, for which reason they call four times. *Return*, that we may be cleansed with thy purity, *return*, that we may be kindled with thy fire, *return*, that we may be illuminated with thy light, *return*, that we may be perfumed with thy fragrance. [Cassiodor. Beda. S. Greg. M. S.Ans.Laud.] [S. Greg. M.] [Cassiodor. Beda.] [Theodoret.] [Tres Patr.] [Thom. Verc.]

If, on the other hand, it be an erring soul which GOD is recalling to the right way; then, as S. Ambrose teaches, He saith well, as a driver to his chariot, *Return, O Shulamite*, that is, Peaceful, for the soul which is peaceful turns herself quickly, and corrects herself, even though she sinned before, and CHRIST all the more readily ascends, and vouchsafes to guide her, as is said to Him, "Ride upon Thine horses, and Thy chariots were salvation." And His reason for four times calling back the soul on which He looks, is perhaps that it may not abide in the habit of sin, nor in consciousness of offences, nor yet in the lukewarmness and sloth of ingratitude, nor in [S. Ambros. de Isaac. 8.] [Hab. iii. 8.] [S. Bernard. Serm. 3, super *Missus*.]

the blindness of conceit. *Return*, He says, first from vain joy; secondly, from useless sorrow; thirdly, from empty glory; fourthly, from hidden pride. The LORD, says one of the profoundest of mystical writers, four times calls her to return, as though He would say, Return from what is Mine, because it is wonderful; return from thine own, for it is evil; return from thyself, because all flesh is grass; return to Me, for I am the Supreme Good. Thou canst not see Me unless We first look upon thee. Thou hast some spot upon thy face, thou art foul, and bearest another image than Mine, cleanse it, therefore, *that We may look on thee.* Return, as a handmaid to her master, as an erring daughter to her father, as a patient to her physician, as a sinful wife to her husband. Return through infusion of divine grace, through direction of thy free-will to faith and love for GOD, of that same free-will to hatred of sin, and through the expulsion and remission of sin itself. Return too, by the four stages of true repentance, knowledge of sin, sorrow for it, confession, and satisfaction. Or, as S. Ambrose once explains it of the holy soul departing out of the world, return from the exile of earth to thy home in heaven. *What will ye see in the Shulamite?* Who asks the question, and of whom? They reply, for the most part, that the Bridegroom addresses the daughters of Jerusalem, and tells them of the aspect which the Synagogue will present when it has returned to the faith. The Three Fathers alone suppose that the Shulamite herself both puts the question and answers it. *As it were the company of two armies.* The ancient versions and the English one have each lost something in translating this verse. The latter, by rendering מְחֹלַת *mecholath*, merely *company*, has missed the true force of the word, which is *dancing company*, preserved in the χοροὶ of the LXX. and the *choros* of the Vulgate. On the other hand, these versions have omitted to take notice of the dual form *Mahanaim*, found here as in Gen. xxxii. 2, and have turned it merely as *camps*, with no mark of number. There appears at first sight, says Theodoret, an inconsistency between the words *choirs* and *camps*, for the one has to do with feasting, and the other with war. But as the Bride is made up of many Saints, she is like to camps because of her valiant soul and warlike panoply, and she is at the same time the choir which has in its mouth the praises of GOD. And after showing how David tells us of the Church's song and S. Paul of her weapons and conflict, the good Bishop continues: That the Saints are not merely like camps, but like choirs also, let us hear the LORD telling: "Then shall the kingdom of heaven be likened unto ten virgins, which took their lamps, and went out to meet the Bridegroom." He says well, then, *What will ye see in the Shulamite, who cometh like choirs of camps?* (LXX.) He does not say, "camps of choirs," but *choirs of camps*. For the choirs are gathered out of the camps, since when brave soldiers in camps have been victorious, they return singing the pæan, and chanting in the dance the song of triumph. So the old Western hymn for All Saints:

<small>Ps. cxviii. 15, 27.
2 Cor. x. 4.
Eph. vi. 13.</small>

<small>S. Mat. xxv. 1.</small>

> Spouse of CHRIST, in arms contending,
> O'er each realm beneath the sun,
> Blend with prayers for help ascending,
> Notes of praise for triumphs won.

<small>The Hymn, *Sponsa* CHRISTI.</small>

What will ye see? Nothing else save these military choirs? No blood of victims, no rite of circumcision? No, all is gone save combat and praise, because "it seemed good to the HOLY GHOST to lay upon you no greater burden than these necessary things." And observe, that as in choirs it is necessary that the singers and dancers should keep time together, we have here a type of the need of harmony and union in the Church. And if we dwell on the phrase *dancing*, we shall remember how the women of Israel went out after Miriam with timbrels and dances, when she sang of the overthrow of the Egyptians; how the Psalmist bids the children of Sion praise their King in the dance and with the cymbals; how the saddest of Prophets can yet declare that in the day of the LORD's redemption "the virgin shall rejoice in the dance." But this dance, as Theodoret has already told us, is not merely one of girls, nor yet of peaceful priests, such as David shared in when he danced before the ark. It is one of tried warriors, whose swords and shields make the music to which they keep step; and it is of *two armies*, not met in deadly rivalry, but in close and perfect alliance, met in her who is the Peaceful, the Church Triumphant, where the two bands move beneath Jacob's staff, Jew and Gentile in the

<small>Rupert.

Acts xv. 28.

Cassiodor.

Exod. xv. 20.

Ps. cxlix. 3; cl. 4.

Jer. xxxi. 13.

2 Sam. vi. 14.

Philo Carp.</small>

Church Militant on earth, men and Angels in the Church Triumphant in heaven. Until the great day of the last battle against the hosts of evil shall dawn, these two choirs join in the mingled Song of Moses and the Lamb, but the time will come when the Song of Moses, with its echoes of war, shall be forgotten, and only the new Song of eternal peace shall be heard from the lips of the Peaceful as she sings the praises of the Prince of Peace, her Spouse.

Dion. Carth.

Rev. xv. 3.

Silius Italicus, ii. 595.

> Pax optima rerum
> Quas homini novisse datum est, pax una triumphis
> Innumeris potior.

> Peace, best of things
> Granted for man to know, peace, which alone
> Excelleth countless triumphs.

S. John Cassian. Ep. i. 11.

For, as a great Saint has said, it is for the glory of the Prince, if peace be loved by all. For what can better proclaim the ruler's virtues than a tranquil people, a united council, and the whole commonweal clothed in dignity of character?

Bern. Cluniac. Rhythmus.

> Yes, peace! for war is needless,—
> Yes, calm! for storm is past,—
> And goal from finished labour,
> And anchorage at last.
>
> That peace—but who may claim it?
> The guileless in their way,
> Who keep the ranks of battle,
> Who mean the thing they say.

And they will truly be *Mahanaim,* the two heavenly armies of the LORD of Hosts, for the ranks of the celestial hierarchies, long broken since the fall of the rebels under Lucifer, shall be filled up with ransomed men, now "like the Angels which are in heaven."

CHAPTER VII.

1 How beautiful are thy feet with shoes, O prince's daughter! the joints of thy thighs are like jewels, the work of the hands of a cunning workman.

There are three views as to the speaker and the person lauded here. Some hold that the virgins are celebrating the loveliness of the Bride, but the majority ascribe the words to the Bridegroom, varying, however, in explaining the Bride here either as the Christian Gentile Church, or as the converted Synagogue. The Chaldee paraphrast comments thus: "Solomon in the spirit of prophecy said before the face of the LORD, How beautiful are the feet of Israel, when they go up to appear before the LORD thrice yearly with their sandals of yew, and offer their vows and free-will oblations." A more literal rendering of the Hebrew than that of the A. V. is found in both LXX. and Vulgate, which read, *How beautiful are thy steps* (or *goings*) *in sandals*. And they agree, for the most part, in explaining the words of the proclamation of the Gospel to distant lands. Her *goings* are commended, but if her feet stood still, their beauty would win no praise. They cite, too, in illustration, the language of the Prophet Isaiah, "How beautiful upon the mountains are the feet of him that bringeth good tidings, that publisheth peace; that bringeth good tidings of good, that publisheth salvation, that saith unto Zion, Thy GOD reigneth!" on which the Apostle gives a comment, saying, "Stand, therefore, having your feet shod with the preparation of the Gospel of peace." So shod, her goings are straight, and keep to the King's highway alone. There is much diversity, however, in explaining what the sandals are with which the Bride hastens on her way. A favourite view is, that they denote the examples of departed Saints, typified by the skins of dead animals, of which the sandals are made. Another cognate interpretation is, that mortification of the flesh is intended, which is not very far from S. Jerome's view that voluntary promises of chastity are the shoes of the Bride. S. Ambrose, however, taking a somewhat wider view, tells us that the soul which subdues the flesh, and keeps it under, using it as a sandal, taking good care also not to defile it with mire nor to plunge it in the waters of sin, is truly beautiful in its progress towards its Country.

And S. Gregory supplies us with yet another interpretation, saying, that the Church, in her task of preaching, is said to be shod, when she is strengthened by the death of CHRIST to endure the evils which rise up against her; while another, confining the words to the faithful soul, teaches that the delight she feels in drawing nearer to GOD preserves her feet from being wounded by the thorns and stones of the steep way of perfection as she climbs. Durandus enters at much length into the mystical signification of the episcopal sandals of the Western Church, saying, amidst much else, that the sole is solid and continuous, and the upper leather of open-work, to denote that the steps of the preacher ought to be guarded below, lest they be defiled by earthly things, according to the LORD's saying, "Shake off the dust of your feet;" while they are open above, to receive the revelation of heavenly mysteries, as it is written, "Open Thou mine eyes, that I may see the wondrous things of Thy law." Nor does the East come behindhand in this symbolism, as the prayers of the priests of the Syriac rite testify while they vest for the Liturgy. Putting on the left sandal, they say, "Shoe me, O LORD, with the preparation of the Gospel of peace, that I may tread upon serpents and scorpions and all the power of the enemy, for evermore. Amen." And then with the right sandal, "Put down, O LORD GOD, under the footstool of my feet every high thing that lifteth up itself against Thy knowledge, that through Thy help I may crush the passions of the flesh for evermore." Observe too, that whereas the Bride began the praises of her Bridegroom with His head, and thence passes gradually to His legs; here, on the contrary, the first commendation of the Bride is for her feet, and the last is her head. And the reason is, because the Bride desires to extol the humility and love of the Incarnate WORD, in that He vouchsafed to descend from His majestic throne to dwell amongst mankind, while He, on the other hand, wills to teach her how He intends to raise her from her present lowly condition to everlasting glory. He begins with the feet in shoes, says one, because the beginning of spiritual life is the trampling the flesh under foot, as we enter on the way of salvation and put away our evil works. He begins with the feet, the lowest members of the body, because the Gospel was first preached to the poor and ignorant, not to the mighty and wise of this world.

And as Moses was commanded to put off his shoes when he drew near the holy ground of the burning bush, so the time will come when the Saints, as they enter the borders of the Land of Promise, will not merely do as

Jews were wont, when reaching Palestine again after a journey into Gentile regions, shake off the heathen dust back on its own soil, not suffering it to pass the frontier, but will cast out the very shoe of mortality over Edom, and tread barefooted those streets of gold where is no mire or defilement.

> Our feet be shod, as pilgrims,
>   With bands of Gospel peace,
> Till life's long march be ended,
>   And strife and struggle cease:
> Till on the ground most holy,
>   Our shoes from off our feet
> We put, with holy gladness,
>   The pilgrimage complete.

<small>W. C. Dix. The Hymn, *O Christ, Thou Son of Mary*, for S. Crispin.</small>

O prince's daughter. What *Prince* can this be, save the HOLY GHOST, the Comforter, Who says in the forty-fifth Psalm, "Hearken, O daughter, and give ear; forget also thine own people, and thy father's house: so shall the King have pleasure in thy beauty, for He is the LORD thy GOD." Others tell us that CHRIST, the Prince of Peace, is meant, in His mysterious relation to the Bride, at once her Father, because she has been born to Him anew in the water of Baptism, when "of His own will begat He us with the Word of truth," and her Bridegroom, the nearest and dearest to her. And this close blending of dissimilar ties in One to Whom all obedience as well as all love is due has been figured for us in the pathetic words of a loving wife, as described by the greatest of heathen poets:

<small>Theodoret. S. Ambros. Ps. xlv. 11. Hugo Card. Dion. Carth. S. James i. 18.</small>

> Ἕκτορ, ἀτὰρ σύ μοι ἐσσὶ πατὴρ καὶ πότνια μήτηρ,
> ἠδὲ κασίγνητος, σὺ δέ μοι θαλερὸς παρακοίτης.
>
> Hector, to me thou father art, and mother dear,
> And brother too, who art my gallant spouse.

<small>Hom. Il. vi. 429.</small>

The Hebrew for *prince* here is נָדִיב *nadib*, which also means "noble" or "generous." And several of the ancient commentators, dwelling on the LXX. reading, *daughter of Nadab*, refer us back to the Amminadab of whom we heard just now, telling us that she is called His daughter, because it is only of His free-will and loving-kindness, not of right, that she has been adopted. Theodoret boldly compares her to that Nadab, son of Aaron, who died for offering strange

<small>Cassiodor. S. Ambros. Serm. 17 in Ps. cxix. Theodoret. Lev. x. 1.</small>

fire before the LORD. For the Bride bore no legal fire into the sanctuary of GOD, but a new fire which she received from her Spouse, that of which He spake Himself: "I am come to send fire upon the earth, and what will I if it be already kindled?" The Bride bearing this new fire of the New Testament into the Divine tabernacle, crieth out and saith, "Old things are passed away, behold, all things are become new." And others tell us that in her title, "daughter of the generous one," we may read her own liberality and nobleness. Observe, too, that as her Bridegroom in this Song is both King and Shepherd, she, that she may be a fitting consort for Him, is shepherdess and princess too.[1] The whole context is also explained by S. Ambrose and many who have followed him as applying especially to that princess of the House of David, that elect daughter of GOD, who was beautiful with the shoes of that pure body whence the Redeemer took His flesh, the sandals which bore His Godhead in its pilgrimage through the world, in that mystery of the Incarnation of which the Baptist said, "Whose shoe's latchet I am not worthy to unloose;" that is, I cannot solve the secret of His birth. For so the Prophet had foretold, saying, "Who shall declare His generation?" "Thy goings, O glorious Virgin," exclaims the Universal Doctor, "are thy noble race, thy purity of body and soul, thy fruitfulness in offspring. Thy shoes are thy thoughts in meditation, thy results in working, thine advance in longings, thy trances in joy. For thou art the princely daughter of that Prince Who is GOD, Prince of princes and LORD of lords, Who begat thee specially by grace, and specially formed thee, so that thou art as truly daughter of GOD as thou art stainless Mother." It was by no swiftness of foot, but by purity of affections, observes another, that she went from strength to strength till she beheld the GOD of Gods in Sion, uniting in herself the innocence of Abel, the obedience of Abraham, the meekness of Moses, the lowliness of David, the patience of Job, and the purity of Daniel. It is recorded of S. Francis Xavier that he cited these words to

---

[1] This term, *prince's daughter*, is one of the most difficult things in the Song to square with the literalist interpretation, and accordingly no little pains has been employed, somewhat ineffectually, to explain it away, by the upholders of that view.

Queen Katharine of Portugal, wife of King John III., and sister of the Emperor Charles V., to induce her to forego a large sum paid annually from the Indian revenue to her privy purse, under the name of slipper-money, that he might devote it to missionary purposes, assuring her that she would enter more easily into heaven shod with the sandals of the prayers of the poor than with the royal buskins which the tribute was intended to provide. And this sense may be not inaptly illustrated by the rude old Border dirge, addressed to the departing spirit, now setting out on its dread journey: Vieyra. Serm. de S. Francisco Xavier.

> If ever thou gavest hosen and shoon,
>   Every night and alle;
> Sit thee down and put them on,
>   And CHRIST receive thy saule.
>
> If hosen and shoon thou ne'er gavest nane,
>   Every night and alle;
> The whinnes shall pricke thee to the bare bane,
>   And CHRIST receive thy saule.

Scott. Minstrelsy. Lyke-wake Dirge.

The joints of thy thighs are like jewels. Instead of *joints*, we should rather have *roundings*, denoting the graceful form of the limb; and so the LXX., which has ῥυθμοὶ μηρῶν, explained by Theodoret as typifying the practical virtues which carry out the intentions of the will, just as the thighs bear us along upon our journeys; or, as another Greek Father takes it, the harmonious outlines of a life guarded by temperance and holiness; or, as a Western writer says, the two thighs are lowliness and purity, the twin supports of sanctification. But the Vulgate, agreeing with the A. V., is usually interpreted in a different fashion. Following the Targum, which explains the clause of the children of the congregation, sprung from the *thigh* (a frequent type of parentage in Holy Writ), and like the precious studs in Aaron's mitre, they take the thighs of the Church to be her spiritual offspring, born of the word of preaching and the laver of regeneration; while the *joints* refer to the union of two natures, Jew and Gentile, in one faith. Theodoret. Philo Carp. Irimbert. Targum. Exod. i. 5, marg. Cassiodor. S. Greg. M. S. Just. Org.

Like jewels. The LXX. and Vulgate, with more exactness, *like necklaces.* And that because as gems shine set in gold, so these good works, done in wisdom, are beautiful to look on; and further, as they are not done independently of each other, but con- S. Greg. M.

Hugo Card. tinuously and regularly, so they are united with the bond of charity, which joins the separate jewels into the necklace which adorns the Bride. And this ornament is the work of no human hands, but of that *cun-*
Cassiodor. *ning workman,* the Almighty LORD Himself. And applying the words to the motherhood of the Blessed Virgin, they bid us think on that costly jewel, the
Honorius. pearl of great price, the glorious ornament of every believing soul, CHRIST JESUS Himself, Begotten, not made, as GOD, but made as Man by the FATHER in the mystery of the Incarnation.

2 Thy navel is like a round goblet, which wanteth not liquor: thy belly is like an heap of wheat set about with lilies.

Targum. Here, as so often, the Chaldee strikes the key-note, and gives an explanation which, with but slight change, is that of many Christian Fathers. It paraphrases the first clause thus: "The Prince of thy school,[1] by whose merit all the ages are ruled, as the unborn child is nourished in its mother's womb by the navel, is resplendent in the Law, like the round disk of the moon, when he comes to purify and to make unclean, and to justify and condemn: and the words of the Law never fail from his mouth, as the waters of the river fail not when it goes forth from Paradise." Very
S. Greg. M. close to this is the comment of S. Gregory the Great: The *navel* is the order of holy preachers, fitly styled a *goblet,* because when the people are taught from its mouth, they are filled with spiritual wine by its ministry. It is *round,* because the preachers' tongue must needs go round all subjects, according to the character of all classes of men. It *wanteth not mixture,* because it must drink more abundantly than others that which it offers to them as a draught, and
S. Epiph. contain more than it gives. S. Epiphanius and Philo
Philo Carp. agree in holding that the Priesthood is here intended, compared to a *goblet* with *mixture* (i.e. wine and water), because of the mystery of the Sacrament of the Body
Cf. S. Cyp- and Blood of CHRIST, whereof it has charge, and with
rian. Ep. ad which the people are mingled by faith and love. The
Cæcilium. Priesthood, as in the centre of the Church, reconciling

[1] President of the Rabbinical College which took the place of the Sanhedrim after the fall of Jerusalem.

the people to GOD, is the *navel;* it is a *goblet* because the people to GOD, is the *navel;* it is a *goblet* because S. Just. Org.
it gives them to drink of the love of GOD; it is *round,* S. Ans. Laud.
because all its angles have been smoothed away according to the will of GOD, that His Hand may find
no inequality in it. The womb of Mary, observes S. S. Ambros.
Ambrose, was in truth a round goblet, wherein was de Inst.
Wisdom, Who mingled that wine, the grace of unfail- Virg. 14.
ing and loving knowledge of Him, the fulness of His
Godhead. As the navel is the weakest part of all Irimbert.
the body, it may not unfitly typify a heart conscious
of its own weakness, holding, as in a goblet, the memory of former sins, which memory, by acting as the
cutter of a lathe to remove all that is superfluous, Luc. Abb.
vain, and evil, makes the goblet *round.* It wants
not liquor, because it is full of the tears of compunction for its past offences. And so the Wise Man saith,
"Be not wise in thine own eyes; fear the LORD, and Prov. iii. 7.
depart from evil; it shall be health to thy navel, and
marrow to thy bones." As the navel is the centre of Honorius.
the body, so temperance is the mean of life. It is a
round goblet, full of liquor, because it is rounded by
circumspection, and is red in wisdom. And as drink
assuages thirst, and gladdens the heart, so temperance
quenches the heat of sin, and checks unruly zeal in
better things.

Thy belly is like a heap of wheat, set about with Targum.
lilies. The Targum, carrying on its paraphrase, tells
us that this denotes the seventy members of the Sanhedrim, gathered round their Prince, and enriched
with all the tithes, oblations, and free-will offerings
set apart for them by Ezra, Zorobabel, and other
chiefs of the Great Synagogue. The *belly* denotes
the multitude of the faithful, say the Fathers, because Dion. Carth.
the womb signifies fruitfulness, and these are here Philo Carp.
denoted, begotten in the Gospel, and born, not of
blood, nor of the will of the flesh, nor of the will of
man, but of GOD. This multitude is compared to a
heap of wheat, because the LORD saith of the fruit of
the Bride: "Except a corn of wheat fall into the S. John xii.
ground and die, it abideth alone; but if it die, it 24.
bringeth forth much fruit." It is a *heap,* and not a
quantity of scattered grains, because as a heap is piled
up with many grains, so the one Church of all the
faithful is formed by the union of many natures,
one in the communion of one Baptism and the Sacrament of the Body and Blood of CHRIST. And as a

heap is wide at the base, growing smaller towards the summit, so in the Church there are many who live self-indulgently, and but few who aim at the height of perfection; as, for instance, there are many more found who will give alms of their goods to the poor than will leave all their possessions for GOD. This heap is *set about with lilies,* because all the good works which the Saints do are for the sake of heavenly sweetness and light. Or, as another Father puts it, the heap of wheat, while awaiting here removal to the granaries of the LORD, is fenced on all sides by the bright and lovely examples of the Saints. Philo takes the lilies to be the good works to which all Christians are bound to devote themselves, and the holy discourses which should fit them for their dwelling in heaven. Others take the heap of wheat, pure, wholesome, and nutritious, to be those divines who are versed in Holy Scripture, and by their teaching win over many not merely to purity, but to vows of perpetual chastity. And with this latter view agrees that explanation of Cardinal Hugo, that the lilies which fence the wheat are the cloistered Orders in the Church. They teach us also that memory is the belly of the soul, containing the food which is her support, those hidden mysteries whereof we can here but just discern the beauty and fragrance. Or, more precisely, the heap of wheat may symbolize the words of Holy Scripture stored up in the mind, and the lilies the pure and lovely thoughts which they supply for meditation. And, spoken of S. Mary, they do not fail to remind us how she bore within her that wheat elected which was ground in the mill of the Passion that it might be made into the Bread of Life, and how He was fenced around by the lilies of her spotless virginity. In the Virgin's womb, comments S. Ambrose, there were at the same time the heap of wheat and the blooming lily-flower, because she bore Him Who is the corn of wheat and the Lily too: The corn of wheat, according to that Scripture: "Verily, verily, I say unto you, Except a corn of wheat fall into the ground and die, it abideth alone." But in that the single grain became a heap of wheat, that prophecy was fulfilled, "The valleys shall be thick with corn," for that grain dying brought forth much fruit. This grain also filled all men with the perpetual food of heavenly gifts, and thereby that other speech of the Prophet's mouth which the same David uttered, was brought to pass: "He fed them also with the finest wheat-flour, with honey out of the stony rock did He satisfy them." And the Divine oracles testify that a Lily too was in this seed, for it is written, "I am the flower of the plain, and the lily of the valleys, as the lily among thorns." CHRIST was the lily among thorns, when He was in the midst of the Jews.

Ps. lxxxi. 17.

Cant. ii. 1, 2.

3 Thy two breasts are like two young roes that are twins.

There is but little to add here to the expositions cited on the previous occurrence of these words.

Taking them, as before, to refer to the preachers of the Church, twofold, as Jew and Gentile, or as deriving their teaching from both Testaments, or, again, as inculcating the two great precepts on which hang all the Law and the Prophets, they have yet a word or two of counsel. Thus, we are reminded that preaching, to be useful to the hearers, must come from those who draw their lessons from a living source, and have not merely got up a single sermon for each occasion by borrowing, or by learning the subject of the day apart from all its true context; a style of preaching often hurtful to the hearers, as the milk given to Sisera out of the bottle was the prelude of his death. Had Jael fed him from her breast, she could not have slain him.

Hugo Card.

Judg. iv. 19.

4 Thy neck is as a tower of ivory; thine eyes like the fishpools in Heshbon, by the gate of Bath-rabbim: thy nose is as the tower of Lebanon which looketh toward Damascus.

Already the neck of the Bride has been likened to a tower, but here the materials of which that tower is formed are first mentioned. Those officers of the Church, whether preachers, through whom comes the voice of doctrine, or priests, by whose ministry the Body and Blood of CHRIST pass to the people for their spiritual food and drink, or Martyrs, because they put their necks under the yoke of CHRIST, and never withdraw them, are all compared to *ivory* because of its whiteness and purity, while the word *tower* serves to remind us that the grace of purity is found allied with

Chap. iv. 4.

Cassiodor.

Philo Carp. Luc. Abb.

strength rather than with weakness. Note, too, that as only that part of ivory which is uncovered by flesh is valuable, and suited for the adornment of a king, so the Martyrs, by putting off their fleshly covering, became a tower of beauty in the City of GOD; and similarly, all those who here mortify the flesh and live, while in the body, as though out of it, are more precious than their fellows. The knowledge of Scripture, observes a Saint, is also the spiritual neck of the Bride, and it is styled a *tower of ivory*, because they who occupy themselves with GOD's Word rise daily higher in spiritual progress, in shining righteousness. The soul has its ivory neck too, that pure and shining observance of the unsullied precepts of GOD, that perfect righteousness and holy bond, which is the means of union between the faithful soul and CHRIST, her Head. Another tells us that as the neck is the channel of speech, so we may here understand penitent confession of sins, compared to a *tower* because it needs strong and steadfast resolution to acknowledge our transgressions, not shrinking back and cowering in shame. And this tower is *ivory*, because confession makes the soul white, firm, and clean. *Thine eyes like the fishpools in Heshbon.* The eyes of the Church, says Cassiodorus, are her Doctors, who watch for the whole body, and point the way it should go. These eyes are compared to *fishpools* built at the gate of the city of Heshbon, because holy teachers wash in the bath of life the people who believe in CHRIST, and refresh them with the draught of saving doctrine. These pools are *by the gates*, because none can enter the Church unless he be first washed in the water of Baptism, and have been given to drink of the fount of saving doctrine. This was typified by the brazen sea which Solomon placed in the porch of the Temple, that the priests, when about to enter the Temple and to sacrifice victims, might wash themselves there. The gate at which it stands is that of *Bath-rabbim*, "daughter of a multitude," because the Church is rightly so named, as daily gathering in the multitude of the Gentiles. This explanation is closely allied to the Chaldee paraphrase, which interprets the clause of the scribes, full of *wisdom* and *calculation*, signified by *Heshbon*, because one of their main duties was to compute the occurrence of the great festivals, and their post was at the door of the Great Council of the people. The spiritual eyes of the soul are also, they tell us, like fishpools in Heshbon; like *fishpools*, because containing the water of heavenly wisdom, ever full of tears for their own sins and those of others, in *Heshbon*, because of the depth of thought with which she ponders in clear and pure meditation, and thus *by the gate of the daughter of a multitude*, because she draws the springs of thought from many lips and various sources. Again, the eyes of devout meditation need to be at the *gate*, at the very entrance of the soul, to guard against all access of foes, to catch the first glimpse of the King as He draws near. And a truly devout soul is called the *daughter of a multitude*, because in her lowliness she is content to class herself as but one of the meanest of GOD's countless elect, and not to claim any pre-eminence as hers by right.

<small>Theodoret.
S. Ambros.
Serm. 16, in Ps. cxix.
Philo Carp.
Dion. Carth.
Hugo Card.</small>

> Amidst the happy chorus
> A place, however low,
> Shall show Him us, and showing,
> Shall satiate evermo.

<small>Bern. Clun. Rhythmus.</small>

Although a few of the Latin commentators rightly follow the Greek in explaining *Heshbon* as "thought" or "contemplation," yet the majority of them prefer to interpret it as "girdle of mourning,"[1] and thus dwell much on penitential sorrow as a special grace of the Bride. There are several reasons assigned for the likeness of the eyes of the devout soul to fishpools. The chief are as follows. First, that as fish is kept alive in these pools, so devout thoughts and affections are retained in the meditations of the heart. They might well add that the fish, from its Greek name, Ἰχθύς, is the familiar symbol of the Ancient Church for her LORD, as the several letters of the word are the initials of Ἰησοῦς Χριστὸς Θεοῦ Υἱὸς Σωτήρ, JESUS CHRIST, SON of GOD, SAVIOUR, and that He is the living tenant of all her thought. Next, these pools are clear and limpid, and reflect images, as the soul, when contemplating GOD, should receive His image in her bosom. Thirdly, as fishpools are deep and full of water, so abundant tears of devotion and contrition flow from

<small>Corn. à Lap.</small>

---

[1] There is a word חֶשְׁבּוֹן, *cingulum*, from the same root חָשַׁב as *Heshbon*, and perhaps אָנָה, *luxit*, may be assumed as the supposed root of the termination. The etymon is thus not so utterly wild as it looks at first.

holy souls. Fourthly, as these pools are at the gates of the daughter of multitude, so meditation and contemplation are by the gates of Paradise, where is the innumerable company of the elect. Fifthly, as the water in such pools is still, and therefore calm and peaceful, so meditation quiets and tranquillizes the soul.

Thy nose is as the tower of Lebanon, which looketh toward Damascus. Because with the nose we distinguish between fetid and fragrant odours, the same holy teachers are rightly understood to be the nose of the Church, as they know how to discern skilfully the sweet teaching of the Catholic Faith, and the deadly stench of heretical error. For among the divine gifts of which distribution is made by the HOLY GHOST, it is said, "To another is given by the SPIRIT discerning of spirits." This nose of the Church is compared to the *tower of Lebanon,* because holy teachers occupy the highest place in the Church, and stand, as it were, on Mount Lebanon, to guard the Church from the assaults of evil spirits. This tower is said to be *toward Damascus.* Damascus is the chief city of Syria, which once, under very powerful and cruel kings, warred against the children of Israel. And Damascus is interpreted, "a draught of blood" or "an eye of blood."[1] They say that Abel was slain there, and it therefore denotes the powers of this world, who thirst after blood, because they delight in the pleasures and allurements of flesh and blood. It also signifies the powers of the air, who thirst for our blood. Therefore this tower is *against Damascus,* because those fortified by the help of CHRIST, always resist the devil and his members. Another, slightly varying from this interpretation, takes the nose to denote all those Saints who perceive the sweet savour of righteousness which is in CHRIST, and transmit it to the body, and who are likened to the tower of Lebanon because of their eminence and purity. And if we take the *tower of Lebanon,* as a third does, to denote the Manhood of CHRIST, holding Lebanon to mean "frankincense,"

---

[1] The true meaning is probably "red land," contrasting aptly enough with the *whiteness* of Lebanon, and sufficiently suggestive of the colour of blood. If the Arabic etymology, "swiftly built," be preferred, we may then see another contrast, that between the hasty, unsubstantial buildings of man, and the "everlasting hills" of GOD.

then those will be like Him who are filled with earnest zeal and ardent faith, and, shining with virtues, overthrow the devil-worship of the Gentiles among whom they dwell. Yet another view sees here the Guardian Angels, keeping ceaseless watch against the enemies of mankind. The nose of the holy soul is also her power of discerning between good and evil spirits, like a lofty tower on the summit of Lebanon, looking towards Damascus, to watch for the approach of any enemy against Israel. It looks towards Damascus in another sense also, taking that word still as implying blood, in that its gaze of contemplation is ever fixed on the Passion of JESUS, and His bloodshedding on the "red ground" of Gethsemane and Calvary. And this is the view taken by S. Jerome, saying of S. Mary Magdalene, "She weeps at the Cross, she makes ready the ointment, she seeks in the tomb, she questions the gardener, she recognizes the LORD, she proceeds to the Apostles, she tells what she had found; they doubt, but she is trustful. Truly towered is she, truly a tower of whiteness and Lebanon, which looks towards the face of Damascus, that is, the Blood of the SAVIOUR, calling her to holy penitence." And another, applying the words to a greater than the Magdalen, exclaims: Thou, O Lady, art that fair nose, of which the Bridegroom saith, "Thy nose is as the tower of Lebanon." The nose hath two orifices, through which it emits the breath from the head; so thou, O Lady, by thy virginity and lowliness drewest down the SON of GOD from heaven, CHRIST the LORD, Whom the Prophet calls "the breath of our nostrils," for He warms us unto charity, and cools our desire, urges us to will what is good, justifies us by faith. Thou therefore art the nose of the Church, and like to a tower; lofty in thy dignity, strong in thy sedateness. Thou art the tower of Lebanon, for Mount Lebanon, which is interpreted whiteness, signifies thine innocence, exalted above all others.

Hugo Card.
Tres Patr.
Irimbert.
S. Hieron. Ep. 140, ad Principiam.
Pseudo-Bernard. Serm. 4, sup. Salve Regina.
Lam. iv. 20.

5 Thine head upon thee is like Carmel, and the hair of thine head like purple; the king is held in the galleries.

Following the Targum, which interprets this head as the King, several of the Fathers tell us that CHRIST

Philo Carp. Cassiodor.

is the Head here promised. They accept also, for the most part, the reason assigned by the Chaldee paraphrase for the comparison, which is a reference to the history of Elijah. But whereas the Jewish expositor dwells on the slaughter of the prophets of Baal, the Christians prefer to remember the descent of the fertilizing rain on the parched and thirsty ground. CHRIST, *S. Greg. M.* comments S. Gregory, is the Head of the Church, and is well said to be *like Carmel,* because He was exalted unto the FATHER by the Passion He endured. Of which is written, " And it shall come to pass in the last days, that the mountain of the LORD's house shall be established in the top of the mountains." For Elijah, praying on Carmel, obtained rain, and we, praying on Carmel, ask for rain, when, believing in CHRIST, we long for CHRIST, and obtain from the FATHER the bestowal of the grace for which we intreat. *S. Just. Org.* And as Elijah and Elisha, Saints of the Old Covenant, often found a refuge on Carmel, so too the dwelling of the righteous is in the LORD JESUS CHRIST, the Head of His Church, from Whom the multitude of the people derive their food. The intellect or reason is also, as many of them add, the head of the soul, as ruling and guiding it, and this is like Carmel, the "fruitful," because, as Theodoret adds, it is filled with all good things. For GOD, when rebuking by His *Jer. ii. 7, marg.* Prophet the ingratitude of the Jews, saith, " I brought you into the land of Carmel, to eat the fruit thereof, and the goodness thereof." Thine head, then, saith He, is like Carmel, bringing forth all kinds of good things, and producing every fruit for Me, its Husbandman.¹ *The hair of thy head like purple; the King is bound in the galleries.* This version, which follows the Masoretic pointing, is practically that of the LXX., save that there, instead of *galleries,* we find παραδρομαῖς, *verandahs,* running round the lower story of a house. *Philo Carp.* This *hair* of the Bride, observes the Bishop of Car-

Isa. ii. 2.

---

¹ The majority of the Fathers interpret *Carmel* as "knowledge of circumcision," and observe that the Head or ruling part of the Church knew circumcision literally under the Law, and spiritually under the Gospel. The marginal reading of A. V., " crimson," is an error, as old as Abenezra, and arises out of confounding כַּרְמֶל and כַּרְמִיל. But it is probable that the reference to *purple* which follows was suggested to the poet by the resemblance of these two words.

pasia, is the innumerable company of the Christian people, which adorns the Church as abundant tresses are the glory of a woman's head. And the epithet *purple* bears a reference to the prophecies and oracles of the coming death of the Bridegroom Himself and of the Martyrs, for as purple resembles the colour of blood, so the Bride, who is the multitude of the faithful, was first washed and dyed with the Blood of JESUS CHRIST, her divine Spouse, and then was further increased and stablished by the death of the Martyrs. This is His royal apparel, of which Jacob prophesies to his son Judah (of whom the Bridegroom was born after the flesh) saying, "He washed His garments in wine, and His clothes in the blood of grapes." For the Holy Church is the robe and garment of CHRIST. Theodoret, dwelling on the word πλόκιον, "twined" or "plaited" hair, and explaining the word to denote the doctrine and teaching of the Church, says that it is so described to point the contrast between the orderly sequence of Christian dogma and the dishevelled opinions of Gentilism, while he agrees with Philo in holding that the purple tinge comes from the Precious Blood. Both fail us in the last clause, Theodoret, because he passes over it altogether, and Philo, because he adopts a reading peculiar to himself (at least found now in no extant text,) *The King is terrible in His goings-forth;* words which he explains, with eloquence and fervour, of the Incarnation, Passion, Resurrection, and Ascension of CHRIST. Ainsworth, however, may supply the lacuna, suggesting as the spiritual interpretation of the A. V. that the King is so tied with the cords of love to the dwelling of His Bride, that He cannot, so to speak, leave it if He would; according to His own saying by the mouth of the Psalmist: "The LORD hath chosen Sion to be an habitation for Himself: He hath longed for her. This shall be My rest for ever: here will I dwell, for I have a delight therein." But it is to be noted that the Hebrew word here found, רְהָטִים *rehatim,* means, in the only other places in the Bible where it occurs, *gutters* or *troughs* for cattle to drink at, and therefore the Vulgate rendering is here to be preferred. *As a King's purple, bound in the conduits (canalibus.)* That is, as they variously explain it, laid in the dye-troughs, and thus in the first freshness of its colouring, before

Gen. xlix. 11.
Theodoret.

Philo Carp.

Ainsworth.

Ps. cxxxii. 14.

Gen. xxx. 39, 41.
Exod. ii. 16.

Cassiodor.
Weissbach.
Leo Juda.

aught has dimmed it; or else, newly washed in running water, and so clean and bright, and shining in the sun. Before passing to the interpretation of this version, the other views proposed may be stated. One is that the word παραδρομὴ or *canalis* does not mean a literal water-trough, but a gold or silver stripe, binding, and yet running like a bright stream across, the purple robe, so that the comparison is then made with the *fillets* wherewith the Bride's dark tresses are bound.[1] The other opinion, which is that of most modern critics, is that the *flowing curls* of the Bride are metaphorically intended, and that the King is caught and tangled in them, as in a net. Mystically, says Cassiodorus, the *conduits* signify the lowliness of the Saints, in which the purple of the Everlasting King is dyed, when those Saints, by imitating the lowliness of their Redeemer, aim at being conformed to His Passion, that they may be changed into the dignity of purple, that is, working for CHRIST may attain to be crowned and to reign with CHRIST. And this purple is said to be *bound*, because the hearts of the Saints are fixed and stablished in the fear and love of their SAVIOUR, so that they can never be separated from His love. The poor of the people, remarks the Chaldee paraphrast, who surround the Prince, because of their need, will one day be clothed with *purple*, as Daniel was in Babylon and Mordecai in Susa, for the sake of Abraham's merit, whom GOD made a king, and for Isaac's righteousness, who was *bound* by his father, and for Jacob's dignity, who peeled the rods at the *water-troughs*. And so, rendering the words in a Christian sense, it is the weakest and lowliest of CHRIST's members who shall inherit the kingdom, and are made true kings for His sake Who is the Friend of GOD, the Father of Nations; for His Who was bound on the Cross for us; for His, the Prince with GOD, Who stripped the Tree of Life, in part at least, of the bark or outer letter, that we might see the wood itself.

Margin notes: Tres Patr. Rosenmüller. De Wette. Ewald. Hitzig. Cassiodor. / Targum. / S. Ambros. / Rupert. in Gen. xxx.

---

[1] And in support of this view two facts may be cited. One is that the Talmud actually uses the word חוטים to denote the ribbons used in decorating the Paschal Lamb, (Talmud, de Agno Paschali, c. 3;) and the other is that the technical name in the modern Greek Church for the wavy stripes on a cope is ποταμοί, "rivers," (Goar. Eucholog.)

And observe, that either of the meanings given to the conduits or ducts yields a spiritual lesson. If they be the actual dye-troughs, then we learn that the first true beauty of the Saints must be derived from conformity with the Passion of JESUS, and that the fairest loveliness of all is martyrdom for His sake. If the reference be to water in which the purple, after being dyed, is washed to make it clean and bright, then we have the font of Baptism for the first such washing, and the tears of penitence to cleanse subsequent defilement. There is a variant of the Vulgate, *joined with canals (juncta canalibus,)* which is explained to mean either Holy Scripture, or the secret counsels of GOD which decreed the Passion and royalty of CHRIST, or else those wise prelates and teachers, who form as it were the ducts for the streams from the Heavenly Jerusalem by which the precious Blood of CHRIST is supplied to the people, that they may be truly a kingly robe for Him, and not, as too often, a prickly hair-cloth on His sacred form; or, yet again, as the rules and ordinances, especially of the Religious Life, which are the outer troughs in which we are placed, that the costly dye may saturate us. Or, again, the examples of the Saints are not inaptly called canals, because the effect of the LORD's Passion does not confine itself to them alone, and sink, as it were, into the ground through them, but the stream passes on after dyeing them, to perform the like office for others, in that they become agents of conversion in their turn.

Note, too, that the praise of the Bride's loveliness is directed to ten beauties of her person successively, denoting thereby that the fairness of the Church consists in fulfilling the commandments of GOD. And, applying the verse to the Blessed Virgin, they tell us how when the nails and spear had made the white Beloved ruddy with the purple of His Passion, then the sword of Simeon's prophecy pierced His mother's heart, so that all her thoughts were dyed in the purple of her compassion, as it lay bound by her perfect obedience in those conduits of GOD's grace which flowed abundantly upon her in that time of suffering, whereby she was crowned as Queen of Martyrs, and therefore fitly clad in royal apparel. It remains only to mention the curious variant found in the Syriac and Arabic versions. *Thy hair is like a kingly purple awning spread above a theatre* (Arab.) or *race-course* (Syr.) And the most obvious mystical import of this seems to be that the examples of the triumphant Saints, the witnesses of our struggle in the arena, serve to alleviate the burning heat of our trial, that we may endure to the end, and conquer.

Heb. xii. 1.

6 How fair and how pleasant art thou, O love, for delights!

Fair in her faith, *pleasant* in her works. Above she was called " fair as the moon, clear as the sun, terrible as an army with banners;" here she is said to be fair and pleasant in *delights*. There seems a contradiction in this, for to be terrible as an army in array and to be in delights are incompatible, since delights enervate the valour of soldiers. But the Holy Church can be both, arrayed as an army in resisting unbelievers, heretics, and evil spirits, to whom she is terrible by her holiness and perfection: and *in delights*, because with her mental palate she ever tastes the dulcet savour of heavenly sweetness, and amidst the troubles of the world seeks to attain those delights and to be ever satisfied therewith. And she who is like this, is rightly said to be *dearest* (Vulg.) to the Bridegroom. She is fair and pleasant in delights also in that she possesses meekness and deep lowliness of heart in the abundance of grace. And all the gifts of grace, and the understanding of the Scriptures, are true delights, while lowliness is true beauty, a pleasant thing, and a virtue loved by GOD. The Carthusian, urging that the Church is never so fair and pleasant in the Bridegroom's eyes as when she is thinking of Him only, and bearing tribulation not merely patiently, but gladly, for His sake, reproduces the Chaldee interpretation, which is, " Solomon the king said, How fair art thou, O congregation of Israel, in the time when thou bearest the yoke of my kingdom, in the time when I correct thee with sufferings because of thy sins, and thou receivest them in love, and they seem delights unto thee." The LXX. rendering, as A. V., *love* instead of *dearest*, gives rise to a slightly different type of exposition. Thou art made *fair*, comments a Greek Father, which thou wast not before, and whereas thou wast full of all unpleasantness, now thou hast at once become *pleasant*, and this thou hast gained because thou delightest in love, for, loving the

Cassiodor.

Rupert.

Dion. Carth.

Targum.

Theodoret.

Bridegroom who loves thee, and counting His affection thy one delight, thou hast slighted all things besides, and art fair and pleasant. And if so even here, what shall be her beauty in the delights of everlasting bless‑ *Honorius.* edness? They apply the verse also to the Virgin Mother, *fair* in her maternity, *pleasant* in her virginity, *dearest* to GOD in both, as He graced her with the *delights* of tending her Divine Son, and of meditating on her own marvellous destiny. *Guilielmus. Card. Hailgrin.*

7 This thy stature is like to a palm tree, and thy breasts to clusters of grapes.

The *stature* of the Church is the uprightness of her *Beda.* good works, because, despising to be bent down towards the desires of earth, she lifts her whole form upwards to attain heavenly things; of which the Apostle counsels, saying, "Watch ye, stand fast in the faith, quit 1 Cor. xvi. you like men." Of which the LORD also saith, "I am 13. the LORD your GOD, Which brought you forth out of the 13. land of Egypt, that ye should not be their bondmen; and I have broken the bands of your yoke, and made you go upright." And, besides, the hand of a conqueror was decked with palm, and also, amongst the ancients, the victors in a contest were crowned with palm. Therefore the stature of the Bride is likened to a palm-tree, when all the intention of the faithful stands erect in love for heavenly things, and meanwhile ponders, when standing in the ranks of battle, that prize which shall be the conqueror's meed when the struggle is over. Moreover, because the palm is rough in its lower portion, but displays its beauty and the sweetness of its fruit at the summit, the stature of the Church or of any faithful soul is fitly likened to it, which bears upon earth harsh troubles for the LORD's sake, but hopes to receive from that LORD a precious reward in heaven. The palm is rough near the ground, because the elect suffer persecution for righteousness' sake. It is fair and sweet at the top, because they rejoice and are glad in their afflictions, knowing that their reward is great in heaven. And as the palm is clothed with enduring foliage, and retains its leaves without intermission; who does not see that it presents a type of the stature of faith, which, amidst the varying conditions of the shifting world, keeps ever to the same words of true confession, as leaves which will never be renewed nor fall, and that it preserves unharmed in its elect unto the end of the world that perfection of works which began from its first origin, just as the palm retains its beauty?

S. Greg. M. Mor. xix. 16.

Further, the palm tree is slender below and expands above, and similarly the holy soul begins in the depths with small things, and growing slowly up to that which is greater, at last branches out into the full beauty of divine love. It is elastic, and springs up under any weight which may be laid on it; it grows in a dry and thirsty soil. And by the palm we may understand also the Cross of CHRIST, for it grows to a great height, and bears sweet fruit, just as the Cross of CHRIST prepared heavenly food for us; and the stature of the Bride is likened to this, because any one who truly loves and imitates CHRIST, does not hesitate to die for Him.

Idem in loc.

And thy breasts to clusters of grapes. Or rather, more probably, clusters of *dates*, as continuing the reference to the palm tree. And so Theodoret takes it: "Tall and exalted as thou art, reaching to the height of heaven, yet thou bowest down to the feeble, and yieldest the breast of thy teaching to those who are in need of teaching. For the palm tree has clusters which hang downwards. And the HOLY GHOST signifies this by blessed David, saying, 'The righteous shall flourish as a palm tree.'" The breasts of the Church, adds Cassiodorus, are, as has been said already, holy teachers, who nourish with the milk of simple doctrine them who are born again in CHRIST. But these breasts are likened to *clusters of grapes* when these same teachers proclaim more perfect things to the perfect. And so the Apostle, when speaking to the less instructed, said, "I could not speak unto you as unto spiritual, but as unto carnal, even as unto babes in CHRIST. I have fed you with milk, and not with meat." These are breasts full of milk, which breasts were turned into *clusters of grapes* when he said, "Howbeit we speak wisdom among them that are perfect." The two breasts are also the two Testaments, the two precepts of love, and the active and contemplative lives of Christianity, all of them yielding sweet and gladdening wine to cheer the heart of those who imitate CHRIST. And as He hung, Himself, as the bunch of grapes upon the pole which the spies brought from the Land of Promise, so the Martyrs, who are close to His heart, and are most like to Him, are fit-

De Wette.

Theodoret.

Ps. xcii. 11.

Cassiodor.

1 Cor. iii. 1.

1 Cor. ii. 6.

Philo Carp.

Luc. Abb.

tingly styled the breasts of His Bride. Spoken of the Blessed Virgin, one devout writer bids us look to that verse of the Gospels, "Now there stood by the Cross of JESUS His Mother," and ponder whether, as she stood beside that palm tree, her stature was not indeed likened to it, nay, whether she was not herself a very cross of suffering then. Another, working out the simile at greater length, comments: Her outer bark was rough, in that she was weak in worldly honour, poor in temporal riches, but yet she possessed vigorous strength in her constancy of soul. She was erect in stem, because shooting upwards to heaven in the resolution of her mind; firm at the summit, by reason of her exalted virginity and lowliness; lovely in flower, because with no thought of sin she conceived the Flower of the plain, the Lily of the valley; sweet in her fruitfulness, because she painlessly bore the Redeemer of the world. She is set before us as an emblem of victory; that as she overcame the world, the flesh, and the devil, so we too may overcome according to our power. The breasts of Mary are her virginity and lowliness, wherein CHRIST delights, and they are set before us for our learning and instruction, that we should follow her footsteps. They are compared to clusters of grapes, because the grape yields perfume in flower and sweetness in fruit. It warms and refreshes, and so too the Maiden's virginity and lowliness are fragrant with the savour of devout thought, warm with love, and refreshing with spiritual fulness.

And it is well to sum up all this description of the Bride's comeliness with the frequent comment of Cornelius à Lapide, that all the eulogy may be interpreted of the Humanity of CHRIST JESUS, that Sacred Body which was, in a sense, the Bride to whom the Eternal WORD united Himself for ever.

Guilielmus.

S. John xix. 25.

Alanus.

Corn. à Lap.

8 I said, I will go up to the palm tree, I will take hold of the boughs thereof: now also thy breasts shall be as clusters of the vine, and the smell of thy nose like apples:

It is more than merely going *to* the palm tree, and the words denote a harder and higher task; *I will climb up into the palm tree*, high enough to reach the fruit which hangs near its summit. Who then is the

S. Cyprian. Serm. de Pass.

Henr. Harph.
Cassiodor.
Honorius.

speaker, and when were the words said? *I said*, quoth the LORD, from all eternity, when I determined to die, of My perfect love and free-will. *I said*, by the mouth of My prophets, that I would *go up to the palm tree*, that is, the Cross, itself formed in part of palm-wood, and exalted on high like a palm, that JESUS, lifted up on it, might draw all unto Him. Of old, too, victory was denoted by the palm, which victory CHRIST won gloriously, as He triumphed upon the Cross. *I said*, unto My FATHER, before all worlds, that I would go up to the palm tree and conquer the tyrant there. And that is the reason why thy stature, in thy perseverance, is like to a palm tree, because I went up to the palm tree for this one thing, and drew thee after Me to victory.

Rupert.

I went up to this palm tree by the hands of the soldiers, who ignorantly fought against My divine majesty. As regards them, they crucified a man to die by a miserable death, as regards Me, I ascended the palm tree as a King about to triumph. And the Jews, unknowing the decrees of GOD, bid Me come down from it, saying, If He be the King of Israel, let Him come down from the Cross. I had gone up to the palm tree, and therefore I willed not to come down while the fruits were not yet formed—the palm tree had already flowered when they so spake to Him—but when, after tasting the vinegar, I said, "It is finished," and bowing My head, gave up the ghost, then, the fruits of redemption were upon the palm. This verse has originated, or at least encouraged, two opinions in the Church. One is the tradition that the Cross was made of four kinds of wood: cedar, cypress, olive, and palm, and that this last formed the transverse beam to which the sacred Hands were nailed. So runs the distich:

Gretser et Lipsius de Cruce.

> De cedro est truncus, corpus tenet alta cupressus,
> Palma manus retinet, titulo lætatur oliva.
>
> Cedar the trunk, tall cypress holds His frame,
> Palm clasps His hands, and olive boasts His Name.

Suarez.

The other view based on this passage is that CHRIST literally went up to the Tree, that is, that it was fixed erect in the ground before He was nailed to it, as the more painful and degrading mode of execution; an opinion followed by SS. Gregory Nazianzen, Bernard, Bonaventura, and Birgitta. But the view more generally accepted is, that He was laid down upon the Cross while it was still flat upon the ground, and even then the going-up may be well interpreted of the weary journey by the Way of Sorrows to the hill of Calvary. There is a secondary meaning of the words, as applied to the Redeemer, inferior to this alone. The palm tree, observes Cassiodorus, signifies the Church, or even the soul of any faithful believer, who is mindful of the LORD his GOD, Who saith, "Be of good cheer, I have overcome the world." For she aims to be victorious over all sin and unrighteousness. He is well said then here to go up to the palm tree, of Whom we read before that He went down into the garden. The garden and the palm are the same, to wit, the one same Church. The LORD both goes down into it, and goes up into it; down, when sending the abundance of that grace from heaven; up, by increasing His gifts to her, and lifting her up to higher things, by progressive advances, as though by steps. ^{Cassiodor.} ^{S. John xvi. 33.}

I will take hold of the boughs thereof. That is, as the Vulgate, with a justifiable paraphrase, reads, *of the fruits thereof,* hidden amongst the *heights* (LXX.) of the tree. And the fruits which the LORD gathered there were, first, the salvation of mankind, and then, as regarded Himself, the glorification of His Body, the hastening of His Resurrection, the splendid pomp of His Ascension, the manifestation of His Name, and the acquisition of authority as Judge. But, though these words belong primarily to the Bridegroom, yet His Spouse, because He endows her with all He possesses, can take them on her lips also. She can say, *I will go up to the palm tree,* to the Cross, by ever bearing CHRIST'S Passion in mind, by sharing in His sorrows, by keeping them alive within me, by imitating them faithfully. And that "because CHRIST also suffered for us, leaving us an example, that ye should follow His steps," and "arm yourselves likewise with the same mind." She can also be like Zaccheus, ascending above the worldly crowd to see her LORD Who is hidden from such as refuse the Cross. *And take hold of the fruits thereof,* not only those fruits of our redemption, by being grateful and giving thanks, but also the fruits of practical perfection, by faithfully imitating that perfection of all virtues. *I will go up,* she saith to her Bridegroom, by imitation in holiness to the perfection of Thy teaching, and will take hold of its heights by contemplation. ^{Henry Harphius.} ^{1 S. Pet. ii. 21; iv. 1.} ^{Tres Patr.}

Or, yet more deeply, interpreting the palm tree, tall and stately, bearing luscious fruit, and growing best in the sands of the " barren and dry land where no water is," to be CHRIST Himself, the Tree of Life, let us hear Hugh of S. Victor: " The toil of the climber is lessened, when he perceives the fragrance of the fruit upon the tree, for the sweetness of its taste does away with the difficulty of the ascent. The palm tree is CHRIST; His fruit salvation; the hope of salvation is in the wood of the Cross. Ascend therefore into the palm tree, that is, give heed to the victory of the Cross, for by the stair of·the Cross thou shalt go up to the throne of the victor." Keeping to the literal Hebrew, *I will take hold of the boughs*, we have two further meanings which the verse bears in the mouth of the Bride, besides that of promised conformity to the Passion. Palm-branches were amongst the green boughs commanded for use by the Jews in token of rejoicing at the feast of ingathering of the harvest, and also at the feast of tabernacles, in token of rest in the fertile Land of Promise after the weary march through the barren wilderness. They were used also, as by the Greeks and Romans, in token of victory, as when Judas Maccabeus took the citadel of Jerusalem, and when Simon dedicated the sanctuary, and thus they typify a more glorious triumph of CHRIST than that entry into the earthly Jerusalem on Palm Sunday, namely, the true feast of ingathering, of tabernacles, of dedication, and of victory, when the LORD's harvest shall have been gathered by His reapers, the Angels, into His garners, when the tents of the great army of heaven shall encamp round the pavilion of their victorious Leader, when the true Land of Promise has been won by the people of GOD under their greater Joshua.

<blockquote>
Here may the band that now in triumph shines,
  And who (before they were invested thus)
In earthly bodies carried heavenly minds,
  Pitch round about, in order glorious,
  Their sunny tents, and houses luminous :
    All their eternal day in songs employing ;
    Joy is their end, without end of their joying,
While their Almighty Prince destruction is destroying.
</blockquote>

And, again, it was the wont amongst the Jews, until after the fall of their city, to use palm-branches as well as nuptial crowns in bridal rejoicings, and therefore the Bride may well declare how she will prepare herself and her companions for the glad procession of that great day when "the marriage of the Lamb is come, and His wife hath made herself ready," and when the great multitude, which no man can number, of all nations, and kindreds, and peoples, and tongues, stand before the throne, and before the Lamb, clothed with white robes, and palms in their hands. And that, because they have "come out of great tribulation," for by the palm which the Bride ascends may be understood the plain of combat and victory, and as CHRIST ascended the Cross to fight for us against the devil, and gathered from that Tree the fruits of redemption and salvation, so the Church went up into her battle-field to fight against tyrants and unbelievers for the faith of CHRIST, and also to war against the flesh, the world, and false brethren. Thus there were four armies that went up to the palm tree for the combat. First went the choir or army of Martyrs, to fight against tyrants, princes, and unbelievers. Secondly, the army of Virgins went up to war against the flesh. Thirdly, the army of Contemplative and Monastic Saints went up to war against the world and its pomp. Fourthly went up the army of Doctors to fight against heretics. And because these four battalions so went up to the palm tree as to a battle-field, the Church was said above to be "terrible as an army in array." *(Rev. xix. 7.)* *(Rev. vii. 9.)* *(Parez.)*

Now also thy breasts shall be as clusters of the vine. "For as the clusters of the vine, when trodden and pressed, yield the pleasant juice of wine to their husbandman and vine-dresser, so righteous and holy men of GOD, when afflicted and tortured like grapes, bring forth and produce from themselves, through their victory of salvation, heavenly gladness to GOD their Husbandman, and to JESUS CHRIST, and to the Bride; and by the fragrance of their holiness and virtue attract and draw on others to be imitators of CHRIST in like manner, for which reason it follows suitably, *And the smell of thy nose like apples:* denoting thereby most plainly the perfume of unconquered faith and hope and glowing charity, according to that saying of the Apostle, 'We are a sweet savour of CHRIST in them that are saved, and in them that perish; to the one we are the savour of death unto death, and to the other the savour of life unto life' everlasting. The *nose* denotes the Orthodox *(Philo Carp.)* *(2 Cor. ii. 15.)*

Church, which inhales the perfume of virtues with both nostrils, that is, the two Testaments. So too, though there is but one nose, to wit, one spirit, one faith, one baptism, one life everlasting, one and the same GOD, the goal of the blessed, yet there are two Churches, divided in name, not in fact, in race, not in faith, by distance of place, not by ultimate aim, to wit, Greek and Latin, Eastern and Western;[1] or, if I mistake not, the Synagogue and the Church may be here understood, derived from the one Author, the SPIRIT of distribution and of unity. And for all this reason, the Bride is compared to apples, because as apples yield both food and drink, both which they contain, so the sweet odour of the Church in true faith and love unfeigned possesses the mystic drink and food of the Body and Blood of CHRIST, and gives them to others."

S. Greg. M. It is by the Cross, observes S. Gregory, that the breasts of the Bride become like clusters of grapes, because in the death of CHRIST the powers of the soul received the two precepts of charity, and when the soul is nourished by them, she is inebriated, so as to forget what is behind, and to reach forward to what is before. *Beda.* Yes, continues Beda, expanding this thought, since the first Doctors of the Church, that is, the Apostles, obtained far more knowledge of the doctrines of salvation when the Passion and Resurrection were fulfilled, than they had before; when He, appearing to *S. Luke xxiv. 27.* them after His Resurrection, opened to them the Scriptures that they might understand, and sending down the SPIRIT upon them, gave them knowledge of all *Acts ii. 13.* languages, that time when it was falsely said "These men are full of new wine." But they were in truth made like clusters of the vine, because they were refreshed with the grace of spiritual gifts, when that *S. Luke v. 38.* saying was truly brought to pass, " New wine must be put into new bottles, and both are preserved." That, *Rupert.* observes Rupert, was the autumn, when men eat of the grapes, and the sweet perfume is everywhere diffused. *Theodoret.* They do not fail to remind us also of that True *Tres Patr.* Vine, from which these clusters hang which yield the *Cassiod.* wine of salvation for mankind. The Vulgate reads *Beda.* *the smell of thy mouth,* and the Latin Fathers accordingly explain the clause as denoting the preaching of

---

[1] This statement of an external severance, not incompatible with internal unity, of the Eastern and Western Churches in the fourth century is noteworthy.

the Word; and S. Gregory, who supposes the *apples* to be pomegranates, dwells, as before, on their ruddy hue, as typifying the Martyrs, chief preachers of the Church either in word or example. Honorius, taking the whole verse of the final glory of the redeemed, comments thus: "The Church Triumphant ascends the palm tree, because by the victory of the Cross she reaches the Tree of Life, of which is written, ' To him that overcometh I will give to eat of the tree of life, which is in the midst of the Paradise of GOD.' She hath already taken hold of its fruit, whereof whoso eateth shall never die. Her breasts are as clusters of grapes, because the joys wherewith she is inebriated in return for her sufferings in the world, are like the joys of CHRIST when He was pressed out upon the Cross. For He is the cluster of the vine, the drink of the Church, the fount of life, wherewith she shall be inebriated, when it shall be said unto her, 'Enter thou into the joy of thy LORD.' Then shall her smell be like apples, that, is, her delights shall be as those of the Angels; and her throat like the best wine, that is, her praise shall be as the praise of them that feast."
S. Greg. M.
Honor. August.
Rev. ii. 7.
S. Mat. xxv. 21.

9 And the roof of thy mouth like the best wine, for my beloved, that goeth down sweetly, causing the lips of those that are asleep to speak.

For *roof of the mouth* or *palate* the LXX. and Vulgate read *throat*. But the inner meaning, that of the speech of the Bride, is alike. The preaching of the Church is *like the best wine*, because it exhibits its great power to the hearers. And whereas the perfume of apples is best when they are new, and that of wine when it is old, this signifies that the preaching of the Church possesses all sweetness and grace alike in its beginning and in its perfection. And wine, pleasant to the taste, and beautiful in colour, denotes also cheerful and devout praise of GOD by His Saints, of whom is written, "Let the praises of GOD be in their mouth." Philo urges that CHRIST Himself is the throat or palate of the Bride, because it is only through Him that she can taste how sweet He is in His own Sacrament of love, wherein He gives her the *best wine*. But the Bride, hearing Him thus speak, can no longer
Heiligstedt.
Cassiod.
Guilielmus.
Ps. cxlix. 6.
Philo Carp.
Cassiodor.

contain herself, and catching up His words, adds, *For my Beloved.* It is, as the Vulgate adds, *worthy for Him to drink,* for the preaching of the Gospel to the world can be effected by Him only, and by no other; for it is fitting that the mysteries of the kingdom of heaven should not be disclosed to the world by any save the "Mediator between GOD and man."

That goeth down sweetly, causing the lips of them that are asleep to speak. In this passage there is much divergence amongst the renderings, and it will be most convenient to take them in order. The LXX. reads, *Going to my Beloved unto straightness, sufficient for my lips and teeth.* That is, as Theodoret paraphrases it, the doctrine which flows from thy throat, preferable to any perfumed wine or to all the pleasures of this life, is that which Thou givest, my Beloved, to guide aright the souls which believe in Thee. And this Thy teaching is enough and sufficient for me, that I should in part disclose it and proclaim it, using the organ of my lips; and partly guard and hide it, using my teeth as a barrier to encompass it. It is sufficient, say others, for my *lips,* in readily satisfying my desires, sufficient for my *teeth* also, in supplying difficult problems for my understanding, needing much careful mastication before they can be assimilated as spiritual food. The Vulgate reads the whole clause thus: *Worthy for my Beloved to drink, for His lips and teeth to ruminate.* The idea here is the slow tasting of very choice wine, sipping it gradually, and allowing it to remain some time in the mouth, in order to perceive its full bouquet and flavour; and they explain it, accordingly, of sedulous meditation in the precepts of the Gospel, in order to extract their full meaning and beauty. And on this S. Gregory says very well: "Such is the wine of the Bride, that it is worthy for her Beloved to drink, because while Holy Church preaches the true faith, and rouses her hearers to holy works, and shows them by word and deed how good it is to love, imitate, and embrace CHRIST alone, what else does she do but make the wine worthy of her Beloved, that it may taste sweet in the Bridegroom's mouth? And on this act it is to be noted, that all drink, but only the lips and teeth ruminate, because while the Church preaches by her Saints, all hear, but not all perceive the whole force of the sayings which are uttered. The lips and teeth ruminate, since the more perfect, after hearing, recall the words to their memory while pondering in earnest thought what they have heard, as those animals which bring again into the mouth the food they have received, taste the full flavour of that food they had eaten. Therefore it is written in the Law that animals which do not ruminate are not clean, implying that any one who does not ponder again on good things which he hears or reads, by not being occupied with holy thoughts, necessarily collects unclean ones." And S. Albert, in a similar spirit, aptly applies the text to meditation after Communion of the Blessed Sacrament. S. Alb. Mag.

The A. V. reading, *Causing the lips of those that are asleep to speak,* may be explained in two ways, either that the sweet wine of the Gospel breathed a new meaning into the dark sayings of the dead Seers and Prophets of the Old Testament, and gave a living force to seemingly inert types and oracles, so that the whole meaning of such mysteries as the sacrifice of Melchizedek, the offering of Isaac, the burning bush, the brazen serpent, and the fleece of Gideon; the inner sense of prophecies like Balaam's, Joel's, and Isaiah's, were revealed, just as sympathetic ink, heretofore hidden from the eye, stands out in relief under the influence of heat; and thus it might be said of each old Seer that " he, being dead, yet speaketh," in bearing witness to CHRIST. The other meaning is the revival of souls dead asleep in the lethargy of sin, roused by the Voice of CHRIST, the sweet wine going down as a medicine *straightly,* in the direct simplicity of the Gospel message, to tell the sinner, "'I say unto thee, Arise,' and he that was dead sat up, and began to speak, and He delivered him to his mother." And this interpretation, which is supported by the Targum, here citing the miracles of Elijah and Elisha, and the awaking of the dry bones which Ezekiel saw, is in the spirit of that ancient hymn in honour of the Cross: Delitzsch. Hengstenberg.

Heb. xi. 4.

A. V. Marg.
S. Luke vii. 14.

Targum.

O branches rich and passing fair, O sweet and noble Tree!
What new and precious fruit is that which hangs for all on thee?
Whose fragrance breathes the breath of life into the silent dead,
Gives life to them from whom, long since, earth's pleasant light had fled! S. Venant. Fortunat. The Hymn, *Crux benedicta.*

Two other renderings are suggested by modern critics, *gliding gently over the lips of sleepers,* which seems to mean that the wine has a gently lulling effect, gradu- Hitzig.

ally bringing a peaceful slumber, which may then be interpreted of the tranquillizing influence of the Word; or, with another version, *causing the lips of sleepers to taste it,* meaning that the wine which was so good at the banquet as to *go down straightly* (because men not only made no difficulty about swallowing it, but bent back the head to drain the cup,) left the memory of its flavour so clear, that the banqueters seemed to taste it again in dreams. And then, it will come to much the same meaning as S. Gregory's explanation of ruminating, to wit, the contemplation in time of rest of all that has been said or done for GOD in the time of action.[1]

Weissbach.

10 I am my beloved's, and his desire is toward me.

This is the third time that the close union and mutual affection of the Bridegroom and Bride is mentioned in the Song. And there is, observes S. Ambrose, a threefold diversity in the manner of expression, to denote the three stages of the Bride's progress in the love of GOD, to wit, her beginning, advance, and perfection. She said, at first, "My Beloved is mine, and I am His; He feedeth among the lilies until the day break, and the shadows flee away," because when she is beginning to learn, the Bride still sees the shadows, not yet disturbed by the approach of the WORD, as, in fact, the Gospel day did not shine upon the Church at her origin. In the second place she says, "I am my Beloved's, and my Beloved is mine; He feedeth among the lilies," for in her progress He gathers her sweet perfumes, untroubled by clouds. And thirdly, in this place she says, "I am my Beloved's and His desire (LXX. and Vulgate *turning*) is toward me," because, now made perfect, she makes herself a resting-place for the WORD, that He may turn towards her, and lay His head upon her, and take His rest. And that, observes Theodoret, because she can say, I have con-

S. Ambros. de Isaac, 8.

Chap. ii. 16.

Chap. vi. 3.

Theodoret.

---

[1] The considerable variants in the renderings of this difficult verse are mainly reducible to two causes, viz., the reading וְשִׁנַּיִם "and teeth" instead of יְשֵׁנִים "sleepers," and the erroneous derivation of דּוֹבֵב, as though connected with דָּבָר *locutus est,* instead of the true etymon דָּבַב *repsit.*

secrated myself to Him, and have looked with loathing on the common fellowship of Gentiles, Jews, and heretics. For He hath preferred me to all others, and turned unto me, and whereas He once had not where to lay His head, He hath now found a place to lay it. I will now, comments another, be the servant of the Son of God, and He will reward me abundantly when He shall descend at His second coming to sit as Judge of all. But we must be turned to Him first, as it is written, "Turn ye unto Me, saith the Lord of Hosts, and I will turn unto you." And Henry Harphius, understanding the word *turning* to denote turning in to dwell in a place, tells us here how the Bride should prepare herself to become the kingdom, temple, and abode of Christ, adorned with that love in the midst of which He is ever pleased to tarry. Of such love a Saint has wisely said: Love divine is fire, light, honey, wine, and sun. Fire, in that it purifies in meditation the soul from all uncleanness. Light, in prayer, illuminating the soul with the radiance of holiness. Honey, in thanksgiving, sweetening the soul with the sweetness of God's bounties. Wine, in contemplation, inebriating the soul with sweet and pleasant delight. Sun, in eternal bliss, giving splendour to the soul in unclouded light, gladdening it with the genial heat of unspeakable joy and everlasting jubilation. He turned to us here long ago in taking our flesh upon Him; He turns again and again in answering our prayers. He loved us sweetly, wisely, strongly. Sweetly, in clothing Himself with flesh; wisely, in being pure from sin; strongly, in undergoing death. Therefore, O Christian, learn from Christ how to love Christ; learn to love Him sweetly, that we fail not when enticed; wisely, that we be not deceived; strongly, that no force can make us yield. And where love is, there is no toil.

But if you will have the other rendering, *His desire is toward me*, the Psalmist can tell us how it has been attracted: "Hearken, O daughter, and consider, incline thine ear, forget also thine own people, and thy father's house, so shall the King greatly desire thy beauty." Hear the Word of God with attention, obey it with alacrity, leave behind all former evil conversation; leave, if need be, country, and home, and closest ties of kindred, and follow Christ, and He will desire thee, and with desire will eat His Passover with thee, feeding thee with His own Body and Blood.

Marginal notes: Philo Carp. | Zech. i. 3. | Henr. Harph. | S. Hrabanus Maurus. | Cassiodor. | S. Just. Org. | Dion. Carth. | S. Bernard. Serm. 20 in Cant. | Idem, Serm. 86. | Ps. xlv. 11. | Ayguan, in loc.

Honorius. And when even Sacraments shall vanish, the Bride will turn to her Beloved as she passes from the world to heaven, and He will turn to her, welcoming her into the fellowship of the Angels.

11 Come, my beloved, let us go forth into the field; let us lodge in the villages.

S. Ambros. Serm. 19 in Ps. cxix. There are three main interpretations of these words of the Bride. And first; it is a prayer for the Incarnation. Observe, comments S. Ambrose, how the Bride invites the WORD of GOD to come unto the earth, and to take away the sins of the world. This *field* was once desert, rough with the brambles of our sins, bristling with thorns. It was the *village* whither Adam was banished, and where he bound his heirs and posterity in perpetual exile. Thither the Church leads CHRIST to set Adam free; and when the exiles were loosed, the field of this world began to have competent tillers, and though it once was barren, it became fruitful with the everlasting plantation of the Vine.

S. Greg. M. Or, as S. Gregory more briefly puts it, the Bridegroom goes *into the field* with the Bride when the WORD is manifested to the world in the flesh which He took in the chamber of the Virgin. He *lodges in the villages* when He visits the Gentiles by that faith which He bestows on them that receive Him.

Secondly; the invitation is to convert the heathen. *Cassiodor.* The field, says Cassiodorus in his Master's words, is the world. *Let us go forth into the field*, that is, let us preach to the world. *Let us lodge in the villages*, that is, let us proclaim faith in Thee even to the Pagans. For every one knows that *Pagan* is derived from *pagus*, a village, and Pagans are fitly so named because they are far from the City of GOD. *Come*, saith the Bride, *my Beloved*. Thou hast already raised Thine assumed Manhood to the heavens by the mystery of Thine Ascension, yet *come*, visiting me often with the presence of Thy divine Majesty. *Let us lodge* in the villages, not merely passing through them as we preach, but tarrying there till we make the Pagans Catholics, and the aliens Thine own.

Thirdly; they take it of the field of the Church, into which the Bridegroom is called, that He may note the progress of the faithful; and as S. Ambrose aptly *S. Ambros. de Isaac, 8.* points out, see not only flowers and spices, as in the

garden, but the firm and solid produce of wheat and
barley, denoting the more vigorous kinds of holiness.
Theodoret varies somewhat from this view, saying, <small>Theodoret.</small>
The Bride urges the Bridegroom to undertake the cure <small>Origen.</small>
of souls as yet poor and lowly, which, as being lowly
and insignificant, she typically calls by the names of
field and *villages*. For she does not say, Let us go
into the City, but into the field. And so Hugh of <small>Hugo Vict.
de Claustr.</small>
S. Victor takes it also: The soul goeth forth from con- <small>Animæ, 7.</small>
templation to look round about her; she goeth forth
from care for herself to care of her neighbour, to comfort the feeble, to rebuke the restless, that the field,
once full of brambles and thorns, may be full of virtues.
And she saith, *Let us lodge in the villages*, to wit, in
them who are villeins; that is, clowns, and slow in
understanding the rules of CHRIST's royal court. *Let* <small>Tres Patr.</small>
us go forth, showing them our spiritual union in holy
principles expressed by action. *Let us lodge* in those
souls, which, as villages, have given up all their inhabitants, faculties, and senses, to Thee. Make there a
dwelling for Thyself in the HOLY SPIRIT, and I will
give myself to them as an example that they may learn
to please Thee. And in this sense, let us hear what a
holy writer of another land and age has to tell us:
"We are made so to abound and be more than full, that <small>Gerlach
Petersen,</small>
we ought to flow out with JESUS over all creation, that <small>Soliloqu.</small>
GOD may be all in all. And we should desire this to <small>Ignit.</small>
be brought to pass no less in every one else than in ourselves, because we ought to have as hearty a desire,
longing, and good will that all should have everything
which is good as GOD Himself has. And thus we
make all good things which belong to others our very
own, an easy and facile matter for them that love,
since wherever true love is, it is impossible for it not
to flow out and love, for there is nought so like and so
peculiar to the Image of GOD, as to flow forth evermore and to share with all. There is no clearer mark
and sign of union with the WORD, than thus without
any straitening of internal breadth to converse in
common love, giving all things, filling all things with
JESUS, that nothing may remain which hath not its
rightful share. Thus, so far as in us lies, we can fill
heaven and earth, and all that therein is, with our
love, which is GOD." Another interpretation sees here <small>Parez.</small>
the Church in the days of persecution, driven out of
the cities where the tribunals of the heathen judges

were set up, and forced to withdraw into desert places, as the Thebaid, or, as we read in far earlier times, "And there was a great persecution against the Church which was at Jerusalem, and they were all scattered abroad throughout the regions of Judæa and Samaria." Wherefore, the Bride, cut off from the visible fellowship of the Saints and from the solemnities of public worship, prays her Beloved not to leave her, but to go with her in her exile. And finally, the Church here in the pilgrimage with CHRIST desires to go with Him into that flowery *field,* the Paradise of delight, and to *lodge in the villages* formed of the many mansions in His FATHER's House. So our own poet:

_{Acts viii. 1.}

_{Honorius.}

_{Francis Quarles, *Emblems,* iv. 7.}

> Our country mansion, situate on high,
> With various objects still renews delight;
> Her archéd roof's of unstained ivory,
> Her walls of fiery sparkling chrysolite;
> Her pavement is of hardest porphyry,
> Her spacious windows are all glazed with bright
> And flaming carbuncles; no need require
> Titan's faint rays, or Vulcan's feeble fire,
> And every gate's a pearl, and every pearl entire.

12 Let us get up early to the vineyards; let us see if the vine flourish, whether the tender grape appear, and the pomegranates bud forth: there will I give thee my loves.

_{Philo Carp.} The Bridegroom had lodged during the night in the villages, where up to the night of His death He was a pilgrim, despised and hated, in the clownish souls, the hard and obstinate minds of the Jews, and when He lay in the grave for two nights, and on the third day before the light *got up early to the vineyards* of His disciples and the Gentiles who should believe, and when He called us and His Bride from the darkness of ignorance of GOD and from blindness of mind, from the night of sin and the worship of devils, to His marvellous light, and to the true and saving Faith. He _{S. Greg. M.} rises early to the vineyards, because, sitting after His Resurrection in the glory of the FATHER, He defends the Churches which He has founded. He sees *if the vine flourish,* because He tests with strict examination every progress of the Church. He sees *whether the flowers are bringing forth fruits* (Vulg.) because He looks to see what progress the weak and imperfect are

making. He sees also *whether the pomegranates bud forth*, because He looks to the perfect also, and sees what profit they are to their neighbours, as though looking for the fruit of a tree amongst its flowers. In the early morning of the new Gospel light, He marks the first rudiments of faith in the healthy growth of the vine, its progress in the appearance of the young fruit, its maturity in the likeness to His Passion in the ruddy pomegranate, fit emblem of His Martyrs. And note, though He says, Let *us* get up early; yet, however soon she may be at the sepulchre, her LORD forestalls her, and she finds the stone rolled away; however early she is at the vineyard, the Gardener is there awaiting her, lest any delay in the Resurrection should weaken her faith. Cassiodor.

Angelomus Luxov.

S. Just. Org.

> I got me flowers to straw Thy way,
> I got me boughs off many a tree;
> But Thou wast up by break of day,
> And brought'st Thy sweets along with Thee.
>
> George Herbert.

Honorius, agreeing in other respects with the interpretation already given, differs in one particular. He takes the night to be the time of Antichrist's persecution of the Church, and the early morning the beginning of the new age, when the Synagogue shall be converted, and CHRIST and the Bride will visit the new Churches formed out of her. Honorius.

The same commentator agrees with several others in explaining the verse of the faithful soul, which *gets up early*, that is, exhibits diligence and zeal, because, as is well said by one annotating this passage, "they who wish to urge others to rise to their tasks must get up early themselves, not sluggishly, but taking the lead in example and activity." *Early*, in the dawning of life, as it is written, "It is good for a man that he bear the yoke in his youth;" *early*, because the manna must be gathered in the cool of the morning, since "when the sun waxed hot, it melted;" *early*, because Joshua must beset Ai before its inhabitants are aware, must come suddenly, by a forced march all night, on the unprepared forces of the confederate kings; *early*, in the most literal sense, that the first-fruits of the day may be offered to GOD. S.Ans.Laud.

Hugo Vict. de Claustr. Animæ, 7.

Lam. iii. 27.

Exod. xvi. 21.
Josh. viii. 10; x. 9.

> When first thine eyes unveil, give thy soul leave
> To do the like; our bodies but forerun

*The spirit's duty. True hearts spread and heave
Unto their* GOD, *as flowers do to the sun.
Give Him thy first thoughts then, so shalt thou keep
Him company all day, and in Him sleep.*

*Yet never sleep the sun up. Prayer should
Dawn with the day. There are set, awful hours
'Twixt heaven and us. The manna was not good
After sun-rising; far-day sullies flowers.
Rise to prevent the sun; sleep doth sins glut,
And heaven's gate opens when this world's is shut.*

Henry Vaughan, *Rules and Lessons.*

Then, in quiet self-examination, it is possible to learn whether the True Vine is flourishing in the soil of our hearts, if the flower promise fruit in the formation of character, if the pomegranate of outward self-restraint and inward fervour be developing within us, if purity of life and true confession of faith be ours.

There will I give Thee my loves. Or, with LXX. and Vulgate, *my breasts.* In the field, in the scene of labour, not in the palace of rest, is it that my love and devotion will be chiefly kindled, there only can I bring forth children to suckle and bring up for Thee, there only shall I be able to train them for martyrdom. Or, taking the *vineyards,* with Honorius, to denote the cloisters of the Religious Life, there, apart from the disturbances of the city, in the still quiet of the field, will the love of GOD be best nourished in the soul. And there comes a time too when this world's night is ended, and the Bride rises *early to the vineyards,* lifting herself up to the Churches on high. The Day of Judgment is the morn of that everlasting day, which is better than a thousand years; or, you may take it that man's life is the night, and the life to come is the morning, in which morning each of the faithful gets up to the vineyards when he arrives after death at the Heavenly Churches. There he beholds the flowers of the vineyard, the fruits of these flowers, and the buds of the pomegranates, that is, the reward for the faithful and righteous, given to those who labour diligently, and the wages which shall be paid to the Martyrs. And *there* the Church will *give* CHRIST *her breasts,* because she will, in eternal glory, present to Him the teachers of the Old and New Law.

13 The mandrakes give a smell, and at our gates are all manner of pleasant fruits, new

Tres Patr.

Angelomus.
Philo Carp.

Tres Patr.

Cassiodor.

S. Just. Org.

Honorius.

Idem.

and old, which I have laid up for thee, O my beloved.

The mandrake, or love-apple, a narcotic fruit, was supposed to have the powers of a philtre, to excite love and to produce fruitfulness; and for this latter reason Rachel asks Leah to give her the mandrakes which Reuben had gathered. The root is also said to resemble a headless human body, and these two opinions about the plant have influenced much of the exposition of this passage. Theodoret, confining himself to the notion of an opiate,[1] holds that the words here imply a further progress in grace beyond that last stage of the previous verse, and denote deadness to the world and sin, and tranquil sleep, free from all disturbance and passion, attained by quaffing the chalice of holy doctrine. S. Gregory, also holding to the view that advance in religious perfection is here intended, refers, following Cassiodorus, to the medicinal use of the mandrake, and takes the plant here to denote those more perfect Saints who are not merely fruitful in good works themselves, but are able to heal others with the wholesome odour of their good example. He does not, however, dwell on the special use which Cassiodorus ascribes to the mandrake, that of being given as an anæsthetic to persons about to undergo severe surgical operations, which, he hints, signifies the power of faith in overcoming the tortures of martyrdom. Philo sees in the shape of the mandrake's root, the buried Saints of the Old Testament, hidden from the glory of GOD, but yielding a sweet savour until the early morning of CHRIST'S Resurrection, when they received the reward of their fragrance in the gift of everlasting life. The Vulgate couples this clause with the succeeding one thus, *The mandrakes give a smell at our gates.* These *gates*, says Cassiodorus, are the Apostles and their successors, because no one enters the Church, which is the City of GOD, save he who has been regenerated in Baptism and taught the doctrine of life by holy teachers. Of these gates the Psalmist said, "The LORD loveth the gates

Gen. xxx. 14.

Theodoret.

S. Greg. M.

S. August. in Faust. Man. xxii. 56.

Cassiodor.

Philo Carp.

Cassiodor.

Ps. lxxxvii.

---

[1] "Not poppy, nor mandragora,
Nor all the drowsy syrups of the world,
Shall ever medicine thee to that sweet sleep
Which thou ow'dst yesterday."
Othello, Act iii., sc. 3.

of Sion more than all the dwellings of Jacob." The *mandrakes* denote the perfume of holiness, and thus the mandrakes gave a smell at the gates of the Church when the Apostles and their successors spread far and wide the fame of their sweet teaching, the fragrance of their holiness. And Rupert, who accepts the view that the mandrake produces fruitfulness, adds: The reason why they give a smell in our gates is because that is now at hand to be fulfilled which the spirit of prophecy spake to the yet barren Gentile race: "Rejoice, thou barren that bearest not, break forth and cry, thou that travailest not, for the desolate hath many more children than she which hath an husband." *In our gates*, while we are still within our own borders, in the land of the Jews, we smell this odour. The Ethiopian eunuch had come to Jerusalem to worship and was returning sitting in his chariot and reading Esaias the Prophet, when, lo, the HOLY SPIRIT, smelling the odour, said unto Philip, "Go near, and join thyself to this chariot." We were even then in our gates when the alms of Cornelius the Centurion gave their smell in the sight of GOD. And to this smell too belongs that vision which appeared in the night to one of the Bridegroom's friends, "There stood a man of Macedonia, and prayed him, saying, Come over into Macedonia, and help us." In these and other like ways the mandrakes gave a smell at our gates, denoting fruitfulness where sterility had been. And the resemblance to a headless body is dwelt on by more than one commentator. The mandrakes, says an early writer, were the Gentiles, living by the law of nature, and so far like natural men, but without the head of faith. These, not in the field, but *at our gates*, at the very utmost limit of our tenure, that is, near the end of the world, will be converted to GOD, and yield their perfume to Him. Another, not dissimilarly, tells us that in the evil times of the latter days, Antichrist will be for a time the visible head of the faithful, but when he has been smitten off, when the body lies as it were headless, then the Bride will call on her Beloved to go with her again for a new preaching of the Gospel and the new foundation of Churches amongst the helpless people lying at her gates. And S. Anselm of Laon reproduces this idea, confining it, however, to the Jews, as lacking CHRIST their true Head, but who will give a pleasant smell at our gates when they exhibit signs of conversion, and seek admission by faith into the Church.

At our gates are all manner of pleasant fruits, new and old, which I have laid up for Thee, O my Beloved. There is a general agreement here that the substantial unity of the Church under the Law and the Gospel is intended, and that the Bride tells her Beloved that she will bring Him her children, the Saints of both covenants, that she will preserve the types and promises of the Old Testament along with the fulfilment of them in the New. There are, however, some additional meanings which they draw from the words. One reminds us that the Church offered her LORD His sacrifices without distinction of sex or age, that child-martyrs like Agnes and Cyriac, young maidens as Lucy and Agatha, and aged prelates such as Polycarp, Urban, and Marcellinus, alike were given as choice fruits for the Master's garners. Another interpretation sees here the comparison made, by co-ordinate study, of secular literature and natural religion along with the teachings of the Gospel, that the superiority of the latter may be clearly manifested, and the soul may profit by all. And a modern commentator wisely adds that the Church has not merely to keep in mind the records of former achievements of the Saints and the imitation of their examples, but also to employ new methods, and to practise duties formerly neglected or, at any rate, not brought into prominence. *At our gates.* Many are these *gates* of the Bride, whether Church or soul, where the fruits must be piled as an offering for her Bridegroom and King as He enters His own City in triumph, that He may accept her service and laud her devotion, according to that saying, "Give her of the fruit of her hands, and let her own works praise her in the gates." These are the gates of faith, hope, and charity; the gates of the Sacraments; the teaching of Holy Scripture and of the Saints; the eight Beatitudes; the two low and narrow gates, through which few are to enter, of patient suffering and of perfect meditation on GOD alone. There are, besides, the five senses, gates through which thoughts pass from the body to the soul. At all these the Bride *lays up*, in the recesses of a devout and thankful heart, fruits for her Beloved, since she knows not where He may choose His place of entrance, and she brings *new and old* alike, all the works she once

Theodoret.
S. Greg. M.
Beda.
Honorius.

Parez.

Tres Patr.

Thrupp.

Prov. xxxi. 31.
Nic. Argent.

Hugo Card.
Vieyra.

did for GOD in fear, and all those she now does in love, all those of her early life and those of her later years, and she lays them up not for herself, but for Him, not because He is her LORD, but because He is her *Beloved*, and all that she has done, all the fruits she has stored, come from Him and are perfected in Him. One and all, they illustrate their expositions by citing those words of the Redeemer: "Every scribe which is instructed unto the kingdom of heaven is like unto a man that is an householder, which bringeth forth out of his treasures things new and old."

<small>Beda.</small>

<small>S. Mat. xiii. 52.</small>

CHAPTER VIII.

1 O that thou wert as my brother, that sucked the breasts of my mother! when I should find thee without, I would kiss thee; yea, I should not be despised.

<small>Cassiodor.</small>

Cassiodorus justly remarks that the expression of this wish, so inconsistent with the conditions of earthly love and marriage, is an incidental proof of the spiritual intention of the Song. Accordingly, the usual exposition of the verse is that it is the prayer of the Synagogue for the Incarnation of CHRIST. There is, however, no little variety in the details of this interpretation. Thus S. Epiphanius and his pupil Philo agree in alleging that the *mother* of the Bride is eternal Wisdom, and her *brother* the LORD JESUS CHRIST in the human form which He took and bore; and that when CHRIST comes to the newly-baptized, as though to the infants of the Church, by the grace of His visitation, then He is said to *suck the breasts*, while, in their persons, He begins, as it were, to know GOD and taste heavenly things, that is, to suck the two breasts of the Old and New Testament and of the twin precepts of love. And Theodoret points out that the LORD condescended even more than in this wise, since He did not merely learn in the persons of those with whom He was pleased to identify Himself, but that He "grew, and

<small>S. Athan.
S. Ambros.</small>

<small>S. Epiphan.
Philo Carp.</small>

<small>Theodoret.</small>

waxed strong in spirit, filled with wisdom," that He "increased in wisdom and stature, and in favour with GOD and man." Thou wast willing to suck the same breasts as I, that in this also thou mightest avouch Thy brotherhood. Thou didst suck, not because Thou needest it, but to teach me how I should suck, and from what breast I might draw grace. Therefore, too, Thou camest to Baptism, not to wash away the stain of sins, for Thou didst no sin, nor was guile found in Thy mouth, nor that Thou mightest receive the grace of the All-holy SPIRIT, for Thou wast full thereof, but to show me what are the gifts of Baptism, and how I might suck the grace of the SPIRIT. Others take the mother of the Bride to imply the substance of human nature, and give a literal turn to the clause, as denoting a longing for the nativity of the Infant SAVIOUR. And only the *mother* is named, because it is only through the Blessed Virgin's flesh that the Redeemer is our Brother, since by the FATHER's side He is Almighty GOD. Another view, however, is that the mother of whom the Bride speaks is neither the Synagogue, nor human nature, nor yet S. Mary, but the Heavenly Jerusalem, "the mother of us all," and that her breasts, which CHRIST is prayed to suck, are that new wine which He has promised to drink with us in His Kingdom, so that the prayer is for the hastening of His second Advent. With this agrees the view of several commentators, that we are to look in this place not to the original proclamation of the Gospel, but to the final conversion of the Jews.

I should find Thee without. Where? Some take it literally, outside Jerusalem, and remind us that "JESUS also, that He might sanctify the people with His own Blood, suffered without the gate. Let us go forth therefore unto Him, without the camp, bearing His reproach." Or, as S. Ambrose prefers to explain it, He was *within* from all eternity, in the bosom of the FATHER, *without*, when He was manifest to the world, coming to seek us, heal us, and be again within us; *without*, ruling among the Gentiles, Who was once *within* the Jewish people only. Again, He was *within*, when hidden under the types and prophecies of the Old Testament, *without*, when the veil was withdrawn and the types fulfilled. Or, once more, *I should find Thee without* this world, myself quitting the flesh in order to find Thee; either spiritually, as S. Ambrose, in another

S. Luke ii. 40, 52.

1 S. Pet. ii. 22.

Cassiodor. Beda.

Rupert.

Tres Patr.

Gal. iv. 26.

S. Mat. xxvi. 29.

Luc. Abb. Honorius. S. Ans. Laud. Rupert.

S. Epiphan. Philo Carp.

Heb. xiii. 12.

S. Ambros. de Inst. Virg. 1. Dion. Carth.

Hugo Card.

S. Ambros. de Isaac, 8.

place, observes: That soul is happy, which is without, that the WORD may be within; without the body, that the WORD may dwell within us; or else literally, passing without the body through the gates of the grave, that the spirit may flee away and be with CHRIST. I would find Thee *without*, publicly honoured, and openly worshipped, as when peace was at last granted to the Church, no longer within, hidden in the secret rites of the catacombs and other lurking-places. I would fain find Thee *without*, even in all my external actions, and the active occupations of my life, being ever mindful of Thee, and doing all for Thee, and unto Thee. I would gladly find Thee *without*, in all Thy visible creation, contemplating Thee as the glorious Maker of all, marvelling at Thy wisdom, majesty, and honour. I would see Thee in the beauty of the order of the universe, in flowers, and shrubs, and trees, in grass, and in jewels, in the fruitfulness of the earth, in the vastness of the ocean, in the wide expanse of air, in the blaze of fire, in founts, and rivers, and seas, in sky, and stars, and planets, and in all living things, fain would I contemplate with pure heart Thy boundless excellence, reverence it fitly, love it fervently, praise it devoutly, and ever honour it with all my might, and so be caught away to inner things, and *kiss* Thee, my Bridegroom, clasping Thee to my heart, embracing Thee with the fondest love.

I would kiss Thee, reaching up to Thy lips upon the Cross, to receive that parting kiss of peace and love which Thou didst offer when, bowing the head, Thou gavest up the ghost; *kiss Thee*, in intimate fellowship with Thy Humanity; *kiss Thee*, in bearing Thy reproach; *kiss Thee*, in loving reception of Thy Sacraments; *kiss Thee*, with the mystical kiss of everlasting peace in the heavenly Country.

I should not be despised. If the words be those of the Synagogue, they mean that the contumely which has for nineteen centuries been the lot of the Jewish race will be turned into honour when their conversion to the Gospel has taken place; if the speech be ascribed to the Church, she, in like manner, looks from her time of depression and suffering to the first ingathering of the Gentiles by the conversion of the Roman Empire, and the later and more ample one yet to come, which will shut the mouths of unbelievers. Applied to the faithful soul, the words are variously taken. Philo supposes the meaning to be that the Angels will no longer regard her with contempt, when they see how great a Deliverer has condescended to interest Himself in her salvation. But Theodoret takes a deeper view, which also avoids the unsuitableness of ascribing such a feeling to the heavenly host. He represents the Bride as saying, " Intoxicated with love for Thee, not only in my chamber, nor in the portico of my dwelling, but in the market-place and publicly I would find Thee, embrace Thee, and kiss Thee, nor would the spectators blame me for it, when they knew the ardour of my love." And in this wise the words may be aptly taken of those pure virgins who were not ashamed to confess their LORD in the arena, stripped before the gaze of myriad spectators, and lying gladly down upon the bridal-bed of martyrdom. There is yet another sense in which the faithful soul utters the words, *O that thou wert as my brother.* She desires not merely union with her LORD, but likeness to Him; she asks not merely for His love, but for the perfect interchange of thought, the unclouded intimacy, which can come only of unbroken fellowship from childhood; the thorough familiarity which, born of kindred, has grown through the advancing years. A bridegroom, however loved and honoured, is most frequently unlike his bride, and is a comparative stranger to her up to the time of marriage. It is only afterwards, in the course of a long and happy union, that the likeness in thought, expression, and even in feature, which is often seen in long-wedded pairs, is slowly developed, that mutual trust and confidence is perfected. But the Bride has no mind to wait for all this. She desires to be conformed to her Beloved at once; to know all His thoughts, even as He knows all hers, to have been His from her tenderest years, and not merely won to Him in later life. And in this sense it is also true that she escapes being despised, since the contumely and derision frequently heaped on one who turns to CHRIST from the world, are rarely directed, even by scoffers, against such as have been always consistent in devotion.

Theodoret.

2 I would lead thee, and bring thee into my mother's house, who would instruct me: I would cause thee to drink of spiced wine of the juice of my pomegranate.

Cassiodor.
Beda.

The favourite interpretation of this verse by the Fathers is that the Bride is looking forward to the joys of heaven. *I would lead Thee*, not in the sense of guiding or influencing, but of processional attendance, clinging to Thee in faith and love, following Thee with eyes and prayers, as did the Apostles, when returning unto heaven at Thine Ascension, back to that Jerusalem which is above, the *mother* of us all. I would follow Thee even more perfectly, not ceasing till I joined Thee; and *there Thou wilt teach me* (as the Vulgate correctly renders the next clause, mistranslated in the A. V.) all that truth and wisdom which man cannot learn in the present life, all that "eye hath not seen, nor ear heard, neither have entered into the heart of man." *I will cause Thee to drink of spiced wine*, the wine of my love and devotion, *spiced* with good works and holiness, *of the juice of my pomegranates*, because I would offer Thee the passion of all the holy Martyrs in proof of the fervour of my affection.

Honorius.
1 Cor. ii. 9.
Cassiodor.

S. Greg. M.

A second view, explaining the verse of the return of the Jews, represents the Church as promising to lead and bring CHRIST, by her preaching, into the house of her mother the Synagogue, and there receive His teaching. She will then give Him spiced wine to drink, in that she will offer the Synagogue the strong rough wine of the testimony of the Law softened and blended with the sweet tidings of the Gospel, and will also bring forth the juice of her pomegranates, by using the examples of the Martyrs as arguments on behalf of the Faith for which they were glad to die. And Rupert, preferring to see here the final conversion of the Gentile world, explains analogously, that the *mother's house* of which the Gentile Church speaks, is to be taken as denoting the palaces of idolatrous kings and the temples of heathen worship, while the spiced wine which she will offer is that Cup of salvation which she takes as the reward of her Bridegroom for all that He has done for her, the Sacrifice of thanksgiving wherein she unites His Passion with that of His Martyrs. And in that case, the spicing of which the Bride speaks, will not be honeyed, but the bitter myrrh of death, the same which was blended in the cup offered to Him on the Way of Sorrows. There is a singular exposition, connected with the idea of the Passion, which sees in the mother of the Bride, the earth, as the parent dust out of which human nature was formed,

Luc. Abb.

S.Ans.Laud.

Rupert.

S. Epiphan.
Philo Carp.

and in the *mother's house* the grave, wherein the Saints are treasured till the Resurrection. Thither the Bride is ready to go with her Lord, thither she did go down with Him, when she brought Him in to conquer the realm of death, and to spoil it of its accumulated wealth. A widely different interpretation sees here the Holy Scriptures, the dwelling of that wisdom whence the Bride has sprung, wherein she holds frequent colloquies with her Divine Spouse, and is refreshed by Him with the wine of understanding and of endurance. Theodoret, who explains the verse of the devout soul, will have it that the Church, God's temple, imitating the heavenly Jerusalem, is her *mother's house,* wherein is the *wine* of wholesome doctrine, and the *pomegranate juice* of practical benevolence, drawn from the fruits of charity. This exposition is akin to that of the Targum, which, as it explains the previous verse of Messiah the King, showing Himself as the brother of the Jewish nation, and studying the Law with them, takes this of His being brought into the sanctuary to teach the will of God, and to sit down with His subjects at the mystical banquet prepared from the creation for the chosen people. The Three Fathers, also taking the clause of the holy soul, will have it that her *mother's house* is that higher understanding in which dwells the grace of the Holy Spirit, of which she was born in Baptism. There she offers her Lord that knowledge of Him which she holds within her, *spiced,* because mingled of various ingredients, of natural religion, which contemplates Him in His creatures, and of Holy Scripture, where He is seen in revelation. And as the juice of pomegranates has a mingled flavour, sweet and yet tart, so the love which the Bride offers her Lord, and which is the one gladness of her spirit, is blended with reverential awe and longing for full possession. And there is yet another way in which the devout soul can bring her Lord into her *mother's house,* when by her own holy conversation and example, she wins those of her own earthly kindred, or of her own local Church, or, again, as another takes it, her own cloister, to serve Him faithfully, and to offer Him the cup of their conversion and instruction, the juice of their zealous works, to drink.

Theodoret.
Targum.
Tres Patr.
Dion. Carth.
Honorius.

3 His left hand should be under my head, and his right hand should embrace me.

Honorius. The *left hand* of the Bridegroom, notes Honorius of Autun, shall be under the Bride's head, because she will see all the glory of the world under the sway of CHRIST; and His *right hand* shall embrace her, because the fellowship of the Angels and the unity of the Saints, who are to stand at CHRIST's right hand in the Judgment, will join her to their company, and in the clasp of that right hand she rests free from all dis-
S. John xvi. 22. turbance, and no one will rouse her from that rest, because her joy no man taketh from her.

4 I charge you, O daughters of Jerusalem, that ye stir not up, nor awake my love until he please.

Hugo Card. This is the third time these words occur, to impress on us the alternations of religious training, and the reciprocal succession of the parts of our holy calling.
Gen. i. 5. For, as "the evening and the morning were the first day," so the soul ought to enjoy seasons of contemplative rest, with nevertheless a set purpose of returning at the proper time and place to active work, and
Job vii. 4. conversely, according to that saying, "When I lie down, I say, When shall I arise, and the night be gone?" And the verse occurs thrice, because sleep is threefold. First in the devotion of love, brought on by memory of bounties, and thanksgiving for them. Secondly, in the contemplation of the truth, which is caused by anxious search and fruitful toil. Thirdly, in the foretaste of future blessedness, brought on by eager longing for our Country, and forgetfulness of earthly things. Wherefore the first of these three adjurations checks the restless, lest by their irreverence they should break the holy repose of their devout Mother, rather than wait patiently till she return from the house of wine, full of blessings for them. Next, she warns the uninstructed, who have no capacity for understanding exalted subjects, that they may be no hindrance to those who can attain to them. And this third adjuration is addressed to the angelic hosts, to which they who have a foretaste of eternal bliss are united as in the third heavens, which hosts are said to stir up or awake the faithful soul when they oblige her to come down and pay attention to the needs of human nature. And in saying *until she* (Vulg.) *will*, it is signified, that

she ought sometimes to be willing to be roused, for sleep draws on work, and work sleep. And it is to be noted that in the two former adjurations it is said, *By the roes, and by the hinds of the field,* by which are signified the angelic hosts, in whose name the adjurations are made; but it is not said here, because the Angels themselves are adjured, and cannot be so by their own name. For as the less is always blessed by the greater, so also is the less always adjured by the greater. And others more briefly tell us that this triple warning against untimely waking is to remind us that the LORD prefers the tranquil listening of Mary to the busy service of Martha, cumbered about many things. S. Just. Org. Rupert.

5 Who is this that cometh up from the wilderness, leaning upon her beloved? I raised thee up under the apple tree: there thy mother brought thee forth: there she brought thee forth that bare thee.

It is, says Cassiodorus, the voice of the Synagogue, marvelling at the Church gathered out of the Gentiles. She had been given up by GOD to idolatry and ignorance of the truth, and she *ascended from the wilderness,* that is, from the error of unbelief, wherein she had been left up to that time, by the gradations of holiness. Here the Vulgate amplifies a little, by giving a double sense to one phrase, and adds, *abounding in delights,*[1] while the LXX. omits *wilderness,* and reads *made white.*[2] She is abounding in delights, because full of holiness and of the graces and gifts of the SPIRIT, she is *made white* in the waters of Baptism, not by her own power or merit, but by His mercy Who saith, "Though your sins be as scarlet, yet shall they be white as snow," and so she is *leaning on her Beloved,* because, unlike the elder Synagogue, which trusted in the Patriarchs and the ceremonial Law, she puts her whole trust in CHRIST, and ascribes all her virtues and good works to His grace, knowing that she can do nothing of herself, and therefore saying with the Apostle, "By Cassiodor.
Rupert.
Philo Carp.
S. Ambros.
Serm. 14 in
Ps. cxix.
Isa. i. 18.
Nic. Argent.
S. August.
de Grat. 6.
Cassiodor.
1 Cor. xv. 10.

---

[1] The verb מִתְרַפֶּקֶת, found here only, means "leaning on the elbow;" but some Jewish interpreters explain it as signifying "delighting one's self."

[2] Reading, possibly, מְלֻבָּנָה, or rather מַלְבֶּנֶת.

the grace of GOD I am what I am." The holy soul, observes S. Gregory, cometh up from the wilderness, because set as she is in the exile of pilgrimage here, she strives towards heavenly joys in spirit and meditation, whence Paul saith, "Our conversation is in heaven." She abounds in delights, because, occupied in study of Holy Scripture, she constantly feeds her spirit with heavenly food. She leaneth on her Beloved, because, trusting in the help of CHRIST alone, she is translated by His bounty from exile to her country. She went down into that wilderness, comments another, by her birth; she comes up through it, by advancing from one virtue to another; she comes up over it, despising all worldly pride; she comes up from it with everlasting blessedness. And this wilderness is threefold: that of the passing vanity of the world, out of which the Bride comes; that of humility, truly a wilderness, because so few Christians are willing to dwell there, through which she must pass; and that of pure and simple innocence, to which she must attain. And akin to this last remark is the stress laid by the Greek Fathers on the LXX. reading, *made white*. It is not *white* simply, but *made white*, for the Bride, herself black, saith of the Bridegroom, "My Beloved is white;" not "made white," because He is such by nature. But though she was dark, since the sun had looked upon her, she hath been made white, and partaker of the whiteness of her Bridegroom, Who, being Himself Light, hath made her and calls her light, being holy, hath made her holy, being the Resurrection, hath counted her worthy of the resurrection, and thus shared His own whiteness with her. S. Bernard suggests yet another meaning of ascending through the wilderness, when the prayer of the Bride goes up in the silent watches of the lonely night.

She is *leaning on her Beloved*, that she may not dread the fear of men, that she may not fail in tribulations which find her out, or in the persecutions of her seen and unseen foes. How would she hold her ground amidst all these, unless she were leaning on her Beloved? Ought she to lean on herself, or on any chance arm? If she did so, she would surely fall, not stand. But now she saith, "The LORD is my light and my salvation! whom shall I fear? The LORD is the strength of my life! of whom then shall I be afraid? Though an host of men were laid against me, yet will

I put my trust in Him." And observe further that this is the third ascent of the Bride mentioned in the Song. The first was when she came up out of the wilderness like a pillar of smoke, denoting compunction and suffering, and answering to the Bridegroom going up to Jerusalem to be crucified. Next is her advance in holiness, when she arose as the morning, and became as the moon and sun, even as her LORD arose in early morning from the grave, in the twofold glory of His Manhood and Godhead; and thirdly, this coming up, when she is abounding in delights, filled with heavenly contemplation, and thus typifying the Ascension of JESUS to the celestial throne. Parez sees here, not inaptly, but with far less beauty, the three stages of the Christian Church: in its first obscure birth, in its long trial and suffering, and its final victory under Constantine. The whole of the picture, representing the Bride as slumbering, as desiring and receiving the kiss of her Bridegroom, and as then leaving all to go with Him, finds a curious type in that old nursery tale, itself a relic of a vanished creed, which tells of the Prince who found the Sleeping Beauty in the wood, and waked her from her mystic slumber to be his bride. *Hugo Card.* *Parez.*

> And on her lover's arm she leant,
>   And round her waist she felt it fold,
> And far across the hills they went
>   In that new world which is the old.
>
> Across the hills and far away
>   Beyond their utmost purple rim,
> And deep into the dying day
>   The happy princess followed Him.
>
> "O eyes long laid in happy sleep!"
>   "O happy sleep, that lightly fled!"
> "O happy kiss, that woke thy sleep!"
>   "O Love, Thy kiss would wake the dead!"
>
> "A hundred summers! can it be!
>   And whither goest Thou, tell me, where?"
> "O seek My FATHER's court with Me,
>   For there are greater wonders there."
>
> And o'er the hills, and far away.
>   Beyond their utmost purple rim,
> Beyond the night, across the day,
>   Through all the world she followed Him.

Tennyson, The Daydream.

Targum. The Targum, which explains the passage to mean the resurrection of the dead of Israel, coming forth from the valley of Jehoshaphát and passing through the opened Mount of Olives, abounding in delights through the mercy of GOD, finds a parallel in the Christian view that the migration of the holy soul from the wilderness of earth to the full enjoyment of the glories of heaven is here intended, viewed with loving admiration by the choirs of Angels. And it has been especially applied to the passage of the Blessed Virgin to her home in a happier world. So runs the mediæval hymn:

Honorius.
Guilielmus.
Card. Hailgrin.

Hymn. in Assumpt. B.V.M.

> Affluens deliciis
> David regis filia,
> Sponsi fertur brachiis
> Ad cœli sedilia,
> Et amica properat
> Sponsum, quo abierat,
> Quærens inter lilia.

> She, abounding in delights,
> Child of David's kingly line,
> Borne to the celestial heights
> In the Bridegroom's arms divine,
> Hastes to seek Him, as His love,
> Thither, where He passed above,
> Where the mystic lilies shine.

Theodoret. *I raised thee up under the apple tree.* It will be easy for us, observes Theodoret, to understand these words, if we remember what the Bride said in the earlier part of this Book. For she said to the Bridegroom, "As the apple tree among the trees of the wood, so is my Beloved among the sons. I sat down under His shadow with great delight, and His fruit was sweet to my taste." For when we, believing the preaching concerning our SAVIOUR, have come to Holy Baptism, so coming, we receive regeneration, wherefore is added, *There thy mother brought thee forth,* for it is the grace of the HOLY GHOST which hath borne us. But the general consent of the Latin Fathers takes the words differently, following also, as they do, the Vulgate reading in the second clause, *There thy mother was defiled, there was she forced that bare thee.*[1] By the *apple tree*, notes Cassiodorus, we should understand the LORD'S Cross, under which

Chap. ii. 3.

Cassiodor.

---

[1] Perhaps reading חֻבְּלָה for חִבְּלָתְךָ.

tree the Synagogue was *raised up*, because she was redeemed by the Cross of CHRIST from the rebellion of original sin, and from the power of the devil; she was raised up, who had been dead in sin. *I raised* Guilielmus.
thee up, saith the Bridegroom, for My redeeming Blood poured on thee in five streams from My Body as it hung upon the Tree. And as the LXX. and Arabic read, *There thy mother bore thee with pangs,* a Greek Father adds, The Church was brought forth Philo Carp. with pangs of heart and body on the Cross; for the Flesh of CHRIST, suffering the torture of the Cross, brought forth a Bride for itself redeemed with His Blood, regenerated and washed with the water from His side, united and bound to Him, and to His abiding Godhead, by the HOLY GHOST.

When we remember how He sought His love, the Church, while she was still under the rule of her mother the Synagogue, how He made His first visit to Delrio. woo her when He went up to Jerusalem at twelve years Corn. à Lap. of age, and sat in the midst of the doctors in the Temple, and how He died by the sin of His people, we may see the aptness of that citation from a heathen poet which several of the later commentators adduce:

> Sepibus in nostris parvam te roscida mala Virg. Eclog.
> (Dux ego vester eram) vidi cum matre legentem, viii. 37.
> Alter ab undecimo tum me jam ceperat annus;
> Jam fragiles poteram a terra contingere ramos,
> Ut vidi, ut perii, ut me malus abstulit error!

> I saw thee, yet a child,
> (Myself your leader) by our garden hedge
> Plucking the dewy apples with thy mother,
> Then my twelfth year of life was just attained,
> And I could reach the frail boughs from the ground,
> I saw, I died, ill error wrought me woe.

Another interpretation, closer to the Hebrew text, Ainsworth. ascribes the words to the Bride, who is here represented as it were in travail with CHRIST, and therefore an especial type of His Mother. She raises her Beloved Lyranus. up under the apple tree when she invokes Him to aid her, in the words, "By Thy Cross and Passion, Good LORD, deliver us." And under that Tree His dear Mother was outraged, when the cruelty of the Jews caused the sword of Simeon's prophecy to pierce her virgin heart. The Vulgate rendering of the latter clause finds its interpretation in that the Synagogue was *defiled* and *deflowered* under the Tree by her own sin in crucifying her LORD, and imprecating the curse of His Blood on herself and her children. S. Ambrose, taking the whole verse in a slightly different sense, understands by the *apple tree* public confession of CHRIST'S Passion and triumph, and by the *mother* who there brings forth the devout soul, the Church, or divine grace. And as the LORD saw Nathaniel under the fig tree, so, he adds, happy is that soul which rests beneath a fruitful and fragrant tree, for if Nathaniel was good, in whom was no guile, and who was seen under a fig tree, doubtless that soul is good which is raised up under the apple tree by the Bridegroom, for it is a greater thing to be raised up than to be seen, and greater still that the raiser should be the Bridegroom. S. Anselm of Laon will have it that the Cross is called an apple tree, to remind us of that tree of knowledge in Paradise whereby our first parents sinned, and he recounts the twofold legend that the Cross was actually made of wood sprung from a bough of that tree, and that it was set up on the very spot where Adam lay buried. And though we may not receive the legend itself, yet there is no need to turn away from the allegory it contains:

> We think that Paradise and Calvary
>   CHRIST'S Cross and Adam's tree, stood in one place;
> Look, LORD! and find both Adams met in me:
> As the first Adam's sweat surrounds my face,
> May the last Adam's Blood my soul embrace.
>
> So in His purple wrapped, receive me, LORD!
>   By these His thorns give me His other crown;
> And as to others' souls I preached Thy Word,
> Be this my text, my sermon to mine own;
> Therefore, that He may raise, the LORD throws down.

But, whereas the all but universal consent of the Fathers ascribes the verse to the Bridegroom, the Hebrew text, as now read, makes the suffixes masculine, and therefore holds that the Bride is the speaker, though many scholars have urged that the points ought to be changed, as the sense clearly makes for the traditional interpretation. If, however, the present pointing stand, there are not wanting expositions. *I raised Thee up*, that is, I brought Thee forth, that Thou mightest in turn bring forth the fruit of life; I raised Thee up under the apple tree, because my sin in eating of the forbidden fruit was the cause of Thy death upon the Cross. Or, I raised Thee up, myself being under Thy Cross, crying to Thee in prayer to help me in my need, that the Cross might be to me for pardon, grace, and salvation. Tigurinus.
Vatablus.

6 Set me as a seal upon thine heart, as a seal upon thine arm; for love is strong as death; jealousy is cruel as the grave: the coals thereof are coals of fire, which hath a most vehement flame.

There is in this verse also a diversity of opinion as to the speaker. The Hebrew points ascribe it to the Bride, the great majority of the Fathers to the Bridegroom. Taking these views in their order, we find, in the first place, that the Targum paraphrases thus: "The children of Israel will say in that day unto their LORD: I pray Thee, set us as the graving of a ring upon Thine heart, and as the graving of a ring upon Thine arm, that we may be exiles no longer." Targum.
The Bride desires to be ever close to her Bridegroom's person, to be His peculiar property, to bear upon herself the inscription of His Name, to be the means wherewith He stamps and marks the sheep of His pasture. Signets were worn upon the breast or upon the arm, amongst the ancient Hebrews and Egyptians, suspended by a cord, as well as set in rings for the finger, and it is to this custom that the verse refers. And the force of the metaphor is clearly brought out in one passage of Holy Writ, "As I live, saith the LORD, though Coniah the son of Jehoiakim, King of Judah, were the signet upon My right hand, yet would I pluck thee thence." Another meaning of the petition may refer to the "breastplate of judgment" worn by the High Priest, with its twelve jewels "with the names of the children of Israel, twelve, according to their names, like the engravings of a signet," that he might never forget them when pleading the sacrifices before GOD, as is written in another place, "Behold, I have graven thee upon the palms of My hands, thy walls are ever before Me." The Bride therefore implores the love of her Spouse and Priest, signified by His *heart*, and His power, denoted by His *arm*, to aid her and commemorate her unceasingly in Jer. xxii. 24.

Ainsworth.

Exod. xxviii. 21.

Isa. xlix. 16.

the perpetual mediation of His everlasting Priesthood before the golden altar in heaven. The one old commentator who takes the words as spoken by the Bride gives, however, a different explanation from this. "O my Beloved," says he, speaking in the person of the Bride, "what is Thy heart in this world, and what Thine arm, save the Scriptures of truth, which are written after Thine own heart, and the record of Thy wondrous works, whence is known how great and mighty is Thine arm? Set me as a seal upon that heart of Thine, set me as a seal upon that arm of Thine. Wherefore? Because of the triple rage which lifts its voice against me, Jewish, pagan, heretical. I am ready, I am prepared, I am sworn, on my part, to defend that heart of Thine, to guard that Thine arm as Thine imperial signet, as Thy faithful testimony, with wondrous vigour, with wondrous hardness, which no man can break through." But the more usual view has been copiously illustrated by the Fathers, and that with sufficient diversity. It is, one of the earlier commentators on the Song of Songs tells us, the seal and sign of the Cross which needs to be impressed first on the heart, and then on the arm of the Bride, that we may learn to imitate our Head, so far as may be, by giving up our own will and all desire of earthly things beyond mere necessaries, as the Bridegroom Himself has taught us, saying, "If any man will come after Me, let him deny himself, and take up his cross, and follow Me." The *heart* is the contemplative, the *arm* the active portion of the soul, which is the reason why the breast and the shoulder of sacrifices were set apart for the priests from the offerings of the people. Our SAVIOUR therefore desires that we should have Him impressed as a seal upon all our thoughts and reasonings, and to stamp His mark upon our words and deeds. For so shall they be royal medals, and no false coin, but bearing the image of the King. Cassiodorus, less forcibly, explains the words merely of keeping CHRIST's benefits to us in our memories; but another gives fresh point to the idea, by comparing the impress on the heart to the private watchword given by a general to his soldiers, by which to distinguish friend from foe, and the seal on the arm to be an outer badge of his service, that none may in error wound his fellow-soldier. And the soul needs to have as the seal on her heart the devout belief that CHRIST is the Wisdom of God, upon her arm the not less deep certainty that He is the Power of God too. Again, as one use of a seal is to protect secrets from prying eyes, so CHRIST, as the Bridegroom, gives His spouse a signet whereby she may seal up the treasures of their house, which are intrusted to her charge. And He is Himself this seal, set upon our heart, when the mysteries of the Faith are committed to our charge, in such wise that when the enemy sees that our hearts are sealed with faith, he dares not attempt to force them open by temptation. We are then to keep our dear LORD as a seal upon both heart and arm, by remembering that all His words and all His actions are alike secrets and mysteries, belonging to Divine Wisdom, and given to us to ponder and imitate. Also, as a seal gives authenticity and force to a deed, so we have CHRIST set as a seal upon our heart and arm, when we accept and follow His commandments as the sure pledges of the reward He prepares for us. CHRIST, observes a Western Father, is a seal on our foreheads, a seal on our heart. On the forehead, that we may ever confess Him; on the heart, that we may ever love Him; and a seal on our arm, that we may ever work for Him. And as the seal is also a mark of ownership, another Saint paraphrases thus: "Set Me as the ruler of thy heart and thoughts, that My friends may plainly see that thou holdest My secrets, and Mine enemies may as plainly know that the secrets thou possessest are closed to them, and that thou hast Me as thy guide in all thy works." The power which presses down this seal, so that it leaves its stamp indelibly upon heart and arms is, they wisely tell us, love. "Be thou printed by Me, as by a seal, clinging to Me closely by love, that thou mayest receive Mine image as from a seal, and derive likeness unto Me from that clearly-cut impression. And as forcible as is the impress of love, so distinct will be the expression of likeness, and the more eagerly thou clingest to Me by love, the more like Me shalt thou be. The more forcibly thou pressest thyself against Me, the more clearly shall I, CHRIST, be formed in thee, and thou be transformed and reformed in Me." So S. Jane Frances de Chantal branded the Holy Name upon her heart, that she might never forget her LORD, but ever ponder upon His marvellous grace, and on the yet more painful graving of our names on

S. Clem. Alex. Prædag. iii. 2.

S. Greg. M. Mor. xxix. 4.

Beda.

S. Ambros. de Isaac, 8.

S. Ans. Laud.

Guilielmus.

His Heart and arms, by the nails of the Cross and the spear of the soldier.

For love is strong as death. Whose love? We may take it in two ways,—the love of GOD towards man, or the love of man towards GOD. The love of CHRIST for us was *strong as death*, because it made Him, though immortal and impassible in His divine nature, endure bitter pangs and death for our redemption.

<small>Cassiod.
Dion. Carth.</small>

<small>Hupton,
The Hymn,
Come, ye faithful.</small>

> Ere He raised the lofty mountains,
>   Formed the sea, or built the sky,
> Love eternal, free and boundless,
>   Forced the LORD of Life to die,—
> Lifted up the Prince of princes
>   On the throne of Calvary.

And man's love to Him, though falling infinitely short of His, may yet be as strong as death, and that in two ways, by the mortification of sin, and by the endurance of martyrdom. Love, observes S. Ambrose, (taking the former of these views,) is strong as death, for love slays guilt and every sin; love destroys the blows of death. And, besides, we die to our vices and to sin when we love GOD's commandments. GOD is love, love is the WORD of GOD, which "is quick, and powerful, and sharper than any two-edged sword, piercing even to the dividing asunder of soul and spirit, and of the joints and marrow." And so too another Saint, working the idea out further: That which death effects in the bodily senses, love does in the desires of the mind. For there are some who so love GOD as to take no heed of any visible things, and while straining in soul towards that which is eternal, they become almost insensible to all temporal matters. In such as these, without doubt, love is strong as death, because as death destroys all the natural properties and desires of the outward bodily senses, so love in men of this stamp, forces them to despise all earthly inclinations, and to keep the thought fixed elsewhere. To those who are dead and yet alive in this way the Apostle saith, "Ye are dead, and your life is hid with CHRIST in GOD." And in the other sense they remind us of the joy with which the Martyrs faced torture and death for the sake of their LORD, not merely bearing, but welcoming the pangs which were bringing them to Him. So in many of their Acts, so in many of the hymns which commemorate them. There is a

<small>S. Ambros.
Serm. 15 in
Ps. cxix.</small>

<small>S. Greg. M.</small>

<small>Col. iii. 3.
Philo Carp.</small>

third reason why love is strong as death, common to God and man; namely, its constraining might, for God's love compels man's salvation, man's love wins answer from God to prayer. And therefore the Doctor of Grace, summing up all these, observes, "Love is rightly called strong as death, either because no one can conquer it, any more than death, or because in this life the measure of love is until death, as the LORD saith, 'Greater love hath no man than this, that a man lay down his life for his friends,' or rather, that as death forces the soul away from the bodily senses, so does love force it from carnal desires." That great light of the Church of France, who earned by learning and holiness the title of the Most Christian Doctor, closing his life, like S. Gregory Nyssen, S. Bernard, Gilbert of Hoyland, and S. Thomas of Villanova, while labouring on the Song of Songs, repeated these words over again and again in his last sickness, as he meditated on the Passion which had ransomed him, and fell asleep at last, saying, "Love is strong as death." *S. Ans. Laud.* *S. August. Ep. 39, ad S. Hieron.* *S. John xv. 13.*

Jealousy is cruel as the grave. The word *hard*, as given in the margin of A. V., is better than *cruel*, and agrees with the LXX. and Vulgate. The varying meaning of the first word in the two great versions has led to different treatment by the Eastern and Western Fathers. The LXX. ζῆλος is usually explained as *zeal*, the Vulgate *æmulatio* as *rivalry* or as *envy*. Taking the former, we observe further that the LXX. correctly renders the Hebrew שְׁאוֹל *sheol*, which means the place of all departed spirits, by *Hades*. Neither the Vulgate *infernus*, which in Christian language denotes the place of punishment, nor the A. V. *grave*, which goes no further than the idea of sepulture, is at all so exact as this. Two widely different interpretations are found in two nearly contemporary Greek Fathers. One tells us that the zeal for God which we ought to feel and display against sin, should be as relentless as death, and like that of Phinehas and Elijah, who slew the rebels against God, a view not very unlike that of Rupert, who explains the words of Ecclesiastical censures and excommunication. Another, in a far more loving spirit, tells us that *zeal is hard as Hades*, for that just as Hades itself formed no obstacle to the Bridegroom, when He descended thither to deliver the souls of them who had gone down there before His *Polychronius.* *Rupert.* *Philo Carp.*

Advent, so it is no barrier now to our prayers, which we can still offer for the faithful departed, who are there undergoing the purification which is to fit them for their dwelling in heaven. The same Father shows that our zeal may be as strong as Hades in another way, that as those who pass into the unseen world are stripped thereby of all their earthly possessions, so too such as are inspired with true zeal for CHRIST are ready to give up father and mother, wife and brethren, houses and lands, for His sake and the Gospel's, and to follow Him with neither staff, nor scrip, nor purse,

Dion. Carth. a thing which is, as a Western writer notes, hard as hell to those who do not truly love GOD. Akin to this *S. Just. Org.* is one Latin exposition, which says that as rivalry is hard as hell, so the Saints, imitating CHRIST, do not hesitate to undergo suffering and death in loving emu-

Cassiodor. lation of Him. His rivalry with hell in contending for man's redemption was hard as it, for as hell never yields up those it has once received, so CHRIST's love never lets go those it has ever embraced; wherefore

Rom. viii. 35. the Apostle saith, "Who shall separate us from the love of CHRIST? shall tribulation, or distress, or persecution, or famine, or nakedness, or peril, or sword?" And as hell knows not pity, nor any alleviation of the pains of sufferers, so CHRIST's love can never cease to be merciful, nor can it be wrenched from the love of mankind by any wickedness on the part of those that

S.Ans.Laud. persecute Him. Again; the yearning of the devout soul for GOD is hard as hell, because of the pain and restlessness it occasions, knowing no satiety in doing and giving all for the Beloved. And so S. Teresa:

S. Teresa, The Rhythm, Vivo, sin vivir in me.

 Oh, what a bitter life is this,
 Deprived of GOD, its only bliss;
  And what though Love delicious be,
  Not so is Hope deferred:
 Ah then, dear LORD, in charity,
 This iron weight of misery
  From my poor soul ungird.
 For evermore I weep and sigh,
 Dying because I do not die.

 Absent from Thee, my SAVIOUR dear,
 I call not life this living here,
  But a long dying agony,
  The sharpest I have known;
 And I myself, myself to see
 On such a rack of misery,
  For very pity moan,
 And ever, ever, weep and sigh,
 Dying because I do not die.

And in that other sense of *envy,* they explain this jea- _{Cassiodor.}
lousy to denote the bitter hostility with which the
Synagogue pursued the LORD and His disciples, persecuting them even unto death; an envy manifested
still by false Christians in the relentless hatred they _{Luc. Abb.}
bear to the Church, the Bride of the Lamb. *The coals
thereof are coals of fire.* For *coals,* (more properly
glowings) the Vulgate reads *lamps,* and the LXX., perhaps having regard to the rapid flashings of fire, or to
the whirling of sparks, reads *wingings round,* περίπτερα.
And this the Greek Fathers interpret as meaning that _{Philo Carp.}
love of GOD serves as wings to the Bride to lift her _{Theodoret.}
above the world and waft her to heaven. And S. Am- _{S. Ambros.}
brose, following the same reading, adds, "Good is that _{de Isaac, 8.}
love which has burning wings of fire, whereon it flies
through the hearts of the Saints, scorching up whatever material or earthly is there, and tries whatever is
genuine, purifying what it touches with its flame. This
is the fire which JESUS sent upon earth, and therewith
faith glowed, devotion was kindled, love enlightened,
and righteousness made glorious. And with this fire
He inflamed the hearts of His Apostles, as Cleophas
beareth witness, saying, 'Did not our heart burn _{S. Luke}
within us, while He opened to us the Scriptures?'" _{xxiv. 32.}
Following the Vulgate reading, *Her lamps are lamps* _{Cassiodor.}
of fire and flames, we find the more usual exposition to
be that which sees here a type of the Saints. The
lamps of love are the hearts of the Saints, in which
love dwells, as though in vessels. These lamps are *of* _{Beda.}
fire and flames; of *fire,* because they glow in hearts
through love; of *flames,* because they shine outwardly
in their works. It is the LORD's will that they should
do so, for He said to us, "Let your light so shine be- _{S. Mat. xxv.}
fore men that they may see your good works." These ^{1.}
are the lamps which the virgins must have when the
Bridegroom cometh, and they are to enter with Him
into the chamber of His everlasting kingdom. These
virgins have set His love and fear on their hearts and
arms, that is, have put all their thoughts and deeds
under His commands. Then are the lamps of the
foolish virgins extinguished, because the works which
they seemed to do before men shall be darkened, when
the inward Judge shall appear and make manifest the
secrets of all hearts, because they did their good works _{Luc. Abb.}
for the sake of human praise. The fire with which the
true lamps shine is the glow of the HOLY GHOST, Who

S. Just. Org.	makes them bright in precept and example, and especially in the fervour of chastity, inasmuch as flame is always pure. And in this sense the title of lamps is given to eminent Saints, as to the Baptist in Holy
S. John v. 35, λύχνος.	Scripture, and to the Apostles in ancient offices of the Church, as, for instance, in the hymn,
The Sequence, *Alleluia nunc decantet*, in Comm. Apost.	These are lamps, with splendour shining In the Face of GOD most High, These the nobles of the Monarch, Who is throned above the sky, Salt of earth and light of mortals, Stars that beam eternally.
Targum.	And if, following the Targum, jealousy be here taken in a bad sense, of the hostility of unbelievers to the
S. Greg. M.	people of GOD, S. Gregory will tell us what its lamps are, "As fire consumes what it kindles, so their envy destroyed all the power of faith in the Jews. This fire of envy shot forth flames when, by the examples of those amongst whom it was kindled, it spread through all the world, even amongst the Gentiles, to the martyrdom of Christians." *Which hath a most vehement flame.* This clause is practically omitted by the LXX. and Vulgate, because they both take it as no more than an amplification of the word *fire*, occurring just before. Nor does the A. V. do it much more justice. The whole passage should run, "The glowings thereof are glowings of fire, *a flame of* JAH." This is the one solitary place in the Song where the Great Name occurs, and then only in a compound word, for it would be a violation of the strict laws of allegory to unite type and antitype in the one composition. The
Ainsworth.	flame of His love, then, which melted the hard hearts of men, purging away the dross and leaving the pure
Cocceius.	gold behind; the flame of His love, which descended in tongues of fire on the Apostles; the flame of His
S. Mat. iii. 12.	jealousy, burning up the chaff with unquenchable fire; are alike divine, eternal, the emanation of His justice and His mercy. A devout servant of GOD has coupled these two ideas together in a hymn to the Holy Paraclete :
Bianco da Siena, The Hymn, *Discendi Amor santo.*	Come down, O Love divine, Seek Thou this soul of mine, And visit it, with Thine own ardour glowing ; O Comforter, draw near, Within my heart appear, And kindle it, Thy holy flame bestowing.

>   O let it freely burn,
>   Till earthly passions turn
>   To dust and ashes in its heat consuming;
>   And let Thy glorious light
>   Shine ever on my sight,
>   And clothe me round, the while my path illuming.

And therefore it follows most fitly:

7 Many waters cannot quench love, neither can the floods drown it: if a man would give all the substance of his house for love, it would utterly be contemned.

The waters and floods might perchance quench the *lamps*, but they cannot quench the exhaustless fountain of heavenly fire at which those lamps are kindled, for that fountain and stream of fire is CHRIST Himself. The Targum here again gives the tone to the most usual patristic interpretations. In it the *many waters* are the nations of the world gathered together against Israel, and the *floods* are the kings of the earth, endeavouring to uproot the chosen people, but alike unable to overcome the mercy of GOD. So the Christian teachers tell us that the waters and floods are the fierce threats of persecutors, or even their flatteries, whereby they endeavour to separate the Saints from the love of GOD. And of these threats the LORD saith in the Gospel touching the man who built his house on a rock: "The floods came, the winds blew, and beat upon that house, and it fell not, for it was founded upon a rock." The holy Martyrs, comments S. Gregory the Great, burned so with charity as to blaze forth marvellously in love of GOD and their neighbours. Many waters could not quench this love, because their sufferings, how great soever, could never change them into hatred. For this would have been the quenching of love, if by the sufferings heaped upon them, they could have been lowered so far as to hate GOD or their neighbours. And Theodoret gives another part of the same picture to our view, by citing the troubles through which the Saints of the Old Covenant, Abraham, Isaac, Jacob, Moses and Joshua, Samuel and David, Elijah and Elisha, Daniel and the Three Children passed. The last example is also cited by S. Ambrose, showing that the miracle wrought in

[margin notes: Hugo Card. / Targum. / Cassiodor. Gerson. / S. Mat. vii. 25. / S. Greg. M. / Theodoret. / S. Ambros.]

the fiery furnace is the exact converse of the spiritual marvel here described, and identical with it in meaning. It is the same thing if fire fail to burn and if waters fail to quench. And the reason is the same in both cases, because beside the sufferer stands the Form of the SON of GOD, Who saith, "When thou passest through the waters, I will be with thee; and through the rivers, they shall not overflow thee: when thou walkest through the fire, thou shalt not be burned; neither shall the flame kindle upon thee." And we know that we can trust His promise, for His love was not quenched nor overwhelmed when that was fulfilled which He spake by the Psalmist: "The waters are come in, even unto My soul; I am come into deep waters, so that the floods run over Me." And as they distinguish between *waters* and *floods*, as noting severally temptations and persecutions, striving to put out the fire of love, so they distinguish also between *quenching* and *overwhelming*, as the first is effected when the light of holiness flickers, wanes, and goes out, utterly exhausted, through the allurements of sin; and the second when terror or violence from without overthrows the lamp, leaving it dark and useless for the time within the heart, the mere corpse of itself, but capable of being rekindled, as it was in S. Peter after his fall. Not only do the waters and floods fail to quench love, but " which is most to be wondered at, the fire had more force in the water, that quencheth all things, for the world fighteth for the righteous." Cardinal Hugo, with a certain aptness, reminds his readers of the Greek fire used in the warfare of his days, which was said to burn fiercely in water, and to be extinguishable by vinegar alone ; whence he draws the lesson that though temptation and suffering cannot hurt love, yet hatred, which is the vinegar put to the lips of the dying SAVIOUR, can quench it, and therefore, "when He had tasted thereof, He would not drink."

If a man were to give all the substance of his house for love, it would utterly be contemned. Once more the Chaldee paraphrase will help us. "If a man give all the substance of his house, that he may gain wisdom in the Captivity, I will render him twofold in the world to come, and all the spoil which he shall take in the camp of Gog, shall be his." The verse, says Cassiodorus, needs no explanation, for no worldly substance and no riches are aught in comparison with love. We read that the Saints gave up all for the love of CHRIST, and yet they seemed to themselves to give up nothing in comparison with that love which was so dear to them. Wherefore the Apostle, when he had not only given up worldly possessions, but the traditions of his fathers, for CHRIST, said, "I count all things but loss for the excellency of the knowledge of CHRIST JESUS my LORD; for Whom I have suffered the loss of all things, and do count them but dung that I may win CHRIST." "O love," exclaims a holy writer of a later time, "if I knew thy worth, I should be ready to pay the price. But it may be that thou exceedest my narrow means, and thy price is not in my power. Yet I will give that I have, and all that I have, and will barter all my house for thee, and when I have given all, I will count it as nothing. All the pleasures of my flesh, all the enjoyments of my heart, I will cheerfully give up for thee, that I may possess thee alone. Thou alone art dearer to me, thou alone more valuable, sweeter, more pleasant, more delighting, more satisfying, preserving more safely, protecting more happily." It needs not, adds another, taking up this saying, that thou shouldest doubt, O man; for He wills that all should be satisfied with this love, Who graciously invites us all to this fountain of life, saying, "Ho, every one that thirsteth, come ye to the waters, and he that hath no money; come ye, buy, and eat; yea, come, buy wine and milk without money and without price." But we must buy the pearl of great price with our own money, not with that which is the LORD's, Whose is the earth and the fulness thereof, to wit, all things temporal, bodily, spiritual, and eternal. The price of this pearl lies hid within ourselves, and we must therefore open our purse, and produce our own money. Our purse is our heart, in which lies hid our money, that is, our faults and sins, which, paid out by lowly contrition and true confession, the LORD and Fount of Love willingly accepts as the price of love. Hear David paying this price, "I said, I will confess my sins unto the LORD." Hear him receiving the pearl of Divine love, "And so Thou forgavest the wickedness of my sin." O boundless sea of love, what doest Thou, what dost Thou endure? O height of the wisdom of GOD, which passest all understanding, how

Phil. iii 8.

Hugo Victorin.

Henr. Harph.

Isa. lv. 1.

Ps. xxxii. 6.

Thou seemest as though made foolish by love, gladly receiving the coins of our sins, and mercifully bestowing the plenteous gift of Thy love, to make us blest therewith for evermore!

The LXX. reading somewhat differs from the Vulgate and A. V., and runs, *If a man give all his substance in love, they will contemn him with contempt.* That is, says Theodoret, whoever gives away all his goods in charity, will be despised by those who are not charitable, as the Apostle saith: "Being reviled, we bless; being persecuted, we suffer it; being defamed, we intreat: we are made as the filth of the world, and are the offscouring of all things unto this day." The Three Fathers say that those who will so despise the liberal giver are the evil spirits. S. Ambrose sorrowfully adds, that such mockers will be found even in the Church of GOD, and among the followers of the Crucified. And no marvel, as another observes, for CHRIST Himself, the Head, fared no better than His members, when He counted all the substance of His house, all the Divine glory of His Godhead, all the time of His mortal sojourn, as nothing, but gave up all for love, and was despised and mocked, spitted on, scourged and crucified by the Chief Priests and Pharisees, who utterly contemned Him.

8 We have a little sister, and she hath no breasts: what shall we do for our sister in the day when she shall be spoken for?

There is a variance as to the speaker here. The Targum and some of the Greek Fathers take the verse as uttered by the Bride, the majority of Latins will have it that it is the Bridegroom's, and S. Ambrose gives it to the daughters of Jerusalem, agreeing therein with Theodoret, who assumes the Saints of the Old Testament to be the speakers. There is no real antagonism between the first and second of these views, since at this part of the Song the Bridegroom and Bride are represented as so united that their possessions are in common. Hence, whichever speaks, says *we*, not *I* have a sister. There is complete agreement in the next point, which is that the condition of an imperfect Church or soul, not yet fitted for spiritual bridal, incapable of producing offspring, or supplying milk to babes, is here symbolized. But the views again diverge as to the particular object intended. The most satisfactory view is also one of the oldest, that the Gentile Church, in its lowly beginnings, when it depended on the Apostles and other Jewish teachers for all instruction in Divine things, is represented under this figure of an immature maiden. Another view sees here the Synagogue, converted at the close of the world, a younger sister of the Church, as but recently born again in Baptism; *little*, because few in number and weak in faith and steadfastness, and without breasts, as having few or no preachers of her own nation, and rather leaning on the aid of the elder sister to teach her children. She is CHRIST's *sister* too, not only because of His descent from Abraham, but because she will come in the latter days to the full glory of being so entitled by Himself. The soul which is just beginning to believe in CHRIST and to be fed with the milk of faith, but is yet uninstructed in the two Testaments and in the two great precepts of the Gospel, is also a *little sister* of the more advanced and perfect Christians, and is not rejected, but permitted and encouraged to pray for increase of knowledge and charity. Cassiodor. S. Greg. M.
Tres Patr. Luc. Abb. Honorius.
Guilielmus.
Luc. Abb. Philo Carp.

What shall we do for our sister in the day when she shall be spoken for? That is, in the day when she shall be asked in marriage, as may be seen by comparing that other text, "And David sent and communed (lit. "spake concerning") with Abigail, to take her to him to wife;" and the difficulty proposed is that which so long disturbed the early Church, as to the relations which were to exist between the new Gentile communities and the race and polity which gave them their doctrines and laws; whether the new Churches of Asia Minor, Greece, and Italy were to be retained in a sort of tutelage under Jewish supremacy, like the proselytes of the old Law, or to be given full powers of self-government, and exempted from the ceremonial precepts of the Mosaic dispensation. But the Hebrew, being a little vague in expression, may be rendered also, *when speech shall be made of her*, whether for or against; or even *in her*. The former of these is the Chaldee explanation, which represents the Angels as asking what shall be done for Israel in the day when the Gentile nations shall speak together of warring Cocceius. Ainsworth. 1 Sam. xxv. 39.

Targum.

against her. And not unlike this is the explanation of some Latin writers, though following the Vulgate rendering, *when she shall be spoken to;* namely, that the words refer to the interrogation put by Nero and other Pagan rulers to the Church, asking her concerning her belief and practice. And when the question was first put, in the earliest persecution at Rome, the Gentile Church was indeed little, and without breasts, in that she had no native teachers and but small acquaintance with the Law out of which the Gospel had sprung. Another view is that the little sister is spoken to when GOD addresses the Church or any faithful soul either by secret inspiration or by outward preaching, and that the HOLY TRINITY debates, as it were, whether she is to be intrusted with only the minor precepts of the Faith, or, to the end that she may become great, with the deeper mysteries of heavenly secrets. And in this sense *the day* in which she was so spoken to was that Day of Pentecost, when CHRIST sent the HOLY GHOST on the Apostles, and speaking to them inwardly, taught them all the languages of the world. And Philo, explaining the LXX. reading, *in the day wherein if it be spoken in her*, as though it stood for *when she hath spoken within herself*, interprets the words as denoting that stage of spiritual progress which leads to careful self-examination and to calls for the aid of the brethren of the young sister, those teachers of the Church whose task it is then to assist her with counsel and prayer. There are yet two other interpretations; one somewhat resembling this, namely, that the words are those of long-established Churches, considering what is to be done to help and encourage a newly-planted one, in the day when its progress and good works are such as to cause it to be spoken of and praised for its zeal. The other, conversely, takes the day to be that of temptation and trial, when the adversary is speaking against the youthful maiden, and there is need that she should be defended against his craft by older and wiser friends, so that nothing may hinder her from being, in good time, the Bride of her Beloved.

9 If she be a wall, we will build upon her a palace of silver: and if she be a door, we will inclose her with boards of cedar.

The Bride of CHRIST, whether Church or soul, is both *wall* and *door*, and therefore fitted to receive the costly decorations promised by the speakers, whether these be the Blessed TRINITY, the Angels, (as the Targum holds) or the daughters of Jerusalem. The Church, comments S. Ambrose, is a wall, which has twelve Apostolic gates, through which access into the City is afforded to the nations. But even though a wall include the circuit of the entire city, yet it is all the stronger, if it have *battlements* (LXX. and Vulg.) prepared, whence the garrison can safely keep a lookout. Yet as this city is rational, and all its hope is in GOD, it needs not iron battlements, but *silver* ones, since it is more wont to repel the attacks of the enemy with the sacred writings than with bodily pleasures. Defended with such a bulwark, shining with such splendour, she is counted fitter for union with CHRIST. And since CHRIST is the Door, Who saith, "By Me if any man enter in, he shall be saved," so the Church also is called a *door*, because through her there is a way made to salvation for the people. Lest this door should be eaten away by the moths and worms of heretics, the daughters of Jerusalem, or the Angels, or the souls of the righteous, say, *We will inclose her with boards of cedar*, that is, the sweet perfume of a lofty faith, which neither worm nor moth can injure. Cassiodorus prefers to divide, instead of blending, the two metaphors, and will have it that the *wall* denotes the abler and more learned disciples won over by Apostolic teaching, to whom, as capable of defending others as well as themselves, the custody of Holy Writ is assigned. The *door* represents the weaker converts, unable to resist any powerful attack, but useful in their degree, as teaching the easier and simpler doctrines of the Faith, and admitting fresh disciples by Baptism and the other Sacraments into fellowship with the Church. These are to be fortified with the examples of the Fathers who preceded them, who, like *cedars* with their incorruptible timber, have works which fade not, and who are broad like *boards* in the width of their knowledge and charity. For the width of the boards denotes the width of the heart (wherein there ought to be width of charity and knowledge,) as the Psalmist saith, "I have run the way of Thy commandments, when Thou didst widen mine heart." With these boards of cedar, then, we inclose this door,

S. Ambros. Serm. 22, in Ps. cxix.

S. John x. 9.

Cassiodor.

Ps. cxix. 32, Vulg.

that is, with the examples of the Saints, that by imitating them, there may be a gate or door of entrance opened for others into the Church. Another ingenious explanation of the *door* is, that as a door is opened and shut only when wanted, so those members of the Church who know when to speak and to be silent are doors too, and are inclosed with boards of cedar when they are taught to glory only in the Cross of the LORD JESUS CHRIST. Again, as the wall denotes firmness and constancy, so the door is the type of docility and obedience, admitting only the Master of the house and His friends, while excluding all others, wherefore the one is adorned with the pure and shining virtues of holiness, and the other with the incorruption of that practical life of devotion whereof is written, "The righteous shall spread abroad like a cedar in Libanus."

S. Just. Org.
Delrio.
Philo Carp.
Ps. xcii. 11.

So far it is obvious that all the ancient commentators have taken the twofold clauses of this verse as parallel, not as antithetical. But a theory was suggested in the seventeenth century that the two sets of ideas are opposed to one another, and that the meaning is, If our sister remain pure, and resist all temptation, we will reward her with great gifts, but if she allow ready access to every one, and yield to pressure, then we will punish her by confining her closely. This view has been adopted by most of the modern literalists, but rejected by others on the very sufficient ground that the silver battlements and cedar panels answer to one another as costly decorations, and are not opposed in any way as rewards and punishments, independently of the tameness and obscurity of this new idea thus introduced into the Song. It only remains to point out the further meaning, that as some commentators have seen in the preceding verse the Angels discussing what should be done for the Blessed Virgin, in the face of her vow of perpetual purity, on the day when she should be addressed by Gabriel's greeting, so they see here the pledge of those graces of shining and constant faith and of incorruptible purity of soul and body wherewith she was endowed, who was that temple through whose gate the King alone had passage.

Sanchez.
Corn. à Lap.
Rosenmüller, Hitzig, &c.
Renan.
Guilielmus. Card. Hailgrin.
Hugo Card. Cantacuzene.
Ezek. xliv. 2.

10 I am a wall, and my breasts like towers; then was I in his eyes as one that found favour.

The younger sister, be she the Gentile Church, the newly-converted Synagogue, or the elect soul, makes joyous and thankful reply to the doubts expressed by her elder, and declares the strength and increase she has obtained through the Bridegroom's love. *I am a wall*, because I am founded upon a sure Rock, and cemented with the mortar of divine love. *I am a wall*, because built up of living and elect stones, the Saints of GOD; *and my breasts like towers*, because I have those within me who are able to nourish others with spiritual instruction, and defend and guard them like *towers*, and who stand eminent, like towers on a high wall, amongst my other members by virtue of their learning and godliness. And this I have not of my own merit or free-will, but by the gift and grace of my Bridegroom, for *then*, from the time when He shed His Blood for me, and propitiated the FATHER on my behalf, *I was in His eyes as one that findeth peace*, (LXX., Vulg., A.V. marg.,) for He put an end to the enmity between GOD and man, and made peace for me with heaven. And so the Apostle saith, "Being justified by faith, we have peace with GOD through our LORD JESUS CHRIST." The *wall* of the Church, observes another, is the Manhood of CHRIST; the towering *breasts*, supported on that wall, and containing within them the arms of the garrison, are the Apostles, whose example and teaching are the weapons of our Christian warfare. Philo, applying the words to the holy soul, represents her as saying: I am now fortified in faith and filled with charity, and my breasts (I call them mine, for they are given to me and to all who do after them,) namely, the two Testaments and the two precepts of love, and moreover the two kinds of life, active and contemplative, are tested by the workings of righteousness. And these, under the guidance of divine grace, have raised me like a tower to the highest grade of approval, and there I have begun to be a stranger to all anxiety, disquiet, and care for human things, and to take my rest. *And I was in His eyes as one that findeth peace*, for He who foreknew me also foreordained me, and knowing that I should seek peace and ensue it, and ensuing, obtain it, called me then Peaceful, and Shulamite, and made me an impregnable wall, terrible to the enemy; and lifted on high my breasts, that is, my moral and theological teaching, and made them like a tower, that warring thence, I might repel the

Cassiodor.

Rom. v. 1.

Luc. Abb.

Philo Carp.

Theodoret.

Bridegroom's foes. *Findeth* peace, as the LXX. and Vulgate more correctly read, for, as a Saint tells us, we are here only searching for it. We know where it is, but so long as we are in this world, we cease not from all kinds of sin, and so long as we are in sin, we do not yet enjoy perfect peace with Him Who lived in the flesh without sin. When we do find peace, it is only as His gift Who said, " Peace I leave with you, My peace I give unto you; not as the world giveth, give I unto you." The verse has also been applied to various classes of Saints, and especially to Religious. S. Jerome bids Virgins take it on their lips when temptation assails them, and S. Ambrose had already taught them how the Church had been their bulwark and nurse through all the days of persecution, until peace was at last granted to the people of GOD. This peace, however, is not perfect. It is merely truce from outer suffering, peace from sin, peace in grace, peace from the noise of carnal nature, not the peace of the Vision, not the peace of an abiding mansion in eternal glory. But that will come too. "For the Church Triumphant, when she sees herself built up with living stones as a dwelling-place for GOD, and that she has been chosen to repair the angelic tower of the Heavenly Jerusalem, says exulting, *I am a wall, and my breasts towers.* I am built up by CHRIST the Builder, of the elect of mankind, a wall of stone to compass the Heavenly Jerusalem, as a wall in the circuit of a city; and *my breasts*, that is, my Doctors, who yielded me the milk of instruction, are erected like towers in the place of the angels who fell thence; and so the City began to be built by skilled workmen, the Apostles and their successors, from that time *when I was in His sight as one that findeth peace.* Mankind had no peace with GOD and the Angels after it transgressed by its first parent the commandment of GOD in Paradise, but it was as one that found peace with Him when it believed in CHRIST, Who is Very Peace. This is the Peace of which the choir of Angels sang to men of good will, when CHRIST the Prince of Peace came from the heavenly hall into the prison of this world. This is the Peace which He left His disciples when He ascended hence. This is the Peace which He brought back to the children of peace, the peace-makers, when, after conquering death and overthrowing the devil, who is the author of wars, He said, ' Peace be unto you.' This is the Peace wherewith the Church ever desired to be reconciled to GOD, saying, 'Let Him kiss me with the kisses of His mouth,' that is, let Him restore me, through CHRIST, that peace which I have lost. This peace she now hath in hope, and after shall have it in deed, when she shall see face to face CHRIST Who is Peace itself, and when all the borders of Jerusalem shall have peace."

11 Solomon had a vineyard at Baal-hamon; he let out the vineyard unto keepers; every one for the fruit thereof was to bring a thousand pieces of silver.

That is, the Church, which is the spiritual vineyard of the faithful, was planted by the Peaceful King in the *multitude of the nations*, for such is the meaning of *Baal-hamon*.[1] *He let out the vineyard unto keepers*, that is, He intrusted the Church to the Apostles and Doctors, who keep it vigilantly, that the multiform sects which arise against it may not lay it waste, and divide its unity into divers opinions. *Every one for the fruit thereof was to bring a thousand pieces of silver. A man* (Heb., LXX., and Vulg.) shall bring this rent, that is, every one who is of the number of the perfect, who is a teacher of holiness, a hearer and doer of the law, and who has put away, in his bringing, the things of a child, *will bring a thousand pieces of silver*, that is, all the saving fulness of GOD's law and commandments, pure and shining, with him in his hand as his reward in his Country, where he will eat in eternal life and perpetual blessedness of the fruit of his hands. Or, if you prefer it, you may take it that it is we who must bring the fruit, and that the Man Who will give a thousand pieces of silver for it, is the LORD of the vineyard Who rewards the labourers, at the close of their toil, with the perfect gift of wisdom and love. Again, that man who spends his goods upon the poor, and gives his whole substance in charity, leaving all

Tres Patr.

1 Cor. xiii. 11.

Philo Carp.

S. Just. Org.

Irimbert. Cassiodor.

---

[1] So Aquila and Symmachus, severally reading ἐν ἔχοντι πλήθη and ἐν κατοχῇ ὄχλου, both close to the Vulgate, *Quæ habet populos*. But the strict meaning is, "Lord of the multitude." And so reads a variant of the LXX., ἐν τῷ δεσπότῃ τοῦ ὄχλου.

that he possesses, that he may obtain the fruit of the heavenly vineyard, brings a thousand pieces of silver for it, according to the LORD's parable in the Gospel. "The kingdom of heaven is like unto treasure hid in a field; the which when a man hath found, he hideth, and for joy thereof goeth and selleth all that he hath, and buyeth that field." In that the vineyard is said to be *in that which hath peoples,* we are taught that the whole Church, uniting the nations of Jew and Gentile, is here depicted, though some of the Fathers prefer to see the Synagogue alone here, because of that saying, "The vineyard of the LORD of Hosts is the house of Israel, and the men of Judah His pleasant plant." And the holy soul also, which is Solomon's vineyard in the midst of a gainsaying world, (for the full meaning of *Baal-hamon* is the "Lord of the multitude," the Prince of this world,) is intrusted to keepers, earthly ones, who are the priests of His Church; heavenly ones, who are the guardian Angels; and yet He Himself is the chief husbandman and keeper, ever present with His vineyard, as He promised, saying, "Behold, I am with you, even to the end of the world." It is not said to whom the man will bring the thousand pieces of silver, but it is doubtless to Him Who intrusted the vineyard to him, and thus, if CHRIST be the Man spoken of, He will bring His elect Saints, purified seven times in the fire, and stamped with His image and superscription, to His FATHER, that they may be stored in the heavenly treasury; and we shall bring the fulness of our works to CHRIST, in return for what He has given us, that at His coming, He may receive His own with usury. His own, for it is Solomon's vineyard, and we are not more than keepers. And being keepers, it behoves us to remember that the rent is fixed beforehand, at a *thousand* pieces of *silver,* the perfection of a pure life. If we be neglectful, if we allow His vineyard in our hands to be as that of a man of no understanding, and the stone wall thereof to be broken down, then, "it shall come to pass in that day, where there were a thousand vines at a thousand silverlings, it shall even be for briars and thorns." Then, too, we shall be debtors, unable to pay what is due, and must abide what followed in a like case: "His lord was wroth, and delivered him to the tormentors, till he should pay all that was due unto him." Nor shall we prosper more, if, while cultivating the vineyard sedulously, we desire to keep all the fruits for ourselves, and not to pay the King His dues. For then we shall be like those husbandmen who beat, slew, and stoned the servants, and even the Son of their Lord, when He came to receive the fruits. And that because a life of selfishness does, as it were, kill the Lord Jesus within us, and cast Him out of our hearts, that His inheritance, our nature, may be ours to employ as we please. Wherefore the doom which follows is : " He will miserably destroy those wicked men, and will let out His vineyard unto other husbandmen, which shall render Him the fruits in their seasons." S. Mat. xxi. 33, 41.

12 My vineyard, which is mine, is before me : thou, O Solomon, must have a thousand, and those that keep the fruit thereof two hundred.

My vineyard, that same vineyard which of old I had not kept, is *mine*, because the Peaceful One has given it back to me, and with it the thousand pieces of silver which I brought Him, because His sole reason for demanding the fruit is His desire for my salvation. Or, as others prefer to take it, this vineyard is distinct from that in Baal-Hamon, belonging to Solomon, which typifies the Synagogue, whereas this one is the Church, called hers, because she is given a co-ordinate share in its management, such as was not permitted to the Church of the elder dispensation, bound down as it was by a special and immutable code received from the Lord of the vineyard. It is, she says, *mine*, not only because of its freedom from any other owner but Christ, but by reason of the Communion of Saints, which is so perfect that each elect soul can truly say of all that the entire body possesses, It is *mine ;* for every grace, every blessing, every promise, every intercession, every thanksgiving made by any one member of the Church belongs to all the rest, and the aggregate of that which the whole enjoys or effects, is the special property of each single partner in that great firm, alike in this world and the next. Wherefore is added, *is before me*, to denote the common vigilance, interest, and care felt by all alike in tending that mystic vineyard whose fruits are common to all without excep-

tion. And so S. Peter Damiani sings of the unity of
the Church Triumphant:

The Hymn,
Ad perennis
vitæ fontem.

They know Him Who knoweth all things, nothing from their
 ken may flee,
And the thoughts of one another in the inmost heart they see;
One in choosing and refusing, one are they in unity.

And though each for divers merits there hath won a various
 throne,
Yet their love for one another maketh what each loves his own,
Every prize to all is common, yet belongs to each alone.

Cassiodor.
Beda.
Tres Patr.

  The more usual interpretation of the Latin Fathers,
however, assigns these words to the Bridegroom, and
represents them as a reply to the remark of the Bride
that He had let out His vineyard to keepers. It is
true that He has so done, but He is nevertheless constantly present with His vineyard Himself, according

S. Mat.
xxviii. 20.
S. Just. Org.

to His own saying already cited, "Behold, I am with
you always, even unto the end of the world," so that
He says, *My vineyard which is Mine.* He ever super-

Ps. xxxiv.
15.

intends all that is done therein, for "the eyes of the
LORD are over the righteous, and His ears are open
unto their prayers," and therefore He adds, *is before
Me.* And it is not only before Him here, but in the
world to come it will be *before* Him in another and
yet more blessed sense, because of the open vision of
Him which the Saints will enjoy.
  Thou, O Solomon, must have a thousand, and those

Tres Patr.

that keep the fruit thereof two hundred. This, say the
Three Fathers, is the Bride's reply to the King's claim
to be the true LORD and Husbandman of His vineyard. *Thou, O Solomon, must have a thousand,* because perfection is Thy gift, Who art the beginning
and end of all things, Who art Peace itself, and the
bestower of peace. *And they that keep the fruit
thereof two hundred.* For the renewal of our nature

Theodoret.

is effected by the keeping Thy commandments, which
is the fruit of the Church. And this renewal is denoted by the number *two hundred,* because it is made
up of twenty, the product of four and five, (signifying
human nature, endowed with five senses and formed
of four elements) multiplied by ten, the number of the
moral commandments. The Latin Fathers have nearly
all mistaken the meaning of this passage, by reason of
an ambiguity in the Vulgate rendering, which is, *Mille*

tui pacifici et ducenti his qui custodiunt fructus ejus. This should be read with the second and third words in the genitive case singular, thus : *A thousand are of Thee, the Peaceful One.* But as these same words may, so far as form goes, be the nominative plural, the Westerns have mostly supposed the meaning to be, *Thy peaceful ones are a thousand.* Cassiodorus, seeing plainly enough that the *thousand* must have reference to the pieces of silver mentioned in the preceding verse, and yet failing to note the true construction of the sentence, gives the very forced explanation that the thousand silverlings are the reward and gifts of peace which certainly await the faithful soul; and that the *two hundred* silverlings are also the peaceful reward of those who have earned a double prize for that perfection which a hundred denotes, either by holiness in faith and works, or by personal devoutness of life and by the conversion of others through preaching. And this double remuneration is implied by the LORD, saying, "Verily I say unto you, There is no man that hath left house, or brethren, or sisters, or father, or mother, or wife, or children, or lands, for My sake and the Gospel's, but he shall receive a hundredfold now in this time, houses, and brethren, and sisters, and mothers, and children, and lands, with persecutions; and in the world to come eternal life." A hundredfold is promised to all who take up the Cross, and it will be doubled for them that persevere. Others, going yet further from the literal construction, suppose that the numbers refer to persons, not to coins, and explain it as though it were, *Thy peaceful Saints are a thousand,* that is, attain to the perfection of bliss which the mystical number denotes; and very nearly the same meaning comes out of another construction, *Thy peaceful ones shall have a thousand.* Yet again, there are some of the Latin Doctors who see the true form of the sentence, though failing to supply the right word after *a thousand;* and interpret either, *They who are a thousand,* who have reached perfection of life and holiness, are *Thine, O Peaceful One;* or, closest of all to the genuine sense of the passage, *A thousand fruits,* that is, all good things done in the vineyard of the Church, *shall be Thine, O Peaceful One,* because every such good thing does as it were return to CHRIST, whence it flowed out, and rewards Him; and *two hundred fruits,* the far less perfect, though yet superabundant

[margin notes: S. Greg. M. S.Ans.Laud. S. Mark x. 29. Nic. Argent. Hugo Card. Dion. Carth. Cocceius.]

glory, shall be given to His servants, the keepers, whether they have been, like prelates and pastors, set over the charge of great tracts in His vineyard, or merely placed to tend the single vine of an individual soul.

13 **Thou that dwellest in the gardens, the companions hearken to thy voice : cause me to hear it.**

The LXX. and Vulgate are at variance here in the Hebrew text which they have severally followed. The LXX., reading the first verb in the masculine form, takes the Bridegroom to be the dweller in the gardens, Whose voice the Bride desires to hear. The Vulgate, conversely, following the present reading of the Hebrew, makes the Bridegroom the speaker, and the Bride the person addressed. Taking the former view, Theodoret paraphrases thus : " O my Bridegroom, Thou Who restest in Thy spiritual and Thy visible creation, planted, like gardens, with them that do Thy will, there are others besides us, who gaze unceasingly on Thee, because not drawn aside by the fetters of the body, namely, the ranks of the Angels, altogether immaterial. But I, who am bound by this chain, am in dread of change, and therefore, eagerly looking for Thy second Advent, I beseech Thee, make me to hear that desirable voice, ' Come, ye blessed of My FATHER, inherit the Kingdom prepared for you.' " But the Vulgate reading, which is also that of the Chaldee, of Aquila, and of Symmachus, is to be preferred. It is, says Cassiodorus, the voice of the Beloved, addressing the Bride, that is, the Church : O Church, *that dwellest in the gardens*, which art busied in cultivating the plants of holiness, *cause Me to hear thy voice*, that is, preach the Gospel to all thou canst, declare the precepts of My law, and also the promise of heavenly rewards. And *the companions hear thee*, for the angelic spirits delight to listen to thy voice, they whom I made thy companions by the shedding of My own Blood, whom I have appointed as thy helpers and guardians against evil spirits. And those other thy companions, the spirits of the just, whom I have taken out of thy congregation to Myself in heaven, they hear thy voice also, for they delight in thy preaching and in the salvation of their brethren. Others will have it that the gardens in which the Bride dwells are those of Holy Scripture, and of delight in holiness; or, as the Eastern Fathers tell us, the churches for public worship, the shrines of the Martyrs, the convents of ascetic life. And Holy Scripture itself is divided into four gardens, —that of herbs, which is the literal sense; that of apples, which is the moral interpretation; that of nuts, denoting the difficult, yet sweet lessons of allegory; that of spices, which is anagoge, the foretaste of heavenly things. And the Religious Life also has this same fourfold classification of its gardens. Its kitchen-garden of pot-herbs denotes the temporal administration of the house, and the supply of necessaries for its inmates, especially the sick. And this garden is to be kept small. No vineyard is to be destroyed, as Naboth's was by Ahab, to widen it. The apples, comely and fragrant, denote ready and cheerful obedience. The nuts, hard without and sweet within, are the austerities of the rule; and the spices the joys of devout contemplation. In all these gardens dwells the truly cloistered soul. Rupert. Tres Patr. Hugo Card.

And observe that there are two distinct and co-ordinate methods of interpreting the verse. It may imply that the Bride is entirely silent, or that she is speaking to the companions only, and not to the Beloved. In the former case, the meaning is, that she is commanded to preach, because she, and she only, is sure to be listened to by those who are willing to love and obey GOD. She is not to spend her time, as she would prefer, in silent meditation and prayer, but must occupy herself for the benefit of her companions. The other sense, conversely, is that in the zeal of active life and the work of bringing in neophytes to the fold, she has forgotten the care of her own vineyard. She has been speaking, earnestly and devoutly enough, in teachings and warnings, to the multitudes: she has failed in her more directly personal service to her Beloved, in prayer, praise, and thanksgiving. *Make Me hear thy voice.* He then saith, Let Martha leave her serving for a time, and sit down with Mary at My feet. And therefore the vow of elect souls must be that which the Apostles made, "We will give ourselves continually to prayer, and to the ministry of the Word." And He calls on her to speak for yet another reason. He it is Who has made her to dwell in those pleasant gardens where Philo Carp. S. Greg. M. Angelomus. Ainsworth. Acts vi. 4. Nic. Argent.

grow His lilies and spices, He has clothed her in royal attire, He has made His companions, the Angels, ministering spirits for her service. They are waiting, watching, listening, to know what they are to do for her next, and He wishes to heap yet more blessings upon her. *Make Me,* then, *to hear thy voice.* "What wilt thou, and what is thy request? it shall be even given thee to the half of the kingdom." And the Bride makes answer at once:

Esth. v. 3.

14 Make haste, my beloved, and be thou like to a roe or to a young hart upon the mountains of spices.

Make haste. The Hebrew is rightly given in the margin, and by the old versions, *Flee away.* But why does the Bride, who has all along been desiring the presence of her Beloved, and union with Him, reply thus to His invitation to speak? They give many reasons, but the best of all seems that of Philo and Cassiodorus, which may be conveniently cited in the words of Nicolas of Strasburg. The Primitive Church, because of those words of CHRIST, "If I go not away, the Comforter will not come unto you;" and again, "It is expedient for you that I go away," desired her Beloved, to *flee away* in His Manhood, that she might more clearly comprehend Him according to His Godhead. And thus she was able to say: Since Thou hast come, and hast kissed me by Thine Incarnation, and hast tarried with me on earth, now *flee away* again, *my Beloved.* from me to the FATHER, that I may know Thy Godhead, and one day be able to follow Thee thither, where Thou hast ascended, since not till then canst Thou hear my voice, for not till Thy earthly work is ended, can I begin to preach Thee. And this is curiously in accord with the Chaldee paraphrase: "At that time shall the elders of the congregation of Israel say, Flee, O my Beloved, LORD of the world, from this unclean earth, and let Thy Majesty dwell in the highest heavens." Or it may be the voice of humility saying with Peter, "Depart from me, for I am a sinful man, O LORD;" and with the centurion, "LORD, I am not worthy that Thou shouldest come under my roof." *Flee away,* then, *my Beloved,* I seek not for glory in this life, but I long for grace. I seek not the renown of working miracles, but I desire the

Philo Carp.
Cassiodor.
Nic. Argent.

S. John xvi. 7.

Beda.

Targum.

Rupert.
S. Luke v. 8.

S. Mat. viii. 8.

remission of my sins. Flee away also, that thou mayest ever be incomprehensible, that Thou mayest always be desired and desirable, that we may never know, while in this body, how great is the abundance of Thy goodness which Thou hast hidden for them that fear Thee. Flee, flee, in Thy care and providence for us, that we may never fancy while we live that we have attained Thee, but that we may still follow in order to attain, " Draw me, we will run after Thee." It is not that she wishes Him to flee, observes a Saint, but that she sees it to be His wont to do so, and her only will is that His will may be done. Or, once more, as others will have, *flee away* from hard and sinful hearts which refuse to admit Thee, unto the hearts of the elect, open to welcome Thee, flee from the unbelieving Synagogue to the faithful Church. *Flee away*, too, by withdrawing Thy visible dispensation, Thine earthly kingdom, retiring, as it were, into the heights of heaven, on the Day of Judgment, and drawing us with Thee from the perishing world. *And be Thou like to a roe or a young hart.* We have here again in the Greek that word δορκὰς, meaning the "clear-eyed," and therefore the Bride asks her Beloved to flee away in such fashion as nevertheless to see her, and not lose sight of her during her toils, that she may be comforted with the thought of His ever-watchful eyes. Though I be unfit for Thy continual presence, yet show Thyself often and swiftly to me *on the mountains of spices*, in moments of contemplation, in the lives of those great Saints whom Thou visitest and inspirest; mount, O Lord, ever higher and higher above the mightiest Angels, that I, though far off, may behold Thee surpassing all, and perfect in majesty, and myself haste after Thee to those true *mountains of spices*, on which the Heavenly Jerusalem stands, and whence the incense of perpetual adoration ascends before the throne of God.

Beda.

S. Greg. M.
Dion. Carth.

Theodoret.

Corn. à Lap.

Hugo Card.

Nic. Arg.
Thom.
Vercell.
Alvarez.
S. Greg. M.
Hugo Card.

Lyranus.

Now, on those eternal mountains
  Stands the sapphire throne, all bright,
Where unceasing Alleluias
  They upraise, the sons of light;
Sion's people tell His praises,
  Victor after hard-won fight.

Bring your harps and bring your incense;
  Sweep the string, and pour the lay;
Let the earth proclaim His wonders,
  King of that celestial day;

Hupton,
The Hymn,
Come, ye faithful.

He the Lamb once slain, is worthy,
Who was dead and lives for aye.

S. August. Meditat. cap. 22.
"O truly blessed kingdom," exclaims the Doctor of Grace, "free from death, having no end, where no seasons follow one another for ever and ever, where the perpetual day without night knows not time, where the victorious warrior, united with the tuneful choirs of Angels, sings to GOD unceasingly the Song of Songs of Sion, while the crown evermore encircles his ennobled brow!" *Make haste*, then, *O my Beloved*, for "the SPIRIT and the Bride say, Come. And let him that heareth say, Come." And Thou, O dear and worshipped LORD, art not deaf to the call, "He which testifieth these things saith, Surely I come quickly; Amen. Even so, come, LORD JESUS."

Lyranus.

Rev. xxii. 17, 20.

Vol. I. Post 8vo., cloth, 10s. 6d.

A COMMENTARY ON THE PSALMS:

From Primitive and Mediæval Writers; and from the Various Office Books and Hymns of the Roman, Mozarabic, Ambrosian, Gallican, Greek, Coptic, Armenian, and Syriac Rites.

BY THE LATE REV. J. M. NEALE, D.D.

Vol. II. 10s. 6d.

Completed by the REV. R. F. LITTLEDALE, LL.D.

"Without any reference to different systems of Biblical exegesis, this Commentary is, both theologically and devotionally, an immense advance upon any Commentary upon any portion of Holy Scripture—not even excepting Dr. Pusey's Minor Prophets—which has yet been written."—*Church Review.*

"To Clergymen who are willing to give time to its study it will prove invaluable for homiletical purposes, as an abundance of new trains of thought will be suggested by the various texts incidentally introduced which will give their sermons that freshness which is as unusual as it is desirable in pulpit utterances. And no less a boon will it be to those of the laity who enjoy a book which, without requiring any great amount of continuous reading, will give food for meditation, and enable them to enter with more interest into that book of Holy Scripture which they are probably more familiar with than with any other."—*Church Times.*

London: J. MASTERS, Aldersgate Street.

September, 1869.

CLASSIFIED INDEX.

BIOGRAPHY.

Autobiography of John Brown	2
Baines' Life of Archbishop Laud	2
Brechin's (Bp. of) Memoir of Helen Inglis	4
Brett's Doctrine of the Cross	5
—— Memorial of M. C. B.	5
Brownlow's Memoir	6
Heygate's Memoir of Rev. J. Cook	15
Life of Sister Rosalie	33
Lives of Englishmen (4 Series)	20
Memoir of M. E. D. and G. E. D.	21
Memorial of Elizabeth A——.	21
Newland's Memoir	25
Suckling's Memoir	35
Teale's Lives of Eminent Divines	35
Walcott's Life of Bishop Hacket	15

BOOKS FOR THE SICK AND AFFLICTED.

Brett's Devotions for the Sick Room	5
—— Companion for ditto	5
—— Instructions and Prayers for Sick	5
—— Leaflets for Sick and Dying	5
Few Words to a Christian Mourner	12
Manual for Mourners	21
Method of Assisting the Sick	21
Monro's Readings and Lessons for Sick Rooms	23
Prayers and Maxims, in Large Type	28
Short Prayers for the Sick	29
Short Devotions from Prayer Book for do.	29
Stretton's Guide to Sick and Dying	34

BOOKS FOR THE USE OF THE CLERGY.

Brechin (Bp. of) Memoriale Vitæ Sacerdotalis	4
Brett's Suggestions for Burial of the Dead	5
Devotional Aids for the Clergy	10
Newland's Essays on Confirmation	25
Paget's Memoranda Parochialia	26
Parish and the Priest	27
Plenderleath's Priest's Visiting List	27
Priest's Prayer Book	30
—— Responsal to	30
Questions for Self-Examination for Clergy	30
Sermons Register	32
Thompson's Concionalia	35
Visitatio Infirmorum	9

CATECHISMS AND CATECHETICAL WORKS.

Arden's Catechetical Manual	1
Brechin's (Bp. of) First Catechism	4
Catechism on the Unity of the Church	6
Catechism on the Incarnation	17
Catechism of Theology	7
Chanter's Exposition of the Catechism	7
Catechism of the Chief Truths	7
Church Catechism, illustrated	8
Collects Catechetically Explained	9
Easy Catechism on the Old Testament	11
Hicks' Lectures on the Incarnation	15
Holden's Anglican Catechist	16
Hyde's Church Catechism with Notes	17
—— Catechism with Easy Explanations	17
Johns' Collects and Catechisings	18
Johns' Questions on the Pentateuch	17
Lea's Catechisings on the Prayer Book	19
Malan's Exposition of the Creed	20
Phipps' Catechism on the Holy Scriptures	27
Questions on Church Catechism	30
Questions on Christian Doctrine	30
Smith's Church Catechism	33
Stretton's Church Catechism explained	34
—— Child's Catechism	34
—— Catechism of First Truths	34
—— Brief Catechism of the Bible	34
Watson's Catechism on the Prayer Book	37
West's Questions and Answers on Chief Truths	37
—— Questions for Higher Classes	37
—— Catechism on the Church	37

CHRISTIAN MEMORIALS.

Carter's Christian Gravestones	7
Forsyth's Monumental Designs	13
Hallam's Monumental Memorials	15
Paget's Tract upon Tombstones	26
Stride's Sketches for Christian Memorials	34
Sunter's Designs for Headstones, &c.	35

CHURCH HISTORY.

Blackmore's History of the Russian Church	3
Book of Church History	3
Brownlow's History of the Church	6
Neale's History of the Eastern Church	24
—— Voices from the East	24
Popoff's Council of Florence	28
Pye's Short Ecclesiastical History	30
Wilkins' Lecture on Early Church History	37

COMMENTARIES.

Acts of Apostles, Exposition of	1
Book of Genesis, Exposition of	3
Brechin's (Bp. of) Commentary on Litany	4
—— on Te Deum	4
—— on Canticles	4
—— on Penitential Psalms	4
Cottage Commentary	9
Deane's Proper Lessons with Commentary	10
Ford's Commentary on the Gospels	13
—— on Acts	13
—— on Romans	13
Littledale's Commentary on Song of Songs	19
Malan's Gospel of S. John	20
Neale's Commentary on the Psalms	24
—— on Hymnal Noted	25

CONFIRMATION.

Brechin's (Bp. of) Seal of the Lord	4
Brett's Guide to Confirmation	5
Certificate of Confirmation	7

Confirmation Medal 9
Ellis' Font to the Altar . . . 11
Helps for Confirmation and Communion . 15
Illuminated Memorial of Confirmation . 63
Laying on of Hands 19
Milman's Meditations on Confirmation . 22
Monro's Preparation for Confirmation . 23
—— Manuals and Prayers ditto . . 23
Newland's Confirmation and Communion . 25
Pott's Confirmation Lectures . . 28
Prynne's Plain Instructions . . . 30
Suckling's Manual for Confirmation . 35
Tracts on Confirmation . . . 60

DEVOTIONAL BOOKS.

Avrillon on the HOLY SPIRIT . . 32
Bourdaloue's Spiritual Exercises . . 32
Brechin's (Bp. of) Christian's Converse . 4
—— Nourishment of the Soul . . 4
—— Meditations from Pinart . . 4
—— Mirror of Young Christians . 4
—— Meditations on the Passion . 4
Brett's Meditations on the Life of our LORD 5
Brettingham's Anniversaries . . 4
Butler's Meditations on the Life of our LORD 6
Clarke's Watch Tower Book . . 8
Daily Events of Holy Week . . 10
Divine Master 10
Edmonstone's Portions of Psalms . . 11
Eighty-fourth Psalm, Treatise on . . 11
Familiar Instructions on Prayer . . 12
Footprints of the LORD . . . 6
Footsteps of the Holy Child . . 6
Gerhard's Meditations . . . 29
Great Truths of the Christian Religion . 14
Heygate's Evening of Life . . . 15
—— Wedding Gift . . . 15
Hidden Life 16
Holy Child JESUS 16
Holy Childhood of our LORD . . 16
Kalendar of the Imitation . . . 18
Kempis' Soliloquy of the Soul . . 18
—— Valley of Lilies . . . 36
Ken's Practice of Divine Love . . 19
Kettlewell's Companion for the Penitent . 29
Legenda Domestica 19
Lowder's Penitent's Path . . . 20
Malan's Meditations on the Passion . 20
—— Companion for Lent . . . 20
—— Meditations for Lent . . . 20
Milman's Voices of Harvest . . 22
Monro's Readings for Holy Week . . 23
Paget's Christian's Day . . . 26
Pathway of Faith 27
Patrick's Parable of the Pilgrim . . 27
Practice of the Presence of GOD . . 28
Shipley's Daily Meditations . . 32
—— Meditations for a Month . . 32
Skinner's Heads of Christian Duty . 33
Spiritual Voices from the Middle Ages . 34

ECCLESIOLOGY.

Best's Plea for Daily Worship . . 2
Badger's Nestorians and their Rituals . 2
Book of Common Prayer (Sealed Book) . 3
Ditto, Church of Scotland . . 3
Browne's Lecture on Symbolism . . 5
Chamberlain's Chancel . . . 51
Church Floral Decoration . . . 8
Dickinson's List of Service Books . 10
Directorium Scoticanum et Anglicanum . 27
Ecclesiastical Embroidery . . . 11
Ecclesiological Society's Publications . 51
Ecclesiologist, the 11

Form of Consecration of Churches . . 13
Form for Laying Foundation Stone ditto . 13
Form of Consecrating Cemetery Chapels . 13
Freeman's History of Architecture . . 14
Goodwin's Art of Polychrome . . 14
Gresley's Treatise on English Church . 14
Handbook of Ecclesiology . . . 11
Helmore's Church Choirs . . . 15
Hierurgia Anglicana 16
Hopkins' (Bp.) Law of Ritualism . 16
Liturgies 19
Masters' List of Daily Services . . 21
Maunsell's Church Bells and Ringing . 21
Neale's Introduction to Eastern Church . 24
—— Ecclesiology of the Isle of Man . 24
—— Church Tourists . . . 24
Organs, a Short Account of. . . 25
Poole's Churches described . . 28
Popoff's Origin of Roman Liturgy . 28
Practical Hints on Church Embroidery . 11
Pratt's Letters on Scandinavian Churches . 28
Reverence due to holy places . . 31
Spelman's History of Sacrilege . . 33
Sperling's Church Walks in Middlesex . 33
Walcott's Interior of a Gothic Minster . 36
—— Precinct of a Gothic Minster . 36
—— Cathedralia 36

EDUCATIONAL.

Bezant's Geographical Questions . . 2
Key to ditto 2
Chamberlain's English Grammar . . 7
Child's New Lesson Book . . . 7
Couper's Hints on Management of Children 9
Easy Lessons for younger children . 11
Ditto, Questions on . . . 11
Finchley Manuals of Industry . . 12
Hints on Early Education . . . 16
Hopwood's School Geography . . 16
—— Child's Geography . . . 16
Johns' Dictation Lessons . . . 18
Lessons for every day in the Week . 19
Companion to ditto for Teacher . 19
Lessons in Grammar for a Child . . 19
Sankey's Bible Exercises . . . 31
—— Ditto, Teacher's Copy . . 31
Sunday Alphabet 35
Wakefield's Charades from History, &c. . 36
—— Mental Exercises . . . 36
Young Churchman's Alphabet . . 38

EUCHARISTIC MANUALS.

Altar Book for the Young . . . 9
Companion to Altar for Scottish Church . 9
Devotions for Choristers at Holy Communion 10
Devotions for Holy Communion . . 10
Eucharistic Month 11
Form of Self-examination before Holy Communion 13
Guide to the Eucharist . . . 8
Holy Eucharist, a Manual, &c. . . 16
Laurence's Assistant at Holy Communion 19
Malan's Prayers for Holy Communion . 20
—— Preparation for Holy Communion . 20
Manual for Communicants . . . 21
Nelson's Guide to the Holy Communion . 29
Prynne's Eucharistic Manual . . 30
Scottish Communion Office in Greek . 4
Scudamore's Steps to the Altar . . 34
Shipley's Eucharistic Litanies . . 32
—— Eucharistic Meditations . . 32
—— Divine Liturgy . . . 32

CLASSIFIED INDEX.

FAMILY PRAYERS.

Book of Family Prayers from the Liturgy . 3
—— By a Layman 3
Bowdler's Family Prayers 3
Carter's Family Prayers 6
Domestic Offices for the Use of Families . 11
Family Prayers by a Priest 12
Family Prayers for Children of the Church 12
Hooper's Prayers for Family Worship . 16
Monsell's Prayers and Litanies . . . 23
Morning and Evening Prayers for a Family 29
—— For a Household 23
Rose's Family Prayers 31
Short Services for Families . . . 33
Suckling's Family Prayers 35

HISTORY.

Arnold's History of Ireland . . . 18
Baines' History of England . . . 2
Cranborne's History of France . . . 10
Flower's History of Scotland . . . 18
Fox's History of Rome 18
Haskoll's History of France . . . 18
Jenkins' Annals of the Kings of Judah . 17
Johns' History of Spain 18
Lectures on History of England . . 19
Moore's Easy Readings on English History 23
Neale's English History 18
—— History of Greece 18
—— History of Portugal 18
Poole's History of England. . . . 28
Wilbraham's Kingdom of Judah . . . 37

HYMNS.

Hymns for Little Children 1
Hymns Descriptive and Devotional . . 1
Hymns for Infant Children 17
Hymns on Scripture Characters . . . 17
Hymns of the Holy Feast 17
Narrative Hymns for Schools . . . 1
Neale's Mediæval Hymns 24
—— Hymns for the Sick 24
—— Hymns for Children 24
Raine's Verses for Church Schools . . 30
Williams' Hymns on the Catechism . . 38

HYMNS FOR PUBLIC WORSHIP.

Anthems, Words of 1
Chamberlain's Hymns for Minor Festivals 7
Fallow's Psalms and Hymns . . . 29
Hymns and Introits 17
People's Hymnal 27

JUVENILE TALES.

Archie's Ambition 1
Baines' Tales of the Empire . . . 2
Baptismal Vows 2
Baron's Little Daughter, &c. . . . 1
Beginnings of Evil 2
Bishop's Little Daughter 2
Bonus's Beatrice 3
Chapters on Plants 44
Chapters on Animals 44
Charcoal Burners 18
Charity at Home 7
Christmas Dream 8
Christmas Present for Children . . . 8
Consecration and Desecration . . . 9
Douglas' Mary and Mildred . . . 11
Drop in the Ocean 11
Dunster's Stories from Chroniclers . . 18
Early Friendship 18
Eccles' Midsummer Holydays . . . 11
Fanny's Flowers; or, Fun for the Nursery . 12

Five Tales of old Time 12
Flower's Classical Tales 13
—— Tales of Faith and Providence . . 13
—— Widow and her Son, and other Tales 13
Flowers and Fruit 43
Forbes' Snowball and Other Tales . . 13
Fox's Noble Army of Martyrs . . . 14
—— Holy Church 14
Frederick Gordon 14
Going Home 14
Gould's Path of the Just 14
Grace Alford 33
Gresley's Henri de Clermont . . . 18
—— Colton Green 18
—— Holiday Tales 15
Heygate's Godfrey Davenant . . . 18
—— Ditto at College 18
Higher Claims 16
Holiday Hours 44
Home for Christmas 16
Island Choir 17
Ivo and Verena 17
Levett's Gentle Influence 19
Little Alice and her Sister 20
Manger of the Holy Night 18
Memoirs of an Arm-chair 21
Mercy Downer 21
Minnie's Birthday 22
Mitchell's Hatherleigh Cross . . . 22
Monro's Stories of Cottagers . . . 23
—— Footprints in the Snow . . . 22
—— Harry and Archie 22
—— Pascal the Pilgrim 23
—— Leila 22
Neale's Christian Heroism 18
—— Christian Endurance 18
—— Heathen Mythology 18
—— Followers of the Lord . . . 24
—— Lent Legends 24
—— Evenings at Sackville College . . 24
—— Egyptian Wanderers 24
—— Afternoons at an Orphanage . . 24
Old Court House 25
Paget's Hope of the Katzekopfs . . . 18
—— Tales of Village Children . . . 18
—— Luke Sharp 18
Parish Tales 27
Pearson's Stories on the Beatitudes . . 27
—— (H. D.) Stories of Christian Joy, &c. 27
Poynings: a Tale of 1688 18
Prisoners of Craigmacaire 30
Rainy Mornings with Aunt Mabel . . 30
Robert and Ellen 31
Roberts' Snowbound in Cleeberrie Grange 31
Root of the Matter 31
Ruth Levison 31
Scholar's Nosegay 43
Stone's Ellen Merton 34
Stories for Young Servants 34
Stories on the Commandments . . . 16
Stories on the Festivals, &c. . . . 43
Story of a Dream 34
Swedish Brothers 18
Tales of my Duty towards my Neighbour . 43
Tales to read to Myself 35
Tales of a London Parish 2
Thinking for Oneself 35
Trust 36
Vidal's Esther Merle 36
—— Home Trials 36
Village Story for Village Maidens . . 36
Voyage for the Fortunate Isles . . . 36
Was it a Dream ? 37
Wilbraham's Tales for Boys 37

CLASSIFIED INDEX.

Wilford's Author's Children	37
—— King of a Day	37
Winter in the East	38
Yorke's Cottage Homes	38

MISCELLANEOUS.

Churchman's Companion	8
Macaulay's Day at Nismes	20
Malan's Bethany : a Pilgrimage	20
—— Tyre and Sidon	20
Mediæval Alphabets	21
Monro's Schoolmaster's Day	23
Newland's Lectures on Tractarianism	25
Our Solar System	26
Plea for Industrial Schools	27
Presbyterian looking for the Church	30
Raine's Summer Wanderings	30
—— Queen's Isle	30
Reminiscences of Forty Years	31
Roberts' Rocks of Worcestershire	31
Selections New and Old	32
Sentences from Sewell's Works	32
Shipley's Purgatory of Prisoners	32
Sisters of Charity	33
Whytehead's College Life	37

MUSIC.

Church Music	38
Sacred	40
Secular	42

PAROCHIAL AND CHURCH BOOKS.

Book of Strange Preachers	3
Burial Service on Card	6
Canticles pointed for Chanting	6
—— Ditto with Blank Staves	6
Consecration Prayer for Altar Desk	9
District Visitor's Memorandum Book	10
Form for Foundation Stone of School	13
Ditto of a Church	13
Form for opening a New School	13
Litany, 4to. rubricated	19
Ministration of Baptism	22
Prayers for Choirs in Vestry	26
Register of Baptisms	31
—— Burials	31
—— Persons Confirmed	31
—— Preachers, Sermons, &c.	31
Sponsor's Duty on Card	34

POETRY.

Athanasius and other Poems	2
Benn's Solitary	2
Bernard's (S.) Sweet Rhythm	2
Bourne's Thoughts on Catholic Truths	3
Braune's Persone of a Toun	3
Chambers' Lauda Syon	7
Churton's Lays of Faith and Loyalty	18
Cornish's Sonnets and Verses	33
Dakeyne's Sword and the Cross	10
Daily Life of the Christian Child	10
Echoes of Our Childhood	11
Evans' (Archdeacon) Daily Hymns	11
Evans' Pietas Puerilis	12
Ford's Thoughts in Verse	13
Freeman's (Archdeacon) Sunday	14
Goodrich's Claudia	14
Hawker's Echoes from Old Cornwall	15
Hopkins' Pietas Metrica	16
Intermediate State	17
Ken's (Bp.) Preparatives for Death	19
Last Sleep of the Christian Child	19
Loraine's Lays of Israel	20
Lyra Sanctorum	20
Magnay's Poems	21
Monro's Lella	22
Moral Songs	1
Morgan's Gifts and Light	23
—— Ascension and other Poems	23
—— Church in Babylon	23
Moultrie's Martyrdom of S. Polycarp	23
—— Hymns and Lyrics	23
Neale's Songs and Ballads	24
Ogilvy's Nun of Enzklosterle	25
Original Ballads	35
Orlebar's Christmas Eve	26
Paradise Kept	26
Poems on Old Testament Subjects	1
Poems. By C. A. M. W.	27
River Reeds	3
Russell's Lays of the Early Church	31
Thoughts in Solitude	35
Tomlins' Tonbridge School Chapel	36
—— S. Mary's Home	36
Tute's Holy Times and Scenes	36
—— Champion of the Cross	36
Verses and Pictures on Life of our Lord	36
Verses for the Christian Year	36
Waring's Annuals and Perennials	37
Williams' Altar	38
Winged Words	38

PRAYERS FOR SCHOOLS.

Liturgy for Village Schools	20
Mouro's School Prayers for a Week	23
—— Ditto for Ecclesiastical year	23
Prayers for Parochial Schools	29
Simple Prayers for Village Schools	29
West's Prayers and Hymns for Children	37

PRIVATE PRAYERS.

Andrewes' (Bp.) Private Devotions	1
Brechin's (Bp. of) Pious Churchman	27
Brett's Churchman's Guide	5
—— Christian's Daily Guide	5
—— Devotions for Schoolboys	5
—— Devout Prayers on the Passion	5
—— Fervent Aspirations	5
—— Offices for Sick and Dying	5
—— Prayers for Children	5
Butler's Prayers for Working Men	6
Carter's Private Prayers	6
—— Litanies	6
—— Night Offices	6
Christian Servant's Book of Devotion	8
Clergyman's Manual of Private Prayers	9
Collects from Prayer Book	9
Cosin's (Bp.) Private Devotions	9
Day Hours of the Church	10
Supplement to ditto	10
Dial of Meditation and Prayer	10
Errington's Prayers for Soldiers	11
Few Devotional Helps for the Seasons	12
Gray's Christian's Plain Guide	14
Heygate's Manual	15
Ditto for General Use	15
Horology, or Dial of Prayer	16
Johnson's (Dr.) Prayers and Meditations	18
Little Hours of the Day	19
Malan's Pocket Book of Prayers	20
Manual of Prayers for a Servant	21
Manual for Sisters of Mercy	26
Morning and Evening Exercises	23
Moultrie's Primer	23
—— Offices for Holy Week	23
Order for Prime, Compline, &c.	25
Paget's Sursum Corda	26
—— Prayers for the Church	26
Pathway of Faith	27

CLASSIFIED INDEX.

Pocket Manual of Prayers . . . 27
Prayers and Maxims 28
Prayers for Seven Canonical Hours . 28
Psalter according to Sarum Use . . 30
Sacramentarium Ecclesiæ Catholicæ . 31
Short Devotions for the Seasons . . 33
Smith's Devout Chorister . . . 33
Stretton's Scholar's Manual . . . 34
Taylor's (Bp. J.) Prayers . . . 35
Young Churchman's Manual . . . 29

RELIGIOUS INSTRUCTION.
Black's Primer of Christian Worship . 3
—— Manual on the LORD's Prayer . 3
Bowdler's Few Words of Instruction . 3
Christian Servant taught . . . 7
Christian Duties 7
Churchman's Library 8
Church Doctrines proved by the Bible . 8
Companion to the Sunday Services . 9
Conversations with Cousin Rachel . 9
Cosin's Sum of the Catholic Faith . 9
Edmonstone's Christian's Daily Walk . 11
Erasmus's Preparation for Death . 24
Evening Meetings, the 12
Explanation of Scriptural Terms . . 12
Fasts and Festivals of the Church . 12
Few Words on Christian Seasons . . 12
GOD's Church on Earth . . . 14
Great Truths of the Christian Religion . 14
Husband's Truths of the Catholic Religion 16
Litany Explained 25
Morning and Evening Prayer Explained . 25
Poor Churchman's Friend . . . 28
Prynne's Few Plain Words . . . 30
Readings on the History of Joseph . 30
Scenes in Lives of Christian Children . 7
Simple Words on the LORD's Prayer . 33
Stone's Handbook to the Christian Year . 34
Tomline's (Bp.) Holy Scriptures . . 36
West's Figures and Types . . . 37
—— Reasons for being a Churchman . 37
—— Tracts on Church Principles . 37
What we are to Believe 19

REWARD BOOKS.
Packets of Books 43
Penny 44
Twopenny 44
Threepenny 45
Fourpenny 45
Sixpenny 46

SCRIPTURE READINGS.
Brett's Scripture History for the Young . 5
Reading Lessons from Scripture History . 30
Readings from Holy Scripture . . 30
Ditto, Second Series 30
Scripture Reading Lessons for Children . 32
Ditto, Second Series 32

SERMONS.
Alsop's Sermons 1
Ashley's Victory of the Spirit . . 2
—— Translation of Rossi's Sermons . 2
Baines' Sermons 2
Bingham's Easter Sermons . . . 2
Bowdler's Sermons on Christianity . 3
Brechin's (Bp.of) Are you being Converted? 4
—— Sermons on Amendment of Life . 4
—— Waning of Opportunities . . 4
—— Grace of GOD and other subjects . 4
Bright's Sermons of S. Leo . . . 5
Browne's Sussex Sermons . . . 6
Butler's Sermons for Working Men . 6
Carter's Sermons 6

Carter's Imitation of our LORD . . 6
—— Life of Sacrifice 6
—— Passion and Temptation of our LORD 6
—— Life of Penitence 6
Chambers' Fifty-two Sermons . . 7
Chamberlain's Christian Worship . 7
—— Seven ages of the Church . . 7
Chanter's Sermons 7
Cheyne's Teaching of the Christian Year . 7
—— Consolations of the Cross . . 7
Codd's Sermons 9
Comper's Teaching of British Churches . 9
Cresswell's Christian Life . . . 10
Davies' Benefit Club Sermons . . 10
Deane's Occasional Sermons . . . 10
Evans' Christianity in its Homely Aspects 12
Flower's Sermons of S. Bernard . . 13
Ford's Sermons at Heavitree . . 13
—— Translation of Segneri's Sermons . 13
Fowler's Parochial Sermons . . . 14
Freeman's Advent Sermons . . . 14
Galton's Lectures on the Revelation . 14
—— on Book of Canticles . . . 14
Goodwin's Cretian Church . . . 14
Gresley's Practical Sermons . . . 14
—— Sermons at Brighton . . . 14
—— Three Sermons on Rome . . 14
Hamilton's Sermons 15
Hill's Short Sermons 16
Hopwood's CHRIST in His Church . 16
Hutchings' Lent Lectures . . . 17
Innes' Five Advent Sermons . . . 17
Irons' Lectures, Holy Catholic Church . 17
—— Lectures, Ecclesiastical Jurisdiction 17
—— Preaching of CHRIST . . . 17
—— Miracles of CHRIST . . . 17
Lea's Sermons 19
Lee's Advent Sermons 19
—— Message of Reconciliation . . 19
—— Miscellaneous Sermons . . . 19
Magnay's Sermons, Practical & Suggestive 21
Michell's Sermons 21
—— Churches of Asia 21
Mill on the Nature of Christianity . 21
—— Four Sermons at Cambridge . 21
Monro's Old Testament Characters . 22
Mossman's Sermons 23
Mountain's Sermons for Seasons . . 24
Neale's Readings for the Aged . . 24
—— Sermons for Minor Festivals . 24
—— Sermons in a Religious House . 24
Newland's Postils 25
Nugee's Words from the Cross . . 25
—— Holy Women of the Gospel . 25
Paget's Duties of Daily Life . . . 26
—— Sermons on Saints' Days . . 26
—— Sermons on Special Occasions . 26
Poland's Earnest Exhortations . . 28
Polehampton's Steps in the Christian's Life 28
Poole's Sermons on Holy Communion . 28
Pott's Confirmation Lectures . . 28
—— Village Lectures on Sacraments . 28
Prichard's Sermons 30
Prynne's Plain Parochial Sermons . 30
Skinner's Revelation of Antichrist . 33
Smith's (C. F.) Sermons . . . 33
—— (W. B.) Lent and Parochial Sermons 33
Smyttan's CHRIST Slighted . . . 33
Stretton's Acts of S. Mary Magdalene . 34
Suckling's Sermons 35
Thompson's Davidica 35
—— Concionalia 35
—— The Sunday School . . . 35
Tomlins' Sermons for Seasons . . 36

CLASSIFIED INDEX.

Tomlins' Advent Sermons	36
Watson's Seven Sayings on the Cross	37
—— Sermons on the Beatitudes	37
—— Sermons for Sundays	37
West's Parish Sermons	37
Wilkinson's Mission Sermons	37
Wilmshurst's Six Sermons	38
Windsor's Sermons for Soldiers	38
Woodford's Sermons at Bristol	38
—— Occasional Sermons	38
Wroth's Sermons on Baptism	38

TALES AND ALLEGORIES.

Adams' Silvio	1
—— Fall of Crœsus	1
—— (C.P.) Cressingham	1
Alice Beresford	1
Apple Blossom	1
Bayliss' Loving Service	2
Birthday, the	2
Cecil Dean	7
Children of the Chapel	7
Chorister Brothers	7
Chronicles of S. Mary's	8
Cudlip's (Mrs.) A Noble Aim	10
Curate of Holycross	10
Enthusiasm not Religion	11
Evans' Tales of the British Church	11
Everley	12
Gertrude Dacre	14
Gresley's Forest of Arden	14
—— Siege of Lichfield	15
—— Coniston Hall	15
—— Clement Walton	15
—— Charles Lever	15
—— Church Clavering	15
—— Frank's Trip to the Continent	15
—— Bernard Leslie	15
—— Part II.	15
—— Portrait of an English Churchman	15
Henrietta's Wish	15
Heygate's William Blake	16
Hilary S. Magna	16
Ion Lester	17
Ivon	17
Lord of the Forest and his Vassals	1
Lucy and Christian Wainwright	20
Macgregor's Somerford Priory	21
—— Deepdene Minster	21
Maiden Aunt's Tales	21
Mason's Old Library and its Tales	21
Meeting in the Wilderness	21
Milman's Way through the Desert	22
Monro's Allegories	22
—— Eustace	22
—— Claudian	22
—— Basil the Schoolboy	22
—— Walter the Schoolmaster	22
—— Leonard and Dennis	22
—— Footprints in the Snow	22
My Birthday Eve	24
Neale's Stories of the Crusades	24
—— Duchenier	24
—— Unseen World	24
—— Theodora Phranza	24
—— Tales on the Apostles' Creed	25
Northwode Priory	25
One Story by Two Authors	25
Paget's Curate of Cumberworth	26
—— Lucretia	26
—— Milford Malvoisin	26
—— S. Antholin's	26
—— Owlet of Owlstone Edge	26
—— Tales of the Village	26
Paget's Warden of Berkingholt	26
Parsons' Life-at-Ease Incumbents	27
Pollard's Avice	28
Reed's Adventures of Olaf Tryggveson	31
Reformed Village	31
Rockstro's Abbey Lands	31
S. Alban's, or Prisoners of Hope	31
Sand's Sylvester Enderby	31
—— Voices of Christmas	31
Spencer's Scenes of Suburban Life	33
Stories for Christmas-tide	34
Summerleigh Manor	35
Sunbeam, the	35
Sydney's Life's Search	35
—— Chronicle of Day by Day	35
Tales of Crowbridge Workhouse	35
Two Guardians	36
Wilford's Play and Earnest	37
—— Master of Churchill Abbots	37
—— Maiden of Our Own Day	37
Wynnes, the	38

THEOLOGICAL.

Atkins' Three Essays	2
Black's Messias and Anti-Messias	3
Blackmore's Doctrine of the Russian Church	3
—— Harmony of Anglican Doctrines	3
Blunt's Atonement	3
—— Essays on Reformation	51
Brechin's (Bp. of) Primary Charge	4
—— Theological Defence	4
Britton's Horæ Sacramentales	5
Browne's Mosaic Cosmogony	5
Carter's Doctrine of the Priesthood	5
—— Doctrine of Confession	6
—— Doctrine of the Eucharist	6
Duke's Analysis of Bp. Butler's Analogy	11
Flower's Three Books of Theophilus	13
Fowle's Epistle to the Hebrews	14
Gresley's Sophron and Neologus	14
—— Idealism Considered	52
—— Ordinance of Confession	14
Heygate's Ember Hours	15
—— Catholic Antidotes	15
Hicks' General View of the Doctrine of Baptismal Regeneration	16
Houghton's Rationalism	16
—— Pauline Theology	16
Incarnation, Tracts on	17
Irons' Whole Doctrine of Final Causes	17
—— Judgments on Baptism	17
Laurence's Essay on Confession	14
Malan's Letters to a Missionary	20
Milman's Love of the Atonement	22
Mossman's Glossary of Scripture Words	23
Moultrie's Lecture on Family Prayer	23
Murray's Catena on Eucharist	24
Newland's Confirmation and Communion	25
Our New Life in CHRIST	26
Owen's Dogmatic Theology	26
Palmer's Dissertations	26
Perry's Analogies	27
—— Declaration on Kneeling	27
Poole's, Rev. A., Case, Statement of	28
Priest in Absolution	30
Revelation of JESUS CHRIST explained	31
Shipley's Treatise on Humility	32
—— Mysteries of the Faith	32
—— Liturgies of 1549 and 1662	32
Saravia on the Eucharist	10
Spirit of the Church	33
Thorndike on the Eucharist	7
West's Treatise on the Holy Eucharist	37
Woodward's Demoniacal Possession	38

www.ingramcontent.com/pod-product-compliance
Lightning Source LLC
Chambersburg PA
CBHW051735300426
44115CB00007B/569